TWILIGHT
IN THE FORBIDDEN
CITY

2nd Edition
Revised & Updated

REGINALD F. JOHNSTON

Simon Wallenberg Press

Warning and Disclaimer

REGINALD F. JOHNSTON

TWILIGHT
IN THE FORBIDDEN
CITY

Simon Wallenberg Press

About the Author

Sir Reginald Fleming Johnston (1874–1938) was a Scottish academic, diplomat and pedagogue and the tutor of Puyi, the last emperor of China, and later appointed as commissioner of British-held Weihaiwei.

Born in Edinburgh, he studied at University of Edinburgh and later Magdalen College, Oxford. In 1898, he entered into colonial service and worked in Hong Kong. After initial service in Hong Kong, Johnston was transferred to the British leased territory at Weihaiwei in 1906 on the coast of the Shandong Peninsula as a District Officer, working with Sir James Haldane Stewart Lockhart.

In 1919, he was appointed tutor of thirteen-year-old Puyi who still lived inside the Forbidden City in Beijing as a non-sovereign monarch. As the British-born Tutor to the Dragon Emperor, Johnston was the only foreigner in history to be allowed inside the inner court of the Qing Dynasty. Johnston carried high imperial titles and lived in both the Forbidden City and the New Summer Palace. After Puyi was expelled from the Forbidden City in 1924, he served as Secretary to the British China Indemnity Commission (1926). In 1927, he was appointed Commissioner at Weihaiwei. He ran the territory until it was returned to the Republic of China on October 1, 1930. The dignity of Johnston's official departure — the first such by a British administrator from a British possession in China — to a waiting Royal Naval vessel, was somewhat spoiled by his obvious irritation at a servant who had failed to pack properly all of his clothes.

Johnston was appointed Professor of Chinese in the University of London in 1931, a post based at the School of Oriental and African Studies. He was not a natural teacher, and hated university administration. He retained his ties with Puyi, which proved an embarrassment after the former emperor assumed the throne of the Japanese puppet state of Manchukuo. Johnston retired in 1937, having acquired the small island of Eilean Righ in Loch Craignish, Scotland, on which he created for himself a Chinese Garden. He died in Edinburgh. After cremation Johnston's ashes were scattered on the island of Eilean Righ and surrounding Loch. He never married but was at one stage engaged to the historian Eileen Power, and was close to author Stella Benson. Mrs Elizabeth Sparshott, to whom he was apparently engaged at the time of his death, destroyed all of his papers.

Johnston's book Twilight in the Forbidden City (1934) describes his experiences in Beijing and was used as a source for Bernardo Bertolucci's film dramatisation of Puyi's life The Last Emperor. He was portrayed by Peter O'Toole in the film.

His ghost is said to reside on Eilean Macaskin, an island just south of Eilean Righ.

CONTENTS

CONTENTS

谨此献给我们的最好朋友梅和杰柯

PREFACE
by
His Majesty the Emperor Hsüan-T'ung

甲子十月予自北府入日本使館莊士

敦師傅首翼予出於險地且先見日使

芳澤言之芳澤乃禮予假館以避亂軍

乙丑二月予復移居天津距今七年而莊

士敦前後從予於北京天津之間者約十

三年中更患難倉皇顛沛之際惟莊士

敦知之最詳今乃能秉筆記其所歷多

他人所不及知者蓋夫喪亂之餘得此目擊

身經之實錄信乎其可貴也莊士敦雄文

高行為中國儒者所不及此書既出乎知其

尚當世所重必矣辛未九月

TRANSLATION OF PREFACE

IN THE TENTH MONTH of the *chia-tzŭ* year,[1] after leaving the residence of prince Ch'un,[2] I took refuge in the Japanese Legation. It was Johnston, my tutor, who was chiefly instrumental in rescuing me from peril. Moreover, he it was who first interviewed the Japanese Minister, Fang Tsê,[3] on my behalf, after which Fang Tsê received me courteously and allowed me to use his Legation as a place of refuge from the wild soldiery. In the second month of the *i-ch'ou* year[4] I made another move, and went to reside in Tientsin. That was seven years ago, and Johnston from first to last, both in Peking and subsequently in Tientsin, was my companion, throughout a period of thirteen years. No one has a more intimate knowledge than he of the disasters and hardships of that critical period. He is therefore well fitted to take up his pen and make a record of events in which he himself played a part. To those who look back upon the sorrows and disorders of that time, this true record of his, based on personal experience and observation, will indeed be a thing of value. As a writer and as a man Johnston is one who is not surpassed by the best of our native scholars. When his book appears I know it will be highly prized by the world.

Ninth month of the *hsin-wei* year.[5]

(Authenticated by two seals of the emperor Hsüan-T'ung.)

---

[1] The *chia-tzŭ* year (which happened to be the first of the present Chinese cycle) roughly corresponds with 1924.

[2] Literally "the Northern Mansion" (*Pei Fu*). It was in the house of his father, prince Ch'un, ex-regent of China, that the emperor was a state-prisoner after the "Christian General," Fêng Yü-hsiang, had forcibly expelled him, in November 1924, from his palace in the Forbidden City.

[3] Fang Tsê—the Chinese name of Mr. K. Yoshizawa, then Japanese Minister in Peking.

[4] *I-ch'ou* year—1925.

[5] *Hsin-wei* year—1931. The Preface was written by the emperor at Tientsin and transcribed by his devoted servant the famous poet, statesman and calligraphist, Chêng Hsiao-hsü, about a week before they both left for Manchuria, to become Chief Executive and Prime Minister, respectively, of the new State.

INTRODUCTION

AT ABOUT ELEVEN O'CLOCK on the morning of July 25th, 1901, there stepped ashore at Hong-Kong a shy and boyish figure attired in the rich silk costume of a Chinese noble and wearing on his hat the red " button " of a mandarin of the highest rank. At the pier, he and his little suite were met by a group of British officials, of whom the writer of these pages was one, who welcomed him to British territory on behalf of the local government. Accompanied by an escort of police whose business it was to keep at a respectful distance the throng of inquisitive but undemonstrative Chinese who lined the streets, four red-coated chair-bearers bore him swiftly away from the water-front. Fifteen minutes later his chair was set down at the front doorway of Government House, where he was received and greeted by the Governor of the Crown Colony.

The distinguished visitor was his imperial highness prince Ch'un, brother of the reigning emperor of China. His host was his excellency Sir Henry Blake, representative in Hong-Kong of his majesty king Edward VII.

The occasion was a memorable one, for this was the first time that a Chinese prince had set foot in British territory. Yet his visit was shorn of most of the ceremonial courtesies that would have been extended to him by the British authorities had he been willing to accept them. No salute from British men-of-war or from the shore-batteries greeted him as he entered the harbour in the German ship *Bayern*, no guard of honour received him at his landing. This was in accordance with his own wish ; for he was travelling on a mission of humiliation, and while it remained unfulfilled he preferred to receive none of the honours due to a prince of the blood-royal of China. One year and thirty-five days before prince Ch'un set foot in Hong-Kong, the German plenipotentiary in China had been murdered by a " Boxer " in the streets of Peking. The shot that killed baron Von Ketteler on June 20th, 1900, reverberated round the world, for it marked

Bc

the beginning of the lamentable episode known to history as the
Siege of the Legations ; and now, in accordance with one of the
conditions of peace imposed by the victorious allies on the abased
Chinese court, a Manchu imperial prince was on his way to Germany to lay the humble regrets and apologies of the " Son of
Heaven " before the throne of one who in Chinese eyes had lately
been at best a tributary prince, at worst a contumelious barbarian kinglet.

Among some notes which I made at the time, and which were
afterwards embodied in a document now in Downing Street, were
the following words: " Though prince Ch'un cannot, according
to the dynastic customs of China, himself become a candidate
for the imperial throne, it is not impossible that if he has any
children his son may eventually become emperor. This would
certainly make prince Ch'un himself a very important factor in
the future politics of China."

This remark correctly foreshadowed what fortune had in store
for prince Ch'un. After his return from Germany, the empress-
dowager married him to a daughter of her trusted friend and
kinsman Jung-Lu, viceroy and grand-councillor. Early in 1906
their first son was born, and that son, whose personal name was
P'u-Yi, became the last sovereign of the Ta Ch'ing (Manchu)
dynasty in China ; while prince Ch'un himself, as regent for his
own son, became for a few disturbed and anxious years ruler of
the Chinese Empire.[1]

Not long after prince Ch'un had come and gone, another
member of the reigning house passed through Hong-Kong on
a mission that involved no degradation for China. In his case,
therefore, there was no abatement of royal honours. This was
prince Tsai-Chên, afterwards (in succession to his father) prince
Ch'ing, who was on his way to England to represent his sovereign
at king Edward's coronation.

It was on these two occasions that I first came in contact with
members of the Manchu imperial family, whom long afterwards
I was to know more intimately than any other foreigner. But
I had already made the acquaintance of a man whose fortunes
were also linked with those of the Manchu dynasty and who will
deservedly occupy a far more honourable place in the annals of
his country than either of the princes I have named. I first

arrived in Hong-Kong, an " Eastern Cadet " fresh from Magdalen, on Christmas Day, 1898. Epoch-making events had been
taking place in China during that year, and the leading figure
in those events had recently arrived in Hong-Kong as a refugee.
It was in Government House that I first met K'ang Yu-wei, the
most admired and the most hated member of the Chinese race
at that time : admired, even reverenced, by those who combined
loyalty to the dynasty with a patriotic longing to see their
country honoured among the nations ; hated, and also feared,
by those who believed that China had nothing to learn from
Western "barbarians" and that the Chinese emperor was *de jure*
King of kings.

When I first met this great reformer and " Modern Sage " he
was in mourning for those six martyrs who, less fortunate than
himself, had fallen victims to the rage and hate of the empress-
dowager and her minions and deceivers. One of the six was his
brother K'ang Kuang-jên. For his own capture, alive or dead,
very large rewards had been offered not only by the central
government at Peking but also by the provincial authorities. At
Hong-Kong, though carefully guarded by the British government, he was in constant danger of assassination. It was under
the protection of a police escort that he called upon Lord Charles
Beresford, then a visitor to the Far East, and had the interesting
conversation with him which is recorded in Lord Charles's
account of his travels and impressions.[2] After a short sojourn
in Hong-Kong, K'ang Yu-wei went to Singapore and ultimately
to Europe and America, always with a price on his head, always
in danger of his life from watchful spies and agents of the imperial
government. As long as the old empress-dowager lived he was
a homeless wanderer, and indeed, even after his return to his
own country, a wanderer he remained to the end of his life.

My main purpose in writing this book has been to give some
account of what I have called the Twilight period of the Manchu
occupation of the Forbidden City—the thirteen years that
elapsed between the establishment of the so-called Republic at
the beginning of 1912 and the expulsion of the emperor P'u-Yi
(or Hsüan-T'ung, to use his reign-title) from the imperial palace
by the " Christian General " and his associates in November,
1924. But to make the story clear to those who are not familiar

with the recent political history of China I have found it necessary to say something about the sunlight that preceded the twilight—a sunlight already obscured by thunder-clouds—and also
about the tempestuous night by which the twilight was followed.

There is a twilight of the dawn as well as a twilight of the
evening ; and it may be that the night which swallowed up the
twilight described in these pages will be followed in due time by
another twilight which will brighten into a new day of radiant
sunshine. That is what all those who admire and respect the
Chinese people (and who, knowing them, does not ?) ardently
hope or steadfastly believe. Many of us are convinced that we can
already detect the first glimmer of that new dawn, in the very
quarter of the heavens which to others seems blackest. It is only
the evening twilight, however, not the morning twilight, with
which we shall be directly concerned in the following chapters.
My story will therefore be confined to the thirty-four years that
began in 1898 with the noble but hopeless attempt of the unhappy emperor Tê Tsung (Kuang-Hsü) to carry out the compre-
hensive programme of reform laid before him by K'ang Yu-wei,
and ended with the return of the last of the Manchu emperors
of China to the land of his forefathers at the end of 1931 and
with the emergence of Manchuria, in the following year, as one
of the storm-centres of world-politics.

CHAPTER I

The Reform Movement of 1898

THROUGHOUT THE NINETEENTH CENTURY the power and the prestige of the Manchu reigning house were crumbling. Internal revolts and disastrous foreign wars not only shook the throne to its foundations but seemed to be the prelude to that " break-up " of China which provided Lord Charles Beresford with what he not unnaturally believed to be the most appropriate of all possible titles for the book published by him in 1899. Four years before that date, China lay beaten and helpless at the feet of the little island-empire which—not for the first nor for the last time —she had despised and defied. Formosa—which indeed had not become Chinese territory until it was annexed by the Manchu dynasty in the course of its triumphant career of conquest— became part of the Japanese Empire ; and but for the intervention of three great European Powers (Germany, Russia and France) she would have lost that important part of Manchuria (the Liaotung Peninsula) which contains Port Arthur and Dairen. She lost it in any case only three years later, when Russia not only seized for herself the very territory which with simulated magnanimity she had compelled Japan to restore to China, but so strengthened her own military position throughout Manchuria that she became the dominant power in that ancestral home of the Manchu imperial family. British merchants residing there in 1898 spoke of " the practical annexation of the country going on under their very eyes," and a leading British missionary " declared that both he himself and all his missions looked upon Manchuria as Russian in all but name."[1] These are facts which should not be forgotten by those who seek to understand the background of the Manchurian problem as it exists to-day. The Chinese took no part whatever in the work of expelling the Russians from Manchurian territory ; and there can be no reasonable doubt that if Japan had not fought and beaten Russia on Manchurian soil in the war of 1904–5, not only the

Liaotung Peninsula but all Manchuria would have been in fact, perhaps also in name, a Russian province to-day.[2]

But Formosa and Manchuria were not the only portions of the Empire that had passed into alien hands before the close of 1898. That was the culminating year of a scramble among the Western Powers for harbours and leased territories on the coast of China and for the delimitation of " spheres of influence." The territory of Kiao-chou, with its splendid harbour of Tsingtao, was seized by Germany ; nearly three hundred square miles of territory were " leased " to Great Britain at Weihaiwei which for the next thirty-two years was administered as a British colony ; another area of similar dimensions was acquired as an annexe to the colony of Hong-Kong on a lease of ninety-nine years ; and the territory of Kuangchou-wan on the southern coast of the Canton province was similarly " leased " to France. Italy put in a claim to a harbour on the coast of the province of Chehkiang, and when this demand was successfully resisted by China (this was in pre-Mussolinian days) the discomfiture of the Italians at their failure to win a prize in the great game of land-grabbing was matched by the astonishment of the Chinese at their own hardihood in withholding it.

If the Western nations thought that the partition of China was likely to go merrily forward without more than a few grimaces from the Chinese government and people, they soon discovered their mistake. Foreign aggression was beginning to turn a " civilisation " into a nation. The Chinese who had hardly known what patriotism meant began to realise that they lived in a world of competing and often antagonistic national groups, and that their group which was numerically the greatest of all and occupied (if dependencies be included) a larger geographical area than any other, exercised less influence and was treated with less respect than many Western countries possessing scarcely one twentieth of the territory and population of China.

The Chinese were then, as they are now, too proud and sensitive a race to reconcile themselves to a position of permanent inferiority among the nations. They could not be expected to acquiesce in the theory that the Western races or the Japanese were their racial superiors ; and as any such theory is (in the

opinion of those who know them best) patently false, it was something better than vanity that made them reject it. Therefore when
the educated and thinking classes contemplated the condition of
their country as it actually was, and compared it with what they
very reasonably thought it ought to be, they were obliged to look
for the causes of that condition not in a law of nature against
which it would be futile to struggle but in circumstances that
could be altered or in mistakes that could be rectified. The rise
of a reform party was therefore inevitable. Equally unavoidable
was the division of that party into two main sections. The section of the right put its trust in gradual evolution without any
catastrophic constitutional upheaval ; the section of the left
insisted that a fundamental reconstruction of the national life
on a new basis was essential to the salvation of the country,
and that such a reconstruction would be impossible so long as
the Manchu dynasty (believed by them to be inert, incompetent
and incorrigibly corrupt) was allowed to cumber the ground.

K'ang Yu-wei, or " Nan-Hai " as he was known to his disciples from the name of his native district, was by far the most
prominent figure in the Chinese reform movement of the last
decade of the nineteenth century. He must be classed among
the moderates on account of his unswerving loyalty to the
throne. Yet in the eyes of the great majority of those who controlled China's destinies in 1898, his memorials to the emperor,
which led directly to the famous " Hundred Days " of helter-
skelter reform, stamped him as the most dangerous extremist
in the Empire. The fear and hate with which he and his writings
filled the orthodox and " respectable " members of the Chinese
and Manchu official hierarchy may be compared with the horror
and detestation which heresy and witchcraft aroused in medieval
Europe, or which Communism, Fascism and Hitlerism arouse
among their respective opponents to-day. If the solecism may
be permitted, K'ang Yu-wei was in 1898 the " arch-bolshevik "
of his time in China ; and although his views underwent no
fundamental change throughout his life, he was destined, only
fifteen years later, to be derided and thrust aside with contemptuous indifference as a " die-hard " and a reactionary.
Such is the fate that has befallen many reformers, religious,
social and political, at other times and in other places.[3]

Long before his " heresies " were embodied in specific recommendations to the throne, K'ang Yu-wei had established a great reputation for himself in his native province of Canton as a zealous advocate of both political and social reform and also as a bold and original commentator on the Confucian canon. He was leader of what is known as " the Modern Text School " (*chin wên*), while Chang T'ai-yen became leader of " the Old Text School " (*ku wên*). Nevertheless, just as he always remained a loyal subject of the emperor, so he never ceased to be a reverent and faithful disciple of Confucius, whom he always regarded as the spiritual father of Chinese civilisation. It is not surprising that by 1898 he had gathered round him a large body of eager and receptive students. His fame as a teacher and inspirer of youth spread from the Canton province to all parts of China, and his teachings eventually attracted the interested attention of men of high official influence and prestige such as the governor of Hunan, Ch'ên Pao-chên,[4] the Hanlin academician and censor Hsü Chih-ching, and Wêng T'ung-ho the imperial tutor.

The last-named, a native of the province of Kiangsu, was one of the greatest scholars of his age. In 1856 he passed first in the triennial Palace examination and attained the highest and most coveted of all Chinese academic distinctions—the rank of *chuang yuan*. His official advancement was rapid. He became president of the Board of Revenue, a Grand Councillor, and head of the T'ung-wên-kuan—a newly-established Language College in Peking. As scholar, poet and calligraphist he is regarded in Chinese literary circles as a spiritual descendant of the eighteenth-century writer Liu Yung, one of the ornaments of the great reign of Ch'ien-Lung. Wêng T'ung-ho's career as a scholar culminated in his appointment to the post of imperial tutor—*Ti-Shih*—in which honourable capacity he served two successive emperors, T'ung-Chih and Kuang-Hsü.

Though a master of Confucian learning, and a first-rate scholar of the traditional type, Wêng T'ung-ho was also a man of broad and liberal views and took a sympathetic interest in the writings of K'ang Yu-wei. After consultation with some of his like-minded friends, among whom were Ch'ên Pao-chên and Hsü Chih-ching already mentioned, he brought the name of K'ang Yu-wei to the notice of the emperor early in the fateful year 1898, and discussed with his imperial pupil the salient points of the Cantonese reformer's political creed. He was able to do this without let or hindrance in spite of the fact that by 1898 the emperor Kuang-Hsü was already nearly thirty years of age and therefore no longer *in statu pupillari* ; for the post of imperial tutor carried with it certain lifelong privileges which included the right of private audience. Moreover, an imperial tutor was entitled to speak his mind to the emperor without reserve, regardless of the conventional formalities by which other officers of state, however exalted, were more or less hampered in their relations with their sovereign.

That a man in Wêng T'ung-ho's high position should have brought K'ang Yu-wei's political opinions to the favourable notice of the emperor was in itself a very remarkable circumstance. On the one hand it throws an interesting light on Wêng's own character and shows him to have been singularly free from jealousy (a besetting sin of court-functionaries in China and doubtless elsewhere), and unfettered by the pedantic conservatism of the *literati* of his period. On the other hand it indicates that the emperor himself was far from being the shallow-witted or muddle-pated nonentity whom some writers would expose to our contemptuous pity. It is practically certain that Wêng T'ung-ho had a better knowledge of Kuang-Hsü's character and abilities than anyone else at court, not excepting the empress-dowager ; and it is highly improbable that he would have thought it worth while to discuss K'ang Yu-wei's reform schemes with a young monarch whom he knew to have neither the wit to understand them nor the will to carry them out.

There is no doubt about the impression which the young emperor made on K'ang Yu-wei when their first meeting took place in the spring of 1898. Many years afterwards I had several opportunities of discussing the events of that year with K'ang Yu-wei, and I never heard him speak of Kuang-Hsü otherwise than in terms of an admiration which bordered on reverence. Had the fiery reformer of those days found his imperial master and patron lacking in intelligence, patriotism or earnestness, he would have joined the slowly swelling ranks of those who believed that the " mandate of Heaven " had been withdrawn from the reigning house and that the Manchu dynasty was an obstruction which must be removed from the path of China's progress. If thoughts of doing so had ever entered the mind of K'ang Yu-wei in his early days, they were driven out as soon as he came into direct contact with his sovereign, whom he found to be not only willing to give support and sympathy to the reform movement but ready and anxious to place himself at its head.

K'ang Yu-wei has sometimes been described as an imperial tutor. He never occupied that position, and his interviews with the emperor were very few. But at one of those audiences the emperor conferred upon him the high privilege of submitting memorials direct to the throne instead of through the ordinary official channels, and the privilege was one which K'ang accepted with eagerness and gratitude. His memorials resulted in the issue of the famous series of reform-edicts which were promulgated with breathless haste one after another during the summer of 1898—the period known as " the Hundred Days." The edicts amazed as much as they gratified the small minority of liberal thinkers in the China of that day, and shocked and violently antagonised the vast conservative majority.

It is customary to criticise K'ang Yu-wei's reform schemes, and the imperial edicts in which they were embodied, as rashly conceived, inappropriate to the conditions of Chinese political and social life at that time, and irreconcilable with the spirit of Chinese civilisation. Such criticisms are not altogether invalid, though they might be applied with far greater force and truth to the later attempt to thrust China, suddenly and without preparation, into the mould of Western parliamentary democracy. K'ang Yu-wei himself admitted, in his late middle age, that a few of his schemes were ill-advised—such as the recommendation that Chinese clothing should be abandoned in favour of Western, which would have meant the ruin of the Chinese silk industry. But there was nothing fantastic or unreasonable in the bulk of his proposals, or in the arguments with which he supported them. K'ang and his imperial colleague failed in their attempt to establish the New China of their dreams not because their dreams were intrinsically absurd or impossible of fulfilment but for reasons which do no discredit to the character or the intelligence of either. Something will be said of them in the chapters that follow.

CHAPTER II

The Collapse of the Reform Movement

FOR A PROPER UNDERSTANDING of the events which led to the abrupt termination of the " hundred days " of reform, it is necessary to devote some preliminary attention to a subject which has never been adequately dealt with by any Western student of modern Chinese political history. I refer to those ethical and constitutional theories and practices which rendered possible if not inevitable the triumph of political reaction under the real or nominal leadership of the empress-dowager.

From the beginning of the reign of Kuang-Hsü in 1875 up to the year 1888 the exercise of the imperial functions was in the hands of the empress-dowager, T'zŭ-Hsi, widow of the emperor Hsien-Fêng (1851–1861) and mother of Hsien-Fêng's childless successor T'ung-Chih (1862–1874). She was known as the " Western empress-dowager " (*Hsi T'ai-Hou*) because she occupied a palace in the western part of the Forbidden City. Her colleague, Hsien-Fêng's senior consort, who predeceased her, was similarly known as the " Eastern empress-dowager." In later years the Western empress-dowager was also popularly known as " the Venerable Buddha " (*Lao Fo-yeh*) and as *Lao Tsu Tsung*—" the Venerable Ancestor."

The position of T'zŭ-Hsi between 1875 and 1888 was practically that of regent, though the title used in China for a regent— *shê-chêng-wang*—was never bestowed on a woman. The process by which an empress or an empress-dowager exercised the functions of regent was known as *ch'ui lien t'ing chêng*—" lowering the screen and attending to state business "—the allusion being to the theory that when transacting affairs of state the empress-regent concealed her august figure behind a screen. The phrase has been in use since the time of the emperor Kao Tsung (650—683) of the T'ang dynasty. An empress-dowager's surrender of the functions of regency to the emperor on his coming of age was known as *kuei chêng*—" the giving back of the government "—or *ch'ê lien*—" the removal of the screen." Two empresses-dowager of the Sung dynasty (tenth to thirteenth centuries) exercised regency functions similar to those conferred upon the " Western empress-dowager."

In 1888 two important imperial edicts were issued, one announcing the forthcoming marriage of the emperor (an event which by Chinese custom implied his " coming of age "), the other stating that in the second month of the following year the empress-dowager would *kuei chêng*—resign the functions of government to the emperor. During the same year it was officially announced that the buildings of the new Summer Palace (the Yi-Ho Park) were nearing completion, and in court circles it was well known that on her retirement from the regency she looked forward to making that palace her country residence.

The wedding duly took place at the beginning of 1889, when the emperor was nineteen years of age, and immediately afterwards he assumed in person the imperial duties and prerogatives —a ceremony known in Chinese as *ch'in chêng*. His empress (afterwards known as Lung-Yü) was a daughter of the empress-dowager's brother Kuei Hsiang. By bringing about this alliance the empress-dowager looked forward to the further consolidation of the influence and prestige of herself and the Yehonala clan to which she belonged.

In accordance with custom the emperor was simultaneously provided with various secondary consorts. Two of these young ladies were sisters, aged fifteen and thirteen respectively. The elder, named *Chin* (" Lustrous ") survived till 1924, under the later name or title of Tuan-K'ang ; the younger, whose name was *Chên* (" Pearl ") met, as we shall see, with a tragic death at the age of twenty-five.

The empress-dowager, with every appearance of willingness, resigned into the emperor's hands the functions of government which she had exercised, without either glory or discredit, during two minorities.[1] She was at that time fifty-four years of age. As an outward indication of her acquiescence in the new order of things she followed a well-recognised palace custom by changing her official abode in the Forbidden City. From the " Palace of Kindliness and Tranquillity " (*T'zŭ-Ning Kung*) she moved to the " Palace of Tranquil Old Age " (*Ning-Shou Kung*).

This change of residence might be described as part of the outward ceremonial connected with the assumption by the emperor of full imperial responsibilities. Its significance was well understood by the Court, and was in strict accordance with precedent. When the emperor Ch'ien-Lung, for example, retired from the throne and went into retirement after completing the sixtieth year of his reign in 1795, he transferred his residence from one part of the Forbidden City to another. The palace chosen by the empress-dowager T'zŭ-Hsi ninety-four years later was indeed the very palace selected for a similar purpose by the great Ch'ien-Lung (more correctly known by his " temple-name " of Kao Tsung), and it is probable that her reason for choosing it was that it had been the last residence of one of the most famous monarchs of Chinese history and had received its appropriate name from him.

Neither the emperor Ch'ien-Lung nor the empress-dowager suffered any diminution of dignity or prestige, or even of power, by reason of their nominal surrender of the imperial functions. This is a point of practical importance in connection with our present subject, and is one which is certain to be overlooked by readers who are unfamiliar with Chinese dynastic custom and ritual. The words " abdication " and " retirement " when applied to the action taken by Ch'ien-Lung in 1795 and by the empress-dowager in 1872 and again in 1889 are likely to create a false impression in Western minds. After celebrating his jubilee with great pomp in 1795, Ch'ien-Lung exchanged the position of emperor (*huang-ti*) for that of super-emperor (*t'ai shang huang*) in virtue of which he took precedence of his successor on the throne for the remainder of his life. Ch'ien-Lung was indeed a more august and splendid personage in the Court and in the Empire after his " abdication " than before it. Nor was his exalted position a purely honorary one. Though relieved of the routine functions of the throne, he had the right and the power to reserve to himself the final decision in all matters of importance and to over-rule and set aside, if he felt so disposed, the mandates of his successor. No doubt a " super-emperor " who was weary of the burden and the trappings of monarchy, or had truly set his heart on imperishable things, would be glad to leave his successor in undisturbed enjoyment of his imperial prerogatives;

but he would still be regarded by ministers of state as the ultimate source of authority and as a final court of appeal. The elevation of his name above that of the emperor in all state documents was only one of many reminders, for all who could read, that there was one living being in the empire to whom even the emperor must kneel.

Now if the position of the empress-dowager after her " retirement " was hardly as exalted as that of the venerable Ch'ien-Lung, it was superior, not only in practice but in theory, to that of the emperor. There was nothing extraordinary about the honours conferred on or assumed by the " Venerable Buddha."[2] They were hers in virtue of her place in the genealogical table of the imperial family ; and even if she had never acted as regent during two minorities she would have taken precedence of the emperor Kuang-Hsü, not merely because she was the mother of his predecessor but also because she belonged to the senior generation. Similarly, it was known to all concerned that if she survived the emperor and thereby became senior to his successor by two generations, she would qualify for the still higher rank of *T'ai-huang-t'ai-hou* or " Grand " empress-dowager. As a matter of fact she did, as we shall see, become " Grand " empress-dowager for the few hours of life that remained to her after the death of Kuang-Hsü in 1908, and it was as " Grand empress-dowager " that she was buried and took her place in the dynastic annals.[3]

Thus we see that our term " dowager " is not an adequate translation of the Chinese term *t'ai*, which indeed has no precise equivalent in our language. It is unfortunate that this is so, because in the case of the " Venerable Buddha " the use of the term " empress-dowager " has in itself tended to create the belief that she must have been a woman of extraordinary ability and strength of character. Otherwise, it is asked, how could she, a mere " dowager," have become all-powerful in the State? Those who ask such a question do not understand that not only did an empress-dowager as such take precedence of the emperor and empress but that even the secondary consort of a deceased emperor—a *t'ai fei*—also took precedence of the reigning emperor and empress. So well-recognised was this precedence that when the emperor and empress visited either an empress-dowager or a *t'ai fei*, or received her in one of their own palaces, they could not sit in her presence until she had invited them to do so. On several occasions I accompanied the emperor Hsüan-T'ung to the palace of Tuan K'ang, one of the secondary consorts referred to above, of his predecessor the emperor Kuang-Hsü, and observed that he never failed to treat her with the respect due to one of rank more exalted than his own.[4] Still more marked would have been his deference to an empress-dowager. Thus when we read in certain popular Western accounts of the empress-dowager and her court that she sat on a throne more elevated than that of the emperor Kuang-Hsü, we should be wrong to assume that there was anything anomalous or humiliating to the emperor in this arrangement. That she took a malicious and vindictive pleasure, after September 1898, in humiliating and insulting him is true, but the mere exaltation of her own state-chair above the emperor's cannot rightly be regarded as a proof of this.[5]

I do not wish it to be inferred that all imperial " dowagers," whether they had occupied the position of empress or not, were expected or allowed to supersede the reigning emperor in the exercise of his imperial functions. It would be impossible, in practice, for a *t'ai fei*—a dowager secondary-consort—to do so in any case, at least until she had been elevated by imperial decree to the rank of *t'ai hou* or empress-dowager ; and even an empress-dowager could not supersede the emperor altogether until (like the " Venerable Buddha ") she had " lowered the screen." The point is that her exalted position " above " the emperor entitled her, in an emergency, to over-rule him temporarily or permanently, by measures which in China would be regarded as constitutional or at least not revolutionary. She would naturally refrain from doing so if she had reason to believe that she would find inadequate support in government circles, for in that case the practical difficulties of the situation would be insurmountable. There might be something of the nature of a " strike " among the officers of state. But her position made her the obvious person to lead the opposition against an emperor whose wings she or others were desirous of clipping.

Perhaps we might say that in China an empress-dowager's functions were to some extent analogous to those exercised by the British House of Lords. Even without going the length of

" lowering the screen " she could act as a constitutional check on " hasty legislation " ; and if she had the country—or the Chinese equivalent of " the country "—at her back, there was hardly any limit to her influence or her authority.

This may help us to understand how it comes about that even among the most loyal of Chinese monarchists it is comparatively rare to find anyone expressing more than lukewarm sympathy for Kuang-Hsü in his misfortunes. The very fact of their loyalty to the throne tends to make them oblivious of or merciful towards the faults and crimes of T'zŭ-Hsi, and more or less indifferent to the fate of Kuang-Hsü, because in their eyes it was the " Venerable Buddha " rather than Kuang-Hsü who represented the apex of the dynastic system and was therefore the proper object of loyalty.[6]

I have often discussed this question with Chinese who prided themselves on their devotion to the throne and to the Manchu dynasty, and who had themselves suffered very severely as a result of their loyalty. Apart from men like K'ang Yu-wei and his disciples, and a small number of political students who realised the dangers and drawbacks involved in the Chinese recognition of a power (sometimes dormant but often active) behind or above the throne, I have found very few who were willing to take the side of the emperor against the empress-dowager. Republicans, of course, and all those to whom the monarchic idea is anathema, are naturally ready enough to denounce the empress-dowager for her opposition to reform ; but even they, as a rule, show but little respect for the memory of their martyred emperor. In their case, this seems to be mainly due to an unwillingness to admit that any good thing could come out of Manchuria—or rather out of the Manchu dynasty. We may expect that after the revolutionary fever has passed away there will be an increasing tendency on the part of Chinese historians and political students to elevate Kuang-Hsü to his proper place in the annals of his country and do justice to his memory.

The theories underlying the exaltation of an empress-dowager over the reigning sovereign may seem to the Western mind puzzling and anomalous. But they are easy to understand when we learn to associate them with the traditional Chinese code of ethics, in which filial piety holds the place of honour as the first and most fundamental of virtues. In Chinese eyes, the elder generation can never wholly abdicate its functions of authority over the younger ; the younger must never fail in respect for and obedience to the elder. This is (or was till recently) the rule in Chinese domestic relationships ; and the imperial family was expected to set an example in these matters to the whole empire. The decrees issued by the great K'ang-Hsi (1662-1722)—certainly one of the strongest and ablest monarchs who have occupied the throne of China—bear ample witness, in their phraseology, to the deep respect and deference shown by him to the empress-dowager of those days and to the filial devotion with which he accepted and acted upon that illustrious lady's " commands." It is needless to ask whether K'ang-Hsi and his successors on the throne of China were sincere in their professions of devotion to the principles of filial piety. Perhaps at times they merely paid lip-service to what they knew to be a fundamental law of Chinese ethics. In any case, they were fully conscious of the excellent effect that their pious language would have on the Confucian *literati* whose support and loyalty were essential to the stability of the dynasty.

A typical illustration of the power exercised by an empress-dowager may be found in an imperial edict of the eleventh month of the second year (1821-22) of Tao-Kuang, which announces that " the emperor has received the commands of the empress-dowager to elevate the *fei* (an imperial concubine) named T'ung Chia to the rank of *huang-hou* (empress)." From this we see that even in so purely personal a matter as the regulation of the rank and precedence of the various imperial consorts it was not the emperor but his mother the empress-dowager who laid down the law. There was nothing whatever peculiar or exceptional about this announcement. It was in strict accordance with precedent, and so long as the empress-dowager lived, the promotion of a secondary consort to a higher rank could have been carried out in no other way. Even the marriage of an emperor had to be ordained by the empress-dowager, and it was she who selected the empress (in theory at least) and fixed the date of the wedding.

Now when we realise how exalted was the position of the
Cα

empress-dowager T'zŭ-Hsi after her "retirement," and how
far-reaching were the powers and prerogatives which were still
at her disposal if she chose to exercise them, we shall find no
great difficulty in understanding how it was that she was able
to emerge from her seclusion, crush the unhappy young emperor,
and put the reform party in China to utter confusion and dismay.   It is quite unnecessary to assume, as the Western-
trained onlooker is apt to do, that her success proved the strength
and vigour of her own character and intellect and that the
emperor's failure proved the weakness and imbecility of his.   It
is unfair to dismiss K'ang Yu-wei, as Morse does, "as a visionary
enthusiast," and the emperor as "an inexperienced weakling."
The empress-dowager's position, both theoretically and practically, was an immensely stronger one than the emperor's :
theoretically, because of her super-imperial rank which she
owed not to her abilities but to the fact that she belonged to
the senior generation ; and practically, because her position
made her the personage to whom all the conservative forces of
the empire would naturally turn in their search for a rallying-
point against the forces of reform.   The conservatives turned
to her not because she possessed consummate qualities of statesmanship and leadership ; not because they regarded her as the
embodiment of wisdom and prudent statecraft ; but because by
inducing her to place herself at the head of militant conservatism
they would be able to annihilate the reform-movement under
cover of what in China would pass for orderly constitutional
procedure.

Had there been no empress-dowager, the conservatives
might have attempted a palace-revolution. They might
have succeeded in getting rid of Kuang-Hsü and replacing him
by a less "dangerous" member of the imperial family. But
palace-revolutions cannot always be confined to palaces ; and
to let loose the dogs of revolution in a wider area than the Forbidden City was the last thing the conservatives wanted to do.
In existing circumstances there was only one obvious way by
which the exigencies of the case might be met, there was only
one method which would be sufficiently drastic to put an end to
the reform movement and yet remain "constitutional" and non-
revolutionary in outward appearance. That method was to

invoke the aid of the one personage in China who could claim the constitutional and (what was in China more important) the ethical right to over-rule the emperor.

It was by no means a foregone conclusion that she would do so. K'ang Yu-wei and the emperor both hoped, at first, not without some reason, that she would refuse to return to the world of politics. She was delighted with her new plaything, the Summer Palace, she took an almost childish pleasure in her picnics and her theatricals (she had two theatres of her own in the Summer Palace), she loved dabbling in art and poetry, and she was, in her peculiar way, a devout Buddhist. There was much to interest her in her quiet life in her new country home, and there was no reason to suppose that she was bored or craved excitement. It is true that she had no sympathy whatever with reform schemes of any kind, but it was mainly in matters affecting the status and privileges of members of the imperial clan, the regulation of precedence and the distribution of rewards and punishments among the ladies and officers of the Court, that she still loved to exercise authority. It was by her command, for example, that the sisters " Lustrous " and " Pearl " were censured, in 1895, for alleged " extravagance " and temporarily degraded to the rank of *kuei jên* or " honourable person "—a lowly degree among the emperor's secondary consorts. The emperor's views on the subject were not known, or if known were ignored. In 1896 prince Tsai Chu disobeyed one of her orders, whereupon he was deprived of his rank and handed over to the Imperial Clan Court (*Tsung-jên Fu*) to receive eighty strokes and to be incarcerated " for ever " in " an empty room." Many other instances of her activities in respect of court and family discipline during the period of her " retirement " might be adduced. The most ominous sign that she might interfere in weightier matters of state consisted in her demand (which the emperor was obliged to obey) that the imperial tutor Wêng T'ung-ho should be dismissed from office on account of his reforming sympathies. Nevertheless the action taken by her in this affair was exceptional, and on the whole she seemed willing to allow the routine business of the State to be transacted by the emperor and his counsellors without reference to her. Thus the young emperor felt justified in at least hoping that she would refrain from interfering with his measures of political and social reform which, after all, had nothing to do with those palace and family matters in which she insisted on having the controlling voice.

There is more than one version of how his hopes were shattered and of the events that led to the dramatic episode of *wu-hsü*.[7] According to a well-attested account, a group of influential Manchu and Chinese officials in the capital, alarmed at the effect which the emperor's policy of drastic retrenchment and reform would have on themselves and their profitable sinecures, sent a deputation headed by the censor Yang Ch'ung-yi to interview Jung-Lu, then commander-in-chief of the Northern Army, at his headquarters in Tientsin, and to convince him of the imperative necessity of inducing the empress-dowager to reassume the regency.

Jung-Lu's upbringing and environment—he was a Manchu of high birth—had been such that his sympathies were naturally with the conservatives ; but he was an able and enlightened man and an honest and loyal servant of the State. Unfortunately, for the reasons already given, and for other reasons of a more personal nature, his loyalty was directed towards the person of the empress-dowager rather than towards that of the emperor. Yet it is very doubtful whether he would have taken any steps against the reformers on his own initiative, for there is justification for the belief that in spite of his conservatism he was one of the few high Manchu officials who realised that if China was to be saved from the internal and external dangers by which she was threatened, she must follow the example of Japan and tread the path of reform. It is questionable whether even the censor Yang Ch'ung-yi and his colleagues would have been able, of themselves, to divert him from a policy of non-interference. What prompted him to take the action he did was something which weighed with him more heavily than the censor's arguments.

The emperor Kuang-Hsü was by no means oblivious of the magnitude of the forces against which he and K'ang Yu-wei had to struggle. This was one of the reasons why they decided to rush the reform-decrees through as quickly as possible, before the opposition could gather momentum. Kuang-Hsü knew that he was taking a serious risk and he took it with his eyes open.

He knew that if the reforms were introduced by gradual stages his opponents would have ample time to consolidate and organise themselves against him. Rightly or wrongly, both he and K'ang Yu-wei felt that a policy of swiftness and boldness, however perilous it might be, had greater chances of success than a timid policy of " wait and see."[8]

Nor was Kuang-Hsü ignorant of the nature of the action which the reactionaries were likely to take if they were given time and opportunity to think out their plan of campaign. He knew that in the empress-dowager they would find a ready sympathiser ; he knew that she hated and despised foreigners and foreign ways, and that any scheme of political or social reform that implied the recognition of foreign methods and institutions as superior to Chinese or worthy of adoption by China would stand in her eyes self-condemned. He knew that her position in the State, in spite of her withdrawal from the regency nine years earlier, invested her with an authority which in the last resort was superior to his own. He knew that she was ignorant and superstitious and extremely susceptible to flattery ; and he was fully aware of the risk that the enemies of reform might find in her a willing, active and all-powerful leader. She had already, as we have seen, compelled him to dismiss from office the imperial tutor Wêng T'ung-ho, and though she had not yet vetoed the reform-edicts already issued she might at any moment order their cancellation. His clear understanding of all these facts and possibilities convinced the emperor that there was only one means by which the danger that threatened him from the Summer Palace might be averted. Something had to be done to make it impossible for the reactionaries to put the empress-dowager at the head of the opposition. In other words, it was necessary for the emperor to summon to his aid someone whose power and influence in official circles were such as to make him feared and respected, who had command of an efficient body of troops, who was a strong and resourceful man of action, who held enlightened views on the subject of reform, and who was incapable of betraying a great trust. The person on whom Kuang-Hsü's choice fell possessed all the desired qualifications except the last.

No blame attaches to the lonely young emperor for his failure to discern a fatal flaw in the character of Yüan Shih-k'ai. How indeed could he or anyone else have foreseen that the man in whom he was placing his trust would reveal himself as one of the arch-traitors of Chinese history? How could anyone have guessed that after betraying his imperial master in 1898 he would betray the throne in 1911 and the Republic five years later?

The emperor entrusted Yüan Shih-k'ai with the delicate duty of preventing the empress-dowager from re-entering public life on the side of the opponents of reform. The secret audience at which Yüan received his instructions and apparently promised to obey them is said to have taken place early in September, 1898. There are varying accounts of the instructions given him, and it is doubtful whether the true story is now known to any living soul. Some people connected with the palace say that the emperor's orders were conveyed to Yüan by a third person who for his own purposes gave them in a distorted form. In any case there is little probability in the story that the emperor ordered Yüan Shih-k'ai to have Jung-Lu put out of the way, by assassination if necessary, and to place the empress-dowager under close arrest.[9] It would not have been to the emperor's advantage, or to the advantage of the cause of reform which he had at heart, to have had either of these acts carried out. Drastic action against the empress-dowager would have caused a public scandal which he could never have lived down; and political assassinations were much less common in the China of that day than they have since become. Nor is there the smallest reason to believe that Kuang-Hsü was by nature either bloodthirsty or vindictive. It would have been amply sufficient for all the practical purposes he had in view if Yüan Shih-k'ai had so disposed his forces as to make it impossible for the reactionaries to get into direct communication with T'zŭ-Hsi, and impossible for T'zŭ-Hsi to return to her quarters in the Forbidden City. This, it seems probable, is all that the emperor desired him to do.

Yüan Shih-k'ai had no sooner received his orders from the emperor than he betrayed the whole secret to Jung-Lu. Whether Jung-Lu had already learned enough from the censor Yang Ch'ung-yi to determine him to place the affair in the hands of the empress-dowager is doubtful. However, the merest suspicion of a plot directed against both her majesty and himself was more than sufficient to make him take decisive action without a moment's delay. Messengers were immediately despatched to the Summer Palace to warn the " Venerable Buddha " that her liberty if not her life was in danger, and that if she now failed to act promptly and with vigour, fresh opportunities for doing so might never arise.

There seems to be no doubt that the old lady was shaken out of any tendency to lethargy by wildly-exaggerated reports of what the emperor and his gang of reformers intended to do with her when they had her in their power. She was to be humiliated, degraded, imprisoned, starved to death. Perhaps the fabricators of these lies were actuated not so much by a desire to blacken the character of the emperor and to magnify his crimes as by the belief that only a sense of imminent peril could stimulate her into effective action. However this may be, the methods adopted were thoroughly satisfactory from the point of view of the conservatives. The empress-dowager's *coup d'état* took place next day. Having issued one bright September morning from the " stately pleasure-dome " that she had created (out of naval funds) for the solace of her old age, she made a sudden and dramatic appearance in the Forbidden City and stood in all the thunderous splendour of outraged majesty before her helpless and shuddering victim. After upbraiding him in unmeasured language for what she described as his treachery and ingratitude, and charging him with having entertained murderous designs against her own person, she had him removed under guard to an island in one of the lakes adjoining the Forbidden City, resumed the position she had vacated in 1889, and promulgated one of the most humiliating edicts ever issued in the name of the monarch of a great State. In this edict the emperor was forced to confess to his subjects that he had realised his own incompetence and unfitness to be their ruler. He was made to say that in response to his earnest and repeated supplications her imperial majesty the dowager-empress had graciously condescended to reassume the onerous duties of the regency which in former years she had discharged with such conspicuous ability and success ; and the edict concluded by saying that he, the emperor, was about to prostrate himself before her imperial majesty's throne in order that he might have the honour of returning thanks on behalf of his people for her gracious benevolence in undertaking once more the oppressive burden of government.

Another and more laconic announcement of very sinister import was simultaneously issued to the public. It consisted of these nine Chinese words : *Ti yu chi, huang t'ai hou fu hsün chêng* —" the emperor being ill, the empress-dowager has resumed the regency."

CHAPTER III

Reaction and the Boxer Movement, 1898–1901

" THE EMPEROR BEING ILL, the empress-dowager has resumed the regency."

The Peking public had a vague knowledge of the grave events that had taken place in " the Great Within,"[1] and they were quick to realise what this brief announcement really meant— that their emperor stood in imminent peril of his life, but not from disease.

There is a curious story, in which some credulous Chinese have expressed belief, that while the " Venerable Buddha " was on her way from the Summer Palace to the Forbidden City—a distance of about seven miles—the emperor Kuang-Hsü, warned of her intentions, made a desperate effort to save himself from her vengeance by fleeing in disguise to the British Legation. There is nothing intrinsically impossible or absurd about this, but the continuation is such as to make the whole story incredible. It is to the effect that the British Minister refused to grant him the hospitality of his Legation and compelled him to return to the Forbidden City—to confront his judge and jaileress. Even if the wildly improbable had happened, and the British Legation had brutally closed its gates in the face of the imperial fugitive, the British was not the only foreign Legation in Peking and there were other Ministers to whom the emperor would have appealed not in vain.[2]

It may be that the unfortunate young monarch contemplated making his escape but was prevented by the palace-eunuchs from doing so. I have been informed by some of the eunuchs of a later day that such was the case, and it may well be true ; for the whole of the enormous palace staff—numbering about three thousand—not only stood in awe of the powerful empress but also had personal and selfish reasons for hating the emperor's reform schemes. Almost to a man—or to a semi-man—they were on the side of the most bigoted of the conservatives. They well

knew that the triumph of the cause of reform would lead, sooner
or later, to a catastrophic upheaval if not in the State at least
in the Forbidden City ; and it was to the empress-dowager that
they looked for the maintenance of the corrupt system by which
they lived and throve.

But though unable to ensure his own safety the emperor had
not been unmindful of the welfare of his friends. He could not
save the lives of all the reformers, but he succeeded in sending an
urgent message of warning to K'ang Yu-wei. One of the first
acts of the empress-dowager on her reassumption of the regency
was to cause warrants to be issued for the arrest of all the leading
men of the reform party ; but by the time this had been done
K'ang Yu-wei and his disciple Liang Ch'i-ch'ao (afterwards one
of the most famous men of letters of his day) were already out
of her reach.

K'ang Yu-wei, as we know, took refuge at first in Hong-Kong,
and it was there that he received the pitiful news of the fate that
had befallen several of his most intimate friends and supporters,
including his own brother.[3]

The victory of the conservatives and reactionaries was complete. Very few of the more prominent leaders of the reform
movement shared the good fortune of K'ang Yu-wei and Liang
Ch'i-ch'ao. Among those sentenced to lifelong imprisonment
was the censor Hsü Chih-ching, whose sole crime was that he
had recommended K'ang Yu-wei for government employment.
Ch'ên Pao-chên, governor of Hunan, was lucky to get off with
mere dismissal from office. The censor Sung Po-lu was dismissed
also, and it was placed on record that he was never to be re-
employed. Wêng T'ung-ho, the imperial tutor, who had already
been dismissed, would certainly have received capital punishment had it not been that his friends in high places were so
numerous and his fame as a scholar so great that his execution
might have led to serious discontent among many of those whom
the conservatives could not afford to antagonise. But he was
deprived of his honours, and special instructions were issued to
the local authorities to spy upon his movements. He died not
long afterwards, poor and disgraced Eleven years later, when
the empress-dowager and her imperial captive were both dead,
the time came for his merits to be remembered and recognised.

In 1909, at the beginning of the reign of Hsüan-T'ung, his titles and honours were posthumously restored and he was " canonised " under the name of Wên-Kung, which may be rendered with fair accuracy as " Scholar and Gentleman."

Among those who were barbarously executed were six whose names deserve a place in China's long roll of political martyrs. They were Yang Shên-hsiu, Yang Jui, Lin Hsü, T'an Ssŭ-t'ung, Liu Kuang-ti, and K'ang Yu-wei's brother K'ang Kuang-jên. Before their execution the Board of Punishments ventured to submit the request that they should be arraigned before a special tribunal ; but the un-Buddhistic comment of the " Venerable Buddha " was brief and to the point : " A trial is unnecessary. Let them be executed at once."

Unfortunately for these and other martyrs, the death-sentences pronounced by China's empress-dowager were not so harmless as those of a royal lady of kindred temper—the Queen of Wonderland. When the " Venerable Buddha " said " Off with his head " there was no Alice to retort " stuff and nonsense."

As for the emperor himself, he would have been saved ten years of misery and degradation had he shared the fate of the six martyrs. It was not from any pity or tenderness that his life was spared. Rumours that he was likely to die were rife in Peking. In China it was customary to break the news of the impending death of an emperor by the issue of public summonses to the leading members of the medical fraternity throughout the land to hasten at once with their bottles and remedies to the imperial bedside. When therefore the high provincial authorities were commanded to hunt out the most distinguished physicians and send them forthwith to the Forbidden City, it was universally assumed that the emperor was on the point of " ascending to be a guest on high."[4] This assumption was confirmed by the reports which were simultaneously noised abroad to the effect that the childless emperor's successor had already been selected from among the eligible members of the imperial clan.

No one seriously believed the stories of the emperor's illness, and although none of the high officers of state were bold enough to demand that the emperor be released from custody and restored to his throne, some of the " liberal " statesmen among

them protested in vigorous language against the arrangements
that were obviously being made to have him put out of the way.
One of the Yangtse viceroys, Liu K'un-yi, sent a strongly-worded
remonstrance to his brother-viceroy Jung-Lu, and a multitude
of other protests, some of them in threatening language, poured
in from various parts of the country, from Chinese merchants
who were living under foreign protection in the treaty-ports,
and from overseas Chinese colonists. The man mainly responsible
for the protests from the merchants of Shanghai was one Yüan
Shan, for whose arrest a warrant was promptly issued. In
Shanghai he felt himself in danger of being kidnapped ; but he
escaped the capital punishment which would have been the
reward of his temerity by taking refuge under the Portuguese
flag in Macao.

Meanwhile, as may be readily understood, K'ang Yu-wei was
not idle. He it was who was mainly responsible for organising
the opposition of overseas Chinese to the threatened removal of
Kuang-Hsü. He founded a society called the *Pao-Huang-Tang*—
" Association for the Protection of the Emperor "—and established branches of it in every country outside China inhabited
by Chinese merchants and colonists. These Chinese had nothing
to fear from the vengeance of the Peking authorities, and used
language which gravely upset the equanimity of the Court. But
T'zŭ-Hsi and her party bowed to the storm, and though the
project of nominating a successor to the throne was not given up,
the idea of dethroning or taking the life of the emperor was for
the time reluctantly abandoned.

Its abandonment brought no joy or relief to Kuang-Hsü,
whose position from that time onwards was always one of nerve-
destroying peril, misery and humiliation. He was fated to become
a pitiable fragment of shattered humanity and to endure a living
death for ten long years. He had done all in his power to save
China and to promote the welfare of his people, but he had been
overwhelmed. Yüan Shih-k'ai, who had betrayed him, never
raised a hand to help him or to soften the rigours of his imprisonment. Nor has the Nationalist China of our own day had the
manliness, the generosity or the chivalry to do homage to his
memory.

When the empress-dowager resumed the regency in September,

1898, she was a physically vigorous and intellectually alert woman of sixty-four. Her imperial captive was twenty-eight. During the ensuing years she divided her time between the Forbidden City and her beloved Summer Palace ; and she always took the precaution of compelling her prisoner to travel to and fro as a humble member of her suite. For her, it was a triumphal progress from one sumptuous palace to another ; for him, a dismal journey from prison to prison. In the Summer Palace his prison was a building called the Yü-lan T'ang—" the Hall of the Waters of Rippling Jade." Those jade-like waters rippled, indeed, against the walls of his prison, but not for his ears to hear nor for his eyes to see.[5] In Peking, his prison was a miniature island known as Ying-T'ai, in the southernmost of the Three Lakes (*San Hai*) just beyond the west wall of the Forbidden City. " Ying-T'ai " has the same signification as *Ying-chou*, which in Chinese mythology is one of the names given to the Isles of the Blest or Fairyland. After the establishment of the republic the " Three Lakes " were included in that part of the palace grounds which were given up to the president, and it was as the guest of the president of the republic that I sometimes visited poor Kuang-Hsü's island-prison—the little " fairyland " in which he died. I may have disturbed the minds of some of my republican friends by my suggestion that it should be maintained for all time by the people of China as a shrine dedicated to the memory of the one sad and lonely spirit by which it will always be haunted.

Only a few months passed before T'zŭ-Hsi felt sure enough of her position to carry out her cherished design of nominating a successor to the throne. The person she selected was a son of prince Tuan, a boy named P'u-Tsun. Tuan was one of the dowager's favourites because he shared to the full her hatred and distrust of all foreigners and all reformers, and because his conservatism was of the same bigoted, ignorant and obscurantist type as her own. Having caused P'u-Tsun to be designated heir-apparent (*huang-t'ai-tzŭ*) she was determined that he should not have access to a more liberal school of thought than that in which she herself had been brought up ; so two fanatical reactionaries—Ch'ung Ch'i and Hsü T'ung—were put in charge of his education.[6]

The public announcement of the nomination of an heir to the throne immediately resuscitated the rumours about the emperor's serious " illness " ; but the dowager, not wishing to stir up another hornets' nest, decided to allow a decent interval to lapse before his majesty's illness should once more become acute.

Meanwhile, however, startling events were occurring in the great world outside the Forbidden City which diverted the attention of the empress and the reactionary Manchu princes from purely dynastic questions and compelled them to face an entirely new problem.

I do not propose to deal at length with the Boxer Movement or with the siege of the Legations. What I have to say may be regarded merely as a footnote to the detailed accounts of those events which are in the hands of all students of modern Chinese history.

The remark has frequently been made that the Boxer outbreak began as an anti-dynastic movement and was " astutely turned into an anti-foreign attack." This statement though repeated with great persistence is not wholly accurate. The movement was a strongly anti-foreign and anti-Christian one from the first, and as Sir Robert Hart frankly and candidly recognised and emphasised, the Boxers were inspired by a very real though blind and ignorant patriotism.[7] That the movement first broke out in Shantung was no accident. The events which culminated in the seizure by Germany of the port and territory of Kiao-chou had made the people of that province vividly conscious of the wrongs and losses which China had suffered in the recent past at the hands of foreigners. That corruption, misgovernment and military incapacity had contributed to their country's shame, and that the Manchu dynasty was partially, at least, responsible for the condition to which China had been reduced, was only dimly recognised by the uneducated masses. What they saw clearly, or thought they saw, was that the evils from which their country suffered were due to the machinations of the " foreign devils," who if China was to be saved must be exterminated or expelled along with all their cunning inventions and contrivances, their strange and intolerant religion, their insufferable airs of superiority.

Had the Boxers appeared a generation later, they would have

learned much from the principles and practices of Hitlerite Germany. They would have sought justification for their anti-foreign activities on grounds almost identical with those on which German anti-Semitism is based to-day. As for the swastika, they would have had at least as good a right as the Germans to make it their badge, for their religion was Buddhistic, and the swastika was and is a familiar object in all Buddhist temples. The Boxers made a mess of things because of their ignorance and superstition. But to-day their less ignorant and more experienced successors are watching with eager interest the progress of Fascist and Nazi Nationalism in modern Europe. Principles which are held (rightly or wrongly) to justify the cleansing of a European State from alien contamination can hardly be held inapplicable to conditions in an Eastern country. If Germany may expel " non-Nordic " elements from her body-politic, we cannot complain if the Chinese claim a similar right to rid themselves of those aliens (European or Asiatic) who threaten or seem to threaten their national integrity. Nor can we justly blame them if they deliberately set themselves to acquire the power that will enable them to enforce that right. Already there are Chinese writers and speakers who in their demand not only for the return of lost territories but also for the cancellation of foreign concessions and the abolition of foreign consular jurisdiction are using arguments directly and admittedly drawn from the utterances of the spokesmen of Hitlerite Germany. Just as Soviet Russia provided them in recent years with useful slogans to encourage them in their struggles against Western imperialism and capitalism, so will Nazi Germany equip them with a new theory of Nationalism and a new technique.

For obvious reasons the Manchu court was ready to encourage the anti-foreign instincts and impulses of the Chinese people whenever it seemed possible that popular rage and discontent might ally themselves with the underground forces that always threatened the stability of the political fabric established in the seventeenth century by the Manchu conquerors. But it is inconceivable that the government would have allied itself with the Boxers if the emperor Kuang-Hsü had been allowed to carry out his schemes of reform. There is no doubt that the movement

could have been crushed with ease, as many lawless movements in different parts of China had previously been crushed, if
the ignorance, fanaticism and superstition of the Boxers had
not been matched by the much less excusable ignorance, fanaticism and superstition of the court. The military forces at the
disposal of Jung-Lu and Yüan Shih-k'ai would have been far
more than adequate to crush a few thousand peasants armed
mainly with bows and spears. It was only when the government
troops under Tung Fu-hsiang and other sympathisers with
reaction were allowed by the Court to join forces with the
Boxers that the latter became more than a rabble.

It is clear that the party in power in Peking " secretly sympathised " as an American writer has said " with these so-called
patriots, and looked upon them as a powerful ally in furthering
the secret plot for driving out foreigners from the Empire."[8]
It happened, most unfortunately for China and the dynasty,
that the governor of Shantung at the time when the Boxers
began to break out in 1899, was Yü-Hsien, a Manchu whose
temperament, upbringing and character made him a hearty
supporter of the policy of blind reaction which had triumphed
so completely over the reforming policy of the emperor. The
advice he tendered to the throne as to how the Boxer trouble
should be dealt with was one of the principal factors which
determined the pro-Boxer policy of the Court. Another American
writer, who was in Peking at the time, goes so far as to say " it
is to him the whole Boxer rising is due."[9] Yü-Hsien was, indeed,
regarded by the Boxers as their patron and defender, almost as
their tutelary divinity; and it must be admitted that he did his
utmost to show himself worthy of their reverence.[10]

At first, the Boxers were regarded (probably rightly) as descendants of the dangerous White Lily Sect (*Pai Lien Chiao*)
which had been responsible for rebellious movements in the past,
and edicts were issued ordering their suppression. Yü Hsien,
however, speedily came to their rescue. His own anti-foreign
proclivities had been greatly intensified by the successful
demand made by the foreign Legations for his dismissal from
the Shantung governorship on the ground that he had failed
to prevent the murder of two German missionaries in 1897—
the murder which quickly resulted in the German occupation

of Kiao-chou. Though dismissed from Shantung, under foreign pressure, he had not lost favour at Court. He was transferred to the governorship of the province of Shansi, where not long afterwards, at the height of the Boxer madness in 1900, he distinguished himself by a particularly brutal and cold-blooded massacre of missionaries in his own provincial capital.[11] The fact that the Boxers were anti-foreign was sufficient to make him sympathise with their cause, and he explained in memorials to the throne that the Boxers were righteous people who could be usefully employed in the great work of rescuing the nation from foreign aggression. He further explained that they possessed miraculous powers which could be turned to excellent account in foreign warfare. To destroy the Boxers, he said, would be a disastrous procedure, " like cutting off one's own wings."

It is unnecessary to continue the pitiful story of how the influence of the Boxers was allowed to spread to Peking and how the tales of their prowess and the potency of their magic charms were accepted as true, first by such men as the brutal and ignorant Kang-Yi and prince Tuan—father of the heir to the throne—and finally by the empress-dowager herself. Men like Yüan Shih-k'ai—who succeeded Yü-Hsien in Shantung— took the measure of the Boxers at once and demonstrated in a practical way the falsity of their claim to be invulnerable ; but the " will to believe " was overpoweringly strong in court circles, and the urgent warnings and entreaties of enlightened viceroys and other high officers of state, including the influential Jung-Lu, fell on deaf or incredulous ears.

The murder of the German minister on June 20th, 1900, and of a Japanese diplomatic secretary, may be said to have marked the beginning of the siege of the Legations. The end of that pitiful episode came with the entry of the allied troops into Peking on August 14th.

It is not surprising that the empress-dowager, with her guilty conscience, was afraid to remain in Peking and face the victorious " foreign devils." What she could and would have done had she been actuated by a lofty patriotism and a noble readiness to sacrifice her private interests for the sake of the people she had so grossly misgoverned, was to resign her regency, reinstate the emperor on the throne from which she had hurled

Dc

him, and trust to his mercy and " filial piety " to escape the
just punishment for her crimes and blunders. The emperor had
nothing whatever to fear from the foreign armies, and she knew
it. That indeed was precisely why, in her rage and jealousy, she
compelled him to accompany her into exile. Not even to save
China from foreign occupation and spoliation would she allow
that presumptuous and rebellious nephew of hers to gloat over
her misfortunes. If ruin must come to her, she would see to it
that he, the emperor, shared that ruin.

Kuang-Hsü himself pleaded in vain that he might be allowed
to remain in Peking. Chên Fei—known to foreigners as the
" Pearl Concubine "—knelt before the frenzied empress and
implored her not to compel the emperor to join her in her flight.
Chên Fei was the emperor's favourite consort, she knew that he
was willing and anxious to remain behind and face the allied
commanders, and she, if anyone, had the right, at this supreme
crisis in the fortunes of their House, to present this humble
petition to the all-powerful arbitress of their destinies. The
common country cart in which the imperial fugitives were to
flee in disguise was awaiting them at the northern gate of the
Forbidden City. At any time the foreign devils might be upon
them. There was not a moment to be lost. According to one
version of what followed, the empress-dowager vouchsafed no
reply to Chên Fei, who was kneeling and pleading before her,
but turned in a tempest of rage and hate to the attendant
eunuchs and ordered them to throw the weeping girl into a
well.

There is another version which I have heard repeated by
palace-eunuchs who were careful to explain that they spoke
from hearsay only, because they took no part in the tragedy and
were not present. (I never came across one who would admit
that he was either participator or witness.) According to this
story, the empress-dowager answered Chên Fei's pleadings with
some such words as these. " We will all stay where we are, but
we cannot allow ourselves to be taken alive by Western barbarians. There is only one way out for you and me—we must
both die. It is easy. You go first—I promise to follow you."
Then at a sign from their mistress the eunuchs seized the girl and
hurled her into the well, where she was left to drown—alone.

The well (never used, I believe, after 1900) was in the eastern section of the Forbidden City, behind that " Palace of Tranquil Old Age " which had been the empress-dowager's official residence since 1889. I have often passed the well in the company of the emperor Hsüan-T'ung. We have sat by its side and talked of the tragedy that had taken place there less than six years before he was born. It is another of the spots that will perhaps be haunted for ever by one lonely Manchu spirit. If the emperor Kuang-Hsü is to have his shrine on the islet of Ying-T'ai or in the Hall of the Waters of Rippling Jade, the people of China should not forget to raise another at the side of this well in the Forbidden City to the memory of his murdered consort.

Many months afterwards, when the empress-dowager had returned from exile and had ordered the cancellation (" in the interests of historic truth ") of her ferocious anti-foreign and pro-Boxer edicts, she deigned to confer posthumous honours on the dead princess by raising her from the relatively humble grade of *fei* to that of *huang kuei fei*—" imperial honourable consort " —and giving her the title of *K'o Shun*—" Respectful and Obedient." Simultaneously it was given out that Chên Fei had committed suicide out of chagrin and dismay at having found herself accidentally left behind when the " tour of inspection to the west " was begun.[12] It is hardly necessary to say that these steps were taken not primarily to do honour to the memory of the dead girl or to placate her spirit, but in order that the empress-dowager might be officially exonerated from the charge of murder.

Did she ever again find tranquillity in her Palace of Tranquil Old Age ?

CHAPTER IV

The Last Years of Kuang-Hsü, 1901–1908

IT IS VERY DOUBTFUL whether the empress-dowager, during the eight years of life that remained to her after the collapse of the Boxer movement, ever realised the depth of humiliation to which her policy—or the policy accepted and carried out by her—had reduced the empire. Still more doubtful is it whether she had any suspicion that she had brought the dynasty to the edge of an abyss. Always surrounded by flatterers and deceivers, always attended by persons whose interest it was to remove any misgivings she might have as to her own wisdom, she was unable to see things as they really were or to profit, except to a very limited extent, from experience. Had she been endowed with outstanding qualities of character and brain she might have risen superior to the corrupt influences that surrounded her ; but she possessed no such qualities. Her ignorance of the world outside China was abysmal. She learned little of any value to herself or to China from previous contacts with the militant West. More than once in her lifetime had she heard the tramp of the legions of the wild men from overseas, and more than once she had bowed low before the blast. What did it matter ? They were only barbarians, and barbarians are here to-day and gone to-morrow.

The " Venerable Buddha " had plenty of time for reflection during her long journey in 1900, and her thoughts must often have carried her back to those far-off days in 1860, when the foreign devils forced the emperor Hsien-Fêng and herself to flee to Jehol, just as now they were obliging her to abandon Peking once more and flee to Hsi-an. Perhaps they would burn the Forbidden City as they had burned the Old Summer Palace forty years before. Perhaps they would even have the effrontery to repeat their performance of 1860 and burn that beautiful new home of hers in the Yi-Ho Park, in which she had hoped to spend a happy and tranquil old age. Be it so. When

they had glutted themselves with booty and burned and an-
nihilated all the beautiful things they could not carry away,
they would return to their own rocky islands, beyond the limits
of the civilised world, and China would be left in peace, to return
to the good old ways. As for herself, she might have to suffer
something like hardship for a few months, but it would soon be
over. She knew those foreign devils. The day would come when
they would be begging her to return to her capital and put
things in order. Her palaces might have to be rebuilt, and new
treasures collected to take the place of those that had been
destroyed or carried off, but that would be an easy matter with
four hundred million loyal and obedient subjects ready to bear
the whole burden. Then, when the last of the barbarian legions
had thundered past, she would plunge again, not into thought—
too much thought was to be deprecated—but into the old
delights of play-acting and flower-painting and calligraphy and
poetry, and picnics in the company of her adoring ladies-in-
waiting and her faithful eunuchs on the jade-like waters of the
K'un-ming Lake. She would have earned some relaxation after
the trouble and anxiety she had endured for the sake of her
loyal but sometimes tiresome subjects. Did not the great sage
Mencius declare that monarchs were justified in enjoying their
parks and lakes and palaces and music and other beautiful
things, and could do so without any prickings of conscience? [1]

No doubt there would be much fatiguing work to be done as
well, and some rather disagreeable duties to attend to. Some of
those princes and ministers who had given her foolish advice
and misled her about the Boxers and their magic charms would
have to be chastised. They deserved it, indeed, for having got
her into such a mess. It might even be necessary to cut off a few
heads, if those ill-mannered foreign devils were tactless enough
to insist upon it. Some regrettable concessions would have to be
made to those queer people who had become infatuated with
what they called Western civilisation, and had ridiculous fancies
about a constitution and popular assemblies and a new system
of education, but no doubt it would be possible to introduce the
essential safeguards. Those pestilential missionaries of the
"Ye-su" (Jesus) and "Heavenly Lord" heresies, who had been
at the root of all the trouble, would probably show themselves

more exacting and arrogant than ever, and as they had the support of their barbarian princes they would have to be placated. As for that troublesome and half-witted young man who had shown her such base ingratitude for his elevation to the throne, let him continue to reflect in solitude on his misdeeds, and be thankful to her for having spared his life when he so richly deserved to die.

Such may have been some of the thoughts that passed through the mind of the " Venerable Buddha " as she was borne in her sedan-chair day after day and week after week on her " tour of inspection " to those parts of the empire to which the foreign devils were least likely to follow her. She knew that some things would have to be mended and ended, that nothing would be again precisely as it had been before the rude awakening of 1900, but she never seems to have realised, to the day of her death, what a narrow escape from destruction the dynasty had had in that year, and what a strenuous uphill task lay before her and her successors if its prestige and power were to be restored. In spite of all the information which she undoubtedly possessed regarding the activities of revolutionary societies at home and abroad, and the anti-dynastic propaganda traceable to men like Sun Yat-sen, she was never told, and she had not the keen vision to see for herself, how dangerously near to the throne was creeping the spectre of revolution.

This is no place to describe the long and tedious negotiations between the allies and the Chinese government which resulted in the empress-dowager's return to Peking in 1901 and in her resumption of power. The settlement arrived at was far from satisfactory, whether it be viewed from the side of China or from that of the allies. A few of the ringleaders of the Boxer movement and perpetrators of anti-foreign outrages, such as governor Yü-IIsien, were executed, and some, like Kang-Yi, would have suffered the same fate had they not died of disease or by their own hands. Hsü T'ung, Ch'ung Ch'i and others were banished to Turkestan, several members of the imperial clan (prince Chuang, prince Yi and duke Tsai-Lan among them) were exiled or subjected to varying degrees of punishment. Prince Tuan was degraded and banished, and the nomination of his son as heir to the throne was cancelled. China was required

to agree to the payment of large indemnities in consideration of
the losses suffered by foreigners during the troubles, and for the
expenses incurred by the various expeditionary forces which
had taken part in the military operations. The story of the
" Boxer indemnities " is a long one, of which the last chapter
has not yet been told.[2] Prince Ch'un, as we have seen, was sent
on a mission of expiation to Germany. Humiliating as this
mission was, much happier was the lot of prince Ch'un than
that of his imperial brother whom he represented. The emperor
would have rejoiced if he could have conducted it in person and
thereby have escaped from the thraldom in which he continued
to drag out his wretched existence for another seven years.

The unsatisfactory features of the settlement were mainly
due to the lack of frankness and cordiality between the representatives of the various foreign powers, some of whom regarded
one another with constant suspicion and jealousy. It was also
due to their ignorance of the background of recent Chinese
politics and palace-intrigues, and to the fact that Russia, while
participating without enthusiasm in the activities of the allies
in north China, was playing a separate game in Manchuria and
sought to negotiate with the Chinese government on lines of
her own.[3] As we know from what British residents in Manchuria
had said two years earlier, that part of the Chinese or rather
the Manchu empire had already become Russian in all but
name.[4] What the Russians did in 1900, therefore, was merely
to extend and consolidate their previous gains. But this they
did with such ability and success that a Chinese historian has
summed up the result in five Chinese characters—*Tung-San-
Shêng ch'üan shih* : " The Three Eastern (i.e. Manchurian) Provinces were totally lost."[5]

The handling by the Powers of the various questions arising
out of the Boxer tragedy was naturally watched with intense
interest and anxiety by K'ang Yu-wei. He heartily approved of
the punishments meted out to such ruffians as Yü-Hsien, prince
Tuan, and other Boxer ringleaders, though the failure of the
allies to insist upon the retirement of the empress-dowager and
the reinstatement of the emperor caused him much distress.
He knew, of course, that so long as the empress held the reins
of power there was no possibility of his own return to court

favour and no hope that he might again become the trusted counsellor of an enlightened and progressive sovereign. His chief concern, however, was not for himself and his official prospects but for the welfare of his imperial master, for whose pitiable sufferings he naturally felt largely responsible.

In June, 1901, after the allies had already dictated their terms of peace to the chastened Manchu court and punishments had been duly administered to most of the guilty—the empress-dowager herself being one of the conspicuous exceptions—K'ang Yu-wei was still an exile from his native land. He was at that time in Penang, living under the protection of the British governor of the Straits Settlements ; and there he wrote a memorandum of which he had an English translation made for the information of two or three English friends. In it he strongly criticised the allies for having failed to insist on the chastisement of those whom he believed to have been the worst criminals, and expressed the earnest hope that they would not leave this very necessary part of their work undone. What has become of the Chinese original of this document I do not know. The English translation, signed by K'ang Yu-wei himself, is in my possession. Although it has never, as far as I know, been published either in Chinese or English, I do not propose to give here even an outline of its contents, which fill twenty-eight quarto pages of manuscript. Of these pages twenty-three are mainly devoted to a denunciation of Jung-Lu, who is described as " the principal culprit." The remaining five contain a similar denunciation of the empress-dowager's favourite eunuch Li Lien-ying.

My reason for not printing or analysing this interesting document is that K'ang Yu-wei, as I happen to have learned in the course of conversations with him in later years, subsequently realised that he had spoken unfairly of Jung-Lu. His strong bias against him was clearly due to the vitally important part taken by Jung-Lu in bringing about the empress-dowager's *coup d'état* of September, 1898. I have little doubt that the chief reason why " Nan-Hai " came to modify his views about Jung-Lu was that as the father-in-law of prince Ch'un, Jung-Lu was the maternal grandfather of Kuang-Hsü's successor on the throne —the emperor Hsüan T'ung. K'ang " Nan-Hai " remained to the end of his life as devotedly loyal to the dethroned

Hsüan-T'ung as he had been to the emperor Kuang-Hsü, and
he could no longer bring himself to denounce the man whose
blood ran in the veins of his revered sovereign.

According to K'ang's memorandum, Jung-Lu was largely
responsible for the Court's adhesion to the Boxer movement
and therefore had a guilty share in the subsequent excesses. In
this matter K'ang was undoubtedly wrong, as he afterwards
frankly admitted to his friends. That he erred in this respect is
not surprising, for there was much circumstantial evidence
against Jung-Lu which was accepted by the allied commanders
and by the diplomatic body in Peking. For a considerable time
the allies regarded him as one of those who were mainly responsible for the siege of the Legations. Thus when the empress-
dowager appointed him to co-operate with prince Ch'ing, Li
Hung-chang and one or two others, in the negotiation of a treaty
of peace, the allies refused to recognise him as a plenipotentiary.
Yet it subsequently became clear that if the empress-dowager
had listened to his counsels there would have been no declaration of war on the foreign Powers, no siege of the Legations,
and no massacres of foreigners either in Peking or in the provinces. We know now that Jung-Lu made strenuous efforts to
oppose the pro-Boxer activities of such princely fanatics as
prince Tuan, and that he risked his own place at court, even
his life, in his steady refusal to let the Boxers get hold of those
heavy guns and other implements of war of which he was the
custodian and the possession of which would have enabled the
Boxers to reduce the Legation Quarter to a heap of ruins in
a few hours.[6] When the Boxer madness was all over, the empress-
dowager realised how wise his counsel had been and she bitterly
regretted that she had not taken it. Until his death in 1903 she
regarded him as the most loyal and trustworthy of her ministers,
and it was as a token of her gratitude that after having brought
about a marriage between his daughter and prince Ch'un she
decreed that their son should succeed the childless Kuang-Hsü
on the throne of China.

Although after 1900 the empress-dowager (acting largely on
the urgent advice of Jung-Lu) threw herself with apparent energy
into various schemes of reform—social, educational, constitutional and military—her conversion from the reactionary policy

of the past came too late to satisfy the radicals, who, though very few in number at first, were active and irreconcilable. Her simulated zeal for reform (the necessity for which she reluctantly recognised) deceived a number of optimistic foreigners but was regarded with cynicism by those Chinese whose antagonism to the reigning House was beginning to become dangerous. Some of the edicts issued by T'zŭ-Hsi soon after her return to Peking— such as that which permitted the intermarriage of Manchus and Chinese—were intended to show that the court wished to obliterate the remaining distinctions between the two races, but they did little to stem the tide of anti-Manchu sentiment. In 1905 an imperial duke (Tsai-Tsê) was appointed head of a commission to visit foreign countries and study systems of government. At the railway station in Peking a bomb was thrown among the commissioners, and the duke himself and one of his colleagues (Shao-Ying) were wounded. Orders were issued for the drawing up of a draft constitution, under which the form of government would approximate to a limited monarchy with popular representative institutions. As the dowager's sincerity was doubted, even this failed to arouse enthusiasm or allay discontent among the small but active band of radicals.[7] In the same year an imperial edict was issued ordering the provincial authorities to suppress with severity *ko-ming p'ai man chih shuo* —" revolutionary and anti-Manchu talk "—but the effect was negligible.

In 1907 Hsü Shih-ch'ang was appointed first viceroy of the three Manchurian provinces. This was an important move, and was the most impressive of all indications that the Court had grasped the necessity of breaking down existing barriers between Manchus and Chinese. Up to that time Manchuria, as the ancestral home of the Manchu dynasty, had always been ruled by military governors under the direct control of the throne. It should be remembered in this connection that the so-called Chinese Empire was really (and had been since 1644) the Manchu Empire. One of the main justifications advanced by the revolutionaries for their rebellion in 1911 was that the Manchus were aliens and conquerors and had therefore no right to rule the Chinese people. These facts should not be overlooked, as they have an obvious bearing on the part played by the Manchu imperial House in recent Manchurian politics. In 1907 Manchuria was for the first time brought into line, for administrative purposes, with the provinces of China Proper, and it was only then that restrictions on free Chinese immigration into that great region were finally abolished.

It should be noted that this administrative change was initiated by the Manchu court itself not because it had any intention of making a present of the " three eastern provinces " to China but for practical reasons of state and in the hope of demonstrating to the Chinese that the reigning House regarded Manchus and Chinese as members of one great family. It should also be noted that the change in the status of Manchuria was brought about after the Russia-Japan war, which had resulted in the expulsion of the Russians from the Liaotung peninsula (with Port Arthur and Dairen) and Southern Manchuria, and in the transfer of the Russian rights in those regions to Japan. It will be remembered that as early as 1898 Manchuria had already (in the words of British residents there) become " Russian in all but name " ; and that the Russian hold on Manchuria had been so strengthened in 1900 that a Chinese historian could state that the three provinces had been " totally lost " to China.[8] After her victorious war against Russia in 1904–5, which had been fought on Manchurian. soil, Japan retained the rights and privileges she had won from Russia on the battlefield, but restored the provinces (subject to those rights and privileges) to the government from which Russia had wrested them. That, of course, was the government of the Manchu dynasty. To describe it as " the government of China " would not be technically correct, for the official designation of the Empire in the Chinese language was not *Chung Kuo* (" China ") but *Ta Ch'ing Kuo*, the nearest equivalent of which is " the Manchu Empire." *Ta Ch'ing* was the dynastic title assumed by the Manchu sovereigns some years before they entered China as conquerors, and it was subsequently retained by them and applied to the whole of their vast dominions, of which China was merely the largest and most important part. This use of the dynastic title as the name of the State was not a Manchu invention. The Manchus followed the practice of former dynasties, foreign and native. The terms " Chinese Empire " and " Emperor of China " were unknown to

Chinese or Manchu constitutional law, though the Chinese authorities acquiesced in the use of these terms by Western foreigners, to whom Chinese constitutional or dynastic terminology was a mystery.

Although Hsü Shih-ch'ang, the first viceroy of Manchuria, was a Chinese, it should be observed that the Court continued to regard Manchuria as still having special associations with the imperial House. Thus we find that Hsü Shih-ch'ang's successor, Hsi-Liang, was a Mongol, who had already held, among other posts, that of governor of Jehol, which like Manchuria had been treated as a special region under the direct control of the throne. Hsi-Liang's successor in 1911, the last year of the reign of Hsüan-T'ung, was Chao Erh-hsün, who being a " Chinese bannerman " was practically a Manchu by adoption.

In 1907 Wang Ta-hsieh (afterwards Chinese minister in London) was sent as head of a second mission to various European countries to study constitutional government. In the same year an attempt at rebellion was made by Sun Yat-sen and Huang Hsing in the province of Kuang-si. It was quelled without much difficulty and Sun Yat-sen was obliged to resume his foreign travels.

About this time was issued the first of many edicts forbidding students to interfere in politics. It had very little effect, though it was not till 1919, long after the Revolution, that the " student movement " in China assumed serious political importance.

We come now to 1908, the year of the death of the dowager-empress and the captive-emperor. As this is not a detailed history of the reform movement in China I have not dealt with the various reforms—political, educational and other—which received the more or less grudging approval of the throne and were in some cases carried into effect during the closing years of the reign.[9] We must pass on to the measures taken to provide for the succession.

As the emperor Kuang-Hsü was childless, it was necessary to select an heir from among his nephews, for in China the throne could not go to a brother or to a member of the same generation, though indeed that rule had been broken in his own case. He had several brothers, the eldest of whom was prince Ch'un. This was the prince who was sent to Germany in 1901 to apologise

for the murder of baron Von Ketteler. Soon after his return
from that mission the empress-dowager, as we have seen, chose
a bride for him in the person of a daughter of Jung-Lu, and
promised that if they had a son that son should become heir to
the throne.

The promise was duly kept. A son was born to prince Ch'un in
February, 1906, and was given the name of P'u-Yi. When Kuang-
Hsü lay dying, the empress-dowager issued commands that this
child, then less than three years old, should be brought from his
father's mansion—the " Pei Fu "—into the Forbidden City,
which remained his home from that day till November, 1924.
In the name of the dying emperor a valedictory edict declared
that he had " reverently received the commands of the empress-
dowager T'zŭ-Hsi " to declare the child P'u-Yi to be his successor.
Whether Kuang-Hsü was in fact told who his successor was to
be is doubtful. It is almost certain that he never saw his own
valedictory edict, and quite certain that he was not consulted
as to its contents. Simultaneously, it may be noted, Kuang-
Hsü's empress (the " Venerable Buddha's " niece) was raised to
the rank of dowager-empress (*t'ai-hou*) and given the name
Lung-Yü by which she was thereafter known[10] ; and T'zŭ-Hsi
herself was elevated from the rank of empress-dowager to that
of " Grand " or " Super " empress-dowager (*t'ai-huang-t'ai-hou*)
and given a new series of honorific titles. All this, as already
explained, was in strict accordance with dynastic usage and
precedent.[11]

Prince Ch'un, the father of the new emperor-designate, was
appointed regent. At first sight the appointment seems a natural
one and almost inevitable. The new monarch was an infant of
less than three years old. There would be a long minority. There
must be a regent. Who could fill that post more fittingly than
the child-emperor's own father ? He was a brother of the late
emperor and an imperial prince of the highest degree. To pass
him over in favour of another member of the imperial family
would surely be an unpardonable slight. Nevertheless in making
this appointment the " Venerable Buddha " committed one of
the last and greatest of her mistakes. Unfortunately for the
Manchu dynasty, and also, as I believe, for China and the
Chinese people, she was blind to the transcendent importance of

selecting as regent a statesman of first-rate ability. Very grave dangers threatened the throne. It was no time to consider the susceptibilities of this or that imperial prince. Unless her knowledge of character and her political sagacity were even less than I believe them to have been, she cannot have been ignorant of the glaring fact that prince Ch'un was too small a man for the enormously difficult task of guiding the ship of the Chinese monarchy through the wild waters that were threatening to engulf it.

When he was appointed regent it was already a matter of common knowledge in official and other circles that he was not qualified to undertake the great task that lay before him, and that the appointment was of ill omen for the dynasty. A current saying was " the Ch'ing House began with a regency and will perish with a regency,"—the earlier reference being, of course, to the great regent Durgan, uncle of Shih-Tsu (Shun-Chih) the first of the Manchu emperors to reign in China. One is reminded of the saying attributed to James V of Scotland on his deathbed —" it cam' wi' a lass and it will gang wi' a lass "—though he was wrong about the " ganging."

There is good reason to believe that Yüan Shih-k'ai strove hard to prevent the nomination of P'u-Yi as heir to the throne, because he knew that this would mean the elevation to power of prince Ch'un, with disastrous results to his own career. Yüan's choice for the throne was prince P'u-Lun, who was senior great-grandson of the emperor Tao-Kuang.[12] Had Yüan's advocacy of P'u-Lun's claims been successful, Yüan, of course, would have remained in office and would doubtless have enjoyed the high favour of the new sovereign. It is difficult to over-estimate the difference this might have made to the course of Chinese history.

Prince Ch'un was, and is, a man of some amiable qualities, free from malice or vindictiveness, sociable, as interested in the Chinese drama as he is uninterested in politics or in the affairs of the great world. He must be given credit for being one of the two Manchu princes (Tsai-Hsün is the other) who has a respectable knowledge of the Manchu language. He is well-intentioned, tries in his languid and ineffectual way to please everyone, succeeds in pleasing no one, shrinks from responsibility, is thoroughly unbusinesslike, is disastrously deficient in energy,

will-power and grit, and there is reason to believe that he lacks
both physical and moral courage. He is helpless in an emergency,
has no original ideas, and is liable to be swayed by any smooth
talker. After he became regent, however, the flattery of sycophants tended to make him obstinately tenacious of his own
opinions, which almost invariably turned out to be wrong.
During several years of fairly intimate contact with prince
Ch'un I came to be so deeply impressed by his fatal tendency to
do the wrong thing or choose the wrong course in matters affecting the imperial House or the interests of the young emperor his
son, that I once made the suggestion to my colleagues in the
Forbidden City that we might actually turn that tendency of his
to good account by adopting the following general principle :
If two possible courses of action present themselves, ask prince
Ch'un which in his opinion should be followed—then follow the
other.

Credit should be given him for having done his best, such as it
was, to honour the memories of his martyred brother and of some
at least of those who had served him. To prince Ch'un it was due
that posthumous honours were conferred upon the imperial
tutor, Wêng T'ung-ho. But he dared not go so far as to recall
K'ang Yu-wei, and the manner in which he dealt with Yüan
Shih-k'ai, whether we regard it as too lenient or too harsh, was
disastrous in its results.

After 1908, and especially after the death of the Lung-Yü
empress-dowager, of whom he stood in awe, he began to develop
a curious strain of vanity which manifested itself in odd ways
and may have been due to what in the fashionable jargon is
called an inferiority complex. To this day he is blissfully ignorant of any political or other shortcomings in himself, or of anything whatever in his career as a ruler or as a statesman that
deserves censure or contempt. He has about him an air of bland
self-satisfaction which seems to be the outward sign of an inward
malaise and which may indeed have its defensive uses ; for if that
malaise were to emerge above subconsciousness it might drive
him mad with shame and despair.

The mere fact that the new sovereign was prince Ch'un's son
did not make the prince's appointment as regent inevitable,
though it would certainly have been difficult or impossible to

appoint another member of the imperial clan in his place. There was another course open to the empress-dowager which, had she adopted it, might have saved the dynasty from ruin and China from decades of chaos and civil war. She could have passed over all the imperial princes and appointed a Council of Regency consisting of a small group of the ablest and most enlightened statesmen in the Empire. A feasible scheme would have been to create a council of five members, two being Manchus (but not imperial princes) and three Chinese. The fact that the Chinese members of the council outnumbered the Manchus would have been gratifying to Chinese pride and might have convinced all except a few anti-Manchu irreconcilables like Sun Yat-sen that the court was sincere in its determination to obliterate all distinctions between the two races and to put the interests of all the peoples of the Empire above every other consideration. To make the scheme workable it would have been essential to surrender once and for all the pernicious theory that the throne was the private property of the ruling House, and to accept the principle that it was an organic part of the Chinese State, existing not for the glorification and profit of one family but for the benefit of the people.

It would have been a difficult but by no means an impossible task to select the members of the Council of Regency. The reactionaries and obscurantists, though still numerous, were no longer in a position to stem the tide of reform by allying themselves with Boxers. Men were not afraid to say openly that changes were overdue and that China must modernise herself or perish ; and there was no dearth of able, patriotic and liberal-minded officials and statesmen in the country who had not yet lost all faith in the dynasty. I need only mention such men as Hsü Shih-ch'ang, Chao Erh-hsün, Chêng Hsiao-hsü, Li Ching-mai (son of the viceroy Li Hung-chang) and at least a dozen other eligible men, besides the strong Cantonese contingent of loyalists headed by K'ang Yu-wei. Had Yuan Shih-k'ai himself been appointed one of the regents, this might have satisfied his ambition and saved the throne. The very knowledge that to the regents were entrusted the interests and welfare of their infant sovereign would in itself have been a spur to their loyalty, if such were needed. One of their principal duties would have been to see that their imperial charge was brought up in wholesome surroundings and shielded from the demoralising influences of the Forbidden City. This would have necessitated the abolition of the eunuch-system and the severe curtailment of the authority and influence of the corrupt and extravagant *Nei Wu Fu*—the imperial household department. It would also have been the duty of the Council of Regency to see that the young emperor's education was entrusted to tutors who were neither bigoted conservatives, blind to the merits of all civilisations but their own, nor extreme radicals, intoxicated with what draughts they had imbibed of Western learning and ready to break up the foundations of Chinese culture. Such tutors could have put him in sympathetic touch with the thought and art and science of both East and West and taught him to fit himself, under modern conditions, for the constitutional rulership of a great world-state.

Under the conditions which I have imagined, the minority of Hsüan-T'ung, so far from being a source of additional weakness or danger to the dynasty, as royal minorities have so often been, might have inaugurated a new era of prosperity and glory both for the Chinese people and for their monarchy. But those conditions were never realised. Instead of a Council of Regency, China was given a prince Ch'un, and the result—or shall we say the sequence?—was Revolution.

CHAPTER V

The Empress-Dowager T'zŭ-Hsi

IF THE JUDGMENTS contained in the foregoing pages are approximately correct, it will be seen that the allies, when they were drawing up the terms of peace in 1901, made a disastrous mistake in failing to insist upon the elimination of the empress-dowager from active politics and upon the reinstatement of the emperor. If it be objected that the mere whisper of such a policy would have condemned the unhappy Kuang-Hsü to immediate death, it may be replied that this risk, though perhaps unavoidable, might have been minimised by the timely issue of a solemn declaration addressed by the united Powers to T'zŭ-Hsi herself giving her a guarantee of personal immunity from all punishment other than removal from the regency but holding her personally responsible for the safety of Kuang-Hsü up to the moment of his re-enthronement.

The great desirability of restoring Kuang-Hsü to the full exercise of his imperial authority (assuming that under the terrible conditions of his imprisonment he had not already become a mental wreck) was fully realised by many of the clearest-sighted Chinese of the day. That K'ang Yu-wei and his party earnestly desired the emperor's reinstatement goes without saying. Instead of quoting K'ang Yu-wei on this subject I will draw attention to some passages in the able letters published in book-form in 1901 under the title *The Chinese Crisis from Within*. The author's name was given as " Wen Ching," but it is now known that this was a name assumed by that well-known pioneer of Chinese educational and social reform Dr. Lim Boon Keng.

" The empress-dowager must be made to resign her regency, unless the allies can get hold of the person of the emperor and can restore him as the *de facto* ruler. In that case he could, with one stroke of the vermilion pencil, deprive the empress-dowager of

all legal authority to interfere in State affairs. . . . The reactionaries are very unpopular in the middle and southern provinces,
and millions would hail with joy the return of the emperor to
power. There is no real difficulty in establishing his authority, for
it is universally acknowledged throughout the Empire. . . . The
most progressive Chinese will come to the front, and with the
assistance of the Powers the new government of Kuang-Hsü is
sure to advance by leaps and bounds. . . . If Kuang-Hsü be not
restored, it would not be surprising to find that the reform
associations would become revolutionary societies, and before
long a great revolution would sweep over China, and entail
untold misery on the land, with incalculable loss to the commerce
of the world. . . . Now the seeds of a great revolution are all
germinating in China. The allies have just now the means of
averting the threatening danger. Will they see it ? "[1]

Alas, the allies did not see it, and " Wen Ching's " prophecy
was verified ten years later.

At first glance it may appear that the passages I have quoted
contain a fatal contradiction, inasmuch as the writer says in one
sentence that the emperor's authority " is universally acknowledged throughout the Empire," and in another that " the seeds
of a great revolution are all germinating in China." But there is
no contradiction. What " Wen Ching " meant and said was that
" a great revolution would sweep over China " if the government remained in the hands of reactionaries like the empress-
dowager. But the emperor was not a reactionary. On the contrary he was, as we know, an enthusiast for reform. Let him be
restored to the throne from which the reactionaries had forcibly
removed him and the world would hear little more of revolution
in China. That was the view of " Wen Ching " and of many
others, and I believe it to have been correct.[2]

The objection will probably be raised that the empress-dowager
herself became a reformer while she was still in exile in Hsi-an,
that reforms of various kinds received her approval and were
carried out with some energy during the remaining years of her
life, yet that the country was not, after all, saved from revolution. But, as pointed out in the last chapter, very few Chinese
took the empress-dowager and her new-born zeal for reform as
seriously as many foreigners have done. It has been declared by

Western writers that after the collapse of the Boxer movement
and the return of the Court to Peking, if not before it, the empress-dowager experienced a real " change of heart," and that
her apparent eagerness both to cultivate friendly relations with
foreigners and to adopt a policy of reform was sincere. Few if any
Chinese, who ought to know best, have said this or believe it.
There was no " change of heart," there was only a " change of
head " ; and a change of both heart and head were necessary if
the " reform associations " spoken of by " Wen Ching " were to
be prevented from becoming " revolutionary societies." Moreover, the head that changed was not a well-endowed head, either
before or after the change. It was a head that possessed no inner
source of illumination and was incapable of borrowing the light
it needed from external sources.

An accomplished writer declares that after 1900 T'zŭ-Hsi
" adopted a policy of modernisation on Western lines and by
sheer force of character compelled a partial observance of her
commands."[3] I believe it would be truer to say that in the post-
Boxer reform movement she followed rather than led. She had
the sense to accept the assurances of wiser people than herself
who insisted that the reforms she hated must come, that the
Westernisation which she detested could no longer be wholly
excluded. Like Charles II of England she did not relish the idea
of setting out on her travels again. Hard facts and the exhortations of men like Jung-Lu and the great viceroy Li Hung-chang
had rubbed it into her that it was not by " Boxer " methods
that the foreign devils could be kept at bay or driven out of
China. But she neither forgot nor forgave those who had ventured to defy her in 1898. She had not the magnanimity to
acknowledge that she had been wrong, nor the sense of justice
to incline her to make such reparation as was possible for the
crimes she had committed. The *K'ang tang* (K'ang Yu-wei's
party) remained on her black list, and K'ang Yu-wei himself
would have suffered the death penalty, probably without any
pretence of a trial, had he come within her grasp. The emperor
continued to be her despised and hated prisoner, and on him she
never ceased to heap insult and indignity. The fact that he
had initiated a policy of reform which she herself was now
reluctantly compelled to endorse and carry into effect,

increased the fire of her hatred by adding to it the fuel of jealousy.

There are two diametrically opposed views of T'zŭ Hsi as a ruler. One view is that she possessed consummate gifts of statesmanship and kept the dynasty alive long after it had ceased to hold the " mandate of Heaven." The other view is that she was largely or mainly responsible for its collapse. I know of no Chinese authority of any standing who takes the former view, but it is a common one among Western students. Stephen King-Hall, for example, tells us that the downfall of the dynasty " was retarded by the genius of a woman "[4]; while Dr. Cameron says that " only her indomitable energy kept life in the dynasty after the Taiping rebellion had brought it perilously near its end " ; and that had she not held the regency the decline " would have been more rapid and disastrous than it was."[5]

Of those who hold the opposite opinion one British and one Chinese authority may be cited as representative. W. E. Soothill says that by the destruction of the reform movement of 1898, the empress-dowager " tore down the last supports of the shaken throne."[6] A Chinese writer already quoted, " Wen Ching," declared in 1900 that for many years T'zŭ-Hsi had been " rushing the empire to the verge of ruin."[7]

Of the two opposing views, I believe the second is nearer the truth than the first, though it fails to take account of the fact, which should be emphasised, that T'zŭ-Hsi was only an ignorant woman who should not be held responsible for all the things done badly or left undone in her name.

Of four American writers, the first describes her as " the most remarkable woman sovereign and the most unbridled despot the world has known "[8] ; the second asks the question, " is it too much to say that she was the greatest woman of the last half century ? "[9] ; the third declares that she was " a strong character such as history has seldom recorded "[10] ; and the fourth has said of her that she was one whom " history will rank among the greatest rulers of mankind."[11]

I do not think so meanly of history's ability to discern true greatness. Several years before I entered the service of the Manchu court and had access to fuller information, I described

the empress-dowager as one " who through the pitiful misuse of
her unrivalled opportunities must be held mainly responsible
for the ignominious collapse of the most ancient of imperial
thrones."[12] I should now substitute " largely " for " mainly " ;
and I should add that her responsibility as a moral agent was
limited by the facts that she was in the grip of a vicious system
which was not her creation (it existed not only before her time
but before the days of the Manchu dynasty) and that she was
bound by corrupt traditions of which she was the inheritor.
Had she been one of the " greatest rulers of mankind," however,
or " the greatest woman of the last half-century," or " the most
remarkable woman sovereign the world has known," she could
have loosened that vicious grip and set herself free from those
corrupt traditions. She had neither the strength of character nor
the will that would have been necessary for so great an accom-
plishment.[13]

Had the " Great " empress-dowager been the statesmanlike,
wise and patriotic ruler some of her Western admirers declare
her to have been, there is far more than a mere possibility that
there would have been no China-Japan war in 1894, no necessity to alienate ports and concessions to foreign Powers in 1898,
no opposition on the part of court and government to measures
of reform, no imperial association with any such movement as
that of the Boxers, no siege of the Legations, no indemnities,
no revolution, no " republic," no collapse of law and order, no
loss of Mongolia, Turkestan, Tibet, Jehol, and Manchuria. All
" unequal treaties " might have been abrogated by mutual agreement long ago without any detriment to her friendly relations
with other countries, and China might now be taking a leading
part in the great task of saving humanity from the economic,
nationalistic and other perils in which the whole world is
involved to-day.

No doubt it is futile to speculate on all these might-have-
beens. Moreover, it is unjust to blame T'zŭ-Hsi for not having
been other than nature made her. It was not her fault that she
was not endowed with great qualities of statesmanship. Nevertheless, that is no reason why we should gratuitously bestow
on her the admiration due to those whom " history will rank
among the greatest rulers of mankind."

Lady Susan Townley, describing an interview with the empress-dowager at the Summer Palace after the Boxer war was over, commented on the difficulty of realising that " this friendly little woman with the brown face of a kindly Italian peasant " was " the mysterious and powerful autocrat . . . who had deliberately debased and degraded the unfortunate emperor sitting beside her, the fiend who had egged on the Boxers to nameless outrages." And she concludes by asking whether T'zŭ-Hsi was " really responsible for all this " or " only a tool in the compelling hand of destiny."[14]

My reply would be that she was indeed a tool but a willing one, and that the compelling hand was not that of destiny but that of patriotic but bigoted conservatives who were themselves the victims of a corrupt gang of Manchu and Chinese knaves and fools. They found her useful for their purposes ; her position in the State and at court, as I have explained, made her their appropriate and indispensable instrument ; and her education, her environment and the limitations of her own character and intellect made it easy and almost inevitable for her to become their nominal leader, their protectress and their dupe.

Among her minor characteristics, vanity was one of the most conspicuous. It was such that if she did not receive from others the full measure of flattery that she craved, she did not hesitate to lay it on herself with a trowel that Lord Beaconsfield would have been delighted to borrow for purposes of his own. " Do you know, I have often thought "—so she remarked to the " princess " Der Ling—" that I am the most clever woman that ever lived and others cannot compare with me."[15] We may take it that neither the " princess " Der Ling nor anyone else at court had the daring or the inclination to contradict her.

But if she loved flattery, she was shrewd enough to know that others loved it too, and her knowledge of human nature was sound enough to enable her to turn the heads of many of the Legation ladies who attended her receptions. She hated them all, but it amused her to observe how readily they absorbed her loving assurances of esteem. She entertained parties of foreign ladies several times before, as well as after, the siege of the Legations ; and it is on record that on one of those occasions she murmured gently to each of the wives of the foreign plenipotentiaries,

" We are all one family," and sent them home full of
admiration for her grace and charm and rejoicing in tangible
tokens of her affectionate regard. Very soon afterwards, as an
American missionary observed, she was issuing edicts ordering
her troops to slaughter all the foreigners within reach, so that
only the Chinese and Manchu contingents of the " one family "
might be left surviving.[16]

After her return from exile her hatred of foreigners was
probably more intense than it had been before. Had they not
caused her to " lose face " to a degree that was never to be
forgotten or forgiven? There was no sincerity in the protestations
of friendship with which she renewed her acquaintance with the
ladies of the foreign Legations after 1900, though some of them
listened to her prattle with childish delight. Perhaps " charming " empresses, like " dear " duchesses, start on the race for
popularity with rather unfair advantages.

She liked to hear herself compared with Queen Victoria,
always provided, of course, that the comparison was made with
due discretion. Much more apt, however, would be a comparison
with Queen Elizabeth in her less Elizabethan moments. Some
of the stories which illustrate the vanity of the " Venerable
Buddha " are comparable with that told by the Scottish ambassador who in answer to one of Elizabeth's questions had to
inform her that her height was not equal to that of his queen.
" Then," said Elizabeth, " she is too high ; for I myself am
neither too high nor too low." And although Queen Elizabeth
may never have ordered an emperor's consort to be flogged in
her presence, far less thrown into a well to drown, we know that
Elizabeth did not shrink from publicly boxing the ears of her
courtiers and ladies-in-waiting. Someone ought to have told the
" Venerable Buddha " about that. It would have amused her.[17]

She liked to compare herself not only with queens but with
divine beings. One of her favourite pastimes in the Summer
Palace was to assume the guise of Kuan-Yin—the Buddhist
bodhisattva whom foreigners know as the Goddess of Mercy—
emerging gracefully from a lotus sea for the purpose of bestowing
the " sweet dew " of her love and compassion on suffering
humanity. The attendant angels on these happy occasions,
standing beside her with clasped hands in attitudes of blissful

adoration, were such persons as her trusty henchman and major-domo, the eunuch Li Lien-ying.[18]

The fact that she liked to think of herself as a Buddhist divinity has nothing whatever to do with the appellation so often bestowed upon her of *Lao Fo-yeh.* The usual foreign rendering of this phrase is " the Old Buddha." I have preferred " the Venerable Buddha," because in this connection the Chinese character *lao* (especially when combined with *yeh*) has a respectful signification which " Old " hardly possesses in English. But although it is respectful, and was actually used by persons addressing her orally at the foot of the throne, it would be erroneous to suppose that it indicated a degree of reverence not accorded to her predecessors. The term *Tang Chin Fo Yeh*—" the Buddha of the present age "—was one of the popular appellations of all emperors. Father Ripa, who resided at the Chinese court early in the eighteenth century, has the following remarks on this subject. The emperor K'ang-Hsi, he says, " was held in such veneration throughout China, that he often received the appellation of *Fo*, a national deity universally adored, both by Tartars and Chinese. I myself very frequently heard him designated as the living *Fo*."[19] Evidently the good Jesuit Father was not aware that *Fo* was the Chinese (Pekingese) word for " Buddha," and that it was a popular designation of Chinese emperors. Another popular title of respect bestowed upon imperial personages was *Chu Tzŭ*— Master or Lord, Mistress or Lady. During my residence at the Manchu court this was the term commonly used by the eunuchs and other palace-servants when they were speaking of the *huang-kuei-fei* or dowager-consorts.

In spite of the reverential language in which her courtiers spoke of and to her, the empress-dowager was not a typical product of Chinese civilisation at its best. Her manners were not always those which Confucian ethics attribute to the *chün-tzŭ*— the fine flower of civilised humanity—or to the royal sages who laid the foundations of Chinese culture. When in 1897 she dismissed from all his posts a high military official named Lin Hsiu-ch'uan merely because at an audience in the palace he was slow in assuming the correct kneeling posture, her reaction to this misdemeanour stands out in startling contrast to that of a certain provincial governor of whom we read in the official history of the Han dynasty. We are there told of a man who failed to make a respectful obeisance to the governor and was brought before him for punishment. Instead of ordering the man's execution, as apparently he might have been expected to do, the governor said " Let him go. It is my fault, not his, that he is bad-mannered. It shows that I have failed to civilise those whom I have been called upon to rule." Someone should have told that story, too, to the " Venerable Buddha." It would not have amused her, but it might have made her think.

Mr. Robert Loraine has recently informed us that if we turn the pages of history we shall find that the outstanding women —with the possible exception of Queen Victoria—were chiefly of the " tiger-cat type." T'zŭ-Hsi was, I think, a woman of that type, though perhaps from deference to the Chinese symbol of imperial dignity it might be preferable to say that she was of the type of the dragon—a creature whose potentialities for both good and evil are of a far more awe-inspiring character than those of a mere cat, however tigerish.

I have said that the empress-dowager loved to pose as the " Goddess of Mercy." It is not surprising that such was the case, for she believed, and was encouraged by the court to believe, that she was actually an incarnation of that bodhisattva. Thereby hangs a tale which we may, if we choose, regard as a tragic one. It happened that in 1908 the empress-dowager was not the only avatar of the bodhisattva Kuan-Yin then existing in China. Every Dalai Lama is—according to Lamaistic doctrine—an incarnation of that divine being, and the Dalai Lama had recently arrived at the sacred mountain of Wu-t'ai in the Chinese province of Shansi. I happened to be travelling in Western China soon after his arrival—he had but recently fled from Lhasa on the approach of the Younghusband expedition—and during a short stay at one of the monasteries of Wu-t'ai in the summer of 1908 I was granted the privilege of a private audience.[20]

Shortly afterwards—in September—the incarnate Kuan-Yin from Tibet proceeded at the invitation of the court from Wu-t'ai to Peking, where he was accorded a state-reception by the incarnate Kuan-Yin of China. For a short time, therefore, there were two Kuan-Yins living in Peking at the same time. Within a few weeks, however, there were no longer two but only one, that one being the Dalai Lama. His rival, the empress-dowager, was dead. In her death the lama fraternity in Peking, and many of the Peking populace, found a striking illustration of the well-known fact that if two " Living Buddhas " or two incarnations of the same bodhisattva are rash enough to manifest themselves simultaneously in the same locality, one of them must perforce withdraw to another world to await in patience the result of one more revolution of the wheel of metempsychosis.

On the subject of the relations between the empress-dowager and the emperor, I have been assured by many of the old palace eunuchs that her dislike for her imperial nephew antedated the events of 1898. A story told by them will be barely intelligible to those who are not acquainted with the ancient and still popular Chinese belief that a sick person may be restored to health by partaking of medicine consisting of a piece of human flesh voluntarily sacrificed by a son or other near relative or by a faithful friend or servant. The theory underlying this repulsive superstition is that the divine powers are touched by the act of filial piety or loyal devotion shown by the painful sacrifice, and therefore allow the patient to recover. Shortly before the China-Japan war, so the story goes, the empress-dowager had a severe illness. The emperor paid her a sympathetic visit. While he was at her bedside—the only third person in the room being the head-eunuch Li Lien-ying—she remarked, with a deep sigh of self-commiseration, " I know I am going to die, because I have no one so devoted to me that he will give me the only medicine that would cure me of my sickness." As she spoke, she gazed first at the emperor, then at the eunuch, but though both well knew what the medicine was which she had in mind, neither of them made any audible response.

Shortly afterwards, the " Venerable Buddha " began to make a rapid and complete recovery. Noticing that Li Lien-ying had apparently been absent from duty for a few days, she enquired the reason. She was told that he was ill. Later on, the nature of his illness was disclosed to her, no doubt by one of Li's own eunuch-subordinates. He had cut off a piece of flesh from his thigh ; it had been cooked, and her imperial majesty had eaten it. From that time, according to the story, Li Lien-ying rose rapidly in his mistress's favour, and the emperor who as her son by adoption had " lost face " by failing to demonstrate the sincerity of his filial piety in the disgusting manner expected of him, became an object of dislike and contempt.[21]

A member of the imperial family is my authority for a little anecdote relating to the emperor's last interview with his august jailoress. One of his regular duties or punishments was to visit her palace at frequent intervals and to prostrate himself before her throne. It was a pure formality, kept up by the empress-dowager partly because she wished to satisfy herself from time to time that he was still her prisoner, and partly because the sight of his humiliation gave her grim satisfaction. One day, in the autumn of 1908, he went to the Ning-Shou palace to perform the usual ceremonial observance, but his illness was entering its last stage and he knew that he was dying. With drooping head and trembling limbs, supported by eunuchs, he tottered into the throne-hall, obviously on the verge of collapse. As he prepared to go down on his knees, in the usual way, the empress-dowager was struck by his extreme weakness and emaciation. The sight moved her, and the attendant eunuchs observed to their astonishment that there were tears in her eyes and on her cheeks. The ceremony of the emperor's *kotow* before the empress-dowager was usually carried out in complete silence on both sides. On this occasion she suddenly broke the silence with these words—*pu yung hsing li*—" you need not kneel." But wearily the dying man sank to his knees, and as he did so he murmured in a scarcely audible voice, " I will kneel. It is for the last time." And the last time, indeed, it proved to be.

A few days later there were two imperial corpses in Peking —one in the " Palace of Tranquil Old Age," the other in the " Fairyland " of the Three Lakes.[22] It may have been that the " Venerable Buddha " had a premonition that they were both about to enter the shadows, in which hatreds, perhaps, are extinguished for ever. Or was it merely that she suddenly remembered that she was the " Goddess of Mercy " and that the time had come for her to show that mercy was a quality not wholly alien to her nature ?

The death of the empress-dowager, on November 15th, 1908,

took place less than a day after that of the emperor. The coincidence inevitably gave rise to the rumour that the " Venerable
Buddha," knowing her illness to be fatal, and determined that
her victim should not survive to triumph over her dead body,
took steps to ensure that he should be the first to die. Another
story is to the effect that certain palace eunuchs, who had been
the agents of her tyranny, had lived in dread of the day when
the emperor would be restored to the plenitude of his power,
and therefore administered the poison that would end his life
and save their own.[23] I do not believe the first story, and although the second one seems much more probable, I am aware
of no evidence to support it. I have in my possession a report
by a well-informed British medical man, prepared from evidence
supplied by the palace physicians, regarding the physical condition and last illness of Kuang-Hsü, and it justifies the belief that
he died a natural death—hastened, no doubt, by the barbarous
treatment of which he had been the helpless victim for ten long
years. After all, perhaps, it would make very little difference to
our estimate of the empress-dowager's character whether she
brought about his death by methods employed over a period of
several years or by a dose of poison taking effect in ten minutes.
But if credit is due to her for having refrained from committing
murder at a moment when she herself was on her death-bed, we
need not begrudge it.

The emperor Kuang-Hsü was born in 1870. He succeeded to
the throne in his fifth year, and till 1889 when he married and
attained his majority at nineteen the government was in the
hands of the empress-dowager. From 1889 to 1898 he was actual
reigning emperor, subject to the old lady's occasional interference. By far the most serious example of her interference during
that period was in connection with the events that led to the
China-Japan war, which first made China's weakness manifest
to the whole world. Her share of responsibility for that catastrophe was very great. From 1898, when Kuang-Hsü was
twenty-eight, to his death in 1908 at the age of thirty-eight, he
was again, as we have seen, emperor only in name. Had he lived
to the present time (1934) he would have been no more than
sixty-four years of age. Had there been no interference with the
reform-schemes of 1898, his reign in spite of the disaster of the

China-Japan war, might have gone on record in Chinese history
as one of prosperity and progress both for the Manchu dynasty
and for the people of China. He might have left a name equal
to that of his illustrious Japanese contemporary, the emperor
Meiji, under whom Japan entered upon her wonderful period
of reform and development. The reign of Meiji began only seven
years before Kuang-Hsü ascended the Dragon throne and ended
four years after Kuang-Hsü's pitiful death.

It is true that during the previous century the Manchu
dynasty had received a series of terrific shocks and had experienced almost overwhelming disasters, that its influence and
prestige had suffered such grave damage that it is legitimate to
doubt whether a recovery was possible. But the dynasty had
suffered shocks and disasters for several decades without collaps-
ing, and even the unprecedented humiliations of 1900 did not
bring about its immediate overthrow. This seems to show that
it possessed reserves of strength hidden from foreign and even
from most Chinese eyes, and that its recuperative powers were
much greater than foreign observers suspected in the latter half
of the nineteenth century. In 1898 the dynasty stood at the
parting of the ways. It might have taken a turning that would
have led it from the valley of defeat and dishonour to the
uplands of prosperity and renewed glory. It took the wrong
turning that led ultimately into a morass of decay and death.

The city of Peking, enclosing the splendid yellow-roofed
palaces of its vanished emperors and surrounded by hundreds
of square miles of great plains and mountains, stands between
the two magnificent mausolea, constructed, in imitation of
those of past dynasties, for the Manchu imperial House. The
body of Kuang-Hsü lies among the *Hsi Ling* or Western Tombs ;
the body of the " Great " empress-dowager—or what remains
of it after the hideous outrage of less than six years ago—lies
among the *Tung Ling* or Eastern Tombs.[24] Just as in their
life-times emperor and empress-dowager were sundered from
one another by a spiritual abyss, so in death they remain
physically sundered by the width of half a province.

Odysseus in *Hecuba* declared that he would be content with
a mean subsistence in this life if in death he could be assured of
the abiding grace of a noble tomb.[25] The " Venerable Buddha"

liked to have it both ways. She loved her costly Summer Palace in the West, which she found a pleasant camping-ground in this transitory life ; and she loved to contemplate that sumptuous tomb in the East, wherein her body—so she fondly dreamed— would rest in everlasting peace amid the mingled glories of mountain and forest and the imperial splendours added thereto by the hand of man. Could she have looked a few years into the future, and have seen what was to become of that peace and those imperial splendours in July, 1928, the stubborn spirit of the " Venerable Buddha " would have been stricken and humbled to the dust.

CHAPTER VI

The Revolution, 1911

THE CHILD P'U-YI ascended the throne in October, 1908. In accordance with Chinese dynastic usage a title was chosen for his reign—Hsüan-T'ung—and it is therefore customary, especially among foreigners, to use that reign-title (*nien-hao*) as if it were his personal name. To do so is, indeed, very convenient, because in China an emperor's personal or private name (what we would call his Christian name) is under a kind of taboo, and throughout his lifetime he is not named, but is referred to by the Chinese equivalent of " his majesty the emperor " (*huang shang*). Even after an emperor's death his personal name is not used ; he is then given a *miao-hao* or " temple-name," under which sacrifices are offered to him in accordance with the rites of ancestor-worship. It is by his " temple-name " that he goes down to history and is properly referred to in speech and writing. The personal (and therefore unused) name of Hsüan-T'ung's predecessor was Tsai-T'ien. This name—or rather the second syllable of it—was taboo, and could not be used by the public or even at court. His " reign-title " was Kuang-Hsü (to which of course no taboo was attached) and the " temple-name " conferred upon him after death was Tê Tsung. In educated Chinese circles it is often considered a mark of carelessness, or ignorance, even of slight ill-breeding, to speak of " the emperor Kuang-Hsü " ; his correct designation is " the emperor Tê Tsung," just as the emperor whom foreigners generally know by his reign-title of Ch'ien Lung is more correctly described as Kao Tsung.

The title of a new reign is not changed till the beginning of the year following the former emperor's death. Hence the whole of the year which roughly corresponds with 1908 was the thirty-fourth and last year of Kuang-Hsü, and 1909 was the first year of Hsüan-T'ung.

One of the first acts of the regent, prince Ch'un, was to remove Yüan Shih-k'ai from all his posts and invite him to go home and nurse an imaginary ailment in his leg. It will be remembered that Yüan had taken a prominent part in the events of 1898 and had betrayed the confidence reposed in him by the emperor. After this he naturally stood high in favour with the empress-dowager to the end of the reign. He became viceroy of the metro-politan province in 1901, a minister of the Army Reorganisation Council in 1903, president of the Board of Foreign Affairs in 1907 and a Grand Councillor in the same year. He doubtless knew that his official life—perhaps his physical life—depended on the maintenance in power of his patroness the empress-dowager, and it is easy to understand why, after the Boxer troubles, he was strenuously opposed to her removal from the regency or to the reinstatement of Kuang-Hsü.

Unfortunately for Kuang-Hsü, Yüan Shih-k'ai's prestige among foreigners stood very high, for he had seen through the pretensions of the Boxers from the beginning, and in 1900 had used his position as governor of Shantung to protect all the foreigners in his province. Moreover, he was an opportunist, and readily adapted his principles to circumstances. Having been clearly conscious of the folly of the empress-dowager in allying herself with the Boxers and in defying the Powers, and being himself a man of comparatively enlightened views, it is very pos-sible that had it not been for the unhappy episode of 1898 and the hopelessness of obtaining forgiveness from the sovereign whom he had betrayed, he would have used his great influence with the foreign Powers to bring about a settlement which would have included the retirement of the empress-dowager and the reinstatement of the emperor. As it was, his fortunes were inextricably linked with hers, and in doing his utmost to protect her interests he had the much greater satisfaction of knowing that he was also safeguarding his own.

Not only was there no possibility of reconciliation between Yüan Shih-k'ai and the emperor, but there was undying hate between Yüan and the survivors of the reform party of 1898. K'ang Yu-wei and his friends not unnaturally regarded Yüan not only as a traitor to his sovereign but also as the person who was mainly responsible for the execution of their six colleagues after the empress-dowager's *coup d'état* of that year. Yüan on the other hand dreaded the vengeance of K'ang Yu-wei and his

Fc

party if they were allowed to renew their activities in China and obtain a footing at Court. This partially explains why it was that even after the inauguration of a new reform policy under the auspices of the empress-dowager herself, K'ang Yu-wei and his friends were never invited to take part in the development of that new policy and never received forgiveness for their past sins.

There is a story that after Kuang-Hsü's death there was found among his papers a document on which was written an order for the immediate execution of Yüan Shih-k'ai. This was regarded by certain members of the imperial family as having the sanctity of a dying wish ; and as they themselves regarded Yüan with jealousy and mistrust they expressed the opinion that Kuang-Hsü's last commands should be obeyed. Prince Ch'un vacillated, and after some delay decided to spare Yüan's life but to dismiss him from all his offices. Hence the command that he should retire to his native village and recuperate his health.

Prince Ch'un acted very rashly and foolishly in this matter, because Yüan's influence with the powerful Pei-yang party and with the new model army was very great, and the regent ought to have foreseen that a man of Yüan's vigour, ability and influential connections would not be content to devote the rest of his life to studying the Buddhist sutras or practising the art of calligraphy. Nevertheless he obeyed orders without an audible murmur and without a moment's delay. The fact that the affair was settled in this prompt and peaceful manner is in itself instructive as showing that even in the last decade of the dynasty's existence the commands of the Throne were still obeyed by the highest and most powerful officials in the land. Had this episode taken place fifteen or twenty years later, under the so-called republic, Yüan's dismissal from office would probably have been followed by a " declaration of independence " on his part and a ruinous civil war. Yüan's influence over the northern army— by far the best-trained fighting organisation in the Empire— was undoubtedly very great ; but armies had not yet become the personal property of their commanders, to be used as the instruments of their private ambitions and aggrandisement. The monarchy, in fact, was still a going concern. The emperor still reigned.

But he did not reign much longer. The remainder of the dismal story is soon told. The prince-regent found himself overwhelmed with difficulties far beyond his capacity to overcome. He wanted, for the sake of peace, to please everyone, but this he soon found he could not do, one reason being that he had to cope with a new empress-dowager, the widow of Kuang-Hsü and niece of the " Venerable Buddha." Kuang-Hsü's valedictory edict contained a clause to the effect that in all matters of importance the prince-regent must consult the new empress-dowager and " take her instructions."[1] It has been supposed that this clause was deliberately inserted with a view to maintaining and strengthening the position of the Yehonala clan ; but though this may have been true, there was nothing in the clause that conflicted with orthodox Chinese principles. As has been explained above, an empress-dowager had rights and privileges merely in virtue of her relationship to the emperor ; and even if she had not been mentioned in the valedictory edict it would have been possible for her (and from the Chinese point of view not illegitimate) to make her will prevail in matters affecting the child-emperor and even in ordinary affairs of state.[2] Not only was she the emperor's aunt by marriage, not only empress-dowager, but she could also claim the relationship and the rights of a mother, inasmuch as by his elevation to the throne he became the adopted son of her consort, the emperor Kuang-Hsü.

The movement towards constitutional reform continued to make progress. It had already gone so far, indeed, that to check its further advance would have been dangerous, and neither prince Ch'un nor his rival the empress-dowager Lung-Yü was anxious to run unnecessary risks. Early in 1909 a decree was issued stating that the Court positively intended to establish a constitutional government, and some conservative officials who opposed reform were removed from office or otherwise punished. Tsai-Hsün, one of the emperor's uncles, was sent to England as head of a mission to investigate naval affairs with a view to building up a modern fleet for China. He spent some time in Europe, and has often spoken to me of his pleasant glimpses of king Edward's court. His brother Tsai-T'ao was sent as head of a similar mission to Germany, to study military affairs, and was so well-treated by kaiser Wilhelm that he never ceased

to be a friend of Germany. Both these missions were costly futilities, for it was useless for China to attempt to provide herself
with a modern fleet and army before she had remodelled the
internal administration of the country and established a sound
fiscal system.[3] It was hoped, however, that the greatest naval
and the greatest military Powers of Europe would feel gratified
by China's evident desire to accept them as models.

Meanwhile petitions were continually being sent to Peking
from all parts of the country pressing for an early opening of
the promised parliament and the establishment of a responsible
cabinet. As a result of these representations it was announced in
an edict by the prince-regent issued on November 4th, 1910,
that the time originally fixed for preparation was to be shortened,
and that parliament was to be opened in the fifth year of the
reign, which would have been 1913. The edict also declared that
the constitution, rules and conditions governing the selection of
members of the upper and lower houses, and all other necessary
things pertaining to constitutional reform should be made ready
and put into force before the opening of parliament.

In the same year an attempt was made by Wang Ching-wei,
a disciple of Sun Yat-sen, to assassinate the prince-regent. The
attempt failed, and prince Ch'un, who wished to be conciliatory,
commuted his death-sentence to one of imprisonment for life.
Wang Ching-wei subsequently became a leading member of the
Kuomintang and of the Nationalist government at Nanking.

In 1911 an edict was issued in the name of the empress-
dowager (Lung-Yü) appointing three imperial tutors under
whom the little emperor (then in his sixth year) was to commence his education in the Yü-ch'ing Kung. This is the building
in the Forbidden City which for a long time past has been used
as the imperial schoolroom. Of the tutors, two of whom were
afterwards my colleagues, more will be said hereafter.

Throughout 1910 and 1911 rebellious mutterings were heard
in various parts of the country. The concessions to liberal ideas
granted by the Throne, the promises to establish a parliamentary
constitution and turn the autocracy into a limited monarchy,
did not allay the unrest; in fact they aggravated it, because all
concessions were regarded by the rebels as indications not of
the sincerity of the Court but of its weakness. A dangerous revolt

took place at Canton under Huang Hsing, afterwards a noted revolutionary general, and the headquarters of the viceroy were destroyed. Huang Hsing was defeated and fled to Hong-Kong, where like many revolutionaries before and after his time he continued to conspire against the dynasty under the protection of the British flag.

The regent then tried to conciliate his foes by appointing a Cabinet more or less on the Western model, but objections were at once raised that it contained too many Manchu princes, which was quite true. This had been a very serious and very just cause of complaint against the Manchu court during its last years. Imperial princes were put into high posts for which they were in no respect qualified, merely because they belonged to the ruling house, and many of them brought discredit on the Throne by their avarice or incompetence or both. Contrary to a common assumption, the imperial clan was very far from being degenerate —it included several men of ability and good character—but unfortunately under the two empresses-dowager and prince Ch'un it was not always, or usually, the ablest and best members of the clan who received high appointments.

The unfortunate attempt to bring the railway system of China under a unified central control—an attempt which for various reasons aroused strong opposition in various quarters though in principle it was sound—is usually mentioned as one of the immediate causes of the revolution. However this may be, the actual outbreaks in Ssŭ-ch'uan in September and at Wu-ch'ang in October, 1911, were only a repetition of what had already occurred at several other centres on a somewhat smaller scale. At Wu-ch'ang, which became the headquarters of the revolutionary movement almost by accident (owing to the fortuitous discovery of a conspiracy), general Li Yüan-hung was forced reluctantly into the position of commander-in-chief of the rebel forces.[4]

The government at Peking, under its ignorant and incapable empress-dowager Lung-Yü and its weak and " feckless " prince-regent, was quickly reduced to a state bordering on imbecility. Prince Ch'un had already committed serious blunders in his short life ; he now proceeded to commit one which was fatal. He decided, or allowed himself to be persuaded, to recall to office a man who was his most dangerous foe—a man whom he had degraded and humiliated three years before.

No doubt an apparently good case could be made out for the re-employment of Yüan Shih-k'ai. His name was still one to conjure with among the rank and file of the only well-trained army in China ; his influence with various political groups was still very great ; no one doubted that he was a capable leader of men and a competent and level-headed statesman ; and his prestige among foreigners stood high. This last point was one of great importance, for the suppression of the rebellion would be a costly business and there would be little chance of raising foreign loans unless there was at the head of affairs a responsible man who enjoyed the confidence of the foreign Legations and had a good reputation in foreign money-markets. Nearly a year before the Wu-ch'ang rebellion broke out—namely on December 17th, 1910—*The Times* published " an excellent, if gloomy, descrip-tion of the plight in which China found herself, together with a plea for the recall of Yüan Shih-k'ai as the only man able to save the situation."[5] This was, indeed, an opinion which was shared by most foreigners in China at that time ; but prince Ch'un knew, or ought to have known, more about Yüan Shih-k'ai's character than foreigners could be expected to know. Foreigners, moreover, were not particularly interested in the preservation of the dynasty ; on the contrary, they nearly all welcomed the revolution when it came, as the dawn of a brilliant new era of peace and prosperity for China, the profits if not the glories of which they confidently looked forward to sharing with four hundred million contented Chinese all longing for ever-increasing consignments of Lancashire cotton. But prince Ch'un had his dynasty to think of as well as the problematical golden age of tranquil commercial activity anticipated by the British and other foreigners of Shanghai, and he should have known, as they could not be expected to know, even if they cared, that Yüan was the last man to be relied on as saviour of the throne of the Manchus.

The first reply sent by Yüan Shih-k'ai to the Court's pressing invitation to Peking was an ominous one on account of its sarcasm. He regretted that he could not obey the imperial sum-mons at the moment because his leg, which three years earlier he had been bidden to go home and nurse, was still giving him trouble. That attitude, however, was not maintained, and merely had the result of driving the wretched prince Ch'un to profounder depths of shame.

No sooner had Yüan arrived in Peking than he perceived that he was master of the situation. He could impose his own terms and feel sure that no one was strong enough to stand in his way. Several of the imperial princes were required to resign their posts ; he himself was made viceroy of Hukuang, commander-in-chief of the imperial forces, and premier in the new cabinet. He then proceeded to take military affairs in hand, and quickly turned the tide of battle against the revolutionaries in the middle Yangtse. Hankow and Hanyang, on the northern bank of the river opposite Wu-ch'ang, were recaptured from the rebels.[6] Yüan struck hard enough to show that he was not to be trifled with, and that in any final settlement of the revolutionary issue his views must be respected ; but he refrained from striking as hard as he could have struck, and loyalists in all parts of the country were both perplexed and indignant when he failed to follow up his initial military successes. Yüan was evidently pursuing a policy of his own, and it soon became clear to all observers that loyalty to the throne was not the guiding motive of his actions.[7]

It is not my purpose to give a history of the revolution, of which detailed accounts exist in English and other languages. I will therefore pass on to the peace conference which took place at Shanghai at the end of 1911 and the beginning of 1912, between the revolutionaries on one side and the Throne on the other. The imperial delegate, T'ang Shao-yi, was the nominee and henchman of Yüan Shih-k'ai. He was a native of the Canton province (his home is near Macao) and in the early days of his official career he was appointed secretary to Yüan Shih-k'ai when the latter was Resident in Korea. During Yüan's governorship of Shantung in 1900 he was again associated with him. Among many other later appointments, he held that of special commissioner to Tibet in 1904, and in 1906 he was the Chinese envoy who negotiated the Tibet Convention with Great Britain. When Hsü Shih-ch'ang was appointed viceroy of Manchuria in 1907 T'ang served under him as civil governor of Mukden.

When we remember that T'ang Shao-yi had had close official relations with Yüan for many years, that their relationsip was that of disciple to master (a binding one in China) and that Yüan had entrusted him with the delicate and responsible duty of acting as imperial delegate to discuss terms of peace with the rebels, we may feel sure that T'ang would not have expressed views at the conference which he knew to be distasteful to his patron in Peking. What secret instructions or advice may have been given by Yüan to T'ang before the latter set out for Shanghai, we do not know ; nor do we know of the secret communications that passed between them when the conference was in session. What we do know is that, to the amazement and consternation of all who were still loyal to the dynasty, T'ang Shao-yi made a public declaration, at the conference, of his conversion to republican principles. Having made this declaration, which in the circumstances was as embarrassing as it was humiliating to the Throne, T'ang Shao-yi resigned his position as delegate, and subsequent negotiations were carried on in a dilatory and unsatisfactory manner between Peking and Nanking.

The upshot of it all was that the parties to the negotiations arrived at a compromise of a most remarkable nature—a compromise which in any country but China would probably be considered too fantastic for serious consideration. A republican form of government was established by imperial decree ; the emperor announced his own abdication ; and in acknowledgment of his willingness to grant the alleged wishes of his people the republic guaranteed that he should be allowed to keep various privileges, including the retention of the full imperial title, and that besides being confirmed in the ownership of his own property he should be granted a large annual subsidy for the continued maintenance of his court in one of the imperial palaces. Details of this extraordinary arrangement will be given in the next chapter.

The imperial edict which announced the abdication of the emperor and the establishment of the republic was issued by the Lung-Yü empress-dowager on February 12th, 1912. The following translation of its essential clauses was made by me shortly after its issue, for publication in an English review.[8]

" The whole nation is now inclined towards a republican form of government. The southern and central provinces first gave clear evidence of this inclination, and the military leaders of the northern provinces have since promised their support to the same cause. By observing the nature of the people's aspirations we learn the Will of Heaven (*T'ien-ming*). It is not fitting that We should withstand the desires of the nation merely for the sake of the glorification of Our own House. We recognise the signs of the age, and We have tested the trend of popular opinion ; and We now, with the Emperor at Our side, invest the nation with the sovereign power, and decree the establishment of a constitutional government on a republican basis. In coming to this decision, We are actuated not only by a hope to bring solace to Our subjects, who long for the cessation of political tumult, but also by a desire to follow the precepts of the sages of old who taught that political sovereignty rests ultimately with the People."

I may perhaps be permitted to quote my own comment on this edict. After observing that " the abdication of the Chinese emperor has been accompanied by the establishment of a republic which has still to prove itself worthy of a patriot's devotion," I wrote the words that follow.

" The Abdication Edict cannot fail to be of interest to students of the science of politics. The Throne itself is converted into a bridge to facilitate the transition from the monarchical to the republican form of government. The emperor remains absolute to the last, and the very republican constitution, which involves his own disappearance from political existence, is created by the fiat of the emperor in his last official utterance. Theoretically, the republic is established not by a people in arms acting in opposition to the imperial will, but by the emperor acting with august benevolence for his people's good. The cynic may smile at the transparency of the attempt to represent the abdication as entirely voluntary, but in this procedure we find something more than a mere ' face-saving ' device invented for the purpose of effecting a dignified retreat in the hour of disaster.[9]

" Perhaps the greatest interest of the decree centres in its appeal to the wisdom of the national sages, and its acceptance of their theory as to the ultimate seat of political sovereignty. The heart of the drafter may have quailed when he wrote the words that signified the surrender of the imperial power, but the spirit of Mencius guided his hand. It now remains for us to hope that the teachings of the wise men of old, which have been obeyed to such momentous issues by the last of the emperors, will not be treated with contempt by his republican successors. Let them remember that those wise men were wise not only in matters affecting statecraft and kingly rule. They were teachers of morals and builders of human character before they were political theorisers. Let the architects of the New China remember that they, too, will assuredly be called upon to choose—not once but many times—between obeying and disobeying ' the precepts of the sages of old,' and that the fate of their country and the welfare of mankind may be dependent on the way in which they exercise their choice."[10]

In the same article I made a brief reference to the unhappy prince Ch'un.

" Those of us who remember prince Ch'un as a courteous and gentle-mannered youth of nineteen years of age, who signalised his entrance into public life by bearing the weight of his country's disgrace at the court of a Western monarch, will not be niggards of our pity for one whose brief and ill-starred career of earthly greatness ended, as it began, in the ashes of humiliation. Brother of a puppet-emperor whose life was ruined by a woman's lust for power, father of an emperor whose three years' reign came to an ignoble end before he had reached his sixth birthday, the ex-regent must now prostrate himself before the shrines of his imperial ancestors and confess to the spirits of the august dead his share in the ruin of their House. ' There is a sacred veil,' said Burke, ' to be drawn over the beginnings of all government.' It is sometimes fitting to draw a sacred veil over the end as well."[11]

The ever-loyal Ku Hung-ming loved telling his friends, in after years, of how he and some others first received the news of the emperor's abdication. They were at a dinner-party in Shanghai, at the house of the well-known scholar Shên Tzŭ-p'ei. " The house-boy," he says, in a published account of the incident,

" brought in an evening express sold in the streets containing the news that the decree of abdication had been issued.
. . . The whole company simultaneously rose to their feet and
turning their faces towards the north fell on their knees and
with weeping and sobbing knocked their heads on the floor. . . .
When, after this, late in the night, before parting from him,
I said to Mr. Shên, ' The catastrophe has come. What is there
more for us to do ? ' he again grasped me by both hands and,
with tears flowing from his eyes, said to me in a voice which I
shall never forget, *Shih shou kuo ên ssŭ shêng i chih*—' For
generations we have received benefits from the Imperial House ;
dead or alive I shall remain faithful to it.' "[12]

At the time when these great events were taking place in
Peking and Nanking, I was at Weihaiwei, where several distinguished Chinese loyalists were glad to take refuge under the
British flag, and where we had found it no easy task to convince
the 180,000 Chinese inhabitants of that territory that the emperor had indeed abdicated. For weeks their attitude was one
of silent incredulity. Enthusiasm for the revolution was wholly
lacking in that little section of Confucius's native province, and
probably not fifty of its inhabitants had the slightest conception
of what a republic was. Nor did they show any desire to learn.
It is doubtful whether five hundred of them could define a
republic to-day, in spite of the fact that since October 1st, 1930,
they have ceased to groan under the lash of British " imperialism " and (in spite of their petitions to be allowed to remain
under that lash) are now " republican " citizens.

The ignorance (or apathy, if it is fair to use that word) of the
people of Weihaiwei was shared by that of the vast masses of
their fellow-countrymen. In the article from which I have already
quoted, and which was written at Weihaiwei, I wrote as follows :

" Whether the Chinese people—as distinct from a few foreign-
educated reformers—do, as a matter of fact, honestly believe that
a republican government is adapted to the needs of the country,
is a very different question. It certainly has not been proved that
' the whole nation is now inclined towards a Republic '—in
spite of the admission to that effect contained in the imperial
edict of abdication. Perhaps it would be nearer the truth to say
that the overwhelming majority of the people of China have not

the slightest idea what a republic means, and how their lives and fortunes will be affected by its establishment, and therefore hold no strong opinions concerning the advantages or disadvantages of republican government."[13]

Nevertheless, if in the days before the revolution a Chinese had asked me what a republic was, I think I should have felt justified in telling him to use his eyes and contemplate his own surroundings. *Si rempublicam requiras, circumspice.* One of the best authorities on Chinese civilisation, writing when the monarchy was still in existence, described China as " the greatest republic the world has ever seen."[14] If we do not insist on too narrow or rigid a definition of the word, that is true. China was far more of a republic under the monarchy than it has ever been since.

If it be true to say that there was no demand among the people of China for a republican government in the Western sense of the term (there has been no " parliament " in China since 1924 and no one seems to show any anxiety for a renewal of the experiment which ended so ignominiously) it is equally true to say that though there was discontent with the feebleness of the government there was no widespread " hate " of the Manchus. The anti-Manchu slogans invented by the revolutionaries were soon taken up by vast numbers of Chinese who had no clear conception of what they were doing or saying. Parrot-like, they learned to cry " Down with the Manchus," just as countless students and others have since learned to cry " Down with capitalism, imperialism, England, Japan, the ' unequal treaties,' " or this or that particular general or politician as the case may be, according to the prevailing mode or the exigencies of the moment. Numberless Chinese were infected in 1911 with the revolutionary germ and suddenly became violently anti-Manchu and anti-monarchic without any distinct idea of what had happened to them. In many cases which came to my own know-ledge they were thoroughly ashamed of themselves afterwards, and admitted that when they were caught in the political maelstrom they temporarily lost their wits. We have witnessed very similar phenomena in other parts of the world, and they only remind us that the Chinese share our common human nature. We have seen something of the kind in contemporary

Europe, and we should not flatter ourselves (though some of us do) that Englishmen are temperamentally incapable of similar ebullitions of unreasoning frenzy. It was Defoe, I think, who said that in his time there were a hundred thousand stout fellows in England ready to fight to the death against Popery, without any notion of whether Popery was a man or a horse.[15]

The Chinese have a saying *Ch'iang tao chung jên t'ui*— " everyone is willing to give a push to a falling wall." Recent Chinese history has verified that saying a thousand times. But it has been verified in many lands besides China.

The Chinese revolutionaries in 1911 made it a point of honour to ascribe all kinds of imaginary virtues to the native Ming dynasty which had preceded that of the Manchus. But this is how the beginnings of that dynasty are described by the distinguished German sinologist Richard Wilhelm. " The Ming dynasty was at the outset distinguished by the cruelty and bloodshed that must accompany the establishment of an absolute monarchy. On the slightest suspicion whole families were slaughtered. Executions frequently ran into tens of thousands. The people had flocked to the standard of the Ming because they were sweeping away the hated foreign dominion [that of the Mongols], but it was soon realised that the oppression of absolutism had become immeasurably worse."[16] In precisely the same way, people " flocked to the standard " of the republic, because they had been stirred up by skilfully manipulated propaganda to take a part in the noble work of " sweeping away the hated foreign dominion," but they have since lived under conditions " immeasurably worse " than those under which they had lived when the " foreign " Manchus ruled the land.

The dynasty had undoubtedly fallen on evil days, and in the hands of rulers like the " Venerable Buddha " and the prince-regent, and the hordes of rapacious palace officials who exercised a malign influence over the dynastic fortunes, it may justifiably be doubted whether the dynasty still possessed powers of recuperation. Yet the common European notion (fostered by the foreign-educated Chinese students, the vast majority of whom were anti-Manchu) that the dynasty was hated by the Chinese people as a whole, is very far from the truth. This is fully recognised by an able Western writer whose freedom from partisanship increases the value of his judgments. " It was only with the decay of the ruling house," says Mr. Owen Lattimore, " the growth of the power of revolt in the south, and the desire to find a scapegoat on which to hang the blame for all the ills of China, that a quasi-racial hatred was worked up against the Manchus, which is now being perpetuated in textbooks and political doctrines."[17]

In view of later events it is interesting to read the considered remarks of the American scholar, Dr. Wells Williams, in his classic work *The Middle Kingdom*, first published more than half a century ago. " Nothing in Chinese politics," he says, " is more worthy of notice than the unbounded reverence for the emperor, while each man resists unjust taxation, and joins in killing or driving away oppressive officials."[18] Perhaps the reverence which so impressed Dr. Wells Williams was rather for the Throne than for the person of the emperor, of whose character and personality no ordinary subject knew anything. Yet the emperor as *T'ien Tzŭ*—Son of Heaven—was accepted, taken for granted, like the forces of nature, and he was regarded from afar with something like religious awe. So perhaps, after all, Wells Williams's word " reverence " was not ill-chosen.

Equally striking is the testimony of Sir Robert Hart, who wrote during the siege of the Legations, when the prestige of the Throne, among both foreigners and Chinese, was at least as low as it had been during the T'ai-p'ing rebellion. " This alien government, the Manchu dynasty," he says, " has been part and parcel of the nation for three hundred years, and the emperor is no more hated by Chinese than the Queen by British."[19] This fully bears out the statement already quoted from the distinguished Chinese who wrote under the name of " Wen Ching."[20] As for the writings of Ku Hung-ming, they are full of enthusiastic, almost fanatical, expressions of devotion and loyalty to the dynasty—a loyalty and devotion which even a foreign education was in his case powerless to shake.

In spite of the allegation—which was part of the anti-Manchu propaganda—that the " alien " dynasty had trampled on the rights of the people and had enslaved the nation, Hart observed that " liberty, real tangible liberty, they all enjoy."[21] The testimony of Dr. H. A. Giles is to the same effect. " Everyone who has lived in China, and has kept his eyes open, must have noticed what a large measure of personal freedom is enjoyed by even the meanest subject of the Son of Heaven."[22] Before the revolution, indeed, foreign visitors and travellers were constantly struck by the fact that the Chinese had more individual liberty—were less interfered with by Government—than any other people in the world. This fact was fully admitted by the great anti-Manchu revolutionary, Sun Yat-sen himself, when the revolution was over and there was no longer any need for him to persuade his countrymen that they had been the slaves of alien despots. In those later post-revolutionary days his complaint was that his countrymen, so far from having had too little freedom in former days, had a great deal too much. The following remarks on this point are quoted from the famous *San-min-chu-i*, the authorship of which is attributed to him and which, in the belief of his idolaters, contains the quintessence of political wisdom.

" The Chinese people never suffered directly any of the evils of despotism. . . . The Chinese, because their liberty has been so complete, have never noticed it, just as because there is so much air in a room we do not consider its importance. . . . Why are the Chinese merely sand ? What makes us like sand is the fact that our liberty is excessive. . . . China at present is the slave of more than ten masters, so the nation is entirely without freedom."[23]

It may well be true that the liberty formerly enjoyed by the Chinese was excessive. The point is that Dr. Sun's own remarks show how baseless was the propaganda that denounced the Manchus for having enslaved the Chinese race and kept them under the heel of a brutal foreign tyranny. The revolt against the Manchus, he says frankly, was not for the purpose of winning liberty, and in that respect it differed from revolutions in Western countries. " To speak plainly," he says, " our object was exactly opposite to that of Europeans. . . . We revolted because our freedom was excessive, we had no cohesive quality, no power of resistance, we were just sand."[24]

The organisation which Sun Yat-sen bequeathed to the nation

—the Kuomintang—has seen to it that in this matter of excessive freedom there shall be no further ground for complaint. It would be difficult to point to an epoch of Chinese history in which the people have been less free than they are to-day ; though whether the restriction of freedom will of itself bring about the desired cohesiveness may be open to doubt.

That the Chinese lack " cohesiveness " is possibly true ; nevertheless there is a sense in which it is among the strongest characteristics of the race. A well-known authority on Chinese affairs is right in referring to " the unconquerable vitality and *power of cohesion* which have preserved Chinese civilisation throughout the ages."[25] In any case, the Chinese people are not likely to increase their cohesiveness by following the rambling, sometimes contradictory and often puerile counsels of the *San-min-chu-i.* There are welcome signs that they are beginning to realise this, and to perceive that the author (or reputed author) of that work is no fit substitute for the great teachers once reverenced by their forefathers. Fortunately for China, she has access to profounder sources of political and social inspiration than the shallow sophistries of the so-called " Father of the Chinese Republic," and the New China that will some day take its rightful place among the great nations of the world should have little difficulty in finding a worthier figure than Sun Yat-sen to occupy the shrine of its patron-saint.[26]

It is with the recent past, however, not with the problematical future, that we are concerned in these pages. With the issue of the edict of abdication, the sun of the Manchu dynasty had set, and the vast regions over which the ten monarchs of its line had ruled, not always inefficiently or unwisely, for nearly three hundred years, entered upon a night of darkness and storm. But the light of day seemed unwilling to withdraw itself entirely from the halls and palaces of the Forbidden City, and the sunset was followed there, as we shall see, by a lingering twilight.

CHAPTER VII

The " Articles of Favourable Treatment " of the Manchu Imperial House

I REFERRED in the foregoing chapter to the very remarkable compromise which concluded the peace negotiations between the Throne and the revolutionary party at the beginning of 1912. Without an adequate acquaintance with that compromise, it is impossible to have a clear understanding of how it was that after the revolution and the overthrow of the monarchy there came to be a long period of " Twilight in the Forbidden City " during which the emperor, shorn of all political power but retaining the imperial status and title, continued to hold his court and to occupy the Dragon throne. Nor is it easy, without having studied the terms of that compromise, to grasp the thread of the long and romantic story which recently culminated in the return of the last of the Ta Ch'ing emperors of China first to the home, and then to the throne, of his ancestors in Manchuria.

Surprisingly little attention has been paid by Western writers to the terms of the abdication settlement. Most of them ignore the subject altogether, or make only the briefest passing references to it, as if the conditions under which the emperor vacated the throne were of no practical importance and had no bearing on subsequent political developments.[1] Still more sedulously is the subject ignored or evaded by Chinese Nationalist writers, but in their case it is easy to see why they wish it to be buried in oblivion. The breakers of treaties and agreements can hardly be expected to be over-zealous in drawing the attention of the world to their " scraps of paper."

We have already considered the pathetic edict in which the Lung-Yü empress-dowager, on behalf of the six-year-old emperor, bowed to what she had been informed was the will of the people and agreed to the establishment of a republic. This edict should not be regarded as standing alone. It was part of the compromise arrived at in the course of the negotiations. The

Gc

emperor's contribution towards the compromise was contained in the edict. The republicans' contribution was embodied in a formal document entitled " Articles providing for the Favourable Treatment of the Ta Ch'ing Emperor after his Abdication."[2] The document begins with the following significant preamble :

" In consideration of the fact that the Ta Ch'ing emperor has publicly announced his approval of the establishment of a republican form of government, the following Articles relating to the Favourable Treatment of the Ta Ch'ing emperor after his abdication are hereby set forth."

Then follow the Articles, which are eight in number.

" 1.   After the abdication of the Ta Ch'ing emperor, his title of dignity is to be retained and will not be abolished ; and he will be treated by the Republic of China with the courtesies which it is customary to accord to foreign monarchs.

" 2.   After the abdication of the Ta Ch'ing emperor, he will receive from the Republic of China an annual subsidy of Tls.4,000,000. After the reform of the currency this amount will be altered to $4,000,000 (mex.).

" 3.   After the abdication of the Ta Ch'ing emperor, he may as a temporary measure continue to reside in the Palace (in the Forbidden City), but afterwards he will remove to the Yi-Ho Park (the Summer Palace). He may retain his body-guard.

" 4.   After the abdication of the Ta Ch'ing emperor, the temples and mausolea of the imperial family with their appropriate sacrificial rites shall be maintained in perpetuity. The Republic of China will be responsible for the provision of military guards for their adequate protection.

" 5.   As the Ch'ung mausoleum of the late emperor Tê Tsung has not yet been completed, the work will be carried out according to the proper regulations (relating to imperial tombs). The last ceremonies of sepulture will also be observed in accordance with the ancient rites. The actual expenses will all be borne by the Republic of China.

" 6.   The services of all the persons of various grades hitherto employed in the Palace may be retained ; but in future no eunuchs are to be added to the staff.

" 7.   After the abdication of the Ta Ch'ing emperor, his private property will be safeguarded and protected by the Republic of China.

" 8.   The imperial guard corps as constituted at the time of the abdication will be placed under the military control of the War Office of the Republic of China. It will be maintained at its original strength and will receive the same emoluments as heretofore."

These Articles of the Favourable Treatment of the Ta Ch'ing emperor constituted only a part, though the most important part, of the revolutionary compromise. They were accompanied by two other documents of a similar nature. The first defined the treatment to be accorded to the members of the imperial clan. It guaranteed that the Manchu princes and nobles should retain their titles of honour, including those which were hereditary. Their public and private rights were to be identical with those of ordinary citizens of the republic, except that they were to be excused from military service. Their private property was to remain in their possession and properly protected. The second document similarly defined the treatment to be accorded to the Manchus, Mongols, Mohammedans and Tibetans. It assumed their approval of the conversion of the form of government into a republic, and in consideration of their approval declared that they would receive equal treatment with the Chinese ; that their rights of private property would be respected ; that the titles of honour of the princes and nobles would be recognised ; that help would be given to those members of the nobility who might be in economic distress ; that the allowances hitherto granted to members of the " eight banners " (the Manchu military system) would continue to be issued, pending reorganisation ; that all the old limitations and restrictions on choice of livelihood and domicile formerly imposed on persons of the races concerned were abolished ; and that religious liberty was guaranteed.

Some account should be given of those other related documents which were issued at later dates.

On August 19th of the first year of the Republic (1912) was published a special announcement relating to the treatment to be accorded under the republic to the people of Mongolia. It contained nine clauses. Their general aim was to provide for the removal of all barriers and distinctions between Mongols and Chinese but to confirm the existing titles and privileges of Mongol princes and lamas. In general respects Mongolia was no longer to be regarded as a dependency but as an integral part of the Chinese republic.

On November 23rd of the same year was issued a presidential proclamation guaranteeing the favourable treatment of Mongols, Mohammedans and Tibetans. It announced that the five races (Chinese, Manchus and the three just named) constituted a *hsin pang*—a new State—and that all alike were to enjoy the blessings of a republican form of government. It referred to complaints which had been received to the effect that the republic was robbing and destroying Mongolia, persecuting Lamaism (the Mongolian form of Buddhism) and putting grazing lands under cultivation. Assurances were given that these complaints must have been made under a misapprehension of the real facts, as the government was determined to carry out all the promises contained in the Articles relating to the favourable treatment of the various races constituting the Republic. The fact was emphasised that the republican government had already conferred new titles and honours on the heads of the Lamaist Church and on various members of the Mongolian nobility, thus demonstrating its desire to respect Mongol rights.

The last of the documents of which I will give a rough translation is one which was not issued till December 26th, 1914. Its seven clauses clearly indicate that during the three years that had elapsed since the abdication, some slight friction or misunderstandings had arisen between the imperial household and the republican government regarding the interpretation of the original articles of favourable treatment.

" 1.   The imperial House should recognise the authority of the republican government and should not act in any way that is inconsistent with the recognition of that authority, apart from the exercise of the special privileges accorded to it in the Articles of Favourable Treatment.

" 2.   In official correspondence with the republican government and in the dating of legal documents the imperial House should use the republican calendar instead of the reign-title of the Ta Ch'ing emperor.

" 3. Although the Ta Ch'ing emperor may confer honours and rewards on members of the imperial clan and on officers and members of his staff, no rewards other than ordinary gifts should be conferred by him upon servants or citizens of the republic. Further, the imperial household department, in sending written communications to ordinary citizens of the republic, should not adopt the style and form of official despatches and notifications ; and in transacting legal business with merchants and others, the imperial household should comply with the laws of the republic, failing which their transactions will have no legal validity.

" 4. The imperial household department should take note that the department of the republican government which is empowered to deal with matters connected with the protection of the imperial temples and mausolea and the private property of the imperial family and similar business, is the *Nei Wu Pu* (Department of Home Affairs).

" 5. The *Nei Wu Fu* (the imperial household department) is the recognised organ through which the affairs of the imperial family are conducted, and should be reorganised with a view to the proper fulfilment of its functions.[3]

" 6. Regulations should be drawn up specifying the functions of the newly appointed *hu chün* (palace guards), whose special duty it is to exercise police functions in the palace, and defining the responsibilities of its commanding officers. Criminal jurisdiction within the palace is abolished. Minor offenders among the eunuchs and other palace employees may be dealt with by the commanding officers of the palace guards and punished in accordance with police regulations ; but criminal offenders must be sent to the ordinary courts for trial and punishment.

" 7. All persons employed by the imperial household are citizens of the republic and should conform to Chinese custom in the matter of dress. They may remove their queues if they wish to do so. Nevertheless on ceremonial occasions within the palace, all those who are employed in connection with ritual observances may suit their own convenience with regard to costume."

At first sight the " Articles of Favourable Treatment " as set forth in the first of the foregoing State documents appear to be very generous. Indeed when the world first learned that the revolutionaries had agreed to the emperor's retention of his title, to his continued residence in one of the imperial palaces and to the payment of an enormous annual subsidy for the maintenance of his court and other expenses, comparisons highly laudatory to China were drawn in Europe and elsewhere between the Chinese and the Western methods of dealing with discarded monarchs.

Now there is so much that is admirable and lovable in the Chinese character, and so much that is noble and gracious in Chinese civilisation, that it is futile and unnecessary to go out of our way to pay compliments to China which she does not deserve or to search in her garden for flowers that never grew there.

As I have already said, the Articles were the outcome of a compromise. The imperialists had not been beaten to a stand-still ; in fact they had already recovered some lost ground in central China, nearly all north China as well as north-western China and Manchuria were in their hands, they had the goodwill of the Mongols and Tibetans, some of the ablest viceroys and generals were loyal, they possessed by far the best-equipped and best-trained fighting force in China, and they still controlled the financial and diplomatic machinery of the State. It was by no means certain that the monarchy could be overthrown by force, at least without a civil war which might have lasted for years. My own impression is that had Yüan Shih-k'ai been faithful to his trust, had he devoted himself heart and soul to the salvation of the throne, he would have succeeded.[4] The more usual belief among foreigners—based mainly I think on the conviction that the dynasty was effete and that its collapse was already long overdue—is that the revolution was bound to win. It may be so ; and it is also pos-sible that even if the crash had not come in 1911 it would have come a few years later. On the other hand the replacement of the autocracy by a constitutional monarchy might under skilful guidance have saved the situation.

But why did the Court give way and agree to a compromise which included the abdication of the emperor, when there was still at least a possibility that the revolutionaries might be defeated ? The " face-making " explanation is that the dowager-empress Lung-Yü could not bear to see the Chinese people suffering the anguish of a protracted civil war. The real explanation is that the compromise accorded with the wishes and designs of Yüan Shih-k'ai who had become master of the situation.

Why was Yüan Shih-k'ai half-hearted in the cause of the monarchy, as all the evidence goes to show that he was ? Partly, no doubt, because he had never forgiven the regent for dismissing him from office in 1908. His loyalty required a great deal of stimulation if it was to be roused out of its three years' torpor, and prince Ch'un was not the man to stimulate anyone's loyalty, least of all that of an opportunist like Yüan Shih-k'ai. For three years the ex-viceroy and grand councillor had brooded in impotent silence over what he doubtless regarded as his wrongs, and his thoughts grew ever more bitter when he reflected that the man who had driven him from office was one whom he despised as well as hated. But if his loyalty continued to lie dormant, its place was usurped by something else that found more than all the stimulation it needed. Yüan had always been an ambitious man. Ambition now became in him an all-consuming passion.

To what heights Yüan's ambition had led him by the end of 1911 probably no living man now knows. But I have discussed the question many times with people who were in close touch with him when he was conducting the negotiations that led to the final settlement, and with others who were present at many of the secret interviews in the Forbidden City at which he pressed his views on the imperial family ; and I believe that in all those negotiations and discussions Yüan was working not for the rebels and their republic, not for the child-emperor and the dynasty, but for his own glory.[5]

An examination of the compromise as embodied in the Articles of Favourable Treatment will lead us, I think, to the same view. It is an extraordinary document, and cannot have been drawn up by anyone who had at heart the true interests of either republic or emperor. But the draftsman was no fool. His skill enabled him to produce a document that deluded each of the contending parties into the belief that it had scored a victory over the other, and at the same time created a situation that left the substance of power in his own hands.

Addressing the revolutionaries, Yüan used arguments which may be paraphrased in terms like these :

" This agreement provides for the abdication of the emperor and will give you what you want—a republic. In return, you are asked to let him keep a purely honorary and empty title, and to pay him an annual subsidy which though seemingly large will be only a trifle compared with the cost of a prolonged civil war. The permission granted him to remain in the Forbidden City is only temporary, and when you desire him to move to the Yi-Ho Park (the Summer Palace) he will be obliged to obey. The other privileges reserved to him and his family are of no practical importance and will be in no way detrimental to the prestige and dignity of the republic. All these privileges may be regarded as a kind of insurance against his taking part in any anti-republican or reactionary activities, and will simplify the task of keeping him under observation. Taking the agreement as a whole, it gives ' face ' to the emperor without causing any loss of ' face ' to you. *You secure the substance ; he is left with the shadow.* Foreign countries will extol your magnanimity, and the new republic will start its career amid general applause and in a blaze of glory. For you, there will be a clear sky and brilliant sunshine : for the Ta Ch'ing emperor, only a slowly darkening twilight."

Turning to his dupes in the Forbidden City—an ignorant and helpless woman, a timid and witless regent, and the Son of Heaven, a child of six—his arguments, in effect, followed lines like these :

" This agreement saves the throne, and the emperor remains emperor. All he sacrifices is *chêng ch'üan*—the right of ruling. That is really no sacrifice at all ; for his majesty is only a child, and could not personally assume the imperial responsibilities for many years to come. By giving up the right to rule, the imperial family will save themselves a great deal of trouble and anxiety. By the time he is grown up, the revolutionary madness will have spent itself, and the emperor will resume the powers he has temporarily delegated to a crazy organisation that calls itself a republic. It will prove itself unable to govern or to keep order, and the people will grow weary of it. Then they will remember that their emperor still lives, that his throne has never been vacant, and that he is ready to respond to the call of his suffering people. The agreement guarantees the maintenance of the ancestral rites and the protection of the imperial mausolea, and large revenues will be provided for the maintenance of his majesty's imperial state. The household department will continue to function and the traditional court ceremonies will be kept up as heretofore. *You secure the substance ; the revolutionaries are left with the shadow.* Foreign countries will extol you for your magnanimity in having laid down your arms because you could not bear to see your people enduring the horrors of civil war. The Throne will regain its lost prestige, and in a few years time the whole world will rejoice to see the Son of Heaven step forth to rule once more over a happy and prosperous China."

I have said above that the Articles of Favourable Treatment could not have been drawn up by anyone who had at heart the interests of either republic or emperor. It suited the sinister figure who was its real author or inspirer, because it enabled him to pose as the wise and disinterested friend of both parties, and gave him time and opportunity to consolidate his own position and prepare the way for what seemed likely to be a dazzling future. It suited also that powerful and equally sinister body of men who stood between the emperor and his people and who controlled the finances and grossly mismanaged the property of the imperial family. I refer to the *Nei Wu Fu*—the imperial household department. The vested interests of this incompetent and corrupt organisation were enormous, and all the facts go to show that it was for the deliberate purpose of protecting those interests that provision was made in the Articles for the maintenance at undiminished strength of the costly and useless imperial establishment.

Obviously, however, it could not be conducive to the stability of a newly-organised republic that the imperial palace in the heart of the capital should continue to be occupied by a personage enjoying the status of emperor. Although this emperor was to have no political power, and his regal dignity was to be purely titular, there would always be a risk that he might, even against his own inclinations, become the centre of monarchist intrigue.

As for the emperor himself, there is nothing in the Articles to suggest that Yüan Shih-k'ai, or the revolutionaries, or the imperial household department, took the smallest interest in his personal welfare, or gave a moment's thought to it. They were concerned with the system which he represented, with the livelihood and perquisites of the host of parasites who enriched themselves out of his revenues, and it suited the convenience of one, at least, of the parties to the agreement that he should continue to reign as titular monarch over a kingdom that was bounded by the walls of the Forbidden City. No one dreamed of raising the question of whether it would be to his physical and moral advantage as a human being that he should be brought up in such unnatural conditions. No one asked whether it would be beneficial to his character or conducive to his happiness that he should be surrounded by hundreds of idle and servile eunuchs and flatterers and taught to believe himself semi-divine, yet debarred from assuming the duties and responsibilities that are the only justification for kingship.

An English writer has recently declared that the Manchus were " tricked into giving up the throne."[6] That is true, but in justice to the revolutionaries it ought to be clearly understood that they were not the tricksters. They were, in fact, victims of the same trickery.

However, in spite of all the adverse criticisms that can be directed against the Articles of Favourable Treatment, the fact remains that they were an integral part of the revolutionary settlement, and that had those Articles not been agreed to by the republicans, the republic, such as it is, might never have come into being. There is no doubt that when the Articles received the formal assent of the republicans and monarchists they were regarded as permanently binding on both parties. There could be no modification of them, far less cancellation,

except by mutual consent. Copies were sent to each of the
Legations in Peking for permanent record and for the information of foreign Governments. In 1917 a commission sat to draw
up a permanent constitution for the Chinese republic. They
never completed their task, but it was moved and seconded at
a meeting of that commission that the Articles of Favourable
Treatment (together with the similar documents relating to the
rights and privileges of Manchus, Mongolians, Tibetans and
Mohammedans) should be inserted in the new constitution so
that their permanency might be given a constitutional guarantee. The proposal was dropped only on assurances being given
that the documents in question were regarded as formal treaties
having perpetual validity. Up to 1924, as we have seen, all the
documents in question were included in the collection of laws
and ordinances issued under official authority.[7] What happened
to them in 1924 (or rather to the document which contained the
Articles of Favourable Treatment of the Manchu Imperial
House) will be described in full in a later chapter.

I have said that if the compromise embodied in these Articles
had not been agreed to, or if Yüan Shih-k'ai had not betrayed
his trust, the Manchu dynasty might have been saved. It should
be remembered that even if a withdrawal from Peking had
proved to be necessary, even if the dynasty had felt obliged to
relinquish the great Manchu conquests in China, it was still open
to the Manchu imperial family to retire to Mukden, its old
capital in Manchuria, and to reoccupy the throne of its great
ancestor the emperor T'ai Tsung. If in the early days of the
revolution the Manchu court had decided to retire temporarily
or permanently to its old Manchurian home, it is extremely doubtful whether it could have been dislodged by the Chinese revolutionaries, or whether Manchuria would ever have become even a
nominal part of the republic of China. It has never been more
than that.

Had the Manchus retired to Manchuria, and had the collapse
of their power in China proved final and complete, it is by no
means improbable that we should have witnessed a revived
Manchurian monarchy, similar to that which existed in the first
half of the seventeenth century, completely independent of
China. A large number of able Chinese loyalists would have

taken office under such a monarchy, and they would have been followed by many Chinese of all classes who were dissatisfied with conditions under the republic. Had such a monarchy been established it is not improbable that before long it would have been joined by Jehol and the rest of Inner Mongolia.[8]

This possibility of retiring to Manchuria was not overlooked by the Manchu court when the revolution in China began to look dangerous. On the contrary it was seriously discussed, and many imperialists both in China and in Manchuria urged that this would be the wisest course to pursue. What finally decided the regent and the majority of the princes to remain in Peking was their honest if fatuous belief in the excellence of the terms secured for them by Yüan Shih-k'ai in the Articles of Favourable Treatment. We have seen what the arguments were which Yüan used when he was persuading the princes to accept the compromise. All but two of them were hypnotised by those and similar arguments, and they also tried to convince themselves that the republican government, having once formally agreed to the terms of the compromise, could be trusted to keep its word.

Two of the princes were amazed and indignant at what they regarded as the shameful pusillanimity of the regent and their brother-nobles. They spoke and voted against the acceptance of Yüan Shih-k'ai's proposed settlement and insisted that abdication was unnecessary. They refused to be parties to what they declared was a base betrayal of a sacred cause, an unpardonable insult to the memory of those illustrious ancestors of theirs who first laid the strong foundations of the Ta Ch'ing empire in Manchuria and then extended its sway over all China. When they perceived that they were outvoted, that the promises and veiled threats of Yüan Shih-k'ai were breaking down all opposition, that the regent and empress-dowager were succumbing to the pressure of a stronger will than theirs, and that the imperial cause was indeed lost, these two princes took their departure from the capital and went into exile, vowing that if they ever returned it would only be when the Dragon flag flew once more over the gates of Peking, or in their coffins. One of these men was P'u-Wei, prince Kung ; the other was Shan-Ch'i, prince Su. The former has lived for many years in the Japanese leased-territory of Port Arthur, thinking and dreaming of little else but the possibility of the revival of the glories of his House. Prince Su returned to Peking in April, 1922—in his coffin.

If the compromise which both parties were persuaded to accept was a thoroughly bad one, as undoubtedly it was, by what other compromise would it have been possible for Yüan Shih-k'ai, had he combined loyalty to the throne with patriotism and far-seeing statesmanship, to save his country from a resumption of civil war? That he and the revolutionary leaders were right in trying to arrive at a peaceful solution need not be gainsaid. Civil war, had it continued, might have ended in the partition of China and in the establishment of a northern monarchy and a southern republic. It might have led to the obliteration of the imperial House amid scenes of tragedy such as had once been witnessed in France and were soon to be witnessed in Russia. It might have resulted in a victory for reaction no less decisive than that of 1898 and in the revival of the imperial autocracy under the old bad conditions, perhaps after the devastation of half China and a carnage more horrible than that which fifty years earlier accompanied the T'ai-p'ing rebellion. Or it might have had the rather barren result of making China just as " safe for democracy " as the Western world was made by the Great War.

A compromise of some kind, then, was essential. If civil war was to be avoided, or rather if the armistice was to be turned into a peace, neither party must expect to have its demands met in full. Nor was it desirable that they should. On the other hand, there was obviously no popular demand for the throne's replacement by a republic, and there was no sound reason for believing that the gap created in the Chinese political edifice by the disappearance of the emperor would be adequately filled by a succession of wrangling politicians or jealous office-seekers. Yüan therefore could and should have advocated and insisted upon the retention of the throne, even if its powers were to be so drastically curtailed as to make it little more than an outward symbol of national unity and of the continuity of the national traditions, the official representative of the State in diplomatic intercourse, the rallying point of loyalty and patriotism, the apex of the political, moral and religious structure of the Chinese Empire.[9]

It is true that the Throne had already agreed to convert the autocracy into a limited monarchy, and that revolution had not thereby been averted. But this could legitimately be ascribed to well-founded doubts concerning the sincerity and good faith of a Court presided over by a woman of the character and antecedents of the old empress-dowager. The situation had undergone a complete change by the accession to the throne of a child who was too young to have been corrupted by evil traditions and an unwholesome environment, and whose education could be entrusted to men imbued with a new spirit.

Yüan could have coupled his demand for the retention of the monarchic system with a proposal of the kind which, as I have suggested above, should have been adopted three years earlier, at the time of the emperor's accession : namely, the appointment of a regency commission, with a majority of Chinese members and with wide powers to initiate immediate reforms.[10] Among the first duties devolving upon such a body would have been to banish the horde of eunuchs who still infested the Forbidden City, withdraw from the empress-dowager and other women of the Court the right of interfering in State affairs, abolish the corrupt and incompetent Nei Wu Fu, and remodel the administration of the imperial household on an entirely new basis of efficiency and economy.

Sun Yat-sen and his party would of course have been opposed to the idea of retaining the Manchu monarchy in any form whatever. But the more moderate members of the revolutionary group could, I think, have been won over by Yüan without much difficulty, especially if he had offered them the alternative of acceptance or a renewal of a civil war in which they were likely to be worsted. By far the most strenuous opposition (though in view of Yüan's unassailable position it would have been ineffectual) would have come not from the revolutionaries but from the Nei Wu Fu. There is not the least doubt that if the choice had been left to the members of that body between the compromise that was actually adopted (which left to the emperor only his empty title but allowed the Nei Wu Fu to continue to function) and the compromise here proposed (which would have retained the emperor on his throne but involved the abolition of the Nei Wu Fu), they would have given their whole-hearted support to the former. Their " loyalty " was not directed towards their imperial master : it was directed towards what the Chinese call their own " rice-bowls."

Yüan can hardly have overlooked the possibility of some such arrangement as I have suggested. That arrangement would not only have saved the dynasty, but would also have prevented China from plunging into dangerous political experiments which after twenty-two years of unspeakable misery for the Chinese people have brought the country to a far worse plight than that in which it lay during the closing years of Manchu rule.

Yüan was no republican, and very soon threw off the pretence of being one. Why then did he not utilise his unique position and the overwhelming powers at his disposal to save the throne ? The only possible explanation is that he was already dreaming of the new dynasty of which he himself was to be the founder.

Thus it was that this golden opportunity was lost of estab-lishing a constitutional monarchy through the medium of a child-emperor who was too young to have any enemies, against whom no one could have any grudge, who could not possibly be suspected of duplicity, and whose education had only just begun.[11]

Of the numerous objections to the compromise embodied in the Articles of Favourable Treatment, one of the most serious was that it left intact the pernicious system which had been the principal cause of the Throne's decay. It put the sovereign in the ignoble position of being a parasite on his own former subjects, a completely functionless monarch, drawing a large pension from the State without being either expected or allowed to perform any corresponding duties and without the power to serve his country in any way. He was to be permitted to retain his empty title and the trappings of imperial state, and to keep up a mock-court, merely in order that the most corrupt organisation in the Empire might have an excuse for continuing to exist. It was not the Nei Wu Fu that was to be maintained for the purpose of serving its imperial master, but the emperor who was to be maintained for the purpose of serving the interests of the Nei Wu Fu. The Articles deprived the emperor of all that was worth having—the privilege of being of service to his people—but left untouched the vampire that had drained the life-blood of the dynasty.

The " Republic " was established amid the rejoicings of many who have since found cause for tears. Of the ardent republicans of early days, some have quietly disappeared. Many have retired, more or less broken-hearted, into private life. Some have exchanged politics for commerce or education. One at least has abandoned China for Europe, and has sought peace—and possibly found it—in a Catholic cloister. There were numerous illustrations of the well-known saying that revolutions devour their own children. Many have had the disconcerting experience of being hailed as heroes and patriots one day and denounced as criminals and traitors the next, and again, soon afterwards, hailed as patriots and heroes. Some have taken refuge, from time to time, in British colonies and foreign concessions. Many have died violent deaths by assassination or in civil war. Some have found tranquil homes in Buddhist hermitages among the hills, where they contemplate waterfalls, read and write poetry, scan the lore of the sages, and fish in mountain pools with hookless lines.[12] Only two or three have come scatheless in body and in reputation through the chances and changes of twenty turbulent years. One, indeed, has had the honour of being elevated to the rank of a national saint and sage, and for him has been constructed a costly and sumptuous tomb. For the present, that tomb is kept swept and clean and in good repair ; while the great white marble Altar of Heaven, once the holiest spot in China, on which the emperor, as the representative of his people, stood and communed alone with God, sinks into slow decay or lies corpse-like under a death-mask of whitewash.[13]

Chapter VIII

The Ta Ch'ing and the Hung Hsien Emperors

FOR THE FIRST THIRTEEN YEARS of the new Chinese republic—
from the spring of 1912 to the winter of 1924—there resided, in
the heart of the capital, a president and an emperor. For the
Ch'ing dynasty, those years were a period of twilight ; for the
republic, they were a period of dawn—a very grey dawn, with
ominous streaks of red in its massed clouds.

The outside world was either ignorant of the apparent anomaly
which permitted a dethroned emperor to retain his imperial
title, or it assumed that the action of the republic in granting him
the formal right to keep his title might be regarded as nothing
more than a final gesture of courteous farewell to the last
monarch of a dead dynasty. Many foreigners resident in China
quickly forgot all about the Articles of Favourable Treatment,
if indeed they had ever read them, and assumed that the
emperor's position was identical with that of other dethroned
monarchs. They therefore spoke of him as the " ex-emperor "
precisely as they might have spoken of any ex-monarch in
Europe ; and from the European point of view they had a good
case, because it was quite obvious that whatever the child in
the Forbidden City might call himself, he was no longer reigning
emperor of China. There were others, however, who were vaguely
aware that he was not exactly in the same position as an abdicated monarch in Europe, as was obvious from the fact that he
still maintained a court and sat on a throne. Observing, therefore, that neither " emperor " nor " ex-emperor " seemed to fit
the case, they compromised by conferring upon him the title
by which, in foreign circles in China, he came to be best known
—" the Boy Emperor."

Nevertheless there were many people who when informed that
the emperor by formal agreement with the republic had been
allowed to retain his title of dignity without the prefix of either
" ex " or " boy," were apt to express incredulity. " How," they
Hc

asked, " can the republic have agreed to tolerate the existence, in its very capital, of a person calling himself emperor of China ? "

Now this is a very reasonable question, and it is easily answered. The republic did nothing so foolish. The emperor retained his imperial title intact, *but that title, in its technical Chinese phraseology, was not, and never had been, " emperor of China.*"[1]

The title assumed by all the monarchs whom Europeans describe as " emperor of China " was a dynastic, not a territorial one. Each dynasty adopted a title of its own which was not passed on to the dynasty that succeeded it. The dynasty founded by Li Yüan in 618 was given the name of Ta T'ang ; that founded by Chao K'uang-yin in 960 was named Ta Sung; that founded by Chu Yüan-chang in 1368 was called Ta Ming. When the sovereigns of these dynasties were actually reigning, their empire (regardless of its size or constituent parts) was known as Ta T'ang Kuo, Ta Sung Kuo, Ta Ming Kuo—which meant the dominions ruled by the T'ang, Sung or Ming dynasty as the case might be. The *Ta* may be regarded as a non-essential honorific, meaning " Great." The usual Chinese custom has been to drop the honorific when the dynasty to which it was applied has passed out of existence. The important point to notice is that in the name of the dynasty there is nothing to indicate the territorial limits of its dominions. Thus if the Ming dynasty after its fall had succeeded in maintaining itself in a remote corner of China, or even in territories beyond Chinese limits altogether, such as Tongking or Burma, there would have been no theoretical necessity for a change of dynastic title. The " Ta Ming " dynasty would have continued to exist outside China, ruling over an area the population of which might have been wholly non-Chinese. The dynasty that succeeded it in China would, as a matter of course, have adopted a new title of its own, and China for the time being would have become " Ta . . . Kuo."

As it happened, the Ming dynasty was completely overthrown, and after a few years its last scions had no foothold anywhere. It therefore ceased to exist. Many foreigners with only the vaguest knowledge of Chinese history, suppose that the Ming dynasty was overthrown by the Manchus. It is quite true that

the Manchu onslaughts had shaken the dynasty to its foundations, but it was not the Manchus who drove the last of the Ming
emperors to die by his own hand on the hill that overlooks the
Forbidden City. That tragic event was brought about by the
capture of Peking by a host of Chinese marauders under the
leadership of a bandit named Li Tzŭ-ch'êng. Having devastated
and made himself master of a large part of China, and having
crowned his career of conquest by seizing the capital, Li Tzŭ-
ch'êng did what other bandit-leaders had done before him—he
declared himself emperor of a new dynasty.

The name selected for the new dynasty was Ta Shun, and Li
Tzŭ-ch'êng chose Yung-Ch'ang for his own reign-title. That is to
say, if his enterprise had not collapsed almost immediately after
what seemed to be his crowning triumph, he would have been the
first emperor of the Ta Shun dynasty, his empire would have
been known as Ta Shun Kuo (Empire or State or Dominions
of the Ta Shun Dynasty) and the first year of his reign (1644)
would have been Yung-Ch'ang 1. Had all gone well with him his
name might have gone down to history as that of the famous
founder of a mighty dynasty, and the Chinese people of to-day
might have been the loyal and contented subjects of the latest of
a long line of illustrious Ta Shun emperors.

Every Chinese schoolboy—if not every English or American
one—knows what happened to this new dynasty. It was as
fleeting as that which, as we shall see, Yüan Shih-k'ai tried to
set up in 1916. It is unnecessary for our present purposes to
describe the events that led to the utter ruin of Li Tzŭ-ch'êng's
great enterprise. The only facts that concern us here are that
the Manchus who had long been watching the gradual decay of
the Ming dynasty, had won over to their service a number of
very able military and civil Chinese officials, and had already to
an enormous extent adopted Chinese civilisation and the Chinese
language, marched through the Chiu-mên-kuan and other famous
passes of the Great Wall, were joined by the Chinese frontier
army under Wu San-kuei, utterly routed the hosts of Li Tzŭ-
ch'êng, entered Peking in triumph, and finally took possession
of the Dragon throne.

The name of the new dynasty from Manchuria was Ta Ch'ing,
and this is the dynasty which reigned in China from 1644 onwards

and was still in existence when the revolution broke out in 1911. Each of the ten emperors of this dynasty was *Ta Ch'ing Ta Huang-Ti*—" emperor of the Great Ch'ing dynasty "—and it is this title, not any such title as " emperor of China," which the last of the line was specifically allowed, by formal agreement with the Chinese republic, to retain. The clause in the Articles of Favourable Treatment which deals with this matter states that his " title of dignity is to be retained and will not be abolished." The title is definitely stated to be " Ta Ch'ing Huang Ti," and as such it appears in the preamble and is repeated in five out of the eight Articles.[2]

As no new dynasty was established in 1912, the question of devising a new dynastic title naturally did not arise. The republic decided to follow the analogy of Western States and to call itself simply " the Republic of China." Such is the meaning of the Chinese words " Chung-Hua Min Kuo " which constitute the name of the republic to-day.

The use of reign-titles (necessitating a different title for each reign, such as Ch'ien-Lung for the reign of Kao-Tsung, Kuang-Hsü for the reign of Tê-Tsung and so on) has also, as a matter of course, been abolished. The year 1934 is simply *Chung-Hua Min Kuo erh-shih-san nien*—" the twenty-third year of the Republic of China."

What would have happened if Yüan Shih-k'ai had succeeded in founding his new dynasty in 1916—his attempt to do so will be discussed in this chapter—is not quite certain. Vanity might have led him to follow the old custom and give it a name of its own. But judging from the inscriptions on certain coins and medals which he had struck in anticipation of his enthronement, and from other indications, it appears that he intended to change only one word or character in the name which had been given to the republic. The *Min* in " Chung-Hua Min Kuo " was to be altered to *Ti*. This would have been sufficient to turn " the Republic of China " into " The Chinese Empire."

To illustrate the readiness with which the Chinese people have always accepted the ancient theory that the name of the State varied with the name of the dynasty, it is only necessary to point out that the Cantonese to this day call themselves *T'ong-yan* or " men of T'ang " (because it was under the T'ang dynasty that they were absorbed into the empire), while northern Chinese call themselves *Han-jên*—" men of Han "—a much earlier dynasty than the T'ang. Similarly, many Chinese in Manchuria (even after the establishment of the republic) called themselves " men of Ta Ch'ing Kuo." It may be added that in Weihaiwei (which was under British rule from 1898 to 1930) the people commonly referred to China simply as *Ta Kuo*—" the Great Country." It is quite true that *Chung Kuo* is a term which has always been in more or less common use as a general term for " China," but that term means no more than " Middle Kingdom or Realm "—the assumption being that the empire's position in the world was the central one—and it did not enter into the emperor's formal designation. Now, however, it forms part of the official name of the republic.

Thus we see that the anomalous position described in the first sentence of this chapter was not, after all, so anomalous as it seemed. The Ta Ch'ing emperor remained in being ; but China had ceased to be *Ta Ch'ing Kuo*, and the fact that a personage styling himself the Ta Ch'ing emperor continued to reside in Peking, however liable it might be to cause misunderstandings among the ignorant, did not in principle affect the authority or prestige of the republic.

All these usages and theories regarding national and dynastic names and titles in China may seem to be very technical and of no significance except for those who are interested in matters remote from the practical issues of to-day. But they have a direct and important bearing not only on the monarchist ambitions of Yüan Shih-k'ai, now to be discussed, but also on the Manchurian problem as it has been agitating the world of international politics since 1931.

Yüan Shih-k'ai betrayed the emperor Kuang-Hsü in 1898. He betrayed the emperor Hsüan-T'ung in 1911. He betrayed the republic of China in 1916.

This able but unscrupulous statesman became president of the republic not because the revolutionary party trusted him but because they could do nothing else. Sun Yat-sen, who accepted his own nomination by the revolutionary party, has often been praised for his alleged magnanimity in yielding the presidency into the hands of Yüan Shih-k'ai, but he had no alternative. He knew that Yüan, having grasped the reality of power, had not the slightest intention of giving it up, and that Yüan's position in the north was unassailable by such forces as the revolutionaries could muster.[3]

Having been " elected " provisional president and having taken the oath as such on March 10th, 1912, Yüan received a pressing invitation to proceed to Nanking, which was to be the republican capital. Yüan, however, was too astute to put himself in the power of a revolutionary clique which distrusted him as much as he hated and distrusted them. He therefore excused himself from going south by alleging that political conditions in the north were unstable and required a firm controlling hand. When the revolutionary leaders were politely sceptical about this, Yüan staged a mutiny of troops in Peking to prove that elements of dangerous unrest really existed. The fact that the mutiny cost a number of human lives and caused considerable destruction of property was to Yüan a matter of indifference. It achieved the desired result, and in Peking he remained.

On March 20th, 1913, occurred the assassination (almost certainly at Yüan's instigation) of the southern leader Sung Chiao-jên. In July a new revolutionary movement took place which was aimed at Yüan's overthrow, but he acted so promptly and decisively that the " rebels "—who included Sun Yat-sen—were disastrously defeated within a month. This movement is sometimes known as " the second revolution." Sun himself resumed his travels and was for some time an exile in Japan, where he was entertained and received much substantial help from numerous Japanese sympathisers who were the sincere and generous friends of the cause of reform in China. Many of them came to be disillusioned by the course of subsequent events in that country, and lost faith both in Sun Yat-sen and in the republic of which he was the reputed " Father."

On October 6th of the same year Yüan was formally elected president for a period of five years, and took the oath as such, amid much pomp and ceremony, on October 10th, the second anniversary of the outbreak of the revolution. Not long afterwards he succeeded, by successful intrigues and by a skilful manipulation of the financial aspect of the affair, in getting himself declared president for life, with power to nominate his own successor. The defeat of the " second revolution " made Yüan feel strong enough to dissolve Sun Yat-sen's party, the Kuomintang (" People's Party "), and this led to the dissolution of parliament. Owing to the expulsion of its Kuomintang members it had been left without a quorum, though its formal dissolution did not take place till January 12th, 1914. In December, 1913, General Li Yüan-hung, who had been elected vice-president, was summoned to Peking, ostensibly that he might the more conveniently exercise his administrative functions (which turned out to be practically non-existent) but in reality in order that he might be prevented from becoming the tool of anti-Yüan agitators. In May, 1914, after the promulgation of the revised provisional constitution, which superseded that of March, 1912, Hsü Shih-ch'ang, ex-viceroy of Manchuria, became prime-minister, and Sun Pao-ch'i, ex-governor of Shantung, became minister of Foreign Affairs.

Towards the emperor and his court Yüan maintained an attitude of " correctness " without cordiality, if " correctness " be compatible with the fact that he helped himself on various flimsy pretexts to funds belonging to the imperial house and showed himself not over-zealous in the fulfilment of that clause in the Articles of Favourable Treatment which related to the subsidy from the republican government. As a matter of fact that subsidy was at no time paid in full, and when, as we shall see, the Articles became a " scrap of paper " towards the end of 1924, many millions of dollars were owing to the emperor by the republic.

Early in 1913 Yüan caused dismay in court circles by inviting the dowager-empress Lung-Yü to comply with the third of the Articles of Favourable Treatment by moving the court from the Forbidden City to the Summer Palace.

The Nei Wu Fu—the imperial household department—was panic-stricken at the idea of a removal which would inevitably be the first step towards its own dissolution, and persuaded its dupe, the dowager-empress, to enter a vigorous protest. In the absence of any better argument in favour of the protest, it was pointed out to the president that the imperial family if required to move to the Summer Palace would be at the mercy of hordes of bad characters, who would find it an easy matter to scale the low wall by which the Summer Palace park was surrounded. To meet this objection, Yüan was obliging enough to give orders that the wall throughout its entire length of about three miles should be raised by several feet. The money necessary for this undertaking was, of course, to be found not by the president of the republican government but by the household department—in other words it was to come out of the imperial privy purse.

This was a disconcerting reply to the empress-dowager's protest, but the astute officers of the Nei Wu Fu had no difficulty in turning it into a source of profit for themselves. Their view seems to have been that if they were shortly to be encompassed by the shadows of night they might just as well continue to labour in their accustomed hayfield so long as a gleam of sunlight remained. The heightening of the wall, therefore, proved to be an extremely costly undertaking. Moreover it was carried out with such amazing inefficiency that pieces of the new wall began to collapse shortly after their construction, sometimes bringing down portions of the original structure.

Several years afterwards this unfortunate wall came to be a source of much trouble and worry to myself ; for during the short period in which I held (in 1924) the post of imperial commissioner in charge of the Summer Palace and its adjacent estates, every heavy shower was sufficient to cause pieces of the wall to collapse, and it was my duty to provide for its repair out of the slender resources which it was my thankless task to administer. Nor was this task in any way lightened by the fact that I found it possible to have the many repairs carried out more efficiently and much more economically than had ever been the case before ; for every attempt on my part to balance the palace budget by reducing expenditure inevitably conflicted with established usages and " vested rights " and deprived the palace staff of tangible if illicit additions to their emoluments.

The heightening of the wall proved to have been a useless extravagance after all, for circumstances arose which enabled the Court to evade the necessity of vacating the Forbidden City. Probably very few people in China or elsewhere are aware of the true reason why Yüan Shih-k'ai reluctantly agreed to an indefinite postponement of the removal. The fact is, he was afraid of antagonising the still powerful and influential monarchist general and ex-viceroy Chang Hsün, who controlled the Tientsin-Nanking railway from his base at Hsü-chou and was therefore in a position to dominate all eastern China north of the Yangtse. Chang Hsün was one of Yüan's " men " and one of the instruments whereby Yüan kept the revolutionary armies from marching northwards ; but Chang's acceptance of Yüan's leadership was strictly conditional on Yüan's scrupulous observance of the compact between the throne and the republic. Chang, in fact, combined loyalty to Yüan with loyalty to the emperor, the difference between the two loyalties being that the latter was absolute while the former was conditional.

In giving his powerful support to the empress-dowager's protest, Chang Hsün acted from motives of pure loyalty to the emperor, but it is very much to be regretted that he was successful. Like the empress-dowager Lung-Yü he was himself the dupe of the imperial household department, which had secretly sent its emissaries to Hsü-chou to implore his intervention, the alleged ground for such intervention being that the honour and personal safety of his imperial majesty were at stake. It professed, of course, to be actuated by the same lofty motives of loyalty as Chang Hsün himself ; in reality it was concerned, as always, not with the emperor's interests but with its own. Chang Hsün innocently thought that by persuading Yüan shih-k'ai to abandon his design of removing the imperial family from the Forbidden City he was fulfilling the obvious duty of a loyal subject, whereas he merely succeeded in perpetuating the evils of a corrupt and extravagant system which, as I have said, had been very largely responsible for the decay and fall of the Manchu monarchy.

Having yielded with a semblance of magnanimity to the protest of the empress-dowager backed by the strongly-worded warnings of Chang Hsün, Yüan Shih-k'ai temporarily abandoned the idea of expelling the Manchu court from the Forbidden City, but there is no doubt that as early as 1913, if not before, he looked forward to the day when he would enter it in pomp and glory as founder of a new imperial dynasty. Meanwhile he had perforce to content himself with that outlying portion of the imperial palace which had been allocated to the president of the republic. This was the Hsin-hua Palace, which with its lakes and pavilions adjoined the Forbidden City on the west side, and which—regarded objectively as a place of residence—was not inferior to the quarters in the Forbidden City occupied by the imperial family.

Yüan allowed his schemes of personal aggrandisement to mature during a period of nearly two years from the date of his formal election as president before he threw off the mask. He walked warily, and for some little time was content with his life-presidency, which indeed was a monarchy in all but name. It was an open secret that he had exercised his right to nominate his own successor by choosing his own favourite son, Yüan K'o-ting, who many years afterwards lived as a refugee under my protection in the British leased territory of Weihaiwei.

The next step was an easy one. The organ through which he proceeded to manipulate " the will of the people " was a society created *ad hoc* which called itself the *Ch'ou An Hui* or " Society for the Planning of Peace." It came into existence in August, 1915.

Although Yüan was of course himself at the back of all the activities of this Society, the nominal leader of which was a politician named Yang Tu, he maintained the pretence of having nothing whatever to do with it. The question of the *kuo t'i*— " the form of government "—was, said Yüan, entirely a matter to be decided by the people. Nevertheless he and his tools took care to ensure that their " decision " should be in accordance with his own secret wishes.

During the period of active propaganda for the establishment of the new dynasty, Yüan was of course surrounded by sycophants and flatterers who looked forward with eager anticipation to the good things that would come their way when they had established themselves securely on the steps of the new throne. The Manchu imperial family found just cause for deep humiliation in the fact that several of its members sought to ingratiate themselves with its arch-enemy. P'u-Lun, a prince who belonged to the same generation as the emperor and whose claims to the throne had been strongly advocated (for selfish reasons) by Yüan Shih-k'ai, now showed his gratitude to Yüan by supporting him in his imperial ambitions.[4] P'u-Lun was

regarded by the imperial family as having disgraced himself by
" kotowing " before Yüan and describing himself as *ch'ên*—the
term by which the servants of an emperor refer to themselves
when addressing the throne.[5] As a member of the republican
senate he posed as the representative of the imperial family in
publicly supporting the proposal that Yüan should ascend the
throne, and Yüan showed his confidence in him by entrusting
him with the delicate mission of persuading the imperial family
to surrender the *yü-hsi*—the imperial seals, which were kept
under lock and key in a building in the Forbidden City known
as the *Chiao-T'ai Tien*—the " Hall of the Blending of the Great
Creative Forces." The source of my information regarding this
affair is the emperor Hsüan-T'ung himself, who when he told
me about it added that though P'u-Lun tried to carry out his
mission he was unsuccessful. On the very day on which he had
made arrangements, with the venal connivance of certain
officials of the Nei Wu Fu, to carry off the seals, Yüan's grandiose
schemes of self-glorification came crashing to the ground. The
seals remained in the Forbidden City and did not pass out of the
emperor's custody until November, 1924.[6]

This curious incident has an interest of its own irrespective
of the doings of prince P'u Lun. The fact that the imperial seals
—to which even greater importance was attached in China than
in other countries—were allowed to remain in the emperor's
custody at the time of the establishment of the " republic " indicates that those who drew up the Articles of Favourable Treatment at the beginning of 1912 had serious doubts about the
reality and permanence of the abdication.

Another of Yüan's flatterers was the well-known Cantonese
politician and financier Liang Shih-yi,[7] who in the course of his
career amassed so large a fortune that he came to be known as
Ts'ai Shên or " God of Wealth." Liang and a few of his friends
went so far in their fulsome adulation of the emperor-expectant
as to submit a memorial begging that one of his ancestors should
be given the rank of a national divinity. It can hardly be doubted
that this suggestion owed its origin to a hint from Yüan himself,
who realised the importance of adding to the prestige of the new
dynasty by establishing its claim to divine descent.

The ancestor in question — if he was one — was Yüan

Ch'ung-huan, a distinguished soldier and administrator who
defended the Great Wall bravely and sometimes successfully
against the Manchus in the seventeenth century, during the
closing years of the Ming dynasty.

It was undoubtedly an ingenious idea on the part of Yüan
Shih-k'ai or his supporters to select for deification an ancestor
who had fought for China against the Manchus, as the fact of
having had such an ancestor would naturally tend to increase
his popularity and prestige at a time when Chinese patriotism
was still flowing strongly in anti-Manchu channels. Moreover, it
would enable the new emperor's apologists to defend him against
charges of disloyalty, for *Hsiao* or Filial Piety—which includes
devotion to ancestral and family traditions—is the corner-stone
of Chinese ethics, and it would be easy to show that in bringing
about the triumph of the great cause for which his ancestor had
fought and died Yüan was showing himself to be not only a
Chinese patriot but a true exemplar of the first and most fundamental of the Confucian virtues.[8]

Going through the form of treating the memorial as though
the subject were one in which he had no personal interest, Yüan
referred it to the Department of Ceremonies—the republican
substitute for the old Board of Rites—for its consideration and
report. It is unquestionable that if nothing had occurred to turn
the thoughts of the department in a different direction, it would
have reported in due course that exhaustive enquiries into the
merits of the illustrious Yüan Ch'ung-huan had proved him to
be well worthy of being raised to the rank of a divinity, and
would have recommended his elevation to a high rank in the
national pantheon. Before the report embodying this recommendation was ready to be laid at the foot of the throne of the
emperor-designate, the throne itself vanished into thin air. The
enthusiastic admiration which had been expressed if not felt by
Liang Shih-yi and his associates for the transcendent and heroic
merits of the hero Yüan Ch'ung-huan suddenly cooled down, and
the half-god was relegated to his humble place among the
common multitude of men who have lived and died. From that
date to this, no one seems to have thought it worth while to
revive the question of his claim to divinity. Yüan Ch'ung-huan
failed to achieve divine honours in heaven merely because his

descendant Yüan Shih-k'ai failed to secure imperial honours on earth. *Sic transit gloria coeli.*

This little episode throws an instructive light on one side of the politico-religious life of the Chinese people, and suggests many thoughts concerning the political or other accidents which in past ages may have raised or depressed the spiritual fortunes of China's monarchs and sages.[9]

The sordid intrigues which were to have ended in the enthronement of Yüan Shih-k'ai as first sovereign of a new Chinese dynasty under the reign-title of Hung-Hsien culminated in the arrival of thousands of petitions and telegrams imploring Yüan to yield to the popular demand for the revival of the monarchy in his person. Yüan's agent had seen to it that these communications came from every province in China. Then followed the summoning of a " great assembly of popular deputies " which in December, 1915, voted almost unanimously for a constitutional monarchy. Yüan's next step was to issue a mandate in which he announced that although keenly conscious of his own unworthiness, he felt it his duty to bow to " the will of the people."

A few days afterwards, at the winter solstice, Yüan took the significant step of reviving the most imposing of Chinese religious ceremonies—the sacrifice to God at the altar of Heaven. This was a ceremony which could be carried out only by an emperor, and was equivalent to a public declaration to the whole empire that he had already assumed the imperial prerogatives and was about to ascend the dragon throne. Unfortunately, the ceremony was shorn of much of its traditional beauty and stateliness by the fact that Yüan thought it necessary to ensure his own safety by proceeding from the palace to the Altar of Heaven in an armoured car. Evidently he was not so sure of the unanimity of " the will of the people " as his public utterances signified.

When Yüan stood in all the splendour of his imperial sacrificial robes on the central square of the great marble altar, with only the stars above him, he was as near to being emperor of China as any man below the throne could be. It would seem, however, that the divine being whom he thus solemnly invoked at dawn on that winter morning was not deceived by the outward display of glittering regalia but looked into the soul of the man who wore them, spurned his sacrilegious sacrifice and rejected his presumptuous claim to be the Son of Heaven.

Strange indeed was the coincidence that while the emperor-designate was praying for the divine approval of his great enterprise, and possibly believed that he had obtained it, mundane forces were already at work to bring his schemes to ruin and compel him to turn his gaze from the stars to the earth. No sooner had he made a safe return in his armoured car to his palace than he was confronted with a danger of which the stars in their courses had given him no warning. One of his generals, Ts'ai Ao, had already made a stealthy exit from Peking, giving no hint of his intentions until he had reached the confines of the empire in the south-western province of Yunnan. There, and in the adjoining province of Kueichou, he and T'ang Chi-yao raised the standard of revolt and called upon all true supporters of the revolution to join them in crushing the tyrant who had trampled on the rights of the sovereign people, the traitor who had broken his oath of fidelity to the republic.

It was in the last week of December, 1915, that this "Third Revolution" broke out. The response to the appeal of the revolting generals from several of the central and southern provinces was so prompt and emphatic that Yüan's heart quailed. Towards the end of February, 1916, he authorised the issue of a public announcement to the effect that the enthronement, for which vast and costly preparations had been made (much of the cost coming from funds extorted under the name of "loans" from the Manchu imperial house) was indefinitely postponed. A month later he retreated still further and announced the definite cancellation of the "Hung-Hsien" monarchy.

Mainly owing to the deceptive assurances of his own partisans, Yüan had gravely under-estimated the forces that might be set in motion against him. He thought he had made success a certainty by the elaborate preparations he had been making for two or three years past, and by putting his own men into all the responsible positions in the army and in the State. His enemies and opponents were more numerous and more influential than he had imagined.

It was of course common knowledge in the country that the whole movement had been engineered by Yüan's heavily subsidised agents, and that the elections whereby the people were made to declare themselves unanimously in favour of a revival of the monarchy were bogus. Nevertheless it is conceivable that had there been a national assembly which really represented the people (at that period no such assembly was a possibility), and had it been allowed to vote freely on the question of the *kuo t'i* (" form of government "), a large majority of votes would have been given for a reversion to monarchy. But Yüan was certainly not the man for whom a free vote would have been given. One of the loyalists—a scholar named Sung Yü-jên, a well-known writer on Confucian philosophy and allied topics—was courageous enough to advise Yüan to resign in favour of the young Manchu emperor. Steps were promptly taken to have him impeached and silenced, and his example was followed by none. The loyal supporters of the dynasty had already retired into private life and refused to take any part in politics even when advantageous offers of employment reached them from republican quarters. In acting thus they were obeying a Confucian doctrine which justifies a good man in refusing to take office under a bad government, but there is no doubt that numerous foreigners, through a complete misunderstanding of the motives that led to the retirement of a host of loyalist statesmen and officials, were misled into assuming that loyalty to the dynasty had practically ceased to exist and that the Manchu cause was dead. Yüan Shih-k'ai himself, not being a foreigner, was under no such misapprehension ; but he undoubtedly made a fatal error in supposing that he had himself become an object of loyalty to so vast a multitude that he could ignore the hostility of both republicans and Manchu-monarchists and could safely ascend the vacant throne.

Yüan tried to throw the whole blame for the disastrous fiasco on to others, and to make China and the world believe that in his heart of hearts he had never ceased to be a sincere republican. It was only with extreme reluctance, he laboriously explained in a long " apologia " addressed to the nation, that he had consented to obey what he had been deceived into believing was " the will of the people " ; and it was with joy and relief that he now found that he could whole-heartedly devote the rest of his life to the maintenance of the republic.

He had no intention of resigning the life-presidency, which was a monarchy in all but name and which if all went well might become so in name in the person of his son. But his prestige had received a shock from which complete recovery was impossible. No one believed in him, and it is very doubtful whether, if his life had been prolonged, he would have been able to retain even the titular headship of the state. His death, on June 6th, 1916, less than three months after the definite abandonment of the preparations for his enthronement, was the best solution of an awkward problem. Inevitably it gave rise to rumours of murder and of suicide ; but there is no sound reason for doubting the accuracy of the medical verdict, which ascribed his death to physical derangements produced by prolonged and intense anxiety and emotional disturbance.

The view suggested above, that a freely elected representative assembly might have voted for a return to monarchy, though not for Yüan Shih-k'ai as emperor, may seem fantastic, but it is one which was held by many prominent people in China whose sympathies were wholly with the revolution and wholly anti-Manchu and anti-monarchic. One of the most striking expressions of this belief which I came across was contained in an article by a certain ultra-radical professor in the Peking National University named Ch'ên Tu-hsiu, who afterwards became one of the most zealous leaders of the communist party in China and is now undergoing a long term of imprisonment as a result of his subversive activities. I translate a few sentences from an article which he published in the radical periodical known as the *Hsin Ch'ing Nien* (*New Youth*) in May, 1917, the year following the fall of Yüan Shih-k'ai.[10]

" I do not share the prevalent optimism about the immediate future of our republic. . . . I am not at all sure that there will be no further attempts to change the form of government. . . . I was by no means surprised when the Ch'ou-An Society suddenly began to advocate the re-establishment of the monarchic system. Now that Yüan Shih-k'ai has come to grief and died, it is generally supposed that the republic is firmly established. But I have serious doubts. . . . Although there seems to be no general opposition to the republican idea, people's minds are still obsessed with the old monarchic notions. They have not the slightest idea of what the civilised democratic societies of Europe and America really are. . . . It was no idle dream of Yüan Shih-k'ai's to make himself emperor. *He knew very well that the great majority of people in China still believed in monarchy and had no faith in a republic.* Even of those who opposed the recent attempt to revive the monarchy, *more than half were not genuinely and fundamentally opposed to the monarchic principle but merely to Yuan Shih-k'ai becoming emperor.* . . . Although Yüan is dead, the popular hankering after a monarchy, of which he tried to make use for his own advantage, is still in existence. It seems to me that it would be easier to climb up to heaven than to establish the republic so securely that no monarchic revivals could ever take place again. If we want to stabilise our republic, there is only one thing to be done—we must clear out of people's minds every trace of the antiquated monarchic ideas that still obsess them."[11]

This is a remarkable commentary on the common Western belief—sedulously fostered by clever Chinese propagandists—that the abolition of the monarchy was in accordance with the sovereign will of the people of China. Since the article from which I have quoted was published, the Chinese government has become even less republican than it was between 1912 and 1917, and the people have suffered from an accumulation of evils which make the worst days of the Manchu monarchy seem like a golden age of peace and prosperity. It is not surprising, perhaps, that the republic has not been a brilliant success. As Jowett, the Master of Balliol, is reported to have said—" You cannot have a republic without republicans." Now this is just the trouble with the Chinese republic. There are no republicans.

It is hardly necessary to say that the members of the Manchu imperial house—all except a few sycophants like P'u-Lun who for sordid reasons had become Yüan's man—were seriously alarmed by the Hung-Hsien monarchy movement. It was obvious, at least to the more intelligent of the Manchus, that if Yüan Shih-k'ai became emperor he would not long tolerate the existence of another emperor in his capital city, even though

Ic

that emperor possessed nothing but his barren title. Yüan sent emissaries to tranquillise and reassure them—he knew they still had powerful sympathisers—but not unnaturally they hesitated to put confidence in Yüan's promises, and during the last months of 1915 and the first half of 1916 their anxiety was very great. Probably no section of the community was more gratified by the success of Ts'ai Ao's rebellion and by the fall and death of Yüan than were the princes and all those who had remained faithful to the old dynasty. They were far more numerous than was generally suspected—especially by foreigners—and were to be found among all the races symbolically represented on the five-barred republican flag—Manchus, Mongols, Tibetans, Mohammedans and Chinese.

Like many greater men, Yüan Shih-k'ai was not superior to the little vanities of ordinary humanity. There is evidence that he looked forward with almost childish delight to the magnificent enthronement ceremonies in which he was to have played the principal part, and there was hardly a detail in the programme that he had not himself carefully scrutinised several months before the great event was to have taken place. He intended to revive some antique customs in respect of dress and ceremonial, and those of his friends who were learned in ancient lore pleased him by producing sketches of what the Han emperors of two thousand years ago looked like when they were offering sacrifices to the mountains and rivers. It is said that he had a gold coin minted " depicting him in the garb of an emperor in ancient dress, with the hat the Chinese emperors wore centuries ago."[12] The authority to whom I owe this statement admits that he could not verify it ; but he gives some interesting illustrations and descriptions of the various coins and medals, some of them bearing Yüan's effigy, which were in fact minted to commemorate the inauguration of the new dynasty. Some of them bear the inscriptions *Hung-Hsien chi-yüan* (" the Hung-Hsien era or reign-period ") and *Chung-Hua Ti Kuo* (" the Chinese Empire"). Hung-Hsien was to have been the new emperor's reign-title, just as Hsüan-T'ung was that of P'u-Yi and Kuang-Hsü that of the late emperor Tê Tsung.[13] So sure was Yüan that his great ambition was about to be fulfilled that he did not hesitate to allow many of these coins to pass out of his control, and some were put into silk-lined cases and given by him as presents to his nearest friends.

Besides the coins and medals which were struck for the purpose of commemorating the new reign there were also silver dollars bearing Yüan's effigy, most of which were minted after his death. These are still in circulation as ordinary coins. They of course represent him not as emperor but as president.

Another indication of Yüan's confidence in his high destiny was that he had porcelain bowls and jars made at the famous old imperial porcelain-factories in Kiangsi, bearing the inscription " made in the Hung-Hsien reign." Some of these pieces he had the effrontery to present to the young emperor, from whom in later years I received the two that form part of my own collection.[14].

It is perhaps when we contemplate these coins and pieces of porcelain that we can best picture to ourselves the torment of soul that Yüan experienced when he saw his throne dissolving into mist and dream. And if in the night-watches the " silent voices of the dead " assailed his spiritual ear with bitter reproaches, and if the thought of the sovereigns he had betrayed took ghostly form, it is scarcely necessary for us to seek in any external agency the cause of Yüan's death. The forces that killed him were the spectres that haunted his own mind.

If Yüan had been content to remain in the great position he had (by dubious means) achieved for himself—which was practically that of life-dictator with power to nominate his own son as his successor—he might have succeeded in leading his country into the way of peace and ordered progress, and in spite of his faults of character his name might have been recorded in history as that of a great man who deserved to be remembered by his country with gratitude. That he had, in his prime of life, great energy and ability cannot be doubted. It is equally true that his ambition was of a thoroughly selfish type and that he was crafty and treacherous.

For the benefit of those who may think that I have dealt unfairly with Yüan Shih-k'ai, I will quote the judgment of a learned and patriotic Chinese who spent several years as a student in England and Germany, who has given good service to the republic, and who is so far from being a monarchist that he is or was a strong believer in "revolution" as China's only hope. What Dr. V. K. Ting has to say about Yüan Shih-k'ai is this :

" He began his public career as China's political agent in Korea and was more than anyone else responsible for the Sino-Japanese war of 1894. By betraying the emperor Kuang-Hsü, who was endeavouring to reform the political system in 1898, he became the favourite of the infamous empress-dowager, and was entrusted with the formation of China's new army, from which have been drawn almost all the present military governors who are by common consent China's greatest curse. During the republican revolution of 1911 he betrayed the Manchu dynasty, to which he was premier, to become president of the republic, which position he retained by first bribing then dissolving parliament. There are at least two murders of his political opponents proved against him, and finally he worked his own ruin by trying to create a monarchy by fraud. He died a miserable failure and unblessed."[15]

I am in agreement with every word of this grave indictment. It has always been a matter of perplexity and astonishment to me that Yüan Shih-k'ai was the man who was honoured with the admiration and friendship, consistently maintained through many years, of a British minister.

Yüan Shih-k'ai professed to be a strong upholder of Confucian principles, but while earnestly recommending them to others he miserably failed to be guided by them in his own life. The true Confucian is a *chün-tzŭ*—a " princely man." Comparisons have been drawn between this noble conception and that English ideal of which the word " gentleman," though " soiled by all ignoble use," is still the best verbal equivalent. The extent to which the English and Chinese ideals coincide may be a matter of dispute ; but the facts stated in this chapter are surely sufficient to show that Yüan Shih-k'ai—who betrayed his sovereign, betrayed the throne and betrayed the republic—was neither a *chün-tzŭ* nor a gentleman.[16]

CHAPTER IX

Chang Hsün and the Restoration of 1917

THE DEATH OF YÜAN SHIH-K'AI made China once more " safe for democracy "—or so thought the optimists. The parliamentary system of government, for which Yüan had shown his hearty contempt, was re-established ; but the results only seemed to show that whatever Yüan's sins or blunders in other matters may have been, in this matter of parliamentary democracy his judgment had not been far wrong.

No sooner had the first of China's parliaments been opened than their incongruity with the existing state of the country's political development began to be apparent. Confident assertions were made in 1912 that what the Chinese people longed for above all else was a national assembly through which they could demonstrate their capacity for self-government. Yet in the middle of 1913, the second year of the republic, political conditions could be summed up by a keen-sighted French father in these few words : " Orages parlementaires incessants à Pékin . . . conspirations et assassinats un peu partout."[1]

Nevertheless parliamentary democracy, such as it was, survived two great crises in two successive years. We have just considered one attempt to restore the monarchic system, and its failure. We have now to witness another. What Yüan tried to do in 1916 was to found a new dynasty ; what Chang Hsün tried to do in 1917 was to restore the old one. Both attempts came to grief, and China's parliamentary experiments were destined to continue till near the end of 1924—the thirteenth year of the republic—and were then to be brought, at least for many years to come, to an ignominious close. They have not yet been resumed, and China, as I have already said, is less of a republic in 1934 than she was when a Manchu emperor still reigned in Peking.

The French writer just quoted was no enthusiast for Yüan

Shih-k'ai, and condemned his imperial ambitions ; yet he believed that the continuance of his dictatorship would have been more likely to benefit the country than its replacement by the only kind of parliamentary system that China at that time seemed capable of creating. " Son coup d'état manqué, livra le pays aux parlementaires, race qui paraît devoir le conduire à sa ruine."[2]

Very few Chinese, after Yüan Shih-k'ai's time, dared to say openly, what they frequently said in private, that republicanism was a failure. Many of them realised the main obstacles to its success, one of which was that about ninety per cent of the Chinese people were illiterate, and that no attempt to make the masses take an intelligent interest in politics could be other than farcical. Graham Wallas estimated that in no county in England did the number of persons really active in politics amount to more than ten per cent of the electorate.[3] If that can be said of England, what are we to say of China ? If we assume that as many as ten per cent of the people of China *who can read and write* could be induced to take an active interest in politics, we should probably be overstating the probable proportion of persons who could be so influenced. Yet that proportion would represent no more than one per cent of the total population of the country. This being so, political power under any conceivable parliamentary system in China must almost inevitably pass into the hands of professional politicians, of whom only a small proportion are likely to be unselfish patriots honestly seeking the good of their country and people.

Another equally grave obstacle is that the family-system in China is so organised that the individual finds it practically impossible to release himself from the social bonds which compel him to put the interests of his family before those of the State.[4] Under the monarchic system he could do so to some extent, because loyalty to the sovereign was a corner-stone of Confucian ethics : so much so that writers like Ch'ên Tu-hsiu (already referred to as a leader of the Chinese communist party) have insisted that Confucianism was incompatible with republicanism and that there would always be attempts to restore the monarchy so long as Confucianism was respected.[5]

Although most Chinese have been afraid to speak their minds

openly on this subject, some have done so guardedly and with
discretion. One of these is an able writer already quoted, Mr.
Sih-gung Cheng, who was educated in England and published
in 1919 a valuable political study entitled *Modern China.* " I am
no lover of the Manchus," he says, " and no monarchist, but I
often wonder whether it would not have been safer and easier
for China to move smoothly towards the ideals of democratic
government, if it had been possible to retain the Manchu
emperor as a figure-head, and establish a constitutional monarchy instead of a republic."

Mr. Cheng knew, from his own observations in England, that
monarchy was not necessarily a synonym for tyranny. This is a
discovery which great numbers of Chinese revolutionary en-
thusiasts, especially those who have never been abroad or whose
personal knowledge of the West is confined to the United States,
have failed to make for themselves. This is probably because
they have not learned to turn from the world of books to the
world of men, and have not had opportunities to exchange
political theorising for practical statesmanship. They have failed
to grasp the truth that " republic " and " monarchy " cover a
considerable variety of political structures, and they have shown
a perilous tendency to allow doctrinaire assumptions to cloud
their political judgments.

In September, 1915, a Chinese daily newspaper published in
Peking contained a lament that the republic, which had then
been established nearly four years, had not brought the " freedom " promised by the revolutionaries—though Sun Yat-sen,
as we have seen, believed that the freedom enjoyed by his
fellow-countrymen under the monarchy had been excessive and
must be curtailed.

" If we Chinese," said the journalist, " cannot enjoy the
privileges of American or French people, we may at least hope
for conditions similar to those under which the British, Germans
and Japanese now live." Here we have an amusing instance of
the naïve assumption that because the United States and France
were " republics " and the other states named were " mon-
archies," there must of necessity be greater freedom under the
former system of government than under the latter.

It is a pity that the attention of this writer was not called

to the words of an American author who in the same month of
the same year wrote as follows :

> " We Americans hold that government by the people means
> liberty and justice. This is not necessarily true. Democracy
> gives us ten thousand bosses, each one more costly than a
> single average monarch of Europe. England is nominally a
> monarchy. Yet in London the American can find more home
> rule and common law justice than in New York or Chicago."[6]

In the case of China, the people not only possessed greater
liberty (which as Sun Yat-sen saw is not necessarily a good thing
in itself) but were also better governed under the old imperial
system, even in its days of decay, than under the constantly
shifting forms of " republican " government that have supplanted it. China, too, has had her " ten thousand bosses," and
many of them if not all have proved more costly to the Chinese
people, in life and treasure, than the most rapacious of her
monarchs.

Li Yüan-hung, who had been forced rather unwillingly into
the leadership of the revolutionary forces at Wu-ch'ang in 1911,
had been the uncomfortable occupant of the vice-presidential
chair during Yüan's lifetime. His position, indeed, was little
better than that of a state-prisoner, for Yüan had reason to
believe that he might, unless carefully watched, go over to the
enemy. Yüan's death placed him automatically in the presidency ; but he was a man of mediocre abilities and the task of
ruling the unwieldy republic was altogether beyond his power.
Like all but an infinitesimal fraction of his countrymen, he had
little knowledge of, and less enthusiasm for, Western theories
of democratic parliamentary government, and he lacked the
stimulus of enthusiasm for a great cause.

The various political and military groups intrigued against
him and against one another, and his feeble attempts to bring
order into what was tending to become chaos met with little
success.

Meanwhile men's eyes turned from Peking—where nothing of
any importance was taking place—towards the town of Hsü-
chou, on the Tientsin-Pukow railway, where General Chang

Hsün, with his army, occupied a position of such strategic importance that no Chinese military or civil leader in north China could afford to ignore him.[7]

The death of Yüan had freed Chang Hsün from the obligations of one of his two loyalties. This only served to add strength to the other. He made no secret of his own views as to how the growing political confusion could best be brought to an end. He had always refused to cut off his queue, and was therefore known to scoffers as " the pigtailed general." Not only did he retain this outward symbol of his continued loyalty to the Manchu dynasty but he required his soldiers to follow his example. His forces were known as " the pigtailed army," and there is no reason to suppose that they resented the appellation.

Late in 1916 and early in 1917 a series of more or less secret political conferences were held at Hsü-chou, under Chang Hsün's chairmanship. They were attended not only by his own friends and supporters but also by several of the semi-independent leaders in different parts of north and central China or by their personal representatives. Very little of what took place at the conferences was allowed to become public, and such reports as appeared in the Chinese press were largely imaginary. There is no doubt, however, that there was a council within a council and that before the members of this inner council concluded their deliberations they had given pledges to Chang Hsün to the effect that any movement initiated by him for the restoration of the Manchu monarchy would receive their support and active co-operation.

Li Yüan-hung was certainly not ignorant of the direction of Chang Hsün's political sympathies, and he must have had a shrewd idea, if not certain knowledge, of the action which " the pigtailed general " was likely to take if the capital passed under his military control. Nevertheless it was Li Yüan-hung who, after the Hsü-chou Conference, invited Chang Hsün to visit Peking and mediate between the rival political groups.

These groups included a Southern party which had set up a rival government at Canton under Sun Yat-sen. One of the main difficulties which president Li had to contend with arose out of the question of whether China should or should not join the allies and declare war on Germany. Sun Yat-sen and his party

were strongly opposed to China's participation in the war,
though subsequently they showed themselves eager to reap all
the advantages that such participation enabled China to claim
as one of the victorious allies. But the political struggle in China
was not merely between north and south. There were northern
and central China groups which also found it difficult to tolerate
one another's existence. President Li had reassembled the
parliament which Yüan Shih-k'ai had got rid of, but it had
learned nothing from experience. It was largely in consequence
of the riotous scenes which took place in the Peking parliament
that Li took the momentous step of invoking the aid of the
monarchist general.

Chang Hsün's greatest mistake from the point of view of his
own policy was that he placed too great a trust in his own
military prestige and in the good faith of the various leaders
who had given him open or secret support at Hsü-chou. He left
his army there and proceeded to Peking with a badly equipped
force which was far too small to give him real mastery of the
situation.

He entered Peking in June, and initiated his attempts at
" mediation " by demanding the dissolution of the inept body
which called itself a parliament. President Li, powerless and
irresolute, obediently issued the mandate of dissolution. Members of the loyalist party, including the redoubtable K'ang Yu-
wei, came to Peking in prompt compliance with the secret summonses issued by the " pigtailed general." A week or two of
subdued excitement culminated in the event which had long
been foreseen. Proclamations (drafted by K'ang Yu-wei with
the assistance of experienced ex-officials such as Liang Tung-
yen, a minister of Foreign Affairs under the empire) were issued
announcing the re-establishment of the monarchy, and at the
beginning of July Hsüan-T'ung resumed his imperial functions.

To say that he was restored to the throne is not strictly
accurate, for he had never ceased to occupy it. According to
the terms of the Articles of Favourable Treatment, and in the
eyes of all loyalists, he had surrendered only *chêng-ch'üan*—the
right of rulership—not the imperial status and dignity. All that
Chang Hsün and his fellow-monarchists, according to their own
lights, had to do was to cancel the imperial edict of 1912 in

which the emperor, bowing to what was assumed to be the will
of the people, and anxious to save his subjects from the horrors
of a protracted civil war, had notified to the empire his " voluntary " retirement from the active headship of the state and the
establishment of a republican form of government. The cancellation of this edict automatically restored the *chêng-ch'üan*
and abolished the republic. The boy who had never ceased to
be an emperor in name now became once more an emperor in
fact.

A long manifesto was issued by Chang Hsün and his colleagues
in the form of a circular telegram to the nation. The following is
a translation of a few passages from this lengthy document. It
is the translation which was produced by an anti-monarchist
English newspaper in Peking called the *Peking Gazette*, the
editor of which was a certain native of the British colony of
Trinidad, of Chinese descent, who was unable to speak, read or
write his ancestral language. He was no other than Ch'ên Yu-jên,
better known to foreigners as Eugene Chen, who afterwards
became a high official of the Nationalist government and
negotiated on behalf of the Chinese the British rendition of the
Hankow Concession in 1927. Towards the end of 1933 he re-
appeared as " Foreign Minister " of the new independent
government of Fuhkien, and on its collapse in January, 1934,
took refuge in Hong-Kong.

" Ever since the uprising at Wuchang and the establishment
of the republic peace and order have been cast to the winds
and good reliable people have been nowhere to be seen.
Anarchists have been holding sway while unscrupulous people
have been monopolising the power. Robber chiefs are called
heroes and dead convicts are worshipped as martyrs. Parliament relied on rebels for support while Cabinet Ministers
used biased parties as their protection. Unscrupulous borrowing of foreign money is called finance ; and bleeding the people
is termed revenue-raising. Oppression of innocent people is
considered self-government ; and defaming old scholars is
considered civilisation. Some spread rumours under the
pretext that they are public opinion while others secretly
finance foreigners and call it diplomacy. All these are treason

practised under the fine name of statesmanship, and corruption under the mask of legislation. They even advocate the
abolition of Confucianism and thus call down the wrath of
God. . . . In name we are a Republic but nothing is known of
the citizens. People are called citizens but they know nothing
about their country. Now the people are poor and financial
resources exhausted, the foundations of the country begin to
shake. All this is the result of the bad form of government. . . .
Look at the matter at its root, we find that Republicanism
is the source of all the evil. . . . Compare this with the con-
tinuous reign of a monarchy, wherefrom the people may
enjoy peace for tens or hundreds of years, the difference is
at once seen to be as great as the distance between heaven
and earth. . . . Carefully weighing present conditions and the
tendency of the people it is preferable to expel party politics
and establish a firm monarchy than to invite ruin by adopting
the empty name of a Republic. . . . Our Emperor, who is in
his boyhood, has devoted himself to study and learning to be
calm in obedience to the demand of the day. The country
has passed many great upheavals but in the palace there has
always reigned peace and calm. Recently His Majesty has
made marked progress in his sacred studies and his virtuous
reputation has spread far and wide. It can thus be seen that
Heaven has smiled on the Ch'ing dynasty by conferring His
Majesty with unusual wisdom so that he might be able to
rise at the proper moment to stop disorder and revert to
right. . . . [Chang] Hsün and others have been accumulating
their energy with their weapons near at hand for the last
six years. . . . On this day we have jointly memorialised His
Imperial Majesty to again ascend the throne in order to
establish the foundation of the country and to consolidate the
minds of the people."

There could be no mistaking the attitude of the Peking
populace towards the revival of the *ancien régime*. North China
had never been enthusiastically pro-republican. Peking, for
centuries accustomed to be the seat of a royal court, had never
ceased to be monarchist. I was not personally an observer of the
stirring events of July, 1917. More fortunate in this respect

was my friend Sir Charles Eliot, then vice-chancellor of the University of Hong-Kong and not long afterwards British ambassador at Tokyo. He was a temporary resident in Peking when the restoration took place, and in a letter written to me on the morning of that event he described his astonishment when on awaking in his room in the Hotel de Pékin he found the city decked with dragon flags.

The docile citizens of Peking or of any other city in China are always ready to display any flag for which the local military or police authorities are known to have a preference, or which will, they think, give them immunity from the unwelcome attentions of any invader, whether Chinese or foreign. But in this instance there is no doubt that the lavish display of bunting was an outward manifestation of popular sympathy with the re-establishment of the monarchy ; and this was the conclusion at which Sir Charles Eliot, as a result of his own observation and enquiries, rather unwillingly arrived.

But the success or failure of the royalist revival lay in other hands than those of the people of Peking. The republic found a saviour in the person of Tuan Ch'i-jui, a general who from his headquarters at Tientsin commanded the largest and best-equipped body of troops in that part of China. On the very day on which the English translation of Chang Hsün's manifesto was published (July 3rd, 1917), the battle of Ma-ch'ang, between Tientsin and Peking, decided the fate of the monarchy. Aircraft, never before made practical use of in Chinese warfare, were part of the equipment of the " Saviour of the Republic " ; and when an aeroplane—a few days after the battle of Ma-ch'ang— unexpectedly made its appearance and dropped a bomb or two among the buildings of the Forbidden City, Chang Hsün knew that he and his cause were beaten. The newly-appointed viceroy of Chihli and regent of the empire had fought and lost his last battle and was compelled to take refuge under the hospitable roof of the Dutch Minister. He was joined there by Liang Tun-yen ; while K'ang Yu-wei became the guest of the American Legation. The emperor retired into the obscurity from which he had emerged less than a fortnight before ; and the dragon flags that had brightened every street in Peking were " carefully folded away against the day when the Son of Heaven" should once more "return in splendour to his Great Inheritance."[8]

Chang Hsün had courage and loyalty but he was not free from selfish ambitions and he held an exaggerated opinion of his own capacity as a general and his own skill as a statesman. He foolishly believed that he was strong enough to act independently of his fellow-monarchists, and in his desire to win the sole credit for having brought about the restoration he acted in such a way as to create the impression among many of his colleagues that there was no hope for them of an equitable allocation of the plums that were awaiting distribution—the princedoms, the viceroyalties, the high military commands and the other great offices of state.

Tuan himself was one of those who were indignant with Chang Hsün for ignoring them when the moment for decisive action had come. "There is no possible doubt," as Mr. J. O. P. Bland says, "that the restoration of the Manchu dynasty as a constitutional monarchy had been discussed and approved by the military governors, including Tuan Ch'-i-jui, at their several conferences." He adds, equally truly, that "the failure of Chang Hsün's colleagues to support him and the restored throne in July, 1917, was not due to any republican sympathies on their part, but solely to the fact that Chang Hsün, a blunt, ambitious soldier and no politician, had stolen a march on his associates and could by no means be permitted to reap the fruits thereof."[9]

One of the supporters of the movement, it may be mentioned, was Chang Tso-lin, who actually submitted a memorial to the throne expressing loyal gratitude for the confirmation of his appointment as governor-general of Manchuria.

Nevertheless there are good reasons for believing that the monarchist *coup* was much nearer success than is usually believed, and that the "midsummer madness," as it has been so often called, had in it more than a streak of sanity. The movement failed not because it lacked sympathisers but because some of the principal participators were selfish, ambitious and jealous of one another and because Chang Hsün had none of the essential qualities of statesmanship.

It is erroneous, then, to describe the movement as a "semi-farcical escapade."[10] A more serious and accurate view of the

episode was that taken by the writer of a leading article in the
North China Standard (Peking) in its issue of September 18th,
1923, from which the following is an extract :

" When he [Chang Hsün] inaugurated his monarchical
restoration movement he had the definite assurance of many
prominent leaders that they would assist him in his scheme.
But when the fateful day arrived he stood practically alone
and although he resorted to the *ultima ratio* of war he was
defeated. When we let the history of China of the last twelve
years pass before our mental eyes we find the same everywhere. Whenever there is a man willing and capable of doing
something he is ignominiously deserted by his so-called friends.
Apparently nobody wants to commit himself definitely, nobody has the courage of his convictions. As long as this state of
affairs exists there is no help for China. Even the strongest
man cannot do everything himself, but must rely on the
support and co-operation of others. But if there are no others
willing to give support and co-operation achievement is
impossible."

However, if the episode of July, 1917, is not correctly described
as mere " midsummer madness " or "a semi-farcical escapade ",
it did actually inspire an enterprising Chinese dramatist to write
a serio-comic play on the subject. It is called *Fu-P'i Ch'ao*—
" The Restoration Movement." Neither author nor publisher is
mentioned by name, and the play is undated. It seems to have
been printed for private circulation, and I never saw a copy in a
Peking bookshop ; nor has it ever been performed. My own copy
was presented to me by the emperor himself in 1921. He spoke
of it with amusement and was by no means offended by its tone.
Indeed he could hardly have complained of its reference to
himself, though he is one of the *dramatis personæ*, for the dramatist treats him with delicacy and respect. Even Chang Hsün
himself receives merciful treatment. The sympathies of the
playwright seem to have been with the monarchist cause. This
we may judge from the contempt and abuse which are meted
out to those of Chang Hsün's followers who pretended to be
loyal to him and to the emperor in the hope of obtaining rich

rewards, but deserted him when it became obvious that the cause was lost. From internal evidence it is clear that the writer of the play had a good knowledge of palace etiquette. The closing scene is a touching one. It describes Chang Hsün's last audience with his youthful sovereign just before his withdrawal to the Dutch Legation.

That Tuan Ch'i-jui's action was inspired by jealousy or mistrust of Chang Hsün rather than by zeal for the republican cause was revealed by the fact that no advantage was taken of the episode of the restoration to humiliate the court or deprive it of any of the privileges it had enjoyed since the revolution. Had there existed at that time among the dominant politicians and militarists of northern China a serious desire to establish the republic on a durable basis or to ensure that the emperor should never again play a prominent part on the Chinese political stage, the republican government could undoubtedly have used the incident as a pretext for cancelling or drastically amending the Articles of Favourable Treatment. Neither Tuan Ch'i-jui, the " Saviour of the Republic," nor Fêng Kuo-chang, the general who succeeded Li Yüan-hung as president, showed the least disposition to adopt any such course. It was officially announced that the emperor had not been a free agent and that the court could not be held to blame for what had occurred. Relations between the two palaces were re-established on the former basis of mutual respect, and the emperor continued to occupy his stately quarters in the Forbidden City and to sit—in twilight— on the dragon throne.

It must not be supposed, however, that the attempt of Chang Hsün to subvert the republic was regarded with equanimity by the radicals of the south. From 1917 onwards they never ceased to demand the punishment of the " traitors," the cancellation of the Articles of Favourable Treatment and the reduction of the emperor's status to that of an ordinary citizen. As they also, however, openly repudiated the authority of the northern government, it is not surprising that their demands for the punishment of the court were ignored by those in authority in Peking.

The oft-repeated charge brought against the emperor by the Kuomintang and other Chinese radicals that in July, 1917, he was personally guilty of treachery to the republic, and was therefore deserving of capital punishment, is of course utterly false. At that time the emperor was only a child of eleven years and five months old, and to suppose that he directed or participated in the intrigues that led to his brief restoration is absurd.[11] Nevertheless the charge is one which has never been abandoned by the left wing of the Chinese revolutionaries, mainly no doubt because it can be made to serve a useful purpose when justification is sought for the unilateral action taken by a small group of irresponsible soldiers and politicians in 1924.

Regarding the young emperor's personal attitude towards the problem of his own restoration, the following little story is told not because it is true but because it has appeared in at least one published collection of anecdotes and has often been told at Peking dinner-tables. My translation closely follows the Chinese original.

" A few days before the restoration, Chang Hsün had a secret audience with Hsüan-T'ung in the palace. Chang knelt and informed the emperor what he proposed to do. Hsüan-T'ung shook his head and refused to agree to the restoration. ' May I invite Your Sacred Majesty to tell your old servant your reasons for refusal ? ' ' My tutor Ch'ên Pao-shên,' replied the emperor, ' keeps telling me all day long about how the Classic of Poetry says this and Confucius says that. There is never an end to it. How can I possibly find time to attend to anything more than my endless lessons ? ' ' If your Sacred Majesty,' said Chang, ' will only ascend the throne again, you will have important affairs of state to attend to and you need not spend any more time at lessons.' Hsüan-T'ung brightened up. ' Do you really mean,' he said, ' that if only I become emperor again I may give up all my lessons ? ' ' History tells us,' replied Chang, ' that the Son of Heaven has always been a horseman. No one ever heard of a *Tu-shu T'ien Tzŭ*—a Book-reading Son of Heaven.' ' In that case,' exclaimed Hsüan-T'ung joyfully, ' let it be as you wish. I will do whatever you want me to do.' "

The teller of the tale marks his disapproval of Chang Hsün with this acid comment: " Alas ! How can it be said that Chang
Kc

Hsün had the least spark of real loyalty in him when he was thus willing, for the sake of his own honour and glory, to hood-wink a little boy.''

, Not only was no attempt made by Tuan Ch'i-jui or any of the other northern leaders to seize the opportunity to cancel the Articles of Favourable Treatment, but nothing whatever was done to punish Chang Hsün or any of his colleagues. Even their property was not seized, though confiscation of worldly goods is one of the first steps usually taken in republican China against those who have been beaten in the game of politics or of war. Before long, as we shall see, Chang Hsün received a free pardon, and spent the rest of his life in dignified retirement.[12] Indeed many of his friends in high places made strenuous efforts to bring him back to public life, and very nearly succeeded in doing so.

There is a story that when Tuan Ch'i-jui was asked by some of his republican friends why he treated Chang Hsün so mag-nanimously, he replied : " Chang Hsün is an old friend of mine. How could I do him an injury ? " Perhaps it was a case of the well-known Chinese love of compromise. Chinese political personages are singularly apt at practising the caution and moderation recommended by Francis Bacon—" to treat our friend as though he might one day be a foe, and our foe as if he should one day be a friend."

It should be added, however, that another theory of the very lenient treatment accorded to the monarchist is based on a very prevalent belief that Chang Hsün possessed documentary evidence of the complicity of many of the leading soldiers and politicians of the country in the restoration plot, and that he threatened to publish it if they adopted harsh measures either against himself and his associates or against the Manchu emperor and his court. The matter is referred to in the following paragraphs from the *Peking Leader* of May 6th, 1924 :

" The Chinese press to-day comments on the report that the important documents dealing with General Chang Hsün's mon- archical restoration movement of 1917 have been taken to Paris. These documents are said to comprise the resolutions of the Hsü-chou Conference, and telegrams from influential Chinese giving approval to the proposed movement, which are supposed to number no less than eighty-two.

"This report traces the history of the documents from the hands of General Chang when he fled for safety to the Dutch Legation, into the keeping of a certain Wang, who was hiding in the French Hospital at the time. Through various stages they are supposed to have passed through safe keeping in the French Legation and then on to Paris. As yet no one seems to have been able to confirm this story."

With regard to Chang Hsün himself, much nonsense has been written about the history and personality of this remarkable man. It has been said and believed by many that he began his career as a groom or carter, that his fine bearing and physique attracted the interest of the old dowager-empress T'zŭ-Hsi during her flight to Hsi-an after the Boxer movement, and that he basked thereafter in the sunshine of imperial favour and was promoted to high military office.[13]

A few years after the events of 1917 I became personally acquainted with Chang Hsün and with many of those who were his most intimate associates. From them I gathered the main facts of his chequered career. Moreover, during the last years of his life—from 1919 to 1923—he spent some of his spare time in the preparation of a brief sketch of his life, and a copy of this document was given to me by his family shortly after his death. As far as I am aware it has never been published or translated. As it is a document of some historic and human interest, a translation of it will be given in the next chapter, with no omissions except a few entries relating to the successive births of the general's children.

One of the names by which he was known to his literary and artistic friends was *Sung Shou Lao Jên*, the literal meaning of which is "Pine-Tree Longevity Old Man." Being an evergreen of exceptional strength and hardihood, the pine-tree is regarded in China as a fitting symbol for a prosperous and sturdy old age. *Sung Shou Lao Jên* was therefore a name of good omen, and it is the name by which the old monarchist leader described himself at the beginning of his autobiographic record.

Chapter X

Autobiography of the Old Man of the Pine-Tree
(*Translated from the Chinese*)

THOSE WHO ARE IN CHARGE of the general Clan Register of the Chang family in the province of Kiangsi have repeatedly asked me for a record of myself. Alas, I am a person of small account, but the Register exists for the purpose of preserving the memorials of the clan, whereby we manifest our respect for our ancestors. Though a man of no outstanding ability I have no right to maintain silence as though I were a disgrace to my ancestors. This being so, I will now, for the benefit of my family, put the main events of my life into the form of a narrative which will I think be free from errors of fact.

My family dwelt for generations in the village of Ch'ih-T'ien ("Red Field"), to the south of the district-city of Fêng-hsin in the province of Kiangsi. I was born between 9 and 11 on the morning of the twenty-fifth day of the tenth moon of the cyclical year *chia-yin*, that is to say the fourth year of the reign of Hsien-Fêng [1854].

In 1861, during my eighth year, the district was over-run and harried by the Cantonese robbers [the T'ai-p'ing rebels] and the inhabitants scattered in all directions, seeking safety. My grandfather, K'un-i, was the only one who did not run away. He fell into the hands of the rebels, who tried to compel him to point out the houses of the rich. He refused to do so, whereupon they fell upon him with curses and blows and slew him. In the same year occurred the death of my mother, whose surname was Wei. In 1864 I went to school for the first time and in the following year lost my father, whose name was Yen-jên. When my half-brother, Hsi-ch'iu, was scarcely a year old, my stepmother, whose surname was Wên, also died.

At this time I was fourteen ; and henceforth my brother and I, alone and helpless, with only one another to look to for sympathy, were daily beset by hardship and poverty. In the tenth moon

of 1881 I married. My wife's surname was Ts'ao. Subsequently
I travelled in Fuhkien and afterwards went to Ch'ang-sha in
Hunan.

In 1884 the French made their attack on Annam, and the
Governor of Hunan, P'an Ting-hsin, went to Kuang-hsi [Kwang-
si] to conduct military operations. I joined his forces, and was
rewarded for my services with the button of the sixth military
grade. I was with the forces when they went through the Southern Frontier Pass [Chên Nan Kuan]. In the fifth moon we followed on the track of the enemy to the Kuan-yin mountain,
and in the eighth moon we fought at Ch'uan-T'ou. I acquitted
myself creditably ; and Governor P'an, with the viceroy of the
Two Kuangs, Chang Wên-hsiang, and the commander-in-chief
in Kuang-hsi, Su Yüan-ch'un, jointly recommended me to the
Throne for a Peacock's Feather and the post of Second Captain
with the brevet rank of First Captain. In 1885, after the reduction of Wên-yüan city, the province of Liang-shan [Langson]
and the two prefectural cities of Ch'ang-ch'ing and Liang-
chiang, I was again commended, in a memorial to the Throne,
by viceroy Chang and general Su and by the acting governor Li
Ping-hêng, and promoted to the rank of major. Subsequently
I received orders from General Su to serve with the right flank
of the Kuang-wu army, which was stationed at the frontier.
There I remained for five years, in the course of which time I was
promoted to lieutenant-colonel with the brevet of full colonel.

In 1893 private business took me to Hupei, where my wife
died in childbirth. In 1894 the war with the Japanese over
Korea broke out. The general officer commanding in Ssŭ-chuan,
Sung Ch'ing, wanted my help in connection with the affairs of
the Manchurian *I Chün* (" Resolute Army ") of which he had
taken command, and in the eighth moon I arrived at Mukden.
There I took command of a body of cavalry of the vanguard
division. One of our objects was to capture Tiger Hill and thus
hold the key of the Yalu river, but this plan did not take effect.

As soon as peace was declared I went to Peking. In 1895
I was appointed by Ts'ên Ch'un-hsüan (minister of the Court
of the Imperial Stud) to take command of the newly-raised
Shantung Guards, but as there was friction between minister
Ts'ên and the governor of the province I gave up my post and

paid a visit to Tientsin. There I first met Yüan Shih-k'ai, whose
substantive post at that time was taotai of Wên-chou in Chehkiang. He was then stationed at Hsiao-chan, beginning the
training of the new model army. He gave me a high appointment
in the vanguard of his troops. I was next placed in command
of the engineer-battalion and the reserve battalion, and entrusted with other military duties in addition.

Just at that time, Grand Secretary Jung Wên-chung [Jung-
Lu, afterwards father-in-law of the emperor Hsüan-T'ung],
in his capacity of Minister of the Council of State, made the
experiment of placing the five Wu-Wei armies under the command of Yüan Shih-k'ai's department, and they became the
army of the right wing.

In the fifth moon of the *kêng-tzŭ* year [1900] the Boxer outbreak took place in Shantung. Yüan Shih-k'ai became governor
of that province, taking the army of the right wing with him,
and he put me in command of the vanguard. He also entrusted
me with the duty of protecting communications. Our battalions
destroyed the rebels [the Boxers] at Hai-fêng and repeatedly
routed them at Yang-hsin, Pin-chou, P'u-t'ai and Li-ching, so
that within the area of our operations there was not a rebel to
be seen.

In the eighth moon Li Wên-chung [Li Hung-chang], then
Superintendent of Trade for the Northern Ports [*Pei-yang
Ta-ch'ên*], sent orders that we were to proceed to the south-east
of Chihli, where affairs were in a critical state. Yüan Shih-k'ai
put me in general control of the cavalry, infantry and artillery
battalions operating against the rebels along the northern roads.
I pursued the Boxers to Yen-shan and to the village of Hei-niu-
wang ["Black-Ox Prince"] in the district of Ch'ing-yün, and
as far as Ts'ang-chou. We had a series of victories. After this
I was placed in command of the first infantry battalion of the
right wing.

In 1901 the Yellow River burst its banks at the village of
Wu-yang-chia in the district of Hui-min. Under my direction
the various units under my command carried out the work of
damming the overflow and constructing dykes. It took more
than four months to complete this task.

When the right wing had been under my training for three

years I was recommended by Grand Secretary Jung-Lu for promotion; and on a second recommendation from him I received the substantive rank of colonel. Subsequently on the ground of my services in extirpating the rebels my name was noted for promotion to the rank of a provincial commander-in-chief and brigadier-general. The Throne bestowed upon me the distinction of Bat'uru with the designation "Strong and Brave."[1]

When Yüan Shih-k'ai became viceroy of Chihli I followed him to Paoting; and at the head of my troops I had the honour of going to meet the Imperial Equipage at Tz'ŭ-chou.[2] On the fourteenth day of the eleventh moon I had travelled as far as the Lin-ming Pass, where I encountered the imperial carriages and was granted an audience.

On my return to Peking I received imperial commands to go on guard-duty at the southern gate of the Forbidden City. The following year [1902] I commanded the detachments of horse and foot which acted as escort during the imperial visit to the Eastern Mausolea. In the eighth moon I was made commanding officer of the forces at Chien-ch'ang in Ssŭ-ch'uan, but did not proceed as I was retained for duty with the imperial guard-corps.

In the third moon of kuei-mao [1903] I was in attendance during the imperial visit to the Western Mausolea. I was similarly employed by imperial command in connection with three other imperial progresses.

In the intercalary-fifth moon I was appointed to take charge of the reorganisation of the vanguard cavalry and the remodelling of the constabulary and field troops beyond the Great Wall. Having marched through the Chü-yung Pass I pursued and chastised a large body of mounted bandits who were infesting the district of Ta-t'ung and Hsüan-hua. It took me a few months to tranquillise that country.

In chia-ch'ên [1904] the Throne graciously advanced me one step in official rank, and in recognition of my services in pacifying the country beyond the Great Wall I received the distinction of Bat'uru with the designation Pa-t'u-lung-a [a Manchu term signifying exceptional military virtue].

The same year witnessed the outbreak of war between Russia

and Japan. Our country was neutral, but the Russians plotted to make a stealthy raid on the Mongolian pasture-lands. So I posted troops at Hsüan-hua and met this danger successfully. From Kalgan I proceeded through Dolonor to Tu-shih. Returning, I prepared a plan for the protection of the frontier and submitted it to Yüan Shih-k'ai, who gave it his approval.

Two years later Yüan Shih-k'ai, who was in charge of army-reorganisation, sent me telegraphic instructions to the effect that when the Russia-Japan war was over it would be necessary for the government to select an officer of high rank who understood military affairs to take over the territory which had been the battleground between those two Powers; and he instructed me to go to Mukden. There, the governor-general Chao Erh-hsün appointed me general commanding the Mukden army in northern Shengking, and also put me in charge of the cavalry and infantry of the rear and right flank, with headquarters at Ch'ang-t'u [a city north of Mukden].

In the same year the Throne recognised my services with the imperial guard corps and conferred upon me the insignia of the highest of the nine official grades. In the following year, northern Shengking having been tranquillised, governor-general Chao mentioned me favourably to the Throne, whereupon I was promoted to the rank of a commander-in-chief.

In the fourth moon, Hsü Shih-ch'ang, then a Minister of the Grand Council of State, became viceroy of the Three Eastern Provinces [Manchuria] and in a memorial to the Throne recommended that I should be placed in charge of the reorganisation of the Manchurian Defence Corps, with command of the mobile forces. Thereupon I visited Ninguta and Fêng-mi-shan in the province of Kirin, and went north as far as Sui-hua in the province of Heilungkiang. As a result of seeking out and destroying the strongholds of the bandits, who were mainly concentrated near the Mu-tan river in the neighbourhood of the East Manchurian railway, I rescued all the Chinese men and women, and the Russian traders and Japanese surveyors, who had been captured.

In *wu-shên* [1908] I was appointed commander-in-chief for the province of Yunnan, but at the same time an imperial edict ordered me to remain in the north in command of troops in

Chihli and Fêng-t'ien. The Throne also conferred upon me the honour of the Yellow Jacket.[3]

My substantive post in Yunnan was shortly exchanged for a similar one in Kansu. But in the ninth moon I was ordered by rescript to proceed to Peking, and on the occasion of the Imperial Birthday I had the honour of receiving a Command to attend the state-theatricals in the Forbidden City.

On the Demise of Their Majesties the empress-dowager and the emperor, I took part in the mourning rites.

In the first year of Hsüan-T'ung [1909] Hsü Shih-ch'ang was summoned to the Grand Secretariat, and Hsi-Liang succeeded him as governor-general of Manchuria. Being dissatisfied with Hsi-Liang's appointment I accompanied Hsü Shih-ch'ang on his journey from Manchuria, and in spite of many messages urging me to return I did not do so. In consequence of this, in the seventh moon Hsi-Liang submitted a memorial of impeachment, charging me with prolonged absence from my post. However I received imperial commands to remain for duty in Peking, and the memorial of impeachment was rejected.

In the tenth moon I accompanied the funeral procession of Her late Imperial Majesty to the Eastern Mausolea, on which occasion I was in charge of the military escort. On the completion of the ceremonies at the Tomb, the empress-dowager Lung-Yü returned to the Forbidden City and commanded me to remain at the Mausoleum in charge of the guard which formed the escort of the four *kuei-fei* [imperial consorts of rank below the empress] so that all ill-feeling between the empress-dowager Lung-Yü and the *kuei-fei* might be set at rest.[4]

After the funeral ceremonies were over I was commended for my services, and the empress-dowager conferred upon me an honorific autograph scroll bearing as an inscription the four characters *shu ch'i ch'ing fên*—" Pure Air Clear and Fragrant."

In the tenth moon of *kêng-hsü* [1910] I was appointed to the command of all the Yangtse Defence troops and joint superintendent of protective measures for the Yangtse Valley with headquarters at P'u-k'ou. The right to memorialise the Throne directly was also conferred upon me. In the seventh moon of the following year [1911] I was transferred to the post of commander-in-chief of Kiangnan [i.e. the provinces of Kiangsu and Anhui].

In the eighth moon of that year the Rebellion broke out.[5] I at once asked for permission to go to the relief of Wu-ch'ang, but this was refused ; and the rebellion spread to Soochow.

The governor-general and the Tartar-general consulted me on the question of fighting or remaining on the defensive. But all the military and civil officials in the city [of Nanking] were timid in face of the revolutionary fury and the advice they tendered accorded with their fear. I promptly told them what I thought of them, and said, " To-day you are all my fellow-officials ; to-morrow, if you raise the white flag, in my eyes you will all be rebels." They dispersed in a state of great agitation, and during the night they all stole away. Next day the ninth brigade revolted. I drove them to the Rain-flower Terrace, and inflicted a severe defeat upon them. But the rebel forces collected in great strength, and as I had no rations and no hope of reinforcements I withdrew my forces to the north bank of the Yangtse, fighting a rearguard action during the withdrawal. I halted at Hsü-chou.

In the ninth moon I was appointed Governor of Kiangsu, and in the following moon received the acting appointment of viceroy of Kiangsu and Kiangsi and also that of Imperial Commissioner for the southern ports (nan-yang ta ch'ên). The Throne also raised me to the sixth order of hereditary nobility (ch'ing ch'ê tu-yü).

In the twelfth moon [beginning of 1912] was issued the imperial edict whereby the form of government was changed to that of a republic, and Yüan Shih-k'ai became provisional president. All the contending forces were called upon to lay down their arms, and, in the public interest, to cease from warfare. The edict also commanded the officers and soldiers of the imperial army to refrain from continuing the struggle through feelings of loyalty to the Throne.

I held myself in restraint, and only stubbornness of character made me still cherish the hope of some day seeing the old order restored. The Yangtse Defence troops were turned into the vanguard of the Military Protection Army and I resigned my command of the anti-rebel forces in Chihli, Shantung and Honan.

In the following year, however, I moved my troops to Yen-
chou [in south-western Shantung], and in the fourth moon
[1912] Hsü Shih-ch'ang accompanied by T'ien Wên-lieh came to
me to report president Yüan's proposal to abolish the governor-
generalship of the Two Kiangs and to make me lieutenant-
general of the Red Bordered Banner Army. When about to
take his departure, Hsü Shih-ch'ang asked me if I had any
message for president Yüan. I replied " I cannot show ingratitude for what I owe to Yüan ; I cannot forget the duty of a
subject to his sovereign. If Yüan does no wrong to the imperial
court, he will never be wronged by me. That is all I have to
say."

In the first moon of *Kuei-ch'ou* [1913] president Yüan
requested their majesties [the empress-dowager Lung-Yü and
the emperor Hsüan-T'ung] to remove to the Yi-Ho Park [Summer
Palace]. I raised strenuous objections to this proposal and it
was dropped.[6] The distress felt by the empress-dowager on
account of Yüan's demand was the cause of her illness and
death.

On the death of the empress-dowager I requested the government to issue a proclamation ordering a state-funeral, and
permitting the people to wear mourning. At the head of the
gentry, merchants, soldiers and civilians of the regions under
my control I conducted memorial rites in the capital of the
prefecture.

About this time there was an agitation to abolish the cult of
Confucius, and people seized the opportunity to begin cutting
down the trees [of the Confucian temple at Ch'ü Fou in Shantung]
and carrying off the sacrificial vessels. I immediately despatched
troops to protect the holy places, and was just in time to save
them from the spoilers. Later on, the government proposed to
take possession of the whole of the sacrificial lands attached
to the temple of Confucius and to grant the Duke of Overflowing
Holiness [*Yen-shêng Kung*, the hereditary title of the head of
the Confucian clan and reputed to be the seventy-sixth lineal
descendant of the sage] a fixed pension in lieu of his hereditary
revenues. This measure was also strenuously opposed by me
and it was abandoned.[7]

I do not venture to say that this happy result was due to my

unaided efforts. I was merely the agent through which the
spiritual might of the Sage was manifested.

In the sixth moon Huang Hsing headed a rebellious rising
at Lêng-chü in Kiangnan, seized Hsü-chou and started an
invasion of the north. Fang Yü-p'u, commanding officer of the
fifth brigade, sent me warning of Huang Hsing's intentions ;
whereupon I sent a detachment of the troops under my command
to go with speed and meet the rebels at Han-chuang. There my
troops fought and captured Erh-lang hill with a view to the
capture of Willow-Spring [*Liu-ch'üan*]. As soon as order was
restored at Leng-chü and Hsü-chou, Yüan Shih-k'ai made me
commander in-chief of the infantry battalions and high commissioner for the north of the Yangtse.

In the seventh moon I went south from T'ai-erh village and the
Grand Canal and travelled over a thousand *li* [about 300 miles]
in five days, receiving the submission of the whole territory
between Tsingkiangpu and Yangchow. Still proceeding towards
the south I gained possession of the munitions of war in the
forts on the north bank of the Yangtse. As a result of this,
Chinkiang [on the south bank] surrendered to me, and from
there I moved on and camped outside the Yao-hua gate of the
city of Nanking. There I fought a critical action which resulted
in victory. During the night I made a successful surprise attack
on Black-dragon hill and occupied the city of T'ien-pao. At
the beginning of the eighth moon I returned to Nanking.

In the course of these operations I was offered various de-
corations including the orders of the Excellent Corn and the
Striped Tiger, but I refused them all.

President Yüan then appointed me Tutuh [an old title which
was revived in the early days of the republic and was equivalent
to viceroy or governor-general] of the province of Kiangsu.
I accepted this post because without it I should have been
unable to retain full military control. Thenceforth north and
south were re-united and Yüan Shih-k'ai was really president
of the whole country.[6]

After this I submitted my resignation but the president
refused to accept it. In the twelfth moon the title of my post
was altered to that of high inspecting commissioner for the
Yangtse (*Ch'ang-Chiang Hsün Yüeh-shih*). I took up my

residence at Hsü-chou and distributed my troops along the river
so as to control the important strategic points.

In the sixth moon of *i-mao* [1915] president Yüan converted
the Wu-Wei Army into the Ting-Wu army, and made me
commander-in-chief. I retained my post of high inspecting
commissioner.

In the eighth moon I visited Peking and went to the Forbidden City to pay my respects to his majesty. I returned to
Hsü-chou in the ninth moon.

About this time the Ch'ou An Hui [Society for the Planning
of Peace] commenced its activities.[9] The central government
despatched telegrams to the provinces inviting expressions
of opinion as to the problem of the form of government. I
replied vehemently opposing the scheme [for Yüan's enthrone-
ment]. Soon afterwards, however, the Hung-Hsien reign-title
was announced and it was decreed that I was to be raised to the
rank of Duke. I declined the honour. At the same time I submitted a memorial praying that the rights and privileges of the
Imperial Family be confirmed and that adequate protection
be given to the palace and court. My memorial was ignored.

In the spring of *ping-ch'ên* [1916] the provinces of Yunnan,
Kueichou, Kuangsi and Kuangtung declared independence
one after another.[10] The Hung-Hsien reign-title was cancelled.
Then the question of using military force to crush the insurrection was discussed. In the third moon as high inspecting
commissioner and military governor of Anhui I telegraphed
to all the provinces inviting them to send representatives to a
conference at Kiang-ning [a town on the right bank of the
Yangtse, in Anhui, close to the border of Kiangsu and south-
west of Nanking] to deliberate on the question of sending a
punitive expedition against the south. In the fifth moon, however, president Yüan died, and the idea of military measures
was abandoned.

In the fourth moon of *ting-ssŭ* [1917], several provinces again
conspired with one another to declare their independence of the
Peking government. The military governors or their accredited
representatives all met at Hsü-chou and chose me as leader
of the confederacy. This having been agreed upon, I proceeded
to the north with some of my troops in order to act as mediator.[11]

On the thirteenth day of the fifth moon I brought about his majesty's Restoration.

By imperial edict I was made Regent, and was also appointed minister for Northern Affairs and governor-general of Chihli.

The views of another military commander did not coincide with mine, and he advanced with his army to attack me. On the twenty-fourth, a battle was fought in the capital. My troops were few and could not maintain their position. The minister for Holland sent a car for me, and received me into the Dutch Legation.

In *wu-wu* [1918], in the ninth month I got rid of the entanglements of the affair described above.[12]

In the fifth moon of *kêng-shên* [1920] I moved from Peking to Tientsin.

During the past few years state-affairs have ceased to be a concern of mine. I have remained in seclusion at home; and having ample leisure I have employed it in a desultory reading of the *T'ung Chien* [a Chinese historical work] and in the practice of calligraphy. I have nothing more to do with worldly matters; but I often call to mind how in my young days I emerged from poverty and obscurity and followed the profession of a soldier, and how my fortunes have changed with the changing times. I have now lived sixty-eight years and find myself afflicted with many infirmities. What indeed have I to say of myself that is worthy of men's attention? Nevertheless as a record must be made in the genealogical register of my family, I have ventured to do as other men have done before me, and have written this brief outline of my career.

I wish my young sons to know how hard and strenuous has been the life that their father has led, and hope they may be fortunate enough to learn, from my history, how to guard against the perils of their own future.

Written and put away for future reference by me, Chang Shao-hsien,[13] this eighth moon of the *hsin-yu* year [September, 1921].

．　．　．　．　．　．　．　．

Chang Hsün (*alias* Chang Shao-hsien, *alias* Old Man of the Pine-tree) made no further additions to this little account of his

career except to record the birth of his eighth and ninth
sons, their names being Mêng-yüan and Mêng-fên. He died in
his house at Tientsin on September 12th, 1923.

The family *Ai-ch'i* or obituary notice (always an elaborate
document in China in the case of important persons) was issued
in the names of his six surviving sons. It records a few facts
which are not given in the autobiography. When he went to
Peking in 1915 and was received in audience by the little emperor, then in his ninth year, he also, as a matter of course,
visited his former patron and chief, Yüan Shih-k'ai. Some of
Yüan's men ridiculed him for keeping his queue ; whereupon
he swore an oath that he would keep it till he died, which he
did. " If anyone tries to deprive me of it," he said, " we shall
die together." No one made the attempt.

After referring to the leading part taken by him in the restoration movement, the *Ai-ch'i* goes on to say that Chang Hsün believed himself to be fulfilling a sacred duty. When the fighting
went against him, and the cause was lost owing to the defection
of certain " faithless generals," there were people who urged him
to seek shelter and save himself, but he replied thus : " The
restoration was not due to the wish of his majesty ; it came about
through reverence for our sovereign. If now, in this hour of
crisis, I were to flee for safety and leave my young emperor in
danger, how could my crime ever be expiated ? To-day there
is no road for me but that of death. From of old, it has
been the custom for whole families to sacrifice themselves for
a great cause. It is not the idea of death or of the loss of wife
and children and property that distresses me. What gives me
pain is the harm I have done to my sovereign." Some of the
bystanders, we are told, were moved to tears. " Then our father
bared his arm and went on fighting with the utmost courage
and energy until the buildings around him were in flames.
Then the Dutch minister sent a motor-car for him and he was
forced against his will to drive in it to the Dutch legation. The
days he spent there were days of deep anguish and bitterness
for him."

" During his last illness," the document continues, " the
emperor sent messages of consolation and also sent one of his
own physicians to prescribe for him. Hearing of this, Chang

Hsün descended from his bed and knelt on the ground, saying these words. ' I am seventy years old. I should have died in the *hsin-hai* year [1911, the year of the revolution], and did not. In the year *ting-ssŭ* [1917, the year of the restoration] I should have died, and did not. Now death comes to me too late. Is it enough that I should merely suffer the agonies of remorse ? Alas, I have not repaid the throne one ten-thousandth part of what I owe.' Then we heard the sound of weeping, and his tears fell on coverlet and pillow. Nevertheless this outburst of emotion was followed by a partial recovery, and on the first day of the eighth moon he was able to take a little nourishment. Then he sank again and on the following day he died."

His funeral took place in Tientsin and was attended by the emperor's representative. The local Chinese papers described it as one of the most magnificent funerals ever seen in that city. Even the foreign newspapers gave prominence to the great spectacle.

" To a Westerner," said the *Peking and Tientsin Times*, " the scene where the general's remains lie in state is a revelation of Oriental magnificence. . . . There is his own silk flag, the banner of commander-in-chief of the Chinese army, and the ' Tiger ' flag, the latter honour bestowed by the Boy Emperor. . . . For over eight hours the procession, the largest and most imposing ever seen in the city, wended its halting way through the British, French and Japanese Concessions, returning through the ex-Austrian, Italian and British Concessions, back to the residence in Parkes Road. About four miles long, and with over 4,000 men figuring in it, this last spectacular show is estimated to have cost well over $100,000. This is probably a modest estimate. There was remarkable evidence of Chang Hsün's high standing in imperial favour, for about thirty costly gifts from the late empress-dowager and the Boy Emperor formed a conspicuous part of the procession."

The last gift of the " Boy Emperor " was one that the stout old monarchist would have prized most highly of all. It was the bestowal of a posthumous title of " canonisation." The title chosen was Chung Wu—" Loyal and Brave." It was one that had been conferred in the past upon several of the greatest warriors that China ever produced, from Chu-ko Liang of the second century of our era to Yang Yü-ch'un, Têng Shao-liang, T'a-ch'i-pu and Li Hsü-pin of the nineteenth.

The Tientsin newspaper was not far wrong when it headed its account of the funeral ceremonies with the words "The ' Tiger ' passes in a blaze of glory."

CHAPTER XI

The Forbidden City, 1919–1924

DURING THE TWELVE DAYS of the Manchu " restoration " in July, 1917, president Li Yüan-hung was in hiding in the Legation Quarter of Peking—a portion of the city in which, since 1900, the Chinese authorities have had no jurisdiction. When Chang Hsün, the kingmaker, met with defeat, he, as we have seen, took refuge in the same sanctuary, though in a different Legation. By all the rules of the game, then, Li Yüan-hung could have emerged in triumph and resumed his presidential chair. But his " loss of face " was too serious for that ; moreover he had incurred the wrath of the parliamentarians for having been weak enough to dismiss them at Chang Hsün's behest ; and as it was he who had invited Chang Hsün to Peking he could not absolve himself from indirect responsibility for the nearly successful *coup* of the monarchists.

The new acting president was Fêng Kuo-chang, at heart a very lukewarm supporter of the republic though he had aided Tuan Ch'i-jui in his brief but successful struggle against Chang Hsün. He was a native of the metropolitan province (Chihli) and under the empire had held various posts including that of Director of the Nobles' College and Chairman of the Military Council of the Board of War. Tuan Ch'i-jui, the " saviour of the republic," became premier and reconstructed the cabinet ; and in the following month (August 12th) a new parliament assembled in the capital.

It was by the authority of this parliament that China declared war on Germany two days after it had assembled. As we have seen, it was partly over the question of whether China should or should not participate in the war on the side of the allies that the violent dissensions had arisen which gave Chang Hsün his opportunity to enter Peking. The question was now promptly settled in accordance with the views of the pro-war party ; but this gave intense dissatisfaction at Canton, which maintained under Sun Yat-sen and his group a practically independent government of its own.

Having conferred upon himself the title of *ta-yüan-shuai* (" generalissimo " or supreme commander-in-chief) Sun Yat-sen made a formal protest against the declaration of war, declared Fêng Kuo-chang and his ministers traitors, and prepared in the usual Chinese way to lead a " punitive expedition " against the north.

It was because China was nominally on the side of the allies that she acquired the right of representation at the Versailles peace conference and was able to bring that indirect pressure on Japan which finally compelled the Japanese government to relinquish to China one of its spoils of war—the German leased-territory of Kiao-chou (Tsingtao). China had taken no part whatever in recovering Tsingtao from the Germans (it had fallen to the Japanese army and navy long before China nominally entered the war), and indeed she protested (and was technically right in doing so) against the Japanese violation of her neutrality by disembarking troops, in connection with the operations against Tsingtao, on Chinese soil.

Early in 1918, Ts'ao K'un, a rising military leader, took command of the northern forces against the seceding south, and by the beginning of April he had captured the key-positions of Yo-chou and Ch'ang-sha, south of the Yangtse, which effectually blocked the advance of Sun Yat-sen's punitive expedition. This led to Sun's resignation ; and in the month of May he found himself (not for the first, second, or third time) an exile outward bound to Japan. The civil war between north and south, however, continued. The members of the Old (first republican) Parliament, who would not have been welcomed in Peking, reassembled in Canton and declared themselves the only legitimate legislative assembly in China. About the same time a new northern parliament was elected in accordance with an electoral law promulgated in February, and it met at Peking in August.

From the time of the establishment of an independent parliament in Canton, China had no central government recognised by all the provinces and exercising control over the whole country. The parliamentary problem in China became an insoluble one, concerning which Father Wieger observes that " seul un coup de balai radical pourra faire cesser des disputes qui paralysent tout." It was, indeed, China's parliaments which for several years did more than anything else to paralyse the administrative organism.

The new Peking parliament proceeded to elect a new president, and it would perhaps be indiscreet to enquire too closely into the reasons why its votes were cast almost unanimously in favour of one candidate. Hsü Shih-ch'ang, formerly viceroy of Manchuria, a friend of Yüan Shih-k'ai, was elected by 425 votes against 11.

The Canton parliament promptly declared his election null and void, but this made no difference to the course of events in the north, and president Hsü retained the presidency for more than three years.

Hsü Shih-ch'ang was a fine scholar of the old school and a man of long and honourable official experience. As early as 1906 he was a grand councillor, and in April 1907 he became first Manchurian viceroy, a portion of the empire that had up to that time been treated as an appanage of the imperial House.[1] On the accession of P'u-Yi to the throne in 1908 he was made a t'ai-pao or " grand guardian "—a high but honorary dignity— and was regarded by the Throne as one of its most trusted servants and counsellors. He was sixty-three years of age when he became president.

In spite of his acceptance of the presidency, Hsü Shih-ch'ang was no convinced republican—few if any of the northern politicians were that—and one of his first official acts was to issue free pardons to those who had taken part in the restoration *coup* of 1917. Chang Hsün was not excepted from the amnesty. His pardon, like that of his colleagues, was unconditional ; and though he made no pretence of changing his political convictions, and never swerved in his loyalty to his monarchist principles, he was allowed to remain unmolested in Peking, the centre of an influential circle of like-minded Chinese and Manchu friends.

President Hsü was elected on September 4th and was formally installed as president on October 10th, 1918, the seventh anniversary of the revolutionary outbreak at Wu-ch'ang. Even before his installation the parliament that elected him gave evidence of its conservative sympathies by declaring that the anniversary of the birth of Confucius was henceforth to be observed as a national holiday. Since that date the official attitude towards Confucius and the whole system of thought which he represents has varied in accordance with the changing fortunes of the different political parties. When the tendency is to the " left," Confucius and all that he stands for is anathema. We have seen that the radical Ch'ên Tu-hsiu, even before he became a communist leader, insisted that Confucianism and republicanism were incompatible. When the prevailing tendency is to the " right," and Old China dares to raise a timid voice in favour of the traditional ways, the iconoclastic hands of the radicals are stayed and fathers of families and school-teachers are no longer ashamed or afraid to manifest their reverence for the teachings of the ancient sages.

Hsü Shih-ch'ang next proceeded to show that he took himself seriously as an imperial " grand guardian " and that he did not consider it incompatible with his duties as president of the republic to take an interest in the welfare of his former sovereign. In 1918 P'u-Yi was a boy of twelve and had already been pursuing his Chinese studies for some years under tutors who were among the most distinguished scholars in China. President Hsü discussed the boy's future with some of his closest friends— one of them being a son of the famous viceroy Li Hung-chang— and having regard to the possibilities of the more or less distant future they decided that P'u-Yi (or rather the Ta Ch'ing or Manchu emperor, to give him the title which was his by virtue of the abdication agreement) should be given an opportunity of acquiring the elements of a Western education, including the English language. They also desired that he should learn something of the evolution of political institutions in Europe and more especially of the principles of the English constitutional monarchy.

It would be wrong to assume that this educational scheme was part of a conspiracy to restore the young emperor to the throne. It is true that most of those who interested themselves in the proposal, not excepting the president himself, were more or less dubious about the prospects of republicanism in China, and that some of them, at least, were still at heart loyal to the monarchy. But all they hoped to achieve by having their former sovereign taught something of the history and institutions of the Western world was that in the event of the failure of the republicans to establish a stable government acceptable to the people of China, followed by a popular revulsion of feeling in favour of the old ways, the emperor might be ready and qualified to play his appropriate part in the building-up of a new China under a limited constitutional monarchy.

It was at first proposed to offer the post of foreign tutor at the Manchu court to a distinguished American who had had a brilliant career in China both as an educationalist and as a diplomat. As he was about to become American Chargé d'Affaires, however, it was impossible for him to accept the appointment. The next choice fell upon myself.

It is unnecessary to explain in detail how it came about that the post of English tutor to the young emperor was offered to me. In the course of my official duties and also during my travels in China I had made the personal acquaintance of several persons in close touch both with the imperial family and with the new president. Among these was Lord Li Ching-mai, son of the viceroy Li Hung-chang, to whom I have referred above. During the critical days of the revolution in 1911 he found refuge for a time in the British leased territory of Weihaiwei where I was then district officer and magistrate. In happier days, under the monarchy, Lord Li had served his country as Chinese minister at the court of Vienna. When prince Tsai T'ao, a brother of the emperor Tê Tsung, visited Germany as head of a military mission, shortly before the revolution, he was accompanied by Lord Li. Since that time he has steadfastly refused all offers of official employment under the republic, though he was repeatedly pressed by his friend president Hsü Shih-ch'ang to accept a high diplomatic post. He and his family have always remained loyal to the old dynasty, and it was mainly through his influence both with the president and with the Manchu court that the appointment of English tutor to the emperor was offered to me.

The offer was made towards the end of November, 1918, a few days after the armistice which marked the close of the Great War. I agreed to accept it subject to the approval of the British authorities both in London and in Peking. Before long, the offer was repeated in a formal manner by the president himself through Sir John Jordan, then British Minister in Peking, and in due course it received the approval of the Colonial and Foreign Offices in London. I was then " seconded " from my duties under the Colonial Office, and left Weihaiwei early in 1919.

My first interview with my imperial pupil took place on March 3rd. Shortly after this interview I wrote, for the information of the British authorities, a brief account of my experiences up to that time. This document (which was dated March 7th, 1919) may perhaps be worth quoting in full as it contains my earliest impressions of the Manchu court and of the thirteen-year-old child who in the eyes of the population of the Forbidden City (and of many other people in China and its dependencies) was still their august sovereign.

MEMORANDUM

On arrival at Peking on February 22nd, 1919, I was met at the station by Mr. Ni Wên-tê, one of the President's secretaries. Two days later I was received by the emperor's father, prince Ch'un (whom I had met many years ago in Hong-Kong) and by prince Tsai T'ao (another brother of the late emperor Kuang-Hsü) at their respective residences. The latter takes a special interest in the boy's education and is generally regarded as the most enlightened and progressive of the Manchu princes. His reception of me was extremely cordial, and he has invited me to call upon him at any time when I wish to discuss matters connected with the boy's welfare. He entertained me at a dinner-party on March 5th, and on this occasion I was presented to several other members of the imperial family, including prince Tsai-Hsün, another of the young emperor's uncles.

On February 27th I paid an official visit to president Hsü Shih-ch'ang ; and on that and following days I exchanged visits with the following officers connected with the Manchu Court : Shih Hsü, Comptroller of the Household and Grand Guardian ; Ch'i Ling, a Manchu who is a relative of the emperor's mother, the princess Ch'un ; Shao Ying, a Minister of the Household ; and the Imperial Tutors Liang Ting-fên, Chu I-fan and I-K'o-T'an. On the 8th inst. I am to be the guest of the officers of the Household and the Tutors at a dinner at the Wagons-Lits Hotel.

My formal introduction to the boy-emperor took place on March 3rd.

He was dressed for the occasion in court dress, and was attended by a number of functionaries in uniform. On being conducted into the audience-chamber I advanced towards the emperor and bowed three times. He then descended from his seat, walked up to me and shook hands in European fashion. He remained standing during the rest of this short interview and asked me a few conventional questions, mainly about my official career in China. When the interview was over I withdrew to a waiting-room and was informed that the emperor wished to begin his English lessons immediately and would receive me again in a less formal manner as soon as he had changed his clothes. In the interval, I received visits from a large number of palace officials and eunuchs who offered congratulations on my appointment. On re-entering the imperial schoolroom in the Yü-ch'ing palace, in which the formal reception had taken place, I found the emperor seated at a table on which were placed the books which I had already selected for him. He asked me to sit down at his side, and from that moment our relations have been those of teacher and pupil and have been quite free from formality.

The young emperor has no knowledge whatever of English or any other European language, but he seems anxious to learn and is mentally active. He is allowed to read the Chinese newspapers, and evidently takes an intelligent interest in the news of the day, especially in politics, both domestic and foreign. He has a good general knowledge of geography, and is interested in travel and exploration. He understands something of the present state of Europe and the results of the great war, and seems to be free from false or exaggerated notions about the political position and relative importance of China. He appears to be physically robust and well-developed for his age. He is a very " human " boy, with vivacity, intelligence, and a keen sense of humour. Moreover, he has excellent manners and is entirely free from arrogance. This is rather remarkable in view of the extremely artificial nature of his surroundings and the pompous make-believe of the palace-routine. He is treated by the court functionaries with all the outward reverence supposed to be due to the " Son of Heaven," he never goes outside the " Forbidden City " and he has no chance of associating with other boys except on the rare occasions when his younger brother and two or three other youthful members of the imperial clan are allowed to pay him short visits. Even his daily visits to the schoolroom are made the occasion for a kind of state procession. He is carried there in a large chair draped in imperial yellow, and he is accompanied by a large retinue of attendants.

Although the emperor does not appear to have been spoiled, as yet, by the follies and futilities of his surroundings, I am afraid there is no hope that he will come unscathed through the moral dangers of the next few years of his life (necessarily very critical years for a boy in his early teens) unless he can be withdrawn from the influence of the hordes of eunuchs and other useless functionaries who are now almost his only associates. I am inclined to think that the best course to pursue in the boy's own interests would be to take him out of the unwholesome atmosphere of the " Forbidden City " and send him to the Summer Palace. There it would be possible for him to live a much less artificial and much happier life than is possible under present conditions, and he would have ample space and opportunity there for physical exercise. It would be necessary, of course, to entrust him to the care of an entirely new set of servants and attendants who should be under the close supervision of some thoroughly trustworthy official specially selected by the president or any responsible member of the imperial clan who (like prince Tsai T‘ao) is fully acquainted with the circumstances and has the boy's welfare at heart. Perhaps I may find it possible, later on, to make some recommendation of this kind. At present it is,.of course, too early for me to take any such action, though I have already, to some extent, made my views known to Mr. Liu T‘i-ch‘ien (a relative of Lord Li and a friend of prince Tsai T‘ao's) and to Mr. Ni Wên-tê, the president's private secretary.

Before my introduction to the mysteries of the Forbidden City, a little incident took place which may be worth recording as illustrating the survival of medieval modes of thought in that last refuge of Chinese conservatism. Before I moved into the spacious Chinese mansion prepared for my use—a house afterwards exchanged for another nearer the Forbidden City— I lived in one of the Peking hotels, and for several days my time was occupied with paying and receiving calls. On the last day of February I was visited by a deputation from the household who informed me that the court astrologers had been duly consulted on the important subject of the selection of an " auspicious day " for the commencement of his majesty's English studies, and that they had just submitted their report. It was to the effect that there were two days in the immediate future which were equally auspicious—one being March 3rd, the other March 28th, or rather the dates in the old lunar calendar (still observed in palace circles though not officially by the republic) which corresponded with those two dates. As there was nothing to choose between them in point of auspiciousness, it had been decided to leave to me the responsibility of the final choice.[2]

I have a suspicion that the promptness and lack of premeditation with which I decided in favour of the earlier of the two dates was regarded as bordering on flippancy.

I may add that during my long service at the Manchu court nothing of any importance was ever done without recourse to divination. It was the court astrologers who really decided the date and hour of the emperor's wedding in 1922. I myself caused much shaking of heads when I failed to take the precaution of selecting an auspicious day for my removal from the hotel to my new house ; for in China a change of abode is regarded as a momentous event.

Some account must now be given of the emperor's immediate environment. He lived, of course, in the Forbidden City—a vast walled enclosure in the heart of Peking—and it was there that he received me.

Amid all the anomalies of Chinese political life, there was one which from 1912—the year of the establishment of the republic—until near the end of 1924 never failed to arouse interest and curiosity among foreign visitors to Peking. They knew that " republican " cabinets rose and fell, that parliaments were dismissed in disgrace and recalled in simulated honour, that ministers of state and army commanders fled periodically for shelter to one or other of the foreign legations, that armies fought one another under the walls of the capital in defiance of presidential mandates and in ruthless disregard of the welfare of the people, that presidents themselves were set up by one clique and pulled down by another. Yet they observed that amid all the familiar scenes of turmoil, disruption, banditry, famine and civil war, the plots and stratagems of parliamentarians and wily politicians, the truculence of military adventurers and the antics of hot-headed students, there was one little stronghold in the midst of the capital which seemed to maintain itself as a haunt of ancient peace, one fragment of Chinese soil which preserved at least the outward appearance of stability and dignity, one virgin fortress in which the manners and rituals of a vanishing past still formed part of the daily routine. That home of stately decorum and tranquillity was surrounded by battlemented walls and imposing gateways that symbolised the spirit of Old China. It seemed as though that spirit had found its last sure refuge in the still mysterious halls and palaces of the *Ta Nei*—" the Great Within."³

And yet the appearances were to some extent illusory. Not only were peace, decorum and stately dignity less conspicuous within the battlemented area of the Forbidden City than was popularly supposed, but a breach had already been made in those imposing walls, and it was obvious to all but those who were wilfully blind to the signs of the times that sooner or later they were doomed to fall. An important part of what had previously been included in the Forbidden City had lost its right to that romantic title. A portion of the southern section of the great enclosure (though not the guardianship of its eastern and western gates) had been taken over by the republican authorities immediately after the abdication of the emperor. Two of the largest of the palace-buildings (the Wu-ying Tien and the Wên-hua Tien) had been turned into a museum in which were housed a portion of the exquisite works of art which had formerly adorned the palaces of Jehol and Mukden and were now understood to be " on loan " from the imperial collection pending their purchase by the republican government. Three of the throne-halls—the T'ai Ho Tien (" Hall of Supreme Harmony"), the Chung Ho Tien and the Pao Ho Tien—had also passed into the hands of the republic, together with some subordinate buildings.

Nevertheless the whole of the northern section of the Forbidden City from east to west, and large portions of the sections on either side of the above-mentioned three throne-halls, still remained in the exclusive occupation of the imperial court and were in the strictest sense " forbidden " to all the world except those who had the entrée. Among large numbers of other buildings it included all the palaces which constituted the living quarters of the emperor and those members of the Imperial family who had the right to live there ; the " imperial garden " (Yü Hua Yüan) ; the Wên Yüan Ko, a large pavilion containing the most valuable portion of the imperial library, including the

vast collection of literature known as the *ssŭ-k'u ch'üan shu* ;
the offices of the Nei Wu Fu or imperial household department ;
the Chün Chi Ch'u or office of the Grand Council of State (an
insignificant building which after the revolution became a
waiting-room for those awaiting audiences) ; the Chien Fu Kung
(" Palace of Established Happiness ") which contained very
valuable portraits, gold Buddhist images and other treasures
and which in 1923 was destroyed by fire with almost the whole
of its contents ; and a large number of other halls, pavilions
and other buildings which in the " twilight " period had ceased
to serve any practical purpose. Mention should also be made
of the Fêng Hsien Tien, or " Chapel of the Serving of Ancestors,"
which was used for the performance of the regular memorial
rites carried out by the emperor or an imperial prince on the
first and fifteenth of every month. It is not to be confused with
the spacious and magnificent T'ai Miao or Supreme Temple, a
southern annexe to the Forbidden City, of peculiar sanctity
because it was the temple in which were preserved the spirit-
tablets of the imperial ancestors and was reserved for use on
occasions of special solemnity.[4]

One of the great throne-halls remained in the possession of
the imperial family. This was the Ch'ien-Ch'ing Kung or Palace of
Heavenly Purity. It was in this palace that the emperor still
held court on great anniversaries, the most important of which
were New Year's Day (by the old Chinese lunar calendar) and
Wan-Shou—the emperor's own birthday which was on the
thirteenth day of the first moon.[5] It was built in 1655, rebuilt
in 1669, and again rebuilt, after a fire, in 1797.

In front of the Palace of Heavenly Purity was a great quadrangle in which the members of the imperial family and court
assembled to do honour to their sovereign ; and on the east,
west and south sides of the quadrangle were various buildings—
small but of historic interest on account of their associations
with the early emperors of the Manchu dynasty. These were
the Shang Shu-fang, formerly the schoolroom of the imperial
princes, more recently used as the private office of prince Ch'un
when he was prince regent from 1909 to 1912 ; the Mou-ch'in-
tien (" Hall of Industrious Energy"), used by the great emperor
Shêng Tsu (K'ang-Hsi, 1662-1722) as a study, afterwards

occupied by those members of the Hanlin Academy who had secretarial duties at court ; and the Nan-Shu-fang or " Southern Study," also used by Hanlin secretaries.

Behind the throne-hall was the Chiao-T'ai Tien, the " Hall of the Blending of the Great Creative Forces," in which, as I have said elsewhere, " the divine and earthly powers of the universe intermingled and interacted in perfect harmony."[6] In that building were preserved the valuable and important collection of twenty-five imperial seals which, as we have seen, attracted the covetous longings of Yüan Shih-k'ai.[7] Here also were deposited a clepsydra or water-clock dating from the time of Ch'ien-Lung ; and the *ts'ê pao*, or what in England might be called the " marriage-lines " of the empresses of the dynasty, written on plaques of gold and attested by golden seals.

Immediately to the north of the Chiao-T'ai Tien was the K'unning Kung or " Palace of Tranquil Earth." This was not, in Manchu times, " the special palace of the empress " as several writers have declared, though it had been so under the Ming rulers. In the Manchu period, the eastern portion of it was used as the imperial nuptial-chamber, but occupied only during the Manchu equivalent of the honeymoon. The central portion was reserved for various religious and quasi-religious purposes, including *chi t'ien*—the worship of Heaven, and *t'iao shên*— the invocation of spirits by means of the mystic rites and dances of the shaman or *wu*. Shamanism was a cult with which the Manchus were familiar in the early days of their history, before they entered China, and they brought it with them to their new home. But they seem to have done so rather shamefacedly, as if conscious that it would be held in contempt by Confucian orthodoxy, and the witches and mediums who understood and practised the rites and incantations of Shamanism were always kept in the obscure background of the life of the Manchu court. Their sacrificial vessels, witches' cauldrons and musical instruments (including bronze bells and wooden clappers) were stored in this building because it was one which was " forbidden" even to those for whom the " Forbidden " City had few closed doors. I myself entered it only once, and that was in the company of the emperor on the eve of his wedding. In accordance with the dynastic regulations, state-sacrifices to the spirits (*ta chi shên*) took place here on the second day of the New Year, in the second of the three spring months and at the beginning of autumn. In former days, tributary princes and *beileh* (a Manchu term for princes below the highest rank) and the heads of the Six Boards received imperial commands to a palace-banquet on these occasions, at which they partook of portions of the flesh of the animals used in the sacrifices.

The palace of the little lady who became empress towards the end of 1922 was known as the *Ch'u Hsiu Kung*—" the Palace of Treasured Beauty." The palace of the secondary consort (the *shu fei*) was the *Ch'ang Ch'un Kung*—" the Palace of Long Spring-time." These residences were both to the north-west of the throne-hall and north of the emperor's own palace, which was the *Yang-Hsin Tien* or " Hall of the Nurture of the Mind." This palace, which was built or rebuilt in 1802, had been the residence of several former sovereigns, including the unhappy Tê Tsung (Kuang-Hsü) before the empress-dowager sent him as a prisoner to the islet of Ying-T'ai. The name contains an allusion to a passage in Mencius—*yang hsin mo shan yü kua yü*—which means " in the nurture of the mind it is of the first importance to refrain from self-indulgence."[8] Not a bad motto to be brought daily to the sight and memory of a royal personage.

In later days I became an almost daily visitor at the " Hall of the Nurture of the Mind." Till near the end of 1922, however, my meetings with my imperial pupil took place as a rule in the Yü-ch'ing Kung, the imperial schoolroom, which is situated immediately to the west of the Fêng Hsien Tien or Ancestral Chapel and to the east of the Chai Kung or Palace of Fasting, where the emperor was expected to undergo ritual purification before taking part in a solemn sacrifice.

I have already mentioned by name the palaces occupied by the empress-dowager T'zŭ-Hsi.[9] One of these, as we have seen, had formerly been the last earthly home of the great emperor Ch'ien-Lung. One of the rooms which he used was perhaps unparalleled in any other royal palace. The floor-space was almost wholly occupied by a pile of rocks arranged to represent a wild and rugged mountain. Among the rocks of this mountain, one of the mightiest monarchs who ever ruled a great empire was wont to sit and meditate, and imagine himself to be a lonely hermit qualifying for the high destiny that awaits those who live on herbs and water and commune with the spirits of hills and rivers. Thoreau, the lover of solitude amid the glories of wild nature, looked forward to the time when every house would have not only its sleeping and reception rooms but also a room for quiet thought, and when architects would be expected, when planning a dwelling-house, to provide a " thinking-room." But even that dreamer never seems to have dreamt of a thinking-room furnished not with tables and chairs but with a mountain.

The great Manchu emperor must have possessed that beautiful quality which according to Mencius is possessed by every great man—the heart of a child. He had real hills among which he could ramble and meditate at will—his own mountain-palace of Jehol was within easy reach, and he loved to travel thither when the cares of state permitted. But there was something in him that craved for a wonderland which, with the aid of a few heaped stones, would be wholly the creation of his own mind— a wonderland within the four walls of his own house, into which he could step merely by descending from an imperial altitude to the level of ordinary humanity, and by turning " a tiny golden key " in the lock of a commonplace door.[10]

Besides the emperor there were in 1919 four other members of the imperial family resident in the Forbidden City. They were all women. The empress-dowager Lung-Yü—niece of the " Venerable Buddha " and principal consort of Tê Tsung—was already dead. The four remaining ladies were all *huang-t'ai-fei*— dowager consorts of the second degree. Three were relicts of the emperor T'ung-Chih (1862–1874), son of the " Venerable Buddha." One of these (Chuang-Ho *T'ai Fei*) died in 1921, in her home in the Forbidden City, which was the Ch'ung-Hua Palace. The other two have died since the expulsion of the imperial family from the Forbidden City in November, 1924. The fourth was Chin *T'ai Fei*, afterwards known by her honorific title of Tuan K'ang, the only surviving consort of Tê Tsung (Kuang-Hsü). She was the sister of the unhappy girl who was murdered by the Venerable Buddha in 1900.[11] She died in October, 1924, in her palace in the Forbidden City. Had she lived a

month or two longer, she would have shared with the two elder
dowagers the ignominy of being turned out of her home by the
armed force of " the Christian General."[12] Tuan K'ang wa⁻ the
only one of the four imperial dowagers with whom I ever came
to have more than a ceremonial acquaintance. I occasionally
accompanied the emperor on his visits to her residence, the
Yung Ho Kung or " Palace of Everlasting Harmony."

The imperial princes—the father and numerous uncles and
other relatives of the emperor—and the other members of the
Manchu nobility did not live within the Forbidden City, which
they visited only when summoned to audience or on ceremonial
occasions. Most of them had spacious *fu* or princely mansions
of their own in other parts of what was known as the " Tartar "
city of Peking. The emperor's father, prince Ch'un, the former
regent, dwelt on the shores of the Shih-ch'a Lake near the Drum
and Bell Towers in the extreme north of the city, in a large
house commonly known as the Pei Fu or " Northern Mansion."
Most of the near relatives of the emperor dwelt in similar imposing residences in other parts of the city. Prince Tsai T'ao's
house was near prince Ch'un's, in a locality known as the
Lung-t'ou Ching—" the Well of the Dragon's Head." Over the
spacious courts and pavilions of a neighbouring mansion, that
of prince Kung, once the resort of the greatest and noblest of
the land, silent gloom had settled ; for they had been untenanted
by their lord since 1912.[13]

Though the emperor and the four *t'ai-fei* or dowager-consorts
were the only imperial residents in the Forbidden City, it must
not be supposed that it was an unpeopled city. Before the
revolution there was a staff of about three thousand eunuchs,
of various grades. In 1919, about a thousand still remained.
The others had retired with their fortunes to their homes on the
borders of Shantung and Chihli, to sanctuaries in the foreign
Concessions of Tientsin, to the shops in which they had deposited
their strangely-acquired capital, or to their monasteries and
hermitages in the Western Hills, ten miles to the west of Peking,
or in the sacred isle of P'u-t'o near Ningpo. Of the thousand
who remained, some were the personal attendants and chair-
bearers of the emperor and the four dowagers, others were in
charge of the various palace-buildings and responsible for the

safe-keeping of their contents, others performed more or less menial duties. Those of the highest grade were *yü-ch'ien t'ai-chien*—Eunuchs of the Presence—who had the honour of serving the Son of Heaven himself. The different grades were kept strictly apart from one another and on ceremonial occasions wore distinctive uniforms. Crimson predominated in the ceremonial garments of the Eunuchs of the Presence. Besides the eunuchs there were numerous ladies-in-waiting (*nü kuan*) and maidservants (*kung nü*), but most of the former did not reside in the Forbidden City.

In those parts of the Forbidden City which were nearest to the outer walls and therefore most remote from the quarters of the imperial personages, resided a large number of servants whose miscellaneous duties were confined to parts of the palace precincts which were seldom or never visited by royalty. There also—in the vicinity of the great northern gateway into the Forbidden City—dwelt the officers and men of the *hu chün* or palace-guard, who had replaced the pre-revolutionary imperial guard-corps. Some of these also occupied buildings immediately outside the gate, on the east and west sides of the great open space between the Forbidden City and the " Coal Hill."

Before the " twilight " period, the main imperial entrance to " the Great. Within " was the magnificent southern gateway known as the Wu-mên, immediately in front of the throne-hall of " Supreme Harmony." *Wu-mên* literally means " Noon Gate." The name had a symbolical reference to the emperor in the supreme glory of his strength and power, comparable to that of the sun in its noon-day brilliance.[14] It was through the central section of this gateway that the emperor passed in and out of the Forbidden City. But after the revolutionary settlement this section of the imperial enclosure passed under the control of the republican authorities, and the northern gateway—the *Shên-Wu Mên*—then became the main entrance to that part of the " City " which was still, in the strict sense, imperial and " Forbidden." Like the Wu-Mên this gate contains three sections, each with its own doorway. The central section was opened for the emperor and his suite alone ; the western section was that which was opened daily for the use of those whose lawful occasions permitted them to enter the " forbidden " precincts,
Mc

such as the princes and nobles, the imperial tutors, and the officials of the Nei Wu Fu. All those who had the entrée were obliged to enter the Forbidden City on foot, unless they had been granted the privilege of entering it on horseback or in sedan-chairs. " One of the highest distinctions," remarks Dr. R. K. Douglas, " which can be conferred on officials whom the emperor delights to honour is the right to ride on horseback within the sacred precincts."[15] But the right to be carried in a chair was a still higher distinction, and it included the lower. One or other of these privileges was sometimes conferred for temporary use on specified occasions only. Those on whom it was conferred as a permanent privilege were entitled to include it in the lists of imperial honours which were inscribed on wooden tablets and hung on the wall at the entrance to their private residences. Most of the princes of the blood and a few of the nobility had the right to a chair, while their sons, and the lesser nobility, had the right to ride on horseback. The imperial tutors, in virtue of the dignity of their office, were always granted the higher privilege.

Those who possessed either of these coveted rights were free to ride or to be carried in their chairs as far as the inner gates that led directly to the precincts of the throne-hall. One of these gates—the *Ching-yün Mên*—was on the east side, the other—the *Lung-tsung Mên*—on the west. These two inner gates led directly into that part of the Forbidden City which was occupied by the Son of Heaven, and it was because we had reached " holy ground " that we were required to proceed the rest of the way on foot. At all the gates there was posted an armed guard whose business it was to keep unauthorised persons from proceeding further and to present arms to those who had the right to pass within. Only one of the princes had the special privilege of being carried in his chair a little further than the rest. This was prince Ch'un, who in virtue of his position as former regent and also as father of the emperor, took precedence of everyone else. He had the right of proceeding in his chair to the *Yang-hsin Mên*—the gate of the courtyard in front of the emperor's own quarters.

The name of the great triple gateway which led into the Forbidden City on its north side—the *Shên-Wu Mên*—may be translated " Gate of the Divine Warrior " or of " Spiritual

Valour." In the Ming dynasty and also in the Manchu dynasty up to 1795 its name was Yüan Wu Mên—" Dark Warrior "— which contains an allusion to ancient astrological ideas about the attributes or qualities of various constellations, and indicates the North.[16] The name *Yüan* was changed to Shên in the reign of Chia-Ch'ing (1796–1820) because, being part of a name given to his father, the emperor Ch'ien-Lung, it fell under an imperial taboo.[17]

Outside the Gate of Spiritual Valour was an open space which on account of its great size usually presented a forlorn and deserted appearance ; but on occasions of solemnity, when the emperor was holding court, almost every available foot of space was occupied by the carriages, cars, horses and personal retinues of the princes and others who were in attendance on his majesty or were being received in audience.

The northern side of the great square was bounded by the walled enclosure of the hill which is familiarly known to foreigners and many Chinese as the Coal Hill (*Mei Shan*) though its more correct name is *Ching Shan* or Prospect Hill. This name is justified ; for it is not only in itself an object of beauty, crowned as it is with its exquisite pavilions with their blue and yellow tiles, but from its summit may be had one of the best views of the gleaming roofs of the Forbidden City.

The name *Mei Shan* has suggested the theory that the hill consists of a vast mound of coal, ready to be put to practical use in the event of a siege of the Forbidden City. That theory is erroneous ; but the hill is, indeed, an artificial structure, as its symmetry should suggest even to the most unobservant visitor. According to the information given to me in the palace, it was built up from the material dug out of the neighbouring " Three Lakes " when the small ponds or marsh-lands that originally existed there were deepened and enlarged. The reason why a hill was created out of this material immediately to the north of the Forbidden City is easily understood by anyone who knows something of the principles of Chinese geomancy. The north is the region whence come evil influences, and the function of the hill is to prevent them from reaching the dwelling-place of the Son of Heaven. It was for a similar reason that the emperor's throne (like the seats of important images in temples) was always placed so that it should face the sunny and auspicious south instead of the gloomy and unpropitious north.

Prospect Hill is described in a Peking topography as *Ta Nei chih chên shan*—" the Protecting Hill of the Great Within," and it was also sometimes known as *Wan-Sui Shan*—" the hill of a myriad years "—" wan sui " being used in China (and also in Japan) as the equivalent of our " God Save the King."

The hill was allowed, after the revolution, to remain under the control of the imperial household because it had always been regarded as an annexe to the Forbidden City, and also because its walled enclosure contained the ceremonial hall (*Shou Huang Tien*) in which the bodies of deceased emperors lay in state before they were conveyed to the imperial mausolea. Here also were kept the *Lieh Shêng Yü Jung*—a series of portraits of the emperors of the Manchu dynasty. Nevertheless the hill was not, like the Forbidden City, wholly closed to the public, who were admitted to the grounds when properly introduced.

It is usually said that the Forbidden City as it stands to-day was mainly built by the emperor Ch'êng Tsu (Yung Lo, 1403–1424), the first of the Ming emperors who chose Peking for his capital. But apart from the outer walls and some portions of the older palaces it is doubtful whether much of the work of that period remains. A great part of the Forbidden City was burned (as well as looted) by Li Tzŭ-ch'êng—the bandit-leader whose attempt to found a new dynasty was baffled by the coming of the Manchus—and there have been several fires and much reconstruction of buildings since that date.

Such was the Forbidden City at the beginning of 1919, when I first became a member of the *Nei T'ing* or " Inner Court " and was the only foreigner so privileged. Practically adjacent to it, on its western side, were the " Three Lakes " and the palaces which had formerly belonged to the imperial family but were now occupied by the real ruler of the country. Here we have a striking illustration of the strangeness of the compromise set forth in the Articles of Favourable Treatment. In the heart of Peking were two adjacent palaces. In that which still retained the distinction of being the " Forbidden City " dwelt a titular monarch ; in the other resided the chief executive of the republic. In the latter was a presidential chair occupied by one who exercised the powers of an emperor without the name ; in the former was a throne on which sat one who was an emperor in name alone. He who ruled the vast realm of China was called a president ; he whose rule did not extend an inch beyond his palace walls was called an emperor. Surely in no other land could circumstances so anomalous have lasted more than a week ; yet they lasted in China for thirteen years.

It was not till near the end of those thirteen years that the emperor saw anything of the world outside the Forbidden City. I myself accompanied him on his first journey beyond the gates of Peking. Visiting China just before the revolution, a Dutch scholar, M. Henri Borel, wrote down his impressions of the Peking of those days. " Behind the walls of the Forbidden City," he said, " ever haughty and unapproachable, remains the solitary emperor whom no one knows, who never surrendered his individuality to anyone, and never will."[18]

M. Borel seems to have thought there was very little prospect of the emperor ever ceasing to be solitary or of ever emerging from those haughty and unapproachable walls. But why did the strange thought come to him that the emperor was a myth ? For he tells us that " behind that pink and golden wall, in the fairy-like palaces of which here and there only a gleaming roof is seen flaming against the deep blue sky " dwelt " the mythological little emperor Hsüan-T'ung."

The little emperor Hsüan-T'ung had passed out of his mythological stage when he stepped down from his chair and shook hands with me on that cold March morning in 1919. But perhaps it is only real emperors that are myths and unreal ones that cease to be myths. It is bewildering ; but to M. Borel the little two-year old Hsüan-T'ung must have been something more than a myth after all, for he also informs us that "properly speaking, Peking is all one immense temple, surrounding the recess which is the Forbidden City, where dwells the Deity who is Emperor."

By 1919 that " Deity " had condescended to lower himself from the order of divinity to that of mere humanity, and was popularly known to foreigners as " the Boy Emperor." Nevertheless there were many Chinese then, and much later, to whom he was still the Lord of a Myriad Years, the Son of Heaven, the de jure ruler of the world.

CHAPTER XII

The Imperial Tutors

NEXT TO A LIMITED NUMBER of the imperial princes, including those of the first degree (*ch'in wang*), the persons who took precedence of all others at court were the imperial tutors.

It is difficult for a foreigner to understand the principles that underlay the extreme deference shown by a pupil to a teacher in Old China—the China that found some of its last refuges in the " alien " Manchu court—especially if his personal experience and observation have been confined to the New China that treats many of the ancient traditions with contempt.

" In no country," says Dr. W. A. P. Martin, " is the office of teacher more revered. Not only is the living instructor saluted with forms of profoundest respect, but the very name of teacher, taken in the abstract, is an object of almost idolatrous language. On certain occasions it is inscribed on a tablet in connection with the characters for heaven, earth, prince and parents, as one of the five chief objects of veneration, and worshipped with solemn rites."[1]

According to a famous passage in the *Kuo Yü*, each human being depends on those persons who should be served by him with equal devotion. One is the father, who gives life ; the second is the teacher, who shows how life is to be lived ; the third is the prince, who provides the conditions of a good life by maintaining the social order. In another passage in the same book the theory is expressed thus. " Without a father, there is no life ; without physical nourishment (provided for by the prince), there is no growth ; without the teacher, there is no wisdom."

If we turn to one of the standard books of Chinese classical literature, the *Li Chi*, we find such utterances as the following :

" When a pupil meets his teacher on the road, he should hasten towards him and bow. If the teacher addresses him, he should give a fitting reply ; if the teacher is silent, he should retire quickly. . . . A pupil should wait upon his teacher and serve him without regard to mere conventions. As long as his teacher lives he must serve him zealously, and should pay him the tribute of sincere mourning for three years after his death. . . . If a prince is anxious to civilise his people or make them courteous and well-bred, it is with the school that he must begin. Uncut jade cannot be turned into a serviceable vessel ; if men are uneducated they do not know how to conduct themselves. Thus it was that the wise kings of old, when settling their states on sound foundations and in ruling their people, made education their primary care. . . . It is from the teacher that the ruler learns the art of government ; thus nothing should be a matter of graver concern than the selection of a teacher. . . . There are two men in his realm whom the ruler cannot regard as his subjects. One is the man who in the ritual sacrifices to the dead personates the royal ancestors ; the other is his teacher.[2] That was a right and proper rule which ordained that when the teacher was addressing the Son of Heaven he should not face the north. That was how honour was done to the office of teacher."[3]

The last sentence may require elucidation. It has always been the custom in China for the ruler to sit enthroned with his back to the north, facing the south.[4] Those who approach him, therefore, must face the north. This marks the distinction between ruler and subject. But this relationship of ruler and subject is not the relationship of teacher and pupil ; therefore the teacher when addressing a ruler who is also his pupil is not expected to assume the usual attitude. The interesting point is that this ancient rule was observed to the last in the imperial schoolroom. At his studies the emperor sat at the north side of a square table, facing south. The place assigned to the tutor was a seat at the east side of the table, facing west. That was my own position during all my formal interviews with the emperor in the Yü-ch'ing palace.

Another mark of respect shown by the emperor to each of his tutors—even the barbarian from overseas—was to rise when the tutor entered the room. The tutor advanced to the middle of the room, bowed once, and emperor and tutor then sat down simultaneously in their proper places. If the tutor, in the course of the lesson-hours, had occasion to rise for the purpose of fetching a book from a shelf or for any other reason, the emperor rose too, and remained standing till the tutor returned to his place.

The profound respect shown by the emperor to his tutors was one of the features of the Manchu court which attracted the attention of the Jesuit fathers who were employed in astronomical and other work at the court of the early Manchu emperors. One of the *Lettres Edifiantes et Curieuses* which narrate the experiences of the Jesuits at court in the first half of the eighteenth century contains an account of a eulogium pronounced in 1726 by the emperor Shih Tsung[5] on his deceased tutor, who was a Manchu named Ku-pa-tai. I translate the following passages from the French.

" Ku-pa-tai," said the emperor, " who formerly held the office of first president of the Board of Rites, was a man of irreproachable character, moderate and well-regulated in all his conduct, and full of knowledge and virtue. My father, the emperor Shêng Tsu,[6] who held him in high esteem, employed him in affairs of a most difficult nature. . . . As he excelled in the military art no less than in scholarship, he was astonishingly successful in the enterprises assigned to him. . . . As he was distinguished for his vast erudition, and his actions were such as to make him a worthy model for our imitation, my father selected him to be tutor to several of the imperial princes. I was one of those whom he taught. Filled with indefatigable zeal, he laboured from morning till night in the work of giving us instruction and in engraving upon our hearts the purest and noblest maxims of fidelity and piety. . . . As soon as I heard of his death, wishing to carry out the duty that a disciple owes to his teacher, I went personally to his house to take part in the last rites and to mourn before his coffin. When his funeral took place I sent several of my officials to represent me and to carry out the prescribed ceremonies in my name. . . . I should not forget so wise a master, and I wish to give him a mark of my gratitude." The emperor concluded by calling upon the Board of Rites to deliberate upon the case of Ku-pa-tai and to submit recommendations regarding posthumous honours.[7]

The Jesuit father who wrote the account from which these passages are translated added that he had not discovered what action the Board took in the matter. From other sources, however, we learn that the deceased tutor was " canonised " (to use the ordinary but not satisfactory term for the conferring of posthumous titles on distinguished people in China) under the name of *Wên Tuan*—" Scholarly and Upright "—and was given a place in the national Memorial Temple dedicated to men who have deserved well of their country.[8] A large sum of money was also conferred by the emperor on Ku-pa-tai's needy relatives.

There was nothing exceptional about the emperor's personal visit to the house of his sick or deceased tutor, nor about the grant of posthumous honours. The tradition was maintained, as we shall see shortly, up to and including the time of the emperor whom it was my privilege to serve.[9]

A parallel to the easy and unrestrained relationship that existed in China between emperor and tutor may perhaps be found in that which existed between the Roman emperor Marcus Aurelius and his friend and tutor Marcus Cornelius Fronto. But in China the position of an imperial tutor was more than that of a privileged friend ; he was also a great " mandarin," occupying a position not inferior to that of viceroys and grand councillors.

There was nothing remarkable about this, because he was naturally selected from among the most distinguished scholars in the land, which meant that he had come successfully through the most gruelling of the state-examinations. As the examinations, under the old system that was abolished a generation ago, were the sole avenue to official employment, those who passed high in the triennial palace-examinations (*tien shih*) were sure of a career. Thus anyone who was so distinguished in scholarship as to be qualified for an imperial tutorship was almost certain to have risen already to high office in the State. In most cases he would have attained the red " button " of the highest of the nine official grades before he entered the palace as an imperial tutor. Had he not done so, he would inevitably be raised to that rank and receive other honours in addition, such as the sable robe, double-eyed peacock's feathers, and the right to enter the Forbidden City in a chair. Later on he would probably become a Junior and finally a Senior " Grand Guardian of the heir-apparent " (a purely honorary dignity, often conferred even when no heir-apparent had been designated), and on his death he would (in all probability) receive " canonisation " or a posthumous title of honour similar to that conferred upon Ku-pa-tai. Even if illness or other cause exclusive of misconduct compelled his resignation he would retain his honours and his title of *Ti Shih*—imperial tutor—to the end of his life. He would always retain the right of private audience, he would invariably be invited to sit in the emperor's presence (when even a viceroy would kneel) and he would continue to be treated by the whole of the palace staff with the same respect that had been accorded to him when he held office.

" Wen Ching " shows a curious ignorance of palace etiquette, and the traditional respect shown to the imperial tutors, when he observes that two temporary tutors from T'ung-Wên College were allowed by the emperor Kuang-Hsü to sit in his presence " while others, even princes and grandees, had to kneel and prostrate themselves."[10] The imperial tutors were always privileged to sit—they performed the obeisance of *kotow* only on solemn occasions such as that described in the foregoing chapter—and Kuang-Hsü was making no innovation when he allowed them to do so.

It is perhaps hardly necessary to say that the extreme deference which pupils (imperial and other) were expected in China to pay to their teachers was not a one-sided obligation, any more than was the loyalty due from a subject or minister (*ch'ên*) to his prince. It was the teacher's duty to perform his functions in such a way that his pupil would grow up to be a Confucian gentleman—a *chün-tzŭ*—which meant that he would be a ripe scholar, honourable, modest, sincere, trustworthy in all his dealings and magnanimous to friend and foe. A teacher who failed in his duty to his pupil was no more worthy of respect than was a ruler who misgoverned his country. The principle *maxima debetur puero reverentia* was enunciated almost in the same words by Confucian teachers long before it reached a Roman ear.

My own appointment as English tutor to the emperor was unprecedented and caused no small commotion at court. There had been strenuous opposition on the part of the conservative members of the imperial family and household department to the appointment of a foreign tutor. They feared, of course, that the young emperor Hsuan-T'ung would gradually come to adopt too " modern " an outlook on life and might fall under Western influences to such an extent as to make him dissatisfied with existing conditions in the palace. It must be admitted that their fears in the last respect proved to have been well founded. When the pressure brought by the president of the republic, Hsü Shih-ch'ang, and one or two of the more liberal-minded princes such as Tsai T'ao, became too strong to be overcome, an attempt was made to effect a compromise. The Englishman was not to be given the rank or title of an imperial tutor, which was altogether above what a mere " ocean-man " (otherwise " foreign devil ") could reasonably expect, but was merely to be engaged for the exclusive purpose of teaching English and was not to aspire to the privileges which gave imperial tutors the right to give advice in matters of policy. He was to be a mere teacher of English without official·rank, and was to be regarded as an employee of the imperial household department and take his instructions from the comptroller. Contrary views were put forward by influential members of the court, who insisted that the emperor's foreign tutor should be put on the same footing as the Chinese tutors ; that any other arrangement would be unworkable in practice and might give offence to the foreign government which had agreed to the appointment of one of its nationals.

The controversy was still going on when I entered the Forbidden City, and needless to say it was one in which I had no desire to take part ; indeed for several months I was unaware that any differences of opinion had arisen with regard to my status. I was treated, from the beginning, with oriental courtesy and consideration, not only by my pupil himself—with whom I was very shortly on the most friendly terms—but also by the various members of the imperial family with whom I came in contact and by the officials of the household department. My first quarrel was with the eunuchs, whom I astonished and dismayed by my reply to their request for the largesse which it was customary for a newly appointed member of the court to distribute among their fraternity. I agreed to pay the amount claimed, but only on condition that they would give me formal receipts. As their demand had been an unauthorised one, and they were unwilling to furnish written evidence that it had been made, it was promptly withdrawn.[11]

Before long, the controversy regarding my status was decided against the conservatives, and I was recognised as *Ti Shih*—an " imperial tutor," with all the dignities and privileges'pertaining to that office. At first the only privilege conferred upon me was that of the right to enter the Forbidden City in a two-bearer chair ; and the chair, and bearers, were provided for me by the palace authorities. In a few months, however, I was placed in the second of the nine ranks and received the " sable robe." Some time afterwards, when " wedding honours " were being distributed in 1922, I was promoted to the first official grade, and thus became a Chinese mandarin of the highest order.

In addition to honours, gifts of other kinds were from time to time bestowed by the emperor upon all his tutors, including myself. On the eve of each of the great festivals it was customary for him to send presents of money, for which we gave formal thanks (*hsieh Ên*) at the audiences in the Palace of Cloudless Heaven. Other gifts, of porcelain, books, pictures, jade and other things from the imperial collections, were also occasionally presented by the emperor in person, merely as tokens of good-will. Sometimes presents of fruit and cakes came also from the imperial dowagers. As the arrival of gift-bearing messengers from the palace often caused a commotion in the neighbourhood of the house of the recipient, paragraphs recording such incidents used to find their way into the Chinese press. I have before me, for example, a paragraph from the Peking *Shih Pao* which may be translated as follows :

" It is reported that Chin Kuei-fei,[12] of the Ch'ing House, fearing that the English imperial tutor Johnston may by his labours in the Yü-ch'ing palace lose the natural moisture of his throat, has bestowed upon him a special present of several pounds of Chinese and foreign ginseng. This is a mark of exceptional favour."

I must now give some account of my colleagues in the imperial schoolroom. When I first entered the Forbidden City in 1919 they were four in number, three being Chinese and one a Manchu. The first to be mentioned is one whom I never met. He was a very sick man, half paralysed, when I arrived, and he died towards the end of the year. He was a Cantonese named Liang Ting-fên.

To refer to the Canton province as a breeding-ground of revolutionaries is a commonplace. Many revolutions, indeed, have broken out there in the past and will probably break out there in the future. What is not so well known to foreigners, in or out of China, is that Canton has also been the home of many of the strongest conservatives and also of the most devoted loyalists and monarchists. It would astonish most people who assume that the monarchic principle in general and the Manchu house in particular were and are anathema to all natives of Canton, if they knew how many of the fallen dynasty's best friends have been Cantonese. Of these men, Liang Ting-fên was typical.

He obtained his doctorate in the ordinary way by passing the old-fashioned classical examinations, in 1880, and rose to be chief justice of the province of Hupei. Before the events of 1898 described at the beginning of this book he incurred the wrath of the " Venerable Buddha " on account of his plain-speaking concerning the shortcomings of certain imperial princes and court-functionaries, and had he not had a powerful patron and protector in the person of the viceroy Chang Chih-tung he would have received drastic punishment. He was a friend of K'ang Yu-wei, and was suspected by the empress-dowager of being among those who " plotted " against her in 1898, but in fact he was too conservative to approve of K'ang Yu-wei's liberalising policy and actually denounced it. After the revolution he pleaded with Li Yüan-hung to disentangle himself from his republican associates and restore the dynasty. When his pleadings failed, he went to the " Western Tombs " and prostrated himself, weeping, before his late emperor's grave.

Subsequently, on the recommendation of Ch'ên Pao-shên, he was appointed minister in charge of the construction of the late emperor's tomb ; and not long afterwards, on the death of Lu Jun-hsiang (one of the three imperial tutors originally appointed in 1911[13]), Liang Ting-fên was appointed to the vacancy.

His poetry—a Chinese scholar is hardly recognised as such unless he can at least express himself gracefully in verse—follows late T'ang and Sung models and is characterised by pensive melancholy and a spirit of unworldliness.

Chiang shui pu k'o hao,
Wo lei pu k'o kan

(" The water in the river never runs dry, nor do these tears ever cease to flow").

This is far from being a fair sample of his poetry, but it indicates that Liang Ting-fên's muse was not given to hilarity. She was less a Euphrosyne than the " pensive muse " of Melancholy, and more likely to express herself in an *Il Penseroso* than in a *L'Allegro.*

In an autobiographical poem he tells us how he first began to study when he was three years old, how his mother was his first teacher and how conscious he was of not always doing credit to her teaching. But in his boyhood, he says, his father's house was frequented by high officials and distinguished scholars, and though he could not understand much of what he heard he took delight in listening to conversation about the two subjects that then interested him most—poetry and swordsmanship.

His mother's death, when he was still young, was his first great grief. His father, who was a government official and brought him up well, emphasised the importance of self-discipline and self-respect, and impressed his mind with the principle that if ever the choice lay between death and disgrace he should choose the former.

Perhaps he had this parental counsel in his mind when the testing time came in the summer of 1917. At the time of his death I heard his colleagues in the palace speak of the courage and loyalty displayed by him at the time of the Restoration episode.

Some of the fighting between Chang Hsün's troops and those of Tuan Ch'i-jui took place in the immediate vicinity of the Forbidden City. When fighting was going on in that locality, the hour came for Liang Ting-fên's usual attendance on his imperial pupil. To reach the palace-gates he had to drive in his pony-carriage through streets thronged with undisciplined soldiers. He refused to remain at home or to turn back when the danger was pointed out to him. On his arrival at the great gates opposite the " Coal Hill," he found his official sedan-chair awaiting him as usual, but the bearers earnestly advised him not to go into the palace as the opposing forces were exchanging shots over the palace roofs and it was perilous to cross the open courtyards. Stepping out of his carriage and seating himself in his chair he ordered the bearers to take him forthwith to the Yü-ch'ing palace. They obeyed with evident reluctance— thinking no doubt of their own safety as well as his—and they had gone only a little way when rifle-bullets struck a wall along- side which they were passing and a shower of fragments of brick and plaster struck the chair. The bearers begged him to let them carry him into one of the side-buildings to take cover till the firing was over. *Pu k'o wu ch'ai shih, pu k'o wu ch'ai shih* (" My duty is not to be neglected, my duty is not to be neglected ") was all he replied, and they had the courage to obey him. It would have been a disgrace worse than death if through seeking safety for his own person he had failed to keep his appointment with his imperial master and pupil. We may surmise that not much was done that day in the way of lessons, but not through failure on the part of the imperial tutor to present himself at the usual hour.

Here is his " elegy in a country churchyard," the grace of which will not be apparent in my clumsy rendering.

Dark is the grove of white poplars in the evening shadows.
The sun sets, and sparks of fire fitfully come and go.
I am followed by the hovering ghost-lights—
I must hurry on, I cannot linger here.

Two things I know of rarest beauty—
One is the courage of manhood, the other the charm of woman.

But quickly they pass away with the fleeting years,
And the graveyards are filled with heaps of mounds.

Among all the myriads to be born in years to come,
Perhaps there will be another " me," just as I am to-day.
The way of immortality is not for me, but this I know—
The more rarefied the dust, the more lightly it falls to earth.

The allusion in the two last lines is to the art of the mountain-dwelling sage, who cultivates purity in body and mind, lives on dew and on strange herbs culled in fairyland, sets himself free from all physical entanglements and becomes independent of all the temporal and spatial conditions of ordinary humanity.

Liang Ting-fên himself has now, perhaps, become nothing more than one of the hovering ghost-lights that thrilled him as he hurried through the graveyard. It would be well for his country if his dream could come true, and if he could reappear, just as he used to be in days gone by, among the myriads yet unborn. China in these days is apt to despise men like Liang Ting-fên but can ill spare them.

When he died, the president of the republic, Hsü Shih-ch'ang, who had been an old colleague of his, sent a representative to his house to take part in the mourning ceremonies, and a gift of a thousand dollars towards the funeral expenses. The emperor Hsuan-T'ung acted similarly, sending an even larger present and conferring upon his old tutor the posthumous title of *Wên-Chung*—" Learned and Loyal."

My senior colleague, Ch'ên Pao-shên, who possessed among his other honours the dignity of *T'ai Pao* (" Grand Guardian of the heir-apparent") and was later to become *T'ai Fu* (" Grand Tutor "), was a man of nation-wide celebrity.[14] In 1919 he was about seventy-two years of age, a man of most charming and courtly manners, vigorous in mind and body, a famous poet, greatly admired for his delicate calligraphy, and a highly accomplished scholar. He was a native of the province of Fuhkien in southern China, and when he conversed with his fellow-provincials in his native dialect he was unintelligible to me ; but he spoke Pekingese with almost perfect purity.

As a young man his brilliance marked him out for a very

distinguished career. He took his doctorate in 1868, and rapidly rose in the official hierarchy until, like Liang Ting-fên, he incurred the disfavour of the empress-dowager. His enforced retirement into private life (nominally occasioned by the necessity of going into mourning for his mother) enabled him to devote more than twenty years to the pursuits for which nature probably intended him—poetry, calligraphy and scholarship. He owned two delightful mountain-retreats, one of them, well known to me, on the Ku-shan mountain near Foochow, and there he lived a happy life of scholarly seclusion. He was visited from time to time by his literary and official friends, and together they would " snuff candles and talk poetry without weariness late into the night." He had "a longing for clouds and streams," and much of his poetry is largely an expression of that longing.

The death of the empress-dowager in 1908 resulted in his reluctant return to official life, and he was offered the governor-ship of the province of Shansi. Soon afterwards, however, it was decided by the court that the time had arrived for the emperor (though only five years of age) to begin his education ; and when the prince-regent (or rather the empress-dowager Lung-Yü) offered him an imperial tutorship he accepted it in preference to the provincial governorship. Two other scholars were appointed simultaneously, one being Lu Jun-hsiang, the other I-K‘o-T‘an. Of the latter we shall hear again presently. Lu Jun-hsiang, like his famous and unfortunate predecessor Wêng T‘ung-ho,[15] was a *chuang-yuan*—that is to say, he had obtained the highest academic distinction open to a Chinese under the old examination system. On his death, as we have seen, he was succeeded by Liang Ting-fên.

The tutorial duties of Ch‘ên Pao-shên and his colleagues in 1911 were not, it is scarcely necessary to say, of an arduous nature. But his position as senior tutor was by no means equiva-lent to that of a nursery governess, for he became, in virtue of his position, an intimate member of the *nei-t‘ing* or Inner Court and was consulted on affairs of state. He had nothing to do, however, with the revolutionary settlement of 1912.

When I became his colleague he had already held his post at court for nearly eight years and had seen his imperial pupil grow up from his sixth to his fourteenth year. If I could not aspire to be

Nc

a fitting companion for him in the sphere of Chinese scholarship, a bond of sympathy between us was quickly discovered in our love of mountains. During the years in which we served together in the Forbidden City, his age did not prevent him from visiting with me some of the most beautiful scenes in the neighbourhood, though it justified him in allowing the bearers of his light mountain-chair to do his share of the climbing. One of our favourite haunts was a remote valley in the Western Hills where, owing to the kindness of president Hsü Shih-ch'ang, I acquired a retreat ("Cherry Glen ") which in time came to possess, among its many shrines, a temple to the Unknown God. Ch'ên Pao-shên commemorated his first visit to this delectable fairy-land—it was at the time of the autumn full moon in 1920—by a poem which is here reproduced in facsimile. It will serve as an example of his skill in a fine art which in China takes precedence of all other arts—that of calligraphy. His calligraphy, I may add, is of the delicate and rather dainty variety (very different from that of K'ang Yu-wei or Chêng Hsiao-hsü, both his friends) which to the Western eye seems appropriate to a man of Ch'ên Pao-shên's temperament, though some of my " modernist " Chinese friends have detected in it a lack of vigour and strong purpose which, they say, must be rooted in the writer's character.

I had, indeed, one fault to find with him ; and that was his failure to press hard enough for reform in the administration of the affairs of the imperial family after the revolution. He knew that great evils existed, and he did not do all that his influential position made it possible for him to do in the eradication of those evils. Nevertheless all failings in this respect may well be forgiven in one who in the evening of his life sacrificed the happiness and tranquillity that he had been enjoying for twenty years among the beloved hills and streams of his native province, solely from motives of loyalty to his sovereign and to his Confucian principles.

Another of my colleagues was Chu I-fan, a native of Kiangsi, about ten years younger than Ch'ên Pao-shên. Early in his career he held a Readership in the Hanlin Academy—a hall-mark of literary and scholastic distinction. In 1904 he became Literary Chancellor of Shensi, in 1906 head of the Education Department of Shantung, and in 1907 a Vice-Director of the

夢回疑雨復疑風身在飛流亂石

中此景故山吾家習天涯老顧與

君同澗谷能為盛夏寒未霜林葉

已微丹灑灑洗出中秋月攤褐深宵

數起看　庚申八月十四日

志道吾友招觀櫻桃溝泉石之勝信宿油葊中口占似正　寶琛

AUTOGRAPH POEM ADDRESSED TO THE AUTHOR BY THE GRAND
GUARDIAN AND TUTOR CH'ÊN PAO-SHÊN

Imperial Clan Court. He had held his imperial tutorship about four years when I made his acquaintance. Though popular in Peking society he seemed to me to lack the personal charm of his senior colleague, and his inability to speak anything but the form of " mandarin " current in his own prefecture —a dialect differing considerably from that of the court—was one of the causes that made our relationship less intimate than that which was soon established between his two colleagues and myself. Nevertheless I admired the frankness and sincerity with which he championed the old order of things in China. He had little use for Western civilisation and was honest enough to say so. Though a younger man than Ch'ên Pao-shên he belonged in spirit to an older generation. His entire lack of enthusiasm for reform made him a very tolerant spectator of the corruption and abuses of the Forbidden City. My repeated efforts to open his eyes to these evils, and to the urgent necessity of a drastic reorganisation of the household department, left him cold. Even the eunuch-system found in him a strong supporter. The fact that there had been eunuchs in the palace since the Chou dynasty, more than two thousand years ago, seemed to him to be sufficient justification for their employment in twentieth-century China.

Chu I-fan had made a hobby of Chinese medicine and thera-peutics and was incredulous of the superiority of Western medical science. He loved to be given opportunities of applying his knowledge, and although the palace staff included a number of court physicians, Chu I-fan was allowed to combine his func-tions as tutor with those of physician-in-ordinary to his majesty. When the emperor was indisposed, Chu I-fan was always the first to be summoned to k'an yü mo—"feel the imperial pulse."

One of his theories was that our imperial pupil should not be encouraged to take strenuous physical exercise in any form, partly because properly conducted emperors should at all times preserve a demeanour of solemn gravity, and partly because all human beings—including emperors—possess a fixed stock of vital energy which cannot be replenished. If that energy is dis-sipated in youth by strenuous physical activity, the inevitable result is early decay and death. The less a man draws upon his original store of vital energy when he is young, the more he has to keep him alive when he is old.

Applying this doctrine to the case of our pupil, Chu I-fan used to insist that it justified us in restraining him from indulging in those idiotic outdoor sports and games which must be rushing foolish foreigners into early graves. I contested his theory with all the arguments at my command, and openly incited his majesty to disregard it—not without some ultimate success. Yet if the statement attributed to a distinguished American biologist is correct, it may be that there is more in Chu I-fan's theory than I was aware of. For the biologist is reported to have announced that the duration of life in certain animals " varies inversely as the rate of living—that is to say, the rate of expenditure of energy." He likened vitality to " the potential energy of the charge of a Leyden jar," and declared that a high mortality—in insects and in man—was associated with " high expenditure of energy." *The Times*, which recently drew attention to this theory, attempted to console its physically active readers by reminding them that those whom the gods love die young.

I-K'o-T'an, who as I have said was one of the first three to be appointed tutors to the emperor Hsüan-T'ung, was a Manchu. The duty assigned to him was to teach the Manchu language, or rather to see that the emperor was not brought up in entire ignorance of what had been his ancestors' native tongue. If there was nothing very striking about his personality, he had a gay and genial temperament and was popular both in the palace and elsewhere. Whether his knowledge of his ancestral tongue was profound or not I cannot say, though I think he was a more fluent speaker of Pekingese than he was of Manchu. The emperor's Manchu lessons were not, as far as I could judge, taken very seriously ; and though he learned to speak a little of the language, and to write it fairly well, he never became a good Manchu scholar. When I-K'o-T'an died, his place as Manchu tutor was not filled up, and the emperor himself announced that English was thenceforth to be regarded as the second language of the Manchu court.

I-K'o-T'an's death took place on September 26th, 1922, shortly before his imperial pupil's wedding, which he had greatly hoped to see before he died. Acting on his own impulse and also in accordance with tradition, the emperor paid him a visit just before his death.[16] Accompanied by one or two attendants he drove to I-K'o-T'an's house in a motor-car, and arrived there at half-past two in the afternoon. I-K'o-T'an was just conscious and made an effort to incline his head to indicate that he recognised his imperial master. By seven o'clock he was dead. This was the first occasion on which the emperor had emerged from the Forbidden City except to pay three or four visits to his dying mother, princess Ch'un. A year later he issued a rescript, which duly appeared in the Court Gazette, extolling the virtues of I-K'o-T'an and conferring upon him the posthumous title of *Wên Chih*—" Scholarly and Upright " together with the rank of *Shao-pao*—" Junior Guardian of the heir-apparent."[17] The rescript also states that one of the princes had been sent to represent his majesty at the funeral ceremonies and to convey an imperial gift of three thousand dollars towards the expenses ; and that one of the late tutor's sons had been given an appointment at court in recognition of the faithful services rendered by his father.

CHAPTER XIII

The Manchu Court in Twilight

THE IMPOSING Gate of Spiritual Valour through which I made
my first entrance into the Forbidden City on March 3rd, 1919, led
me into a new world of space and time. It was through that
portal that I passed not only from a republic to a monarchy but
also from the New China of the twentieth century into a China
that was old before the foundation of Rome. On the outer side
of that gateway lay a million-peopled city throbbing with new
hopes and new ideals—many of them, perhaps fortunately, never
to be realised ; a city that was striving to bring itself up to date
and make itself worthy of its position as the capital of a great
democracy ; a city with a University thronged with eager
students who in their reckless impatience were putting modern
science and philosophy, together with Esperanto and the writings of Karl Marx, in the places lately occupied by the outworn
sages of the Confucian tradition ; a city in which cabinet-
ministers had been seen at presidential tea-parties in morning
coats and top-hats ; a city with a parliament that had yet to
produce its Pitts and Gladstones but had already equipped itself
with movable inkpots, and had hopes—also never to be realised
—of some day possessing a duly-elected Speaker.

On the inner side of the same gateway were to be observed
palanquins bearing stately mandarins with ruby and coral
" buttons " and peacocks' feathers on their official hats and white
cranes and golden pheasants on the front of their long outer
garments of silk ; high court officials in loose-sleeved sable
robes, with tufts of white fur (taken from the neck of the sable)
as an indication that the wearer was one who had gained the
favour of his sovereign ; young nobles and court-chamberlains
on horseback, their loose embroidered ceremonial gowns hiding
both saddle and stirrups ; eunuchs standing respectfully to attention, each attired in the uniform of his class ; long-coated
sula waiting in readiness to assist the great men out of their

palanquins or to dismount from their ponies, and to conduct
them to the waiting-rooms where they would be handed, with
due ceremony, the indispensable cups of tea ; officers of the
household scrutinising the lists of those who were to be admitted
to audience ; and finally, in an inner room of the palace of the
Nurture of the Mind, a boy of thirteen, slim of figure, gentle
in manner and simply clad, the last occupant—perhaps—of the
oldest throne in the world, the Son of Heaven, the " Lord of
Ten Thousand Years." And indeed in those innermost palaces of
the Forbidden City the Chinese republic might have been ten
thousand miles away in space instead of only a few hundred
yards, a thousand years away in time instead of contem-
poraneous.

The emperor was addressed as *huang shang*—the equivalent
of " imperial majesty." The same term was also used by the
members of the " Inner Court " when speaking of the emperor
in his absence, though among the tutors and high officers of the
household an equally common expression was *shang-t'ou*,
signifying " he who is above " or " the enthroned one." The
eunuchs more often used the expression *wan-sui-yeh*—" the
Lord of a myriad (or ten thousand) years," and this was also
the term used by palace servants—eunuchs or *sula*—when sent
to the houses of the tutors and other officers of the court, to
convey imperial gifts or messages.

In the Forbidden City the lunar calendar was still observed,
along with innumerable other customs and practices of Old
China. More remarkable, perhaps, than the maintenance of the
lunar calendar was the continued use of the emperor's reign-
title. Outside the Forbidden City, the year 1919 was the eighth
year of the republic of China. But for all those who had the right
to pass through the Gate of Spiritual Valour, the same year was
the eleventh year of Hsüan-T'ung.

The famous Court Gazette, which is said to have been first
issued in the T'ang dynasty more than a thousand years ago,
continued, after the Revolution, to be issued in the Forbidden
City, though in a miniature and much abbreviated form. As its
circulation was confined, however, to members of the Inner Court
(those who had the right of audience) the numbers issued were

very small and each copy was therefore written by hand. One of the issues of this Gazette—which has been called the oldest newspaper in the world—is reproduced in facsimile in these pages. It is dated the first and second days of the first moon of the fourteenth year of Hsüan-T'ung (January 28th and 29th, 1922), and as it was a festival season the date is written on a strip of red paper. It announces that various officials (including a republican general, Wang Huai-ch'ing and some of his men), having been in receipt of the imperial bounty in the shape of many gifts, have duly returned thanks ; and that certain Mongol princes and lamas and the Chang-chia Living Buddha (Hutuketu) have been received in audience and have submitted tribute in the shape of images of Buddha and ceremonial scarfs (*katag*).

In the days when the emperor still ruled, the Gazette (*Ching Pao* or *Kung-mên Ch'ao*) contained important imperial rescripts and edicts, lists of promotions and degradations of officers in the higher ranks, memorials from ministers of state and others, and miscellaneous information of a purely official character. It was not, properly speaking, a newspaper, for it contained no general news and no editorial matter. Still less was the miniature Gazette published in the Manchu court's " twilight " period entitled to be called a newspaper. It contained the names of those received in audience, notifications concerning the recurrent court festivals and functions, announcements about honours conferred upon living and dead servants of the throne, and miscellaneous edicts and rescripts issued by the emperor on matters connected with the administration of the affairs of the Forbidden City and the duties assigned to princes and others in connection with ritual observances.

Here are one or two translations of typical announcements :

" The master of ceremonies memorialises that at the *ch'ên* hour [between 7 and 9 a.m.] of the 20th day of the eleventh moon work was commenced on the making of the spirit-tablet of Kung-su *huang-kuei-fei* [the deceased dowager-consort of that name]. He also memorialises that the 24th day of the eleventh moon will be the date of the winter solstice, at which the usual sacrifice to Heaven must take place, and

requests instructions. Rescript by his imperial majesty : Let
the sacrificial ceremonies be performed on Our behalf by
Tsêng P‘ei."

This refers to the famous ceremony which used to be carried
out by the emperor in person at the Altar of Heaven. After the
revolution the ceremony at the Altar itself was given up (to be
revived, as we have seen, by Yüan Shih-k‘ai on the eve of his
expected enthronement), but it was still kept up on a small scale
within the Forbidden City itself, and performed by a member of
the imperial clan on the emperor's behalf.

" Memorial from the imperial household department. The
master of ceremonies having requested a date to be named for
the changing of winter hats for cool hats at court, an imperial
edict has been issued ordering that the change be made on the
28th day of the third moon." [In 1922, the year of this entry
in the Gazette, the 28th of the third moon fell on April 24th.]

The young emperor has always loved simplicity, and his
ceremonial robes gave him so little pleasure that it was fortunate
for him that the occasions on which he was obliged to wear them
were few. The great ceremonies were conducted in strict accordance with the rites that had been handed down through untold
centuries, for the Manchu sovereigns had been careful to maintain the ritual observances that had the sanctity of immemorial
usage. Apart from such relatively unimportant details as the use
of the Manchu language for certain ritual utterances and words
of command, and the wearing of the Manchu official costume,
there would have been little to perplex and startle the ghosts of
the sovereigns of former dynasties had they returned to visit
the scenes of their earthly splendour.

Something has already been said of the maintenance of the
old religious rites. But the most spectacular of the court-
ceremonies still carried out in the Forbidden City were those
held on the emperor's own birthday and on New Year's Day.
Similar ceremonies of a less elaborate nature were held on the
fifth day of the fifth moon (often called by foreigners the
" dragon-boat festival "—a misnomer in the north) and on the

fifteenth of the eighth moon, the mid-autumn festival. All dates
in the Forbidden City were those of the lunar calendar (hence the
use of the word " moon ") which though officially abolished by
the republic was always observed in court circles, as indeed it was
and is still observed by the people of China in general in spite of
repeated official efforts at suppression. Only once a year did the
Manchu court take any notice of the Gregorian calendar. That
was on the occasion of the Western New Year's Day. It passed
unobserved, indeed, in the Forbidden City itself, but the emperor on that day deputed a Manchu prince to present his personal greetings to the president of the republic. This courtesy
was reciprocated by the president, who regularly sent one of his
staff—usually the master of ceremonies in the presidential
palace—to offer his good wishes to the emperor on his birthday.
On such occasions, presents were given and received, and the
deputy took his seat at the feast which in both palaces followed
the formal ceremonies.

The emperor's birthday was always known at court as *wan-
shou* or (in full) *wan-shou shêng-chieh*. *Wan*, literally " ten thousand," is used to denote any indefinitely large number. *Shou*
stands for " long life." *Shêng-chieh* means " the holy anniversary." The four Chinese characters taken together may be
taken to signify " the holy birthday of the Lord of a Myriad
Years."

The principal ceremony of the day took place in the throne-
hall and great quadrangle of the Ch'ien-Ch'ing Kung—the
Palace of Cloudless Heaven.[1] On the early morning of the
anniversary the first duty to be performed, either by the emperor or by one of the princes as his deputy, was to make a
formal announcement of his majesty's birthday to the spirits of
his august ancestors. This ceremony took place in the *Fêng
Hsien Tien*, the chapel of the " Serving of Ancestors."[2]

By eight o'clock in the morning the princes, tutors, principal
officers of the household and other officials had entered the
Forbidden City in their palanquins or on horseback, and had
assembled in their ceremonial costumes in the Mou-ch'in-tien
and other buildings that open on to the great quadrangle in front
of the Palace of Cloudless Heaven. There they were regaled with
refreshments while the grand marshal and his staff and a corps of

palace musicians took up their positions on the marble terrace in front of the throne-hall. Smaller officials and others who had the right to attend the ceremony but not to draw so near to the throne as their superiors in rank, assembled in the large rectangular open space to the south of the main gateway leading into the great quadrangle.

The musicians, clad in crimson, stood in front of their instruments, which were hung on wooden frames or pedestals erected for the occasion on the marble terrace in front of the windows of the throne-hall. They included bells, gongs, drums of various kinds, sonorous stones, bell-chimes, bowl-gongs, tongued bells and gong-chimes. These instruments were used only in the performance of antique ritual music such as was heard in China at solemn ceremonies of this kind or at the equally stately observances held periodically in the Temple of Confucius. The ritual music performed in the palace was not, however, accompanied by the slow and decorous " dancing " (rather posturing) and the solemn waving of plumes and peacocks' feathers which are features of the impressive Confucian ritual.

" It is the duty of the minister in charge of education," said the Chinese philosopher Hsün Tzŭ more than two thousand years ago, " to prohibit any grossness in songs, to regulate musical performances by the seasons, and to see that the music of our cultured land is not corrupted by the uncouth cacophonies of the barbarians."[3]

This injunction (which reaffirms similar utterances by Confucius) has been kept in view throughout the centuries, though it is very doubtful whether there is much resemblance between the ritual music of modern times and that of the Confucian age.

Short chants accompanied by the striking of one or more of the instruments marked each stage of the extremely simple but deeply impressive ceremony. The arrival of a richly-embroidered state-umbrella, or canopy, which was temporarily set down outside the central door of the throne-hall, was the signal for all the officials to leave their waiting-rooms and arrange themselves according to their rank on the long white causeway, with its noble balustrades of exquisitely-carved marble, that occupies the middle of the quadrangle at right angles to the slightly higher

terrace in front of the throne-hall. The princes of the blood went
up to the higher terrace ; the others, with the imperial tutors in
front, stationed themselves on the lower terrace.

Another short chant, and a few bars of music were immediately followed by the raising of the canopy and the placing of
it in the middle of the open doorway, so that it became a screen,
hiding the interior of the throne-hall even from the princes closest
at hand. This was the moment of *Shêng Tien*—the arrival of the
emperor and his ascent of the Dragon throne. From the quadrangle the throne was only dimly visible even when there was no
obstruction in front of the door. The canopy rendered it impossible to see either the throne or its occupant. The Son of
Heaven seated in his robes on the dragon-throne was too sacred
an object to be gazed upon by mortal eyes—with certain exceptions to be noted shortly—and the state-umbrella was the
curtain that made such gazing impossible.

The rhythm of the music changed, and thereby announced to
those who could understand it that the emperor was on his
throne. Those to whom the music was a mystery, knew it from
the raising of the canopy. Not otherwise could it be guessed, for
there was nothing in the nature of a state-procession, as there
would have been in a Western country, no sight of the sovereign
seated in an open carriage bowing right and left to his loyal
subjects. The emperor was conducted from his own palace to the
throne through an invisible entrance at the back of the hall, the
only persons walking by the side of his great state-palanquin
being one of the chamberlains of the household and four eunuchs
of the Presence. They alone were in the hall when he ascended
the throne and remained in attendance on him throughout the
ceremony.

A momentary pause was followed by another short strain of
music. One of the princes issued from the group on the upper
terrace and entered the hall by one of the side-doors, which was
opened to let him pass. This was prince Ch'un, the emperor's
father. A minute or two elapsed, and he emerged again, having
greeted his emperor in the manner which the rites prescribed.

What the rites prescribed in this case was that the prince
should advance to the throne holding in both hands a curved
blackwood jade-topped symbol of good wishes which is known by

the Chinese term *ju-i*. Foreigners often describe this peculiar-looking article as a " sceptre," and assume it to be a symbol of authority. In fact, however, it is (at least in modern times) regarded merely as a tangible token of respectful greetings. The words *ju-i* mean " in accordance with wishes," an abbreviated way of saying " may happiness, peace and prosperity be yours in abundance."

As prince Ch'un advanced to the steps of the throne and began to ascend them, the emperor rose from the throne and took the symbol from the prince's hands. The prince then bowed and retired, and the emperor resumed his seat. No words were spoken on either side.

What this little ceremony signified was that as prince Ch'un was the emperor's father, it was impossible for him to kneel, because Chinese principles of filial piety forbade a son to assume a position of superiority over his own father. On the other hand the prince was never addressed by the emperor as " father " but as *wang yeh*—" your imperial highness." This was because the emperor, when nominated as heir-apparent to the throne, had become the adopted son and heir of his uncle Tê Tsung (the emperor Kuang-Hsü). The relationship between prince Ch'un and the emperor had then technically ceased to be that of father and son. Prince Ch'un's present heir is not his eldest son, the emperor, but his second son P'u Chieh, and it is the latter who will in the ordinary course of events succeed to the princedom. Nevertheless neither in public nor in private was it possible to ignore the fact that prince Ch'un was indeed the emperor's own father, hence the prince enjoyed exceptional privileges and was the only male member of the imperial family who did not kneel to the emperor. Several women, however, shared the same privilege, namely the four imperial dowager-consorts (because they were the widows of the emperor's two predecessors on the throne) and his own mother, the princess Ch'un.[4]

Prince Ch'un having paid his respects to the emperor, it was the turn of the other princes, who were standing in rows on the upper terrace outside the throne-hall, to do so. The grand marshal gave his word of command and the silent and obedient princes went down on their knees and three times in succession rested their hands on the ground and touched it with their heads. They rose to their feet, and another word of command sent them down again, when they repeated the triple obeisance ; and finally it was repeated once more.

Such is the triple-*kotow*, thrice repeated, so that the head touches the ground nine times. Then rang out the words *Hsieh Ên*—" offer thanks for the imperial bounty "—which necessitated an immediate repetition of the obeisance. The first ninefold *kotow* was the princes' New Year or birthday greeting to their sovereign—a greeting without a word spoken ; the second was in recognition of and gratitude for the gifts (of money or articles of porcelain or jade) which it was customary for the emperor to bestow upon the princes and high mandarins on each of the great annual festivals. These presents had already been distributed to their recipients on the day before the ceremony.

The princes having done their duty, next came the turn of the imperial tutors, the great officers of the household, and of officials whose rank was not below the second of the nine grades. Their obeisances were identical with that of the princes. Before going down on their knees they moved in a body slowly up the causeway with " eyes front." This slow movement towards the throne was an essential and impressive part of the ceremony.

Among those who participated were men who had attained high office under the monarchy but had declined to accept employment under the republic. Some of them travelled from distant provinces at least once a year to have the honour of paying their respects to the sovereign to whom they were still loyal. They wore the costume of the rank they had held under the empire—a costume which, together with the old nine-grade " mandarin " system, had been abolished by a republic careless of the beauty which it was sacrificing to their new god of modernisation.

" For a little while," as a thoughtful writer on Chinese affairs has said, " these men who call themselves republicans may be content to see earth's most beautiful song without words, the Temple of Heaven, abandoned to sordid uses or neglect ; they may see fit to wear frock-coats and top hats, instead of the most dignified and decorative garments ever devised by man ; but surely, before long, they—or others in their place—will be compelled to restore the ancient faith, the ancient ways."[5]

In view of these remarks, with which I am in heartfelt sympathy, it is a dreadful thing to have to confess that I myself was one of the black blots on the harmonious colouring of the great annual ceremonies of the Palace of Cloudless Heaven. The Chinese and Manchus were of course in their splendid official costumes. As the two great ceremonies of New Year's day and the emperor's birthday both took place in the cold weather, the mandarins wore their winter dress. Those who had been granted the right to wear the court sable cloak, with the sable-fronted hat that went with it, naturally did so. I had not been an imperial tutor very long before that honour was conferred upon myself. Had I worn the cloak at a court function, however, I could hardly have done otherwise than join my colleagues in the performance of the *kotow*. Some of my European friends (perhaps thinking of the poem which tells us how an English soldier preferred to die rather than carry out this rite) have been horrified to hear me say that if I felt assured that I could *kotow* as gracefully as my palace colleagues could do, I should have had no objection whatever to performing this act of obeisance, which used to be customary, on certain occasions, among all ranks of the Chinese people and was in no sense regarded by them as a humiliation. But to *kotow* with the ease and grace which seemed to come naturally to the Chinese and Manchus would be almost an impossibility for the average untrained European, even if he were to discard his own utterly unsuitable garments and adopt the loose flowing raiment of the Chinese. I was therefore glad to find that even after I had been invested with the sable cloak and had acquired the right of wearing the gorgeous embroidered garments of a mandarin of the highest rank, I was not expected to join my fellow-tutors and other court-officials in the performance of the *kotow*.[6] It was also satisfactory to know that I was not the only black blot on the gorgeous colouring of the court-ceremonial, for there was another in the person of the representative of the president of the republic. He and I were the only two persons who attended the ceremony in European morning coats.

Fortunately the two blots were not conspicuous enough to mar the proceedings very seriously ; for we remained at the side of the quadrangle, apart from the other participators in the function, until the sable-robed princes and mandarins had completed their part of the ceremony, and we were then summoned, separately, into the throne-hall itself, where the mode of salutation expected of us was merely to bow three times. In my own case, as I had on each occasion been a recipient of the imperial bounty in the shape of gifts, the three bows were repeated. While I bowed, the emperor sat motionless upon his throne. Etiquette required that he should not speak or smile or move hand or head in acknowledgment of the homage of his courtiers. The salutation of his own father was the only one to which the emperor could make any kind of response.

Besides the two black blots there were a few grey ones too, for the ceremonies were always attended not only by the president's official representative but also by about half a dozen uniformed officers of high military rank who though servants of the republic were ready and anxious to show their respect for their former sovereign. They also were admitted, as a special courtesy, into the interior of the throne-hall, and perhaps it was fortunate that this was so, for their sorry imitations of Western military uniforms would not have harmonised well with sable cloaks and silk embroideries. Their uniforms would also have marred the ceremony from the point of view of the ancient traditions, for the emperor of China was one of the few great potentates in the world in whose court the trappings of military rank had to be discarded, and who never, when seated on his throne, wore the garb of a warrior or carried a sword. Anything that tended to the glorification of war was incompatible with the Chinese theory of kingship and would have been utterly inconsistent with the principles that lay behind the music and ceremonial of the imperial court.[7]

While the high mandarins and officials on the marble terraces of the great quadrangle were doing obeisance in front of the screened throne, the crowd of lesser officials and others in the rectangular space to the south of the gateway did obeisance simultaneously and in the same manner. The words of command were called out to them by heralds who stood at the gate, for they were too far away to see or hear what was going on in the quadrangle above them. This crowd included all the subordinate members of the palace staff. In former days it had included great numbers of officials below the second rank.

When the grand marshal had declared the proceedings at an end, the musicians struck their instruments for the last time and the sounds they gave forth were an announcement that his majesty was descending from the throne. The withdrawal of the canopy was the sign that he had left the throne-hall.

As soon as he reached his own palace of " the Nurture of the Mind " he made haste to get rid of all the outward symbols of royalty, and received those members of the imperial family and others who had been invited to visit him informally. An elaborate banquet often followed, but it was held in the emperor's own quarters or in one of the pavilions of the imperial garden, and not in the throne-hall itself.

In former times, however, the Palace of Cloudless Heaven had been the scene of many gorgeous feasts, some of which are famous in court-annals. On several occasions the representatives of vassal states were royally entertained here. In 1713 the great emperor Shêng Tsu (K'ang-Hsi) gave in this throne-hall a great banquet to celebrate his sixtieth birthday. His guests were more than nineteen hundred old men, all chosen from the ranks of the common people. In imitation of this precedent, the emperor Kao Tsung (Ch'ien-Lung) on the occasion of his jubilee (the fiftieth anniversary of his succession) gave a similar banquet to almost four thousand old men, each of whom also received an imperial present of a jade-topped *ju-i*. This took place in 1785.

Until the year 1924 I was the only foreigner privileged to witness and to participate in the great ceremonies of the " twilight " period. The imperial household department was strongly opposed to the admission of strangers—foreign or Chinese—into the Forbidden City, and its opposition was intensified on the occasions of the great ceremonials of New Year's day and the imperial birthday. The emperor himself, however, had no objection to the admission of strangers—indeed it gave him pleasure to meet them—and after his marriage, which took place at the end of 1922, when he was almost seventeen, he was able to assert himself in a way that had previously been impossible. During 1923 and 1924 foreigners introduced by myself were admitted to the Forbidden City on many occasions, but it was not without
Oc

difficulty that even the emperor was able to break the existing rules and accede to my request to be allowed to invite a few " ocean-men " to witness the New Year ceremonial which took place on February 5th, 1924. It was fortunate that on this occasion I was successful, for it turned out to be the last occasion on which the ceremony was performed. Before another year had passed, the emperor had been driven out of the Forbidden City, the life of the Manchu court had come to an end, and twilight had darkened into night.

One of my guests on that memorable occasion was the well-known correspondent of the *Daily Telegraph*—the late Perceval Landon. His long and graphic account of the ceremony was telegraphed to his newspaper and appeared in its issue of the following day. One of his remarks is worthy of quotation, because of his prophetic words concerning the evil days to come.

The ceremony, he says, had been curiously impressive, not only on account of its outward splendour and " the complete silence except for the wailing music," but also because " in these turbulent days of chaos the yellow silken cord which republican China has deliberately retained in order to bind together her present and her past, *may in some dark week be suddenly and irrevocably frayed and torn*. More than all, perhaps, the scene was poignant as the last echo of the pomp and panoply of the most gorgeous of all human courts."[8]

The dark week came, as we shall see, exactly nine months later, and the silken cord was suddenly frayed and torn.

CHAPTER XIV

The Imperial Household Department
(Nei Wu Fu)

SOMETHING HAS BEEN SAID in the foregoing chapters about the Forbidden City as it was when I first entered it in 1919 and for several years thereafter. This chapter will deal with the evil results of the revolutionary compromise arrived at between the throne and the republic. That compromise, it will be remembered, deprived the emperor of all political power but left him with his empty title and with the enormously expensive and barren privilege of maintaining an unnecessary and otiose court. The monarchy was overthrown ; but the costly and corrupt system which had been one of the main causes of its overthrow was left intact.

Like most foreigners and many Chinese I had formerly assumed that the dynasty collapsed through the incompetence, ignorance and avarice of the imperial princes, through the blunders and crimes of the empress-dowager or those in whom she foolishly placed her confidence, through the staggering blows inflicted upon it by Eastern and Western " barbarians," through the enervating results of the vices and luxurious excesses common in oriental courts, through the inrush of Western democratic ideals and their devastating effect on the unprepared mind of " Young China," through the hatred of the Chinese for a " foreign " dynasty, and through the growing conviction among them that the " alien race " by which they had been ruled for nearly three hundred years had " exhausted the mandate of heaven."

The conclusion I came to after I had had opportunities of observing the imperial system of the post-revolution era from within, was that although most of these things may have helped —some of them certainly helped—in varying degrees to bring the monarchy to its doom, the most serious factor of all had been the gradual tightening of the stranglehold of the imperial

household department or *Nei Wu Fu*, which I have already
likened to a vampire draining the life-blood of the dynasty.[1]
Very little has been said about this powerful body by Western
writers on the court-life of imperial China, presumably because
they did not possess the inside knowledge that would have compelled them to give it their attention. The evils of the eunuch-
system were, of course, notorious, and were often denounced by
both foreigners and Chinese. It was inadequately realised, however, that the eunuch system was itself a part of the much
greater system of the Nei Wu Fu, and not the part that was the
most powerful or the most dangerous. The eunuchs were, in
practice, servants of the Nei Wu Fu rather than servants of the
emperor, and they have received far more blame for the corruptions of the court than they really deserved. The abolition
of the eunuch-system was, indeed, a thing greatly to be desired.
It was one of the objects which I tried from the beginning of my
service in the court to achieve. What I did not understand at
first, though I came to see it later, was that the dismissal of the
eunuchs without the abolition or drastic reformation of the
whole system of which they had formed a part, would not
be sufficient to purge the court of the poisons that menaced
its life and endangered the welfare of the emperor and his
family.

The Nei Wu Fu supported the reactionaries against the
reformers in 1898, it acquiesced with complacency—indeed with
entire satisfaction—in the virtual dethronement of Kuang-Hsü,
it applauded the action of the old empress-dowager in aligning
the court with the Boxers, and finally, at the time of the revolution, bestowed its benediction on the Articles of Favourable
Treatment. It approved of those Articles—there is reason to
believe that it inspired them and helped to draw them up—not
because they would be advantageous to the true interests of the
emperor but because they were the best obtainable guarantee of
its own continued existence and the Magna Carta of its own
privileges.

The question will be asked, how was it that the Nei Wu Fu
came to dominate the imperial court to so disastrous an extent ?
How was it able to acquire such immense strength that it stood
firm in a tempest which brought the monarchy itself crashing to

the ground ? Does not its very success in doing so prove that the monarchy was rotten ?

At first sight, indeed, it might appear that only culpable slackness, incompetence or indifference on the part of former emperors could account for the court having passed into the firm grip of its own servants—men who in addressing the throne described themselves with abject humility as *nu-ts'ai*—slaves. But such would not be an adequate explanation. Perhaps the matter may become clearer if something is said about the manner in which the financial and other material affairs of the individual princes of the imperial clan were administered. Each of the princes had his own establishment in which he lived in semi-regal state with the various members of his family and a swarm of retainers. Most of the princes possessed, or had once possessed, large private estates. Some owned valuable real property in Peking, others had country properties from which they drew, or were supposed to draw, substantial incomes. Those who held government posts or court-appointments also received salaries and perquisites.

Now the fly in the ointment was that very few, if any, of the Manchu princes knew the extent of their own property or even where it was situated. They had no exact notion of their own incomes. The affairs of each were in the hands of a *kuan-shih-ti* —a major-domo or steward—who employed his own staff, had complete control over his lord's financial transactions, and was the only person who had any accurate knowledge of his income and expenditure. If the *kuan-shih-ti* were an honest man—and no doubt many of them were honest according to their lights— and if he also happened to be a good man of business—though it was rarely if ever that he owed his position to his business acumen—the prince's affairs might be maintained in a flourishing condition, especially if occasional deficits in the family budget were made good by official perquisites or imperial gifts. But even among " honest " men the pernicious " squeeze " system was rampant, and the venerable Chinese custom which obliges every prosperous office-holder to provide " rice-bowls " for his less affluent relations was responsible for a ruinous system under which ten men drew twenty men's salaries for doing the work of one.

Fortunately it was not to the steward's interest that his
" master " should be reduced to penury. He had, in fact, a
vested interest in his lord's maintenance in a condition of at
least apparent opulence. Many of the princes suspected they
were being robbed, but felt helpless because they knew that if
they dismissed their stewards they might find themselves
floundering in a morass of debt. As a rule a prince made no complaint so long as his steward provided him with the cash that he
might need at any particular moment and acted as a buffer
between himself and his creditors. The steward, for his part,
made it a point of honour—" face " would perhaps be a better
word—never to fail his lord in the hour of financial need. The
money required was always forthcoming, and the prince neither
asked nor expected to be told where it came from.

The revolution naturally hastened the impoverishment of the
Manchu princes, and some of them, when I came to know them
in 1919, had long ceased to be rich men. Those who had depended
—or whose stewards had depended for them—on constant sup-
plies of money from official sources were reduced to a deplor-
able condition, and lived partly on the proceeds of the secret sale
of the treasures of art which had been bestowed upon them or
their ancestors by the court. Considerations of " face " made it
impossible for them to hold public auctions of their treasures.
The prices which they obtained were in most cases ridiculously
low, and as such transactions were wholly in the hands of their
stewards their own share of the proceeds was precisely what
their stewards chose to let them have.[2]

To visit some of these princes in their palatial homes—or
homes that had once been palatial—was a saddening experience.
Weeds grew in the great courtyards, roofs leaked, stables were
empty, and in many cases the kitchens were not too well provided with food. One such prince used to give one or two annual
dinner-parties (at which I was a guest on several occasions) to
celebrate the flowering of his famous hawthorn tree. We sat in
an open pavilion in the gardens, and as we manipulated our
chopsticks and sipped our hot wine, a light breeze would sometimes waft the hawthorn-blossom down to our table. Alas, those
delightful hawthorn-dinners were almost the only occasions on
which this prince—a descendant of the great Ch'ien-Lung in the

fifth generation—could exercise his talents as one of the most charming of hosts. He had become a very poor man. He died during my stay in Peking, his rambling *fu* has passed into alien hands, and only last year I heard that the hawthorn tree is dead.

I must mention the case of another prince because as far as my knowledge goes it was unique. He will not, I think, take offence at my mention of his name. He was prince Tsai T'ao, a brother of the late emperor Kuang-Hsü and therefore an uncle of Hsüan-T'ung. He was devoted to horses—he presented me with one which was famous in Manchu stables for its long white tail—and besides being an excellent horseman he was a keen motorist with a predilection for German cars,[3] an intelligent and active man who had seen something of foreign countries, a polished man of the world. These were admirable qualities, but he possessed another even more remarkable. He was the only member of the imperial family who knew how to conduct his own affairs and who actually did so. I had been told of this phenomenon but I perceived it for myself when I accompanied him and his eldest son (a boy of eleven) on a visit to his family burial-ground near the hot-springs of T'ang-shan, a few miles north of Peking. He was having extensive repairs carried out at the sacrificial and other halls connected with the mausoleum, and in the park-like enclosure were a large number of workmen with their bricks and timber. As we dismounted at the gates, the custodians of the mausoleum knelt and handed him a bundle of papers. These he deposited on a table and proceeded with his son to do obeisance before the family tombs. This essential duty accomplished, he returned to the papers and spent the next hour in a careful scrutiny of them, making numerous annotations and calculations and closely questioning the contractor on the subject of prices and materials. It was clear enough that this member of the imperial family did not allow his business affairs to pass wholly under the control of his steward.

Of another prince, who shall be nameless, I have a different tale to tell. Once among the wealthiest men in China, he is now poor. He lives in Tientsin, because in these days of alarms and excursions he is afraid to occupy his spacious *fu* in Peking. His steward lives there, however, and when the prince is in need of money he sends word to the steward to raise the required amount by selling some of the jade, porcelain, jewellery, pictures or other valuables (mostly gifts from the imperial collections) which still remain in his *k‘u*—the family treasury. The steward takes out as much as he chooses, disposes of the articles in any way that seems good to himself, and sends to Tientsin as much or as little money as he thinks fit. The fact that the *k‘u* in question has recently been robbed by republican soldiers acting under the orders or with the connivance of a very prominent military personage will doubtless hasten the day when the *k‘u* can be adapted to other uses than the storage of treasure.

Now the system under which the Forbidden City was controlled was in principle identical with the system existing in the *fu* of each of the Manchu princes. The officers of the Nei Wu Fu were to the imperial household what the *kuan-shih-ti* or steward was to the ordinary Manchu prince. Even the eunuch-system of the Forbidden City was reproduced in miniature in the princely mansions ; for by a standing regulation of the imperial clan each of the princes possessed the privilege (for such it was accounted) of maintaining a small corps of eunuchs, the number allowed in each case being regulated by the prince's rank.

This being so, it seems probable that if we can discover a reason, other than mere negligence and incompetence, for the almost invariable failure of the Manchu princes to protect their own material interests and to look after their own property, we shall have a clue to the cause that led to the concentration of power in the hands of the Nei Wu Fu, with all its disastrous consequences.

Such a reason can, I think, be found in a strange and generally overlooked defect in the Chinese scheme of education. In the old-fashioned school and state-examination system of China, all the stress was laid on classical learning. To quote the words of an authority on Chinese life and culture, " except with those who, within recent years, have come under the influence of Western education, *arithmetic forms no part of a schoolboy's work.*" He adds that a Chinese " is content to get through life with as scanty a ' knowledge of addition, subtraction, multiplication, and division as would serve an English youngster of six or eight years of age.' "[4]

Now it is true that arithmetic is, or was, almost wholly neglected in the schools, yet every foreign visitor to China knows how extraordinarily skilful the Chinese are in the use of their calculating-frame, the *suan-p'an* or abacus. It is obviously absurd to say of the Chinese book-keepers and accountants who manipulate that little instrument with a speed and dexterity which astonish foreign observers, that they have no better knowledge of addition, subtraction, multiplication and division than an English child of six. The point is, however, that the skilful use of the abacus is an art which is rarely acquired except by those who intend to follow a commercial career. It is handled clumsily, if at all, by scholars who have followed the old traditions. Nor are they ashamed of their lack of skill in this respect. On the contrary they are rather proud of it, just as a Chinese gentleman used to be proud of his long nails which were a visible proof that he belonged to the *literati* and was not under the necessity of using his hands except for the purpose of manipulating his chopsticks or practising the art of calligraphy.

It may be that the abacus became the universal instrument in China for carrying out numerical calculations owing to the comparative clumsiness of the Chinese written system of arithmetical notation. If so, it is perhaps the abacus which is itself responsible for the low place taken by arithmetic in the educational curriculum; because in spite of the remarkable speed and accuracy with which a Chinese shopkeeper will use it in making up his accounts, the fact remains that the manipulation of the abacus has what Dr. H. A. Giles calls " the signal disadvantage of not being able to work backwards in search of a fault, each step disappearing as the work proceeds."[5]

Whether it is the abacus that is to be blamed or not, it is a fact that arithmetic has been regarded by the Chinese mandarin-class with almost supercilious contempt.; and along with this contempt, or in consequence of it, we find a strong tendency in that class to regard mere money-matters as beneath the notice of a scholar and a gentleman.[6] Is it fanciful to suggest that the " signal disadvantage " which Dr. Giles points to as inherent in the abacus has extended from the working of that useful instrument to many of the other activities of the Chinese people ? There is much to lead us to suspect that they are often unable or unwilling to " work backwards in search of a fault." They seem to be only too willing to acquiesce in " each step disappearing as the work proceeds."

However this may be, there seems to be some justification for the hypothesis that the Chinese and Manchu mandarin-class, from the imperial princes downwards, allowed their material interests to pass into the hands of the steward-class mainly because they would not or could not learn how to make simple arithmetical calculations, and therefore could not manage their own finances. This does not mean that they cared nothing about money : far from it. It means that having got it they did not know how to keep it or how to regulate their expenditure in accordance with their incomes. Nor is there anything surprising about this if, to repeat the words of a writer just quoted, they had as much knowledge of arithmetic as would serve a European child of six.

I have said that the system in vogue in the mansions of the Manchu princes was in principle the same as that which existed in the Forbidden City. But emphasis must be laid on two important differences. In the first place, the stewards of the princes were not of mandarin-rank and were therefore not likely to be tainted by the almost snobbish contempt of the mandarin-class for mere book-keeping ; whereas the stewards of the imperial household—that is to say the high officials of the Nei Wu Fu— were not only of mandarin rank but were among the highest mandarins in the land. The inevitable result was that the Nei Wu Fu was not only corrupt but incompetent. The heads of this great department were either unable or unwilling to descend to the sordid details of account-keeping and the financial side of estate-management. That part of their duties was delegated to a host of subordinates, who, whether they were individually honest or not, all belonged to a gigantic system of organised corruption.

The other great difference between the princely and the imperial systems was that a steward's sphere of action was limited to a single family, while the Nei Wu Fu could not be prevented from extending its activities to affairs of state. It was not merely an office entrusted with the management of the property of the Throne, it was also the organ through which the

Throne transacted business with the great departments of state. Had it been merely the office that looked after the domestic affairs of the sovereign and regulated the routine of his court within the limits of the imperial palaces, its activities—however evil they might sometimes be—could hardly have affected the stability of the Throne as the apex of the political structure. Unfortunately its power and influence were not so confined ; they extended to the great world of politics and contributed to the notorious corruption of Chinese public life. The Nei Wu Fu, though not one of the six Boards (or Ministries as we should call them) was itself, in fact, one of the great departments of state, and its intimate relationship with the sovereign endowed it with an influence and prestige which no other department could hope to acquire. The meetings of the Grand Council of State— the emperor's privy council—took place under its auspices, and the comptroller himself was often a member of that Council. In any case he ranked with the most exalted officials in the empire. Shih Hsü, who was comptroller at the time of the revolution and retained his position till his death early in 1922, was also a Grand Councillor, and his principal subordinates were mandarins of the first or second grade with the title of *ta-ch'ên*— minister of state.

While emphasising the almost incredible incompetence and gross corruption which disfigured the Nei Wu Fu and proved so disastrous both to the dynasty and to China, I should like to draw a clear distinction between the system and the men whom fortune—good or bad—placed at its head.

These men were not all scoundrels—perhaps very few if any of them were that. Some—including those whom I will mention by name—were excellent and worthy people when one met them in private life. The Nei Wu Fu was thoroughly corrupt long before any of them had had anything to do with it ; they may not have improved matters, but I am not sure that they can fairly be held morally responsible for making them worse.

" Let him who would be pure, from courts retire."

One of the wisest of men, Montaigne, quoted this line from Lucan, and also cited Plato as witness to the truth that " the man who escapes with clean hands from the management of the world's affairs, escapes by a miracle."[7]

If no miracle was worked on behalf of my friends of the Nei Wu Fu, the blame would appear to rest not with them but with the powers that work miracles. Where they were very gravely at fault was in failing to recognise that the only excuse for their existence as a department was loyal and useful service. It was not sufficient for them to be their sovereign's very obedient " slaves " in a formal or conventional sense ; it was necessary that they should render him such service that he would be the poorer—morally, physically and materially—if they disappeared. So far from doing this, they so conducted themselves both before and after the revolution as to make it clear that they regarded the Nei Wu Fu as an institution in which they had vested interests and as an end in itself. It was not the *raison d'être* of the Nei Wu Fu to serve the emperor ; rather it was his *raison d'être* to provide the Nei Wu Fu with an excuse for continuing to exist.[8]

All the officers of the department were Manchus. They were so numerous, and belonged to so many different grades, that there were many whom I never learned to know even by sight. Moreover a large number of them were not employed within the Forbidden City but at the imperial mausolea, the Summer Palace, and in various other places where the imperial family possessed landed property. Their control did not extend to the vast Manchurian estates, for those properties were looked after by a separate Nei Wu Fu with headquarters at Mukden. This body, as far as I could ascertain, was at least as corrupt as its " opposite number " in the Forbidden City, but with its doings I am not concerned in these pages.

At the head of the Peking Nei Wu Fu was the comptroller—*Tsung Kuan Nei Wu Fu Ta-ch'ên*. Shih-Hsü, who held this exalted position in 1919, had held a variety of important posts in pre-revolution times, including those of director of the imperial armoury, vice-president of the Board of Works, president of the Boards of Ceremonies and Civil Office, a Grand Councillor, Secretary of the Grand Council of State, and a member of the special department of historiography appointed to compile the history of the Manchu dynasty. In virtue of his membership of the Grand Council he was always addressed at court, even after the council had ceased to exist, as *chung-t'ang*, the usual designation of Grand Councillors. Shortly before the revolution be became a *t'ai pao* or " Senior Guardian of the heir-apparent."

Shih-Hsü was undoubtedly a man of ability and force of character. Though conniving at the financial irregularities of his subordinates (perhaps because he knew that without them the whole system would collapse) it was generally believed that he was personally incorrupt. Old-fashioned and thoroughly conservative in his outlook, he was the stout opponent of reform in his own or any other department, yet his dignified appearance and manners, and the tactful tolerance with which he allowed even an overseas barbarian like myself to express views that he abhorred, gave the impression that he was more liberal-minded than he really was.

He was one of the high officials who joined Yüan Shih-k'ai in persuading the court to abdicate its functions in return for the guarantees contained in the Articles of Favourable Treatment. In other words he consented to the destruction of the imperial power in return for the maintenance of the Nei Wu Fu *in statu quo*. When he died, in February, 1922, the president of the republic sent a representative to his funeral, and an official statement was given to the Chinese press that the action of the president was prompted by the knowledge that " the late comptroller had acted meritoriously in persuading Lung-Yü, the empress-dowager, to agree to the abdication of the emperor and the establishment of the republic."

Under pressure from several quarters, the strongest being from the Nei Wu Fu itself, the young emperor conferred a posthumous title (*Wên Tuan*—" Scholarly and Upright ") and other honours on the late Shih-Hsü, sent prince Tsai-Ying to take part in the mourning ceremonies, and gave eight thousand dollars towards funeral expenses.

Next in authority to Shih-Hsü as a minister of the household was Shao-Ying. In 1905 this Manchu was appointed a member of the Commission which was to go abroad to study constitutional systems. Just as they were about to leave Peking a bomb was thrown among them and the chairman (duke Tsai-Tsê) and Shao-Ying were both wounded. This event, which caused a great sensation in China and considerable alarm in court-circles, took place on September 24th, 1905. The departure of the Commission was postponed, and when it actually set out Shao-Ying was no longer one of its members. Shortly afterwards he became vice-president of the Board of Finance.

He was a kind-hearted and well-meaning man but timid and unenterprising. He pretended to be interested in reform yet always avoided action that might make him unpopular with his colleagues or subordinates. He cultivated friendly relations with a few foreigners in Peking mainly in order that he might call upon them to give him protection in times of danger. Close to his own house near the east gate of Peking he owned another for which he was always careful to find European tenants who might be a ready help to him in the hour of need. Rent was a secondary consideration. He would have lent it to a European for nothing rather than rent it to Chinese tenants. Some years after I first knew him this house happened to remain untenanted for a considerable time because its distance from the Legation Quarter made it unacceptable to European families in search of houses. When I succeeded in persuading an English friend of mine to rent it from him—it happened to be one of the most delightful houses in Peking, with a typical Chinese garden—he overflowed with gratitude.

Shao-Ying succeeded Shih-Hsü as comptroller of the household. After the catastrophe of November, 1924, to be described later, he followed many well-known examples in developing a convenient sickness which necessitated a prolonged residence in the German hospital in the Legation Quarter. A couple of years later his feigned sickness became a real one, and mortal.

Ch'i-Ling, next in authority to Shao-Ying, was connected by marriage with the family of the emperor's mother, the princess Ch'un. He had been a sub-chancellor of the Grand Secretariat, with the rank of vice-president of the Board of Ceremonies. He was alert and intelligent, and at first I had great hopes of him as one through whom a policy of reform and retrenchment in the Forbidden City might be carried out. But his interest in reform, such as it was, showed itself in words only, never in action.[9]

Pao-Hsi did not become a minister of the Nei Wu Fu till 1923. He had been Literary Chancellor of Shansi and ranked as a vice-president of one of the Boards. Shortly before the death of

Kuang-Hsü he became vice-president of the Board of Education.
He was connected by marriage with the families of prince
Ch'ing and of a former governor of Shantung—Sun Pao-ch'i. He
is now a member of the council of the new State of Manchuria.

Jung-Yüan, subsequently known as duke Jung, also became
a minister of the household in 1923, and owed his appointment
to the fact that he was father of the young empress. His addition
to the staff produced no good results.

The only other member of the Nei Wu Fu whom I will mention by name is T'ung Chi-hsü. His position in the department
was only a minor one, but his honesty and real loyalty to the
emperor make him deserving of special notice. He did not receive
his appointment till early in 1924, though I had known him since
my arrival in 1919. He belonged to an old Manchu or " bannerman " family long resident in the province of Fuhkien and was
recommended for office by his fellow-provincial the imperial
tutor Ch'ên Pao-shên. He is one of those who in 1931 followed
their imperial master to Manchuria.

I have said that the officers of the household were all Manchus,
and this was true up to the year 1923. This generalisation does
not, however, apply to one very large and important body of
persons employed by the Nei Wu Fu—the court-eunuchs. During the later decades of the dynasty, and especially in the days
of the empresses-dowager Tzǔ-Hsi and Lung-Yü, the eunuchs—
or rather a very small group of *yü-ch'ien t'ai-chien* or " eunuchs
of the Presence "—wielded enormous power. On account of their
direct relationship with, and attendance on, the emperor and his
consorts they were often, in practice, independent of the Nei
Wu Fu and carried on their own financial and other dealings
without reference to that body. Nevertheless they were in theory
subject to its jurisdiction and discipline. Western readers of
books on the court-life of the " Venerable Buddha " may never
have heard of the Nei Wu Fu, but they have all read of the
notorious eunuch Li Lien-ying ; and his successor under Lung-
Yü, though less well-known to foreigners, was at least as powerful and corrupt as Li.

Some Western writers have made the serious mistake of supposing that the eunuchs were Manchus. One of them repeats a
baseless story of how some of the empress-dowager's eunuchs

once played a spiteful trick on the great Li Hung-chang, and she explains their conduct by the fact that they hated him " as only Manchus can hate a Chinese."[10] The fact is that the dynastic house-law strictly forbade the employment of Manchu eunuchs. All the eunuchs of the palace were Chinese, and most of them came from one district on the borders of Chihli and Shantung.

We have seen that the Articles of Favourable Treatment contained a clause to the effect that although " all the persons of various grades hitherto employed in the Palace " might be retained, no more eunuchs were to be added to the staff. This proviso was strongly opposed by the Nei Wu Fu and by the Lung Yü empress-dowager, but it was a point on which they were obliged to give way. Up to 1923 there were still more than a thousand eunuchs employed in the Forbidden City. What happened to them in that year will be narrated in another chapter.

A few words should be added to elucidate what has been said concerning the financial iniquities of the Nei Wu Fu.

Practices which we with our different standards cannot regard as other than corrupt are not always so regarded in China. All European residents in that country have tales to tell of their experiences of the notorious system of " squeeze," and most of them will agree that as the eradication of the evil is impracticable, the only hopeful course to be adopted by those who aim at a quiet life is to abstain from interference unless it becomes obvious that the partition between " squeeze " and sheer robbery is in danger of breaking down. They would probably also admit that what may be tolerated as more or less " legitimate squeeze " in one domestic establishment may be " illegitimate " in a less affluent household.

On this principle it would have been no easy task, in pre-revolutionary days, to determine what " squeezes " might be regarded as legitimate in the Manchu Court. There was no budgetary limit to its revenues, and there were abundant sources of income which were capable of almost indefinite expansion. But this was very far from being true of the greatly diminished and less affluent court that survived the abdication and passed into what I have called its period of twilight. Even if the stipulated annual subsidy from the republican government had been paid in full—which it never was—the imperial revenues would have been inadequate to meet the insatiable demands of a huge staff who possessed what they regarded as a vested interest in a colossal squeeze-system inherited from the days of inexhaustible wealth.

The authors of that entertaining work *Annals and Memoirs of the Court of Peking*, describing the conditions of pre-revolutionary days, observe that the palace " squeezes " helped to make posts in the imperial household " amongst the most coveted in the Empire," and they add that the income of a senior officer of the household " was estimated at over a million taels "—worth at that time about £200,000 a year. They also draw attention to the important fact that any attempt to cut down the perquisites of these posts " naturally made the emperor unpopular with the imperial clansmen, many of whom were directly or indirectly beneficiaries in these Palace squeezes."[11] This is true, and it may explain why the Articles of Favourable Treatment, which enabled the Nei Wu Fu to survive the dynastic *débâcle*, were so readily assented to not only by the imperial household but also by all but two of the imperial princes.

All these people showed an astonishing blindness to the fact that the palace organisation with its financial obliquities had been one of the main causes of the lowering of the prestige of the Throne and the gradual spread of apathy and hopelessness among many of its loyal supporters. Long before the revolution broke out, people were asking how the emperor could expect his people to look up to him for guidance in the affairs of life if he himself proved incapable of regulating the affairs of his own household and of curbing the malpractices of his own servants. They recalled the teachings of one of the great Confucian sages, and wondered why those teachings were ignored by their sovereign : " *so wei chih kuo pi hsien ch'i ch'i chia . . . ch'i ch'i chia jên erh hou k'o i chiao kuo jên* "—" the proper regulation of the household must precede the right government of the State. . . . Only when the ruler has shown himself capable of ordering rightly his own household is he competent to be the teacher of his people."[12]

Pc

Other courts have had, and must have, household departments, and no doubt many of them have been as corrupt and
extravagant as that of China. It appears, for example, that the
caliph Harun Al Rashid's court was in the grip of a body very
similar in important respects to that of the Forbidden City in
China.[13] But the caliph's court at least had the merit of providing
a setting for *The Arabian Nights*, which perhaps justified expenditure on a scale of some magnificence. Similar excuses might
be made for the brilliant if ruinous splendours of the Chinese
court in the golden days of Ming Huang, the imperial artist and
musician, the patron of poets, painters and players, the adoring
lover of his evil genius, the fatally beautiful Yang Kuei-fei. But
more than a thousand years have passed since those golden days
came to a pitiful close on the blood-stained slopes of Ma-wei ;
and even in the dazzling days of the Sung dynasty there was no
more than a partial and fleeting revival of the glories of T'ang.
No credit is due to the Nei Wu Fu for any of the great political
and cultural achievements of the Manchu dynasty. That dynasty
gave China two at least of the greatest monarchs of Chinese
history, but the Nei Wu Fu contributed nothing to that greatness. On the contrary, it was largely answerable for the failure
of the dynasty to maintain the greatness of its early days. The
corrupt eunuchs of the Ming period had brought about the
decay and fall of an imperial house which had been powerful
enough to rid China of the world-conquering Mongols. The
eunuchs of the Manchu house, bad though their influence was,
especially in the days of the empress-dowagers T'zŭ-Hsi and
Lung-Yü, never attained under the Manchus the great political
power that their predecessors had wielded in the Ming period ;
but the powerful organisation to which they belonged—the Nei
Wu Fu—did more than any other single agency to wreck the
fortunes of the proud race of conquerors and administrators
that had emerged from the forests and mountains of Manchuria.
During the years that followed the revolutionary settlement of
1911, the Manchu court, still wholly dominated by that sinister
organisation, repeatedly put itself into a mortifying and ignoble
position by its grovelling appeals to the republican government
for the payment of instalments of its overdue subsidy. Unfortunately its appeals frequently found their way into the Chinese

press and were the subject of much cynical comment. In the *Pei-Ching Jih Pao* of October 1st, 1919, for example, appeared a paragraph stating that Shih-Hsü, comptroller of the imperial household, had begged the president of the republic to authorise the payment of $600,000, without which the household would be unable to meet its obligations. Similar requests were made three or four times every year, with varying results, and were nearly always reinforced by the remark that a payment on account was essential for *wei-ch'ih hsien chuang*—" the maintenance of existing conditions " in the Manchu court. At no time did it ever seem to occur to the comptroller and his staff to ask whether " the maintenance of existing conditions " was desirable in the true interests of the one person who was the theoretical *raison d'être* of those conditions. The phrase *wei-ch'ih hsien chuang* was one with which I became distressingly familiar during my residence at the Manchu court and which to my ears came to have a hateful sound. In conversation with the emperor I once made the remark that *wei-ch'ih hsien chuang*—" the maintenance of existing conditions "—might be adopted as a suitable inscription for the tomb of every deceased member of the Nei Wu Fu, but that however appropriate it might be to a dead past it was utterly unfit to be applied to a living present.

CHAPTER XV

The Dragon Unfledged

THE YEARS OF MY SERVICE in the Forbidden City may be regarded as having been divided into two periods. The first was from March, 1919, to November, 1922, and closed with the emperor's marriage. The second was from the latter date to that of his summary expulsion, in November, 1924, from the palace which had been his home since infancy.

The division is a convenient one, because it marks a transition in his mode of life. Up to the time of his wedding, which took place shortly before his seventeenth birthday, he was a minor and was not expected to act on his own initiative in any but trifling matters. After that event he was regarded as having come of age and although he was still very far from being a free agent, his right to be master of his own time and to regulate his life in his own way was not contested, provided that he did not gaze too longingly at the world that lay beyond the Forbidden City.

Throughout the earlier period he attended daily at the Yü-ch'ing Kung (" Palace of the Bringing-Forth of Blessings ") which had been the imperial study or schoolroom for many years. It was the private residence of the emperor Chia-Ch'ing (1796–1820) after he had been nominated heir-apparent, and it contains autograph scrolls by him. It had a gateway of its own which led into a small courtyard. In the courtyard, to the left of the gate, was a waiting-room for the exclusive use of the tutors. A staff of servants (known by the Manchu term *sula*) had the sole duty of waiting upon them and serving them with tea from ever-ready and inexhaustible sources. The main building faced eastwards, at right angles to the waiting room. Each tutor entered the Forbidden City by the Gate of Spiritual Valour, or, if more convenient to himself, by the Gate of Eastern or the Gate of Western Glory. Leaving his car or carriage outside the gate (I was the only one of the tutors who used a car in preference to a pony-carriage) he was carried through the gate in his official chair, acknowledging, as he went, the salute of the armed sentries. I was again alone among the tutors in occasionally exercising my alternative right to ride into the Forbidden City on horseback. On arrival at one of the inner gates—that known as the Ching-yün Mên—the tutor's chair was set down, or he dismounted from his horse, and the short remaining distance to the Yü-ch'ing palace was traversed on foot.

The tutor sat in the waiting-room, sipping tea, until the arrival of the emperor. He came in an enormous palanquin draped in yellow silk and carried by twelve or more bearers. As it entered the courtyard, etiquette forbade the tutor to go out and meet him. But he rose from his seat and stood in the waiting-room (though it was impossible for him to be seen by the emperor) until his majesty had entered the schoolroom. The tutor then resumed his seat until a loud cry of *chao* (a word denoting the imperial summons) uttered by a eunuch at the door of the main building, and repeated by one of the *sula*, announced that his majesty was ready to begin his studies.

The tutor immediately entered the schoolroom and bowed once in the direction of his pupil who was standing at the north side of a square table. Both then sat down simultaneously, the tutor's seat being at right angles to that of the emperor, who sat facing the south.[1]

When I first entered the palace the tutors' hours with their pupil were arranged thus. Ch'ên Pao-shên was the first to enter the palace every morning, and did so at the early hour of half-past five in summer and six in winter. This was in conformity with the ancient tradition of the imperial court, when audiences used to be held at dawn. At about half-past seven Ch'ên Pao-shên would take his departure, unless he wished to confer with one or other of his colleagues or to share with them the morning meal. It may be mentioned that meals were furnished for the tutors freely and without notice at any time they happened to want them. They were served in the tutors' waiting-room and came straight from the imperial kitchens. They consisted of very daintily served Chinese food of the best quality, from the hands of *chefs* who knew their business and incidentally made very comfortable incomes.

At about half-past eight the emperor would receive his Manchu

tutor, I-K'o-T'an ; and between ten and eleven the latter's place
was taken by Chu I-fan. At half-past one my own turn came, and
lasted as a rule about two hours.

Holidays were not very frequent, though towards the end of
the Yü-ch'ing period (which came to an end with the emperor's
marriage) unofficial holidays tended to increase in number.
Apart from a month's vacation in summer and about three weeks
at the time of the old (lunar) New Year, which included the date
of the emperor's birthday on the thirteenth of the first moon, the
only days on which the emperor did not receive his tutors in their
official capacity were the festivals of the fifth and eighth moons
and the anniversaries of the death of the previous sovereigns of
the dynasty. On the latter solemn occasions the emperor was
supposed to fast, but this, I discovered, did not really mean that
he went hungry to bed. It is probably needless to say that
Sundays and other Western holidays and festivals were not
recognised in any way.

During the first few weeks of my tutorship I was not allowed
to be alone with the emperor. There was always a solitary
eunuch in attendance ; and we were also joined either by one of
the Chinese tutors, usually Chu I-fan, or by one of the ministers
of the household, usually Ch'i-Ling.[2] The eunuch stood motionless against the wall ; the tutor or minister sat with us at the
table, facing north. The reason given for the presence of the
latter was that his majesty, never having spoken to a foreigner
before, might feel nervous or embarrassed. Of nervousness,
however, I detected no sign ; and when our companion showed
obvious signs of somnolence, which happened almost daily, the
emperor made no attempt to wake him up or to remind him that
his function was to keep a sleepless eye on the barbarian from
overseas whose innocent appearance might be the cloak of a
black heart.

Before the second month had elapsed the emperor was assumed
to have recovered from whatever nervousness or embarrassment
he felt at first in his foreign tutor's presence, and the Chinese
tutor or minister ceased to give us the pleasure of his company.
The eunuch, however, remained. As I discovered that no eunuch
was present during my colleagues' hours of attendance on his
majesty, it was clear that the Nei Wu Fu were still unprepared

to leave the Son of Heaven completely at the mercy of a member of that terrifying race of foreign devils who—according to well-authenticated accounts—were in the habit of eating the hearts and livers of children and making medicine of their eyes.

The eunuch stood in silence just inside the doorway. At the end of half an hour he made a noiseless exit, and another equally silent (and shoeless) eunuch took his place. This one was, in his turn, relieved by a third. The process was repeated every half hour.

It was not till the summer of my second year (1920) that my pupil and I were relieved of the constant presence of a eunuch. Before that time, however, I had come to the conclusion that the emperor would make more rapid progress with his English studies if he had a fellow-student, and the student I selected was one of his cousins, a boy about two years his junior, named P'u-Chia. This boy was the eldest son of one of the emperor's uncles, prince Tsai-T'ao. The appointment of young members of the imperial clan as *pan-tu* (literally " companion-readers ") in the imperial schoolroom was a well-recognised custom, and my suggestion caused no surprise. Nevertheless it created a small storm in a teacup because (unknown to myself at that time) considerable jealousy had long existed between prince Ch'un and prince Tsai-T'ao, and the former being the emperor's father, and also ex-regent, was annoyed at the suggestion that one of his own sons (who were of course the emperor's brothers) should be passed over in favour of a son of Tsai-T'ao. The trouble was quickly got over, however, by the appointment of two *pan-tu*— one, the son of Tsai-T'ao, as *pan-tu* in English studies, the other, second son of prince Ch'un and younger brother of the emperor, as *pan-tu* in Chinese studies.

There was already, indeed, a *pan-tu* in the emperor's Chinese studies in the person of a boy of fourteen named Yü-Ch'ung, a son of prince P'u-Lun. It will be remembered that P'u-Lun was the prince whose claim to the throne at the time of the death of the emperor Tê Tsung had been strongly advocated by Yüan Shih-k'ai.[3] Had Yüan been successful in his advocacy, this boy Yü-Ch'ung or his brother P'u-Tsun would doubtless have become heir-apparent, and if there had been no revolution he would have been emperor of China at the present day ; for his father P'u-Lun died several years ago.

P'u-Lun, as we have seen, either from gratitude to Yüan Shih-k'ai for trying to put him on the throne, or from other motives, had supported Yüan in his imperial ambitions and had been entrusted by the latter with the duty (which Yüan's death prevented him from carrying out) of obtaining possession of the imperial seals. After the death of Yüan, P'u-Lun was for some time in disgrace at court. Later on, however, he made his peace with the imperial family (the young emperor himself seems to have no trace of vindictiveness in his nature) and it was as a sign that he had been forgiven that the honour of becoming the emperor's fellow-student was conferred upon one of P'u-Lun's sons.[4]

The name of the emperor's brother, who also became a *pan-tu* or " companion-reader," was P'u-Chieh. The three youths who now shared this much-coveted privilege were P'u-Chieh, P'u-Chia and Yü-Ch'ung, P'u-Chia being the only *pan-tu* in English studies. In virtue of their position they had an official status at court, and the court-gazette which contained the announcement of their appointments also recorded the fact that the right of " riding on horseback in the Forbidden City " had been con-ferred upon them by imperial authority.

It should perhaps be explained that among both Manchus and Chinese there is a generally recognised practice whereby all the boys of a family or clan who belong to the same generation have one part of their personal names in common. Thus all the mem-bers of the imperial clan who belong to the emperor's generation share the name P'u. The emperor is P'u-Yi, his younger brother is P'u-Chieh, his cousin is P'u-Chia, and among numerous other living members of the clan of the same generation are P'u-Kuang, P'u-Ju, P'u Hsiu, and P'u-Wei. P'u-Lun, of course, belonged to this group.

It will be seen from this that to describe the emperor who bore the reign-title of Hsüan-T'ung as " Mr. P'u " (as at least one prominent English newspaper has done) is not only dis-courteous and objectionable for other reasons but is also in-adequate as a designation, because there are many members of the imperial family who share that name.

P'u-Wei—one of the " P'u " generation named above—is prince Kung, who for many years has resided under Japanese protection in the Liao-tung peninsula.[5] His name was frequently mentioned in the press in connection with the beginnings of the recent political upheaval in Manchuria, and English newspapers in China often referred to him as the emperor's uncle, presumably because he was old enough to be so. But age has nothing to do with the matter. He belongs to a collateral branch of the imperial family but to the same generation as the emperor, and is therefore properly described as a cousin.

The members of the generation senior to that of " P'u " similarly share the name " Tsai." Thus the late emperor Kuang-Hsü (more correctly designated since his death by his " temple-name " of Tê Tsung) was named Tsai T'ien, and his brothers are Tsai-Fêng (prince Ch'un, the emperor's father), Tsai-Hsün and Tsai-T'ao. The generation next above that of " Tsai " bore the name " Yi," and so we hear of the emperor Tê Tsung's father Yi-Huan, and also of Yi-Ho and Yi-Shao. The generation junior to that of " P'u " share the name Yü. So we have Yü-Lin (son of P'u-Wei), Yü-Ch'ung (the " companion-reader "), Yü-Tsun, Yü-Lang, and so on. If the emperor has any sons they also will all bear " Yü " as the first part of their personal names.[6]

It should perhaps be mentioned that the surname—if it can be so-called—of the Manchu imperial family is Aisin-Gioro, which is very rarely heard of or mentioned except in Chinese historical accounts of the rise of the Manchu ruling house, and is then represented by four Chinese characters

愛　新　覺　羅

read in Pekingese as *Ai-hsin Chiao-lo*. As " Aisin " is a Manchu word meaning " gold " many of the imperial clansmen have adopted the equivalent Chinese word Chin as their Chinese surname. This enables them, if they so desire, to pass for Chinese, as *Chin* happens to be a common surname among the Chinese people.

About two years after the emperor had begun his English studies he asked me to give him an English name, not for the purpose of prefixing it to his Chinese or Manchu name but for

separate use, as when signing English letters, photographs or
other non-Chinese documents intended for myself or for other
Europeans. As I have explained above, the personal name of an
emperor always lay under what may be called a kind of taboo.[7]
He could not therefore use it in the way in which foreigners use
their names, and when he began to make use of his knowledge
of English he found this inconvenient. From a list of English
royal names which I gave him to choose from he selected
" Henry." There was never any intention that " Henry "
should be used along with " P'u-Yi," nor would there have been
any such intention even if the name P'u-Yi had not been under
an imperial taboo, for he shared my dislike for the *mo-têng*
(" modern " or fashionable) practice—prevalent in the student-
class—of prefixing Western " Christian " names to Chinese sur-
names. Thus the journalistic habit that has grown up in recent
years of referring to him by the uncouth hybrid " Henry P'u-
Yi " is not only unpleasant to eye and ear but is at least as
incorrect as the absurd designation " Mr. P'u." When he uses
" Henry "—which he does only on rare occasions and never
officially—it is not prefixed to any other name.[8]

My relations with my pupil were friendly and harmonious
from the first, and became increasingly so as time went on. The
qualities that I found most attractive in him were his general
intelligence, his frankness, his eager interest in the affairs not
only of China but of the world, his impulsive generosity, his
artistic gifts, the lack of any indication of vindictiveness or ill-
will against those who had wronged him or had been the enemies
of his house, his kindliness and sympathy with suffering, his
courage in the face of grave physical danger, and a keen sense
of humour. He was completely ignorant of English when I
entered his service, and indeed he never made much serious
effort to become proficient in that language. His interest in
purely linguistic studies was not great ; what interested him
most were the current affairs of the world (including the events
in Europe which preceded and followed the Peace of Versailles),
geography and travel, elementary physical science (including
astronomy), the science of politics, English constitutional history, and the drama that was being enacted day by day before
our eyes on the political stage of China itself. On such topics we

conversed freely and unsystematically in Chinese ; and there is
no doubt that our conversations on these and other subjects
took up time that might have been occupied—not necessarily
more profitably—in the study of English.

His proficiency in Chinese calligraphy, however, gave him an
interest in penmanship, and he soon wrote English in a good
formed hand that many an English schoolboy of his age might
envy. At the end of this chapter is reproduced a specimen of his
English handwriting after he had been learning English for about
a year, and when he was fifteen years of age. The subject-matter
consists of three well-known passages, selected and translated by
myself, from one of the Confucian classics—the Book of Mencius.
They have a special interest as illustrating those strongly democratic ideas which, as every Chinese schoolboy knows, infuriated
an emperor of the Ming dynasty and induced him to make an
unsuccessful attempt to degrade Mencius from his place of honour
among orthodox Confucian teachers. It was this democratic
aspect of the Confucian theory of kingship, so disturbing to the
equanimity of the first of the imperial Mings, which I made it
my business to impress on the mind of the last of the imperial
Manchus.[9]

The emperor had an active and intelligent mind, but he had
a frivolous as well as a serious side to his nature. At first I
ascribed the manifestations of frivolity to youthful irrespon-
sibility, and assumed that as he grew up he would put away
childish things. There were times, however, when I seemed to
detect signs in his nature of something like a permanent cleav-
age, almost suggesting the existence within him of two warring
personalities. When he had grown out of childhood I used to
discuss this matter with him very frankly. I often told him that
there were within him *liang ko huang-shang, pu chih i ko huang-
shang*—" two emperors, not one "—and that he would never be
able to do justice to himself and to his ancestors unless the better
of the two imperial personages succeeded in reducing the other
to a permanent state of obedient vassalage.

He invariably took my criticisms of his character and my
admonitions very good-humouredly, even if they did not always
have the desired effect. Indeed the patience and good temper
with which he listened to my complaints, and the complete lack

of any signs of resentment, were among the most conspicuous and charming of his characteristics. I was often told by my Chinese colleagues, however, that he was not equally submissive and receptive with them ; and as it gradually came to be recognised in the palace that the emperor would listen more patiently to his English tutor than to anyone else, I was repeatedly appealed to not only by his Chinese tutors but also by his father and uncles to make representations and suggestions to him which they themselves despaired of doing with any hope of success.

It was one thing, however, to listen quietly to criticisms and quite another to act upon them. There were many occasions on which I spoke seriously to the emperor on what I believed to be his faults. He never showed the slightest ill-feeling or petulance when I did so, and would often tell me that he knew he was wrong and intended to begin a new way of life forthwith. He certainly made efforts in that direction, even if they were not always successful or permanent.

What I have inadequately described as the " frivolous " side of his nature was fully recognised by my Chinese colleagues, especially by Ch'ên Pao-shên, who had been his tutor since he was six years old. The Chinese word which he used to describe the failing which we both recognised was *fou*, of which the dictionary meanings are " to float, to drift ; volatile ; unsubstantial ; thriftlessness ; fickle ; unsteady ; wanting in fixity." It sometimes occurred to me that most of the emperor's good qualities, including his undoubted intellectual ability, probably came from his mother's side—she, it will be remembered, was a daughter of the great Manchu viceroy Jung-Lu—and that the frivolous or *fou* features of his character were an inheritance from his father prince Ch'un. I was also inclined to ascribe to paternal heredity a curious strain of obstinacy in little matters. Nevertheless it was difficult to say which imperfections of character might be due to heredity and which to the thoroughly unwholesome atmosphere of the court in which the boy had spent his whole life. If the former were incurable, there was at least a chance that the latter might gradually pass away in a healthier environment.

I have said that he had a keen sense of humour. On one occasion this delightful characteristic manifested itself in connection with my attempt to explain, in crude language, the difference between absolute and constitutional monarchy. As an illustration of what irresponsible despotism meant I said that the potentate who wielded such power might indulge his whims by summarily ordering the execution of any of his subjects, or might delegate the arbitrary power of life and death to a favoured minister. " Then my predecessors " remarked the emperor, " have all been irresponsible despots." A couple of days later, when I was sitting in the cloistered garden of my Chinese house, a servant announced that a palace-eunuch was at the gate bearing an important message from the emperor which he had been ordered to deliver in person. On being admitted he held out to me a gleaming object which turned out to be a sword-stick. " This sword," said the eunuch without the least flicker of a smile, " is from *Wan-sui-Yeh* (' the Lord of Ten Thousand Years ') and he ordered me to say that he confers upon you the privilege of killing anyone you like—*sui pien sha jên.*"

On my next visit to the palace the emperor was eager to learn from me whether the eunuch had carried out his instructions. I was able to assure him that he had done so to perfection. When reminded, about ten years later, of this little incident, the emperor (who by that time had become head of the new Manchurian government) enquired how often the privilege conferred upon me had been exercised and was interested to learn that up to that time the sword had not been stained with human blood.

He was much less susceptible to flattery than might have been expected. By the time he had reached his middle " teens " he had already acquired a fairly shrewd notion of the corruption and rascality that existed in the Forbidden City, and his opinion of his courtiers was too low to allow him to take their flattery as seriously as he might have done if they had been men whom he trusted and admired.

But flattery of the servile kind that oozed from the lips of the sycophantic eunuchs and officers of the Nei Wu Fu was much less dangerous to the stability of a boy's character than the more subtle flattery that came in all good faith from the hearts and mouths of good men and true. His Chinese tutors indeed were almost, if not quite, free from that semi-superstitious awe and reverence for the person of the emperor that found expression in such words and beliefs as *chên lung tzŭ yü fan jên pu t'ung*—" the true Dragon has a nature different from that of common humanity." They knew very well that he was just a human boy, neither better nor worse than multitudes of other boys. But the same can hardly be said of many devoted servants of the dynasty for whom an audience with the emperor was an awe-inspiring event, and to whom loyalty was a religion. Such men used to come to Peking solely to gratify a craving to kneel at the feet of the personage who was still, in their eyes, the Son of Heaven, and for whom many of them would gladly have died ; and it would have been strange indeed if the spontaneous expressions of devotion uttered by men like these had left the object of their idolatry wholly free from any trace of unhealthy exaltation.

Yet it may be said with confidence that the emperor was under no delusions as to his real position. It certainly never entered his mind that his imperial dragonship had endowed him with a nature different from and superior to that of ordinary men ; and he was so little in love with the grand ceremonial in which, on important occasions, he had to participate that his first anxiety, after he had descended from his throne in the palace of Cloudless Heaven, was to divest himself of his state robes as quickly as possible. He had, indeed, a strong objection to being seen—especially by foreigners—in any but the simplest Chinese clothes, and the photograph of himself seated on the dragon throne which is reproduced in this book is, I believe, the only photograph of the kind that he ever allowed to be taken. It was taken at my own special request, to which he agreed with reluctance.

I have mentioned his proficiency in Chinese calligraphy. The system under which he was educated required him to spend a considerable part of his time in the practice of this art, in which several of his ancestors excelled. It has always been the custom for Chinese emperors to bestow on deserving officials, and also on temples and monasteries and other important buildings, specimens of the imperial calligraphy in the form of large-character inscriptions which are reproduced in facsimile on lacquered and gilded wood. My pupil was expected to follow his ancestors' example in this matter, and it was usual for him to present the principal members of his court, old servants of the dynasty and well-disposed officials of the republican government with written scrolls as ceremonial gifts on New Year's day, birthdays or other important occasions. Imperial autographs of this kind were always authenticated by one or more of the square seals used exclusively by the emperor. In the case of my pupil, the seal ordinarily used bears (in " seal " script) the characters standing for *Hsüan-T'ung Yü Pi* : " imperial autograph of the Hsüan-T'ung reign-period."

Both the emperor and his equally intelligent brother P'u-Chieh have artistic gifts which manifested themselves at a very early age. Their calligraphy is greatly admired for its intrinsic merits, and each has a decided talent for drawing. The emperor's sense of humour often led him in the direction of skilful carica-ture, and I have many specimens of his work in this genre, drawn rapidly in my presence on any odd scraps of paper that happened to be at hand, generally for the purpose of illustrating an anecdote or a newspaper-paragraph or some episode that had amused him in the daily life of the court.

From his Chinese tutors, all of whom were poets, the emperor learned the technique of Chinese verse in his early years and soon became skilful in applying his knowledge. During 1921 and 1922 he became an anonymous contributor of verse to several Peking periodicals, more especially to a daily newspaper called the *Yu-hsi Jih Pao*. His verses appeared under the fictitious name, chosen by himself, of Têng Ch'iung-lin. Têng is an ordinary Chinese surname, Ch'iung-lin is a name which may be rendered " Luminous Unicorn." The editors of the papers to which he contributed were kept in ignorance of his identity, though the editor of the *Yu-hsi Jih Pao*, who published every-thing that was sent to him by the " Luminous Unicorn," made several ineffectual attempts to discover who the poet was. I was of course aware that he wrote a good deal of verse—nearly all educated Chinese do so—but it was not till July, 1922, that he confessed his secret to me and showed me some specimens of the poems which had already been published. As far as I am aware it never became known to the Peking public that the poet who was writing and publishing verse under the name of

the "Luminous Unicorn" was no other than the Manchu
emperor, and my present disclosure of the fact will probably
surprise Chinese as well as foreigners.

In spite of his keen interest in new literary and other movements, the emperor was not attracted by the vogue for *vers libre*
in colloquial Chinese. His verse therefore always followed
classical models. His favourites among the Chinese poets were
Po Chü-i, Han Yü and Li T'ai-po of the T'ang dynasty, and he
also had a very high regard (which was not based merely on
filial piety) for the poetry of his own imperial ancestor Kao
Tsung—the emperor known to foreigners as Ch'ien-Lung.

Here are three samples of his work, all published in 1922
in the *Yu-hsi Jih Pao*, and translated by me from the Chinese
originals. The first consists of forty Chinese characters divided
into eight 5-character lines, and the title is "Parrots."

Parrots can mimic human speech,
Unconscious of the meaning of the words they use.
Many are the readers of the lore of the sages,
But where shall we find one who acts as the sages teach ?
Alas, if we note the ways of birds and men
There is hardly a hair's breadth of difference between them.
Look at the people who are never without their writing-tablets—
How they scribble and scribble and cannot tell us what they really
mean !

The second, in two stanzas of four 7-character lines each, is
entitled "Drifting Moon."

Lightly comes the evening breeze, dissolving the heat of the summer
day ;
Gradually in the void of infinite space emerges the ice-wheel of the
moon.
Cicadas chirp, fire-flies dart over the winding stream.
The wu-t'ung *sheds its leaves, the lotus-blooms have gone, the night*
is clear and still.[10]

A boat lies motionless, like the pavilion that overlooks it ;
Countless little mirrors flash in the rippling waters.

Most wonderful of all is the radiance of the stars in the clear expanse above.
Now is the time for the viols and flutes that will heighten the joys of the wine-cup.

The last of which I will attempt a rendering is entitled " Lotus Month." It is in eight 7-character lines.

Silver and red are the evening clouds ;
The rain is over, and fragrant scents from afar float through the window-gauze.
Beyond all painter's skill is the scene that lies before me,
With its unmatched glory of spring flowers.
A lonely wild duck flies across the sky to a mystical region beyond the waters ;
A light skiff drifting along the water's edge is the only link with human things.
It is a land of faery,
Where no worldly longings stir the heart or check the flowering of the spirit.

When he wrote these verses (my translations of which preserve nothing of the original grace), the emperor had indeed arrived at an age which is often—not in China alone—the beginning of the flowering-time of the spirit of poetry. He was a boy of sixteen.

My readers will not be surprised to learn that I found in my imperial pupil an attractive and lovable personality, and that the days and years spent by me in his company were as agreeable while they lasted as they are pleasant in retrospect.

It would be foolish to pretend that he possesses all the qualities which are the necessary attributes of a successful leader of men of the dictator type. For many years he has been a keen admirer of the great statesman who has put new life into Italy, and he was proud of the signed photograph which was sent to him from Rome through the Italian minister at Peking. But he is, I think, well aware of the fact that he himself has not been cast in the mould of a Mussolini.

Both foreigners and Chinese have often asked me the direct question whether I consider that he possesses the qualities that

Qc

he would need if he were called upon to re-ascend a throne as the constitutional sovereign of a progressive modern state. My answer to that question is Yes, provided he turned a permanently deaf ear to those evil counsellors who would seek by all the means in their power to revive the bad old system of palace-administration which, as embodied in the Nei Wu Fu, was the main cause of the fall of his dynasty in China.

The uniqueness of my appointment as English tutor to the " Boy Emperor " or " the Son of Heaven " (whichever of the titles be preferred) attracted some attention in the Chinese press. The attitude of the Peking and North China papers was, on the whole, courteous and friendly. The Cantonese and Southern press was inclined to be sarcastic and suspicious. I was soon burdened with a heavy Chinese correspondence, though many of the letters that reached me were anonymous and quickly disposed of. Some of my correspondents gave me advice as to how I should educate my pupil ; others begged me to obtain situations for themselves or their relatives at court ; others gave me what purported to be secret information about monarchist movements in Manchuria and elsewhere ; some sent me memorials addressed to the throne and asked me to see that they reached his majesty's own hands ; some made scurrilous accusations against members of the palace staff ; some asked me to procure for them audiences with the emperor as they had secret communications of vital importance to make to him ; others (anonymous) accused me of plotting against the security of the republic and advised me in my own interests to resign my post forthwith, lest worse befall. Explicit threats of assassination did not begin to reach me till 1923. Several fathers of families begged me to undertake the education of their sons, so that the latter might achieve the glory of being taught by the Son of Heaven's own teacher. This request was often put in the form of a hope that I would allow their sons to stand beside me and hold my ink-slab—that is, the grooved slate which is used for the liquefying of Chinese ink.

More troublesome than letter-writers were the strangers who persisted in attempting to pay personal visits. My gatekeeper—a Manchu who understood his job—kept most of them at bay, but I was often waylaid by would-be visitors who having been denied entrance to my house waited till they caught me entering or leaving my car. One of these persistent people was a yellow-booted, Chinese-gowned and American-hatted young man with a pimply white face who explained to me (when he had succeeded in forcing an interview upon me) that he was a Seventh-Day Adventist and had been inspired by some unnamed power to approach me with a view to the emperor's conversion to the true faith. Under his arm he carried a pile of tracts and pamphlets, and he assured me that if I would consent to present them to his majesty they would undoubtedly bring him the spiritual illumination through which comes salvation. To what darkened soul the books eventually brought illumination I do not know. They never illumined the twilight of the Forbidden City.

One duty which fell to me was to deal with the emperor's foreign correspondence. All his letters from Western correspondents were sent by arrangement with the Peking postal authorities direct to myself, and most of them, I must confess, went no further. They were of a very miscellaneous and not always edifying character. Several contained proposals from unknown females who desired to enter the imperial harem. Many contained harmless requests for autographs. One came from a man who explained that he was the rightful czar of Russia, and was now an exile in America. It was his intention, he said, to form an association of ex-monarchs with a view to the concerting of measures for the recovery of their several thrones. He exhorted my pupil to become a life-member of the proposed society. I showed this communication to his majesty, and the idea of an association consisting solely of ex-monarchs made an immediate appeal to his sense of humour. He suggested that the society would add to the gaiety of nations if each ex-monarch were to learn to play a musical instrument, so that the whole society could constitute itself into an orchestra consisting exclusively of heads that had once been crowned. We agreed that bunches of peonies—a flower for which the " imperial garden " in the Forbidden City was justly famous—might fittingly take the place of the missing crowns. His own instrument might be selected from the gongs, bells, drums and stone-chimes that provided the ceremonial music at the Palace of Cloudless Heaven. The combined royal efforts at a " concord of sweet sounds " might turn out to be other than mellifluous, but it seemed improbable that the general effect could be less harmonious than that produced by an orchestra of which his majesty had learned something in the course of his historical studies—that of " the concert of Europe." One suggestion of my own met with instant approval—that the society of musical and peony-crowned ex-monarchs would do well to retire to a little uninhabited island and form a polity of their own, and that it would add to the piquancy of the situation if the dethroned potentates were to adopt a republican form of government and elect one of their own members as president.

During the years I spent in the Forbidden City I wrote numerous letters and memoranda in which I recorded my impressions and made notes of events within that mysterious Forbidden City to which I was still the only European who had access. Two letters written during my first few months contain passages which may perhaps throw a light on the subject of this chapter. They will show that the opinions expressed in this and earlier chapters concerning the evil conditions that existed in the Forbidden City, and the advisability of finding more wholesome surroundings for the emperor were formed at a very early date.

On May 18th, 1919—about two months after I had entered upon my duties—I wrote as follows :

" It is still too early for me to make any formal recom-mendations regarding reforms in the palace ; but I am strongly of opinion that it would be better for the Emperor—physically, morally and intellectually—if he could be taken out of his present surroundings and accommodated in the Summer Palace. But it would be no use doing this unless drastic changes were made in the constitution of the Nei Wu Fu, and I do not think any eunuchs should be allowed to accompany the emperor to his new residence. There is plenty of room in the Summer Palace for all the attendants the emperor should require, and all necessary household officials, and also for the tutors. I had a long talk with prince Tsai T'ao on these subjects a few days ago, and we agreed that

certain reforms are badly needed and that there is no hope
of having them effected by the Nei Wu Fu as at present constituted."

Two months later—on July 17th to be exact—I wrote to an
English-speaking Chinese friend who took a strong interest in
the emperor's welfare a long letter from which the following
are extracts.

" Before I go [on a visit to the Western Hills] I think I ought
to warn you that in my opinion the highly artificial life that
the emperor leads must be detrimental to his health, physical,
intellectual and moral ; and I sincerely hope for his sake that
some means will be devised whereby he may be enabled to
live more naturally and rationally. Although he is an emperor (a titular one) he is also a boy, and if this fact is ignored,
especially during the next three or four years, the results may
be very serious for him. In the first place I am convinced that
he is badly in need of change of air and surroundings. It would
do him a world of good if he could put away all his books for
two months or so and go off to the sea or the mountains.
There may be grave difficulties in the way—some of them
political—but they ought to be faced. It is cruel to keep the
boy cooped up in a palace in the heart of Peking, where he can
get neither fresh air nor adequate exercise.
    " I quite understand that you and other loyal Chinese
regard him primarily as emperor, whereas to me he is primarily a very human boy. But surely it is of far greater importance that his physical and moral health should be safeguarded
than that he should be prepared for an imperial position which
he is never likely to reoccupy. Even if he were de facto emperor,
or were likely to recover his throne at some future date, I
should still adhere to my present views as to his training and
surroundings. In Western countries the theory that monarchs
should be kept rigidly apart from the ordinary life of the
world, that they should be regarded as sacred persons and as
having natures different from the natures of ordinary human
beings, has long been given up as radically unsound. Spain,

perhaps, is a partial exception, but there the monarchy is by
no means stable, and the country is seething with revolutionary forces. The present is not a very promising epoch for
monarchs anywhere in the world. If any type of kingship is
likely to maintain itself through this revolutionary age I suppose it is the English type ; certainly the old-time monarch
who held his throne by " divine right " belongs to an age that
has passed away. When the Prince of Wales was at Oxford
he lived much the same sort of life that I myself lived when
I was at the same college ; and during the war he has played
the part of a young English officer with credit to himself, and
certainly has lost no prestige thereby. Your young emperor
knows a good deal about Western customs now. I often show
him illustrated magazines with photos of the various members of our royal family going about freely among the people ;
and I have tried to make him understand something of the
principles that underlie the modern conception of a sovereign's
position. As a matter of fact there is no difficulty about teaching him these things ; it is hardly necessary for me to do more
than refer him to Mencius. In China the idea of a democratic
kingship is very much older than it is in the West : therefore
no violence need be done to Chinese traditional teaching.

" But what I want to emphasise is the supreme importance
of training the young emperor in such a way that whatever
his future may be—whether the country calls him to the
throne of his ancestors as a constitutional king, or whether
he is forced to surrender even the last vestige of his imperial
dignity and become simply a unit among the four hundred
million people of China—he may have no cause to reproach
those who were responsible for his education and upbringing.
In my opinion everything, if necessary, should be sacrificed
rather than that his physical and moral health should suffer
injury. If he continues to be treated as a being whose nature
is essentially different from that of ordinary humanity, he
will almost certainly be a failure as a man, and it is very
improbable that he would be a success as a king. If he is
brought up solely with a view to a visionary throne, there is
little hope that he will be capable of playing a man's part
in the world when the last hope of a Restoration has faded

away ; whereas if he were trained to be a liberal-minded patriotic and cultivated Chinese gentleman—a real *chün-tzŭ* —he would adorn whatever position he might be called upon to occupy, whether it were that of a king or that of a simple citizen.

" I need hardly say that if the household could be entirely reorganised, and all officials, servants and eunuchs whose services were not actually required could be discharged, there would be an enormous saving of expense and probably a vast improvement in efficiency. But this is a matter upon which I am unwilling to say much at present, and in any case it hardly comes within my province."

When I wrote the letters from which the foregoing extracts are taken I did not know as well as I came to know later how exceedingly difficult, if not insuperable, was the task that lay before anyone who tried to reform the abuses of the Forbidden City. Nor did I fully understand the nature and strength of the objections that would be raised to my suggestion that the emperor should act in accordance with the third of the Articles of Favourable Treatment and move the Court from the Forbidden City to the Summer Palace. These were matters concerning which I still had much to learn.

Mencius held converse with king Hsüan of Chi. "Let us suppose," said Mencius, "that one of Your Majesty's servants, who is about to start on a journey to Chü, entrusts his family to the care of a friend. On his return, he finds that his friend has allowed his family to suffer from hunger and cold. What should he do with such a friend?" "Cut him," answered the King. "And suppose," continued Mencius, "that Your Majesty had a minister of justice who was incapable of controlling his subordinates. How would you deal with such a one?" "Dismiss him at once," replied the king. "And if throughout your realm there is a lack of good government," Mencius went on, "what is to be done then?" The king looked this way and that, and changed the subject.

———————

King Hsüan of Chi put this question to Mencius. "Is it true that Tang dethroned king Chieh, and that prince Wu promoted an insurrection against king Chou?" "History assures us that such was the case," answered Mencius "Is it lawful, then," asked the King, "for a minister to put his sovereign to death?" "He who act in defiance of the highest moral principles of humanity" answered Mencius "is a ruffian. He who outrages every principle of honour is a villain The man who acts in a ruffianly. and villainous way is properly described —

whatever his position may be — as a contemptible rascal. I have heard about the killing of a rascal named Chou: I have not heard about the killing of a king"

———————————

Mencius said "The most important element in a State is the people; next come the altars of the national Gods; least in importance is the king."

———————————

CHAPTER XVI

Monarchist Hopes and Dreams

I HAVE SAID that the emperor took a keen interest in the drama that was being enacted day by day on the Chinese political stage. He had free access to the Chinese press, of which he was an eager student. When I used to find him seated among piles of newspapers from Peking, Tientsin, Shanghai and Canton, and gently remonstrated with him for wasting precious time over ephemeral trash, he would reply that from the multitude of witnesses, all of whom contradicted one another, he was trying to form his own judgment as to what might be the truth. Fortunately his sources of information regarding public events were not confined to newspapers. He frequently received written or oral reports on current Chinese politics from intelligent if not always unbiased ex-officials of the old régime and other friends of the Manchu court, and he also took a lively interest in such information as I was able to give him of current affairs in Europe.

We were living in stirring times. When I first became his tutor in 1919, the Great War was over, but in Paris the " Big Five " were drawing a new map of the world and framing a lamentable treaty which they fondly dreamed would inaugurate a warless world. In China, the interest of the politically-minded public was centred on the problem of the former German colony of Tsingtao which had remained in the hands of Japan since the early days of the war. The Chinese demand was that Tsingtao and all the German railway and other rights in Shantung should be handed back unconditionally to China, and that this should be provided for in the treaty of peace. They were not content with the Japanese proposal that the question of the final disposal of the German rights should be dealt with by direct negotiation between Japan and China, and that meanwhile Tsingtao should be left in Japanese hands. When it seemed likely that the Japanese view would prevail at

Versailles there was an unprecedented outburst of public indignation in China. This marked the beginning of the famous Student Movement which was afterwards to have a profound influence, for both good and bad, on Chinese internal and external politics. The movement quickly spread throughout the whole country, but at first, and for a considerable time afterwards, its leaders were to be found among the students, and certain members of the teaching staff, of the National University of Peking. To their activities, far more than to the efforts of the Peking Government, was due the refusal of the Chinese Government to sign the treaty of peace. This refusal, it will be remembered, necessitated the conclusion of a separate peace-treaty between China and Germany.[1]

All these and subsequent events, and also the endless intrigues of politicians, militarists and parliamentarians (at times there were three co-existing parliaments, each claiming to be the one that represented the people), were followed with the closest interest by the emperor, with whom I frequently discussed them not only in the imperial schoolroom but also in his own living quarters. It would however take us too far from our immediate subject if we were to follow the devious course of Chinese politics throughout the troubled period of Hsü Shih-ch'ang's presidency and they will not be touched upon in these pages except in so far as they have a distinct bearing on the fortunes of the imperial house.

When I entered the service of the Manchu court in February, 1919, only nineteen months had passed since the failure of Chang Hsün's attempt to restore the monarchy. I have already said, when dealing with that episode, that the collapse of the movement was not due to the lack of sympathy and approval on the part of many of those who held strategic positions in civil and military life. It was due very largely to Chang Hsün's foolish belief that he could play the part of kingmaker without taking his monarchist colleagues into full and frank consultation at critical moments and without giving them the expected and necessary guarantees concerning the distribution of such plums as regencies, princedoms and governorships.

It is not to be supposed that this brief space of nineteen months was sufficient to erase all thoughts of a restoration from the minds of the Chinese public. The election of an old friend and servant of the Manchu dynasty to the office of president would have revived the hopes of the monarchists even if one of Hsü Shih-ch'ang's first official acts had not been to grant a free pardon to Chang Hsün. As to public opinion, there is no doubt that at this time the people of many parts of China were thoroughly disillusioned with the republic, which had promised so many good things and had brought them so little but misery. The European newspapers in China provided much evidence to this effect, in the form of reports from their correspondents in the interior. Most of these correspondents were missionaries, who at the time of the revolution had almost unanimously given a hearty welcome to the republic, in the sincere belief that it would inaugurate a new and happy era of prosperity for China and of goodwill between the Chinese people and the Western Powers and also, incidentally, open wide the gates that had hitherto barred the way to the progress of the Christian evangel. The following paragraph, which appeared in the *North China Daily News* of June 23rd, 1919, may be taken as typical. It referred to conditions in the far-western province of Kansu.

" The multiplication of taxes, the corruptness of the officials, cause the people to long for the return of the Manchu dynasty. Bad as it was, they consider the republic ten times worse. Not only in this far-off corner do we hear the sighings for the Manchu dynasty, but from other provinces we hear that there is still a hope of its being re-established."

Testimony to the same effect may be found in the most unexpected places, including the writings of fiery radicals who had nothing to gain by over-estimating the extent to which the Chinese masses were still at heart loyal to the principles of monarchy. The revolutionary propagandists who had succeeded in persuading the West that the revolution was welcomed by the Chinese people were much more frank and truthful when they addressed their own countrymen in their own language. They knew they could deceive foreigners ; they also knew it would be useless to attempt to deceive one another. Such revolutionary journals as the *Hsin Ch'ing Nien* (" New Youth "), *Kai Tsao*

("Reconstruction") and *Shu Kuang* ("Dawn") which were published by the leaders of radical political thought during the years that immediately followed the revolution contained innumerable admissions of their bitter disappointment with their failure to instil revolutionary ideas into the minds of the agricultural masses who constitute ninety per cent of the Chinese population. The following paragraph which I translate from an article published in the *Shu Kuang* ten years after the revolution (1921), will surprise many who assumed that monarchist hopes and dreams had by that time been wholly extinguished.

" Of the agricultural population, eight or nine out of every ten are illiterate and as obtuse as deer or pigs. It is a pitiful state of things. They have no conception whatever of the meaning of liberty, political rights and government. All they know is that they must pay their land-tax and provide themselves with the means of livelihood from day to day. One comes across people in the village-markets who ask questions like these : ' How is the emperor Hsüan-T'ung? ' ' Who is now ruling in the imperial palace? ' Again and again they can be heard to sigh and utter complaints of this kind : ' What is to become of us with such miserable harvests ? We can't expect any good thing to happen to us until the real Dragon, the Son of Heaven, comes forth again.'

" Just think of it ! These country louts will not be satisfied unless a Chang Hsün brings about an imperial Restoration. Let a Chang Hsün start enrolling soldiers, and you will see them press forward eagerly enough. Nothing else will move them. Try to put a new idea into their heads and they will turn away with indifference."[2]

Even among the educated classes there has never been a time when the monarchist cause was regarded as dead. I had not been long at the Manchu court when it came to my knowledge from various sources that many influential leaders in different parts of China more or less secretly sympathised with that cause ; and I also learned that monarchist hopes were mainly centred on Manchuria.

Manchuria was the old home of the imperial house, and in spite of the gradual passing away of the Manchus as a separate race with its own language and customs, the Manchurian province still contained large numbers of people—Chinese, Mongols, Manchus, and many of mixed descent—who were loyal to the dynasty. Manchuria had taken no active part in the revolution, and if the imperial family had taken refuge there instead of entering into negotiations with the revolutionaries, there is no reason to believe that it would have met with any hostility or opposition from the local military authorities (among whom Chang Tso-lin was already prominent) or from the civil government. It is by no means improbable that a " Man-Mêng " (Manchuria-Mongolia) empire under the Ta Ch'ing dynasty would have succeeded in declaring and maintaining its complete independence of China,[3] and before long it might have been joined not only by Jehol and Chahar but also by Chinese Turkestan, the Mohammedan parts of Kansu, and even by Tibet.[4] In that case the Chinese Republic would have found itself faced by a solid block of potentially-hostile states consisting mainly of just those regions which the Manchu emperors, either at the time of their conquest of China or soon afterwards, had added to the empire. Many people would have regarded this development as a just punishment inflicted on the Chinese for having expelled the dynasty under which these vast territorial gains had been made.

This *Man-Mêng Ti Kuo* (or " Manchuria-Mongolia Empire ") would perhaps never have become a single centralised State ; it would have been a federation of autonomous principalities each of which would have enjoyed something like " dominion status " and among which Manchuria might have had a more or less nominal precedence. With or without the other principalities, " Manchoukuo " would have come into existence in 1912 (when there was no League of Nations to question its status) instead of in 1932 ; and it is more than probable that if the attitude of China had seemed likely to threaten its stability as a separate State, it would have entered into a close partnership with Japan. This would have brought about a situation very similar to that which confronted China and the world exactly twenty years later.

" Up to 1911," says Mr. Watkin Davies in an article published
in October, 1933, " Outer Mongolia was subject to China, and
that willingly. The Mongol chiefs had lent valuable aid to the
Manchus in their conquest of China ; and that great adventure
was regarded as a joint victory. But it was to the Manchu emperors in person that the Mongols felt bound ; and so when they
were deposed and China became a republic they considered their
allegiance forfeited. . . . Accordingly in 1912 Outer Mongolia
proclaimed its independence. That was Russia's opportunity ;
and in the last years of its existence the Tsardom greatly
strengthened its hold upon the country."

These remarks are true except for the fact that Outer Mongolia did not regard itself, up to 1911, as " subject to China " but
to " Ta Ch'ing Kuo "—the empire ruled by the Ta Ch'ing or
Manchu dynasty, as indeed Mr. Watkin Davies himself proceeds
to point out in the same paragraph. It must again be emphasised
that the term " Chinese Empire " did not exist except in
Western phraseology. The empire was that of " Ta Ch'ing Kuo "
and its emperor was the " Ta Ch'ing Kuo Ta Huang Ti," the
nearest English equivalent of which is simply " the Manchu
Emperor." Similarly, the official title of the " Venerable
Buddha " was *Ta Ch'ing Kuo . . . Huang T'ai-Hou*—" Empress-
dowager of the Ta Ch'ing Realm," not " Empress-dowager of
China."[5]

Mr. Watkin Davies also says : " Nominally, Inner Mongolia is
still subject to China [" subject to China " is again a misleading
phrase, as I think he would himself admit] but it is hardly necessary to add that the great Republic, convulsed with anarchy,
wields no real authority there." Again : " It is likely enough
that Japan could, at any moment, rally all the Mongols to her
side by a promise of autonomy, and by pledging her protection
to a united Mongol state. To make the issue doubly sure she
would only have to revive the imperial title in the person of the
Manchu Chief Executive of Manchuria. The emperor P'u-Yi
would be gladly acclaimed by every Mongol who reveres the
past."[6]

This, in view of events which have taken place since October,
1933, when Mr. Watkin Davies's article was published, is a
noteworthy statement.

The now familiar term " Manchoukuo," it should be unnecessary to point out, is merely the Chinese for " Manchuria " (or
rather " Manchuria " is merely " Man-chou " or " Manchoukuo "
adapted to English ears) and it is unfortunate that Western
journalists and others insist upon using that form when writing
English instead of the well-established and much more eupho-
nious " Manchuria." We might just as well speak of *Chungkuo*
instead of " China " (as of course we do when we are speaking
Chinese) or of *Mêngku* instead of " Mongolia." " Manchoukuo "
(a more correct transliteration, by the way, than Man*chu*kuo) is
not a new term in the Chinese language, for it was one of the
names given more or less tentatively by the Manchu rulers to
their independent state in Manchuria some years before their
conquest of China. The title " Manchoukuo Huang-Ti " or
" Emperor of Manchuria " replaced the title " Chin-kuo Khan "
formerly used by the founders of the Manchu power, and it was
adopted (as was the later dynastic title Ta Ch'ing) for the express
purpose of asserting equality with the Ming emperor of China.
Therefore if in 1911 the Manchu emperor had returned to Mukden
and declared himself *Ta Manchou Kuo Huang Ti*, he would not
merely have been returning to the throne, but also reassuming
an ancient title, of his Manchu ancestors.

That Manchuria was unwilling to participate in the revolution is fully admitted in the Lytton Report. " When the revolution broke out in 1911," it tells us, " the Manchurian authorities,
who were not in favour of the Republic, succeeded in saving
these provinces from the turmoil of civil war by ordering Chang
Tso-lin, who was later to become the dictator of both Manchuria
and North China, to resist the advance of the revolutionary
troops."[7] It is true that, as the Report continues, after the republic
had been established Manchuria " accepted the *fait accompli*
and voluntarily followed the leadership of Yüan Shih-k'ai," but
that was because the emperor had issued his edict of abdication,
had accepted the Articles of Favourable Treatment, and had
remained in Peking. Manchuria—as I have been personally
assured by Chang Tso-lin himself—would have followed a very
different course had the emperor, or rather the regent on his
behalf, refused to abdicate and had he transferred the court to
Mukden.

Rc

Thus it is not surprising that during 1919 and the succeeding years, with which we are now concerned, the hopes of the monarchists were still, as I have said, mainly centred on Manchuria. I had not been long in Peking, however, before I discovered that the monarchist cause was labouring under the same kind of disability that had brought about its failure in 1917. The monarchists did not trust one another—past experience, perhaps, had made them suspicious—and there was a persistent lack of harmony in their aims and methods. At least two groups were associated with the exiled princes of the Manchu house, and they were distrusted by other groups because they were suspected of aiming at restoring the monarchy not in the person of the young emperor in Peking but in that of one of the imperial exiles. That some of the monarchist party had this aim is true. Their arguments were, firstly, that the young emperor had done nothing for the cause and had already abdicated ; secondly, that one, at least, of the exiled princes had devoted his life and fortune to the cause and had never recognised the republic ; thirdly, that so long as the young emperor remained in the Forbidden City it would be impossible to take any active steps towards restoring him to the throne without endangering his life.

As far as I could ascertain, the people who held these views were much less numerous than those who uncompromisingly rejected the idea of displacing the young emperor and who refused to consider the claims of any rival. But these again were subdivided into various groups who held more or less irreconcilable views as to procedure. Some were in favour of taking no direct action until it was found possible to put the emperor himself openly at the head of the movement, and that was an impossibility so long as he resided in the palace. Others again were in favour of taking no action at all, *so long as the republic kept faith with the emperor by observing the Articles of Favourable Treatment.*

Meanwhile, the monarchists who had always cherished the idea of a new state in Manchuria and Mongolia under the emperor found themselves faced by a difficulty which had not existed in 1911. Manchuria actually, and Mongolia in theory, had become parts of the Chinese republic, and by 1919 the republican system, such as it was, had been extended to Manchuria and was in control of the administrative machine. Chang Tso-lin had no republican sympathies, but he was watchful over his own interests and was not at first the dictator that he afterwards became. It was no longer true to say that if the emperor fled to Manchuria he would be allowed to take peaceable possession of the throne of his ancestors at Mukden. There were already strong vested interests that would oppose him ; and a monarchist movement in Manchuria would lead to civil war just as certainly as would a similar movement in Shantung or any other province of China proper. This was recognised by most of the monarchist party, and the recognition led them to acquiesce in the postponement of all action until the republic should perish through its own inward rottenness—a consummation to which they looked forward hopefully—or until something should happen in Manchuria which would lead to foreign intervention. What the " something " might prove to be, no one knew ; but there were many who felt convinced that the day would come, sooner or later, when Japan would find herself forced to take active steps to protect against Chinese encroachment the vast interests acquired by her in Manchuria as a result of the two wars she had fought on Manchurian soil. A conflict between Japan and the Chinese republic—or those who posed as representatives of the republic in Manchuria—would, thought these monarchists, give them the opportunity they desired. To those who might reproach them with treachery to China in allying themselves with a foreign Power, they would be able to reply that China had already declared the Manchus to be aliens (i tsu) and had driven them from the throne on that ground. An alien race or an alien family owed no allegiance to China. The Chinese could hardly say " we owe no allegiance to this alien race, but this alien race owes allegiance to us." And being aliens, there was no logical reason why the Manchus and those who had remained loyal to them should not choose their own allies.

As early as March, 1919, the *Peking Leader* gave a fairly full account of mysterious events which were said (not, as I knew, without partial justification) to be taking place in both Mongolia and Manchuria. It described the " Pan-Mongolian movement for the establishment of a new Mongol State under the

protection of Japan . . . with the Living Buddha of Outer Mongolia as President " ; and added that " the agitators *are endeavouring to extend their field of activities to Manchuria through
the media of prince Su, prince Kung* . . . and other members of
the Manchu nobility who are dissatisfied with the overthrow of
the Imperial house." It concluded by saying that the Peking
government were taking steps " to watch the movements of
those Manchu and Mongol princes who assisted ex-general
Chang Hsün to restore the boy-emperor in 1917, as there is a
report that the Imperial Restoration Society is taking an interest
in the movement."[8]

On July 20th in the same year (1919) I received the following
report from private sources : " Chang Tso-lin is plotting to
restore the monarchy, his intention being to make an attempt
next autumn to install the young emperor on the throne at
Mukden, simultaneously declaring Manchuria an independent
kingdom under Japanese protection."

Here it may be mentioned that this possibility was again
hinted at three years later. Mr. Rodney Gilbert, writing in the
North China Herald of March 18th, 1922, observed that if Chang
Tso-lin were to be worsted in an anticipated struggle with the
forces of his rival Wu P'ei-fu, his " part in national politics
would be at an end, and *the only refuge would lie in the independence of Manchuria under Japanese patronage.*"

On September 9th, 1919, the *North China Daily Mail*, of
Tientsin, published a leading article entitled " Is Another
Restoration Near at Hand ? " in the course of which the follow-
ing remarks occurred :

" The record of the republic has been anything but a
happy one, and to-day we find North and South at daggers
drawn. The only conclusion to be drawn from this is that
republicanism in China has been tried and found wanting.
The mercantile classes and the gentry, the back-bone of the
land, are weary of all this internecine strife and we firmly
believe they would give their whole-hearted support to any
form of government which would ensure peace to the eighteen
provinces.

" It must not be forgotten that there exists a very strong

phalanx of pro-monarchical people who have never become reconciled to the republican form of government, but they have kept quiet for the last few years for obvious reasons. That they are in sympathy with the present militaristic movement goes without saying and the comings and goings of some of the better known of them to various places where officials are known to congregate are not devoid of significance.

" The contention of those who secretly favour and hope for a successful restoration of the ex-emperor is that the republicans are destroying the country, and that means, however drastic, must be taken to bring it back to its former prosperous and peaceful condition.

" A reversion to a monarchy is not by any means likely to be well received in all quarters. On the contrary, it will probably meet with considerable diplomatic opposition in more than one Legation, but even opposition of that kind is bound to evaporate if a successful *coup d'état* is brought off, as we all know that nothing succeeds like success."

Still more significant was the following paragraph, emanating from Mukden, which appeared in the *Peking Leader* of December 27th, 1919 :

" During the course of the last few days, the rumour of the coming resuscitation of the Manchu monarchy in Peking in place of the existing so-called republican government of China has been in circulation among all classes of the natives especially among the militarists under general Chang Tso-lin. According to current allegations, the monarchy this time will be started by general Chang Tso-lin with the co-operation of certain monarchical and military leaders of north-west China, and ex-general Chang Hsün, who actually placed the young Manchu Emperor, Hsüan-T'ung, on the throne for twelve days in July, 1917, will play a very important part in it. The story adds that at the present moment, the only serious obstacle to the monarchy movement is marshal Tuan Ch'i-jui and certain leaders in the south-west and that even president Hsü and ex-president Fêng, in view of the existing unsettled political situation of the country and external dangers, are inclined to accept the resuscitation of monarchy without strong opposition or dissatisfaction. With regard to Ts'ao K'un, Li Shun and other lesser military leaders, it is said that these men can be satisfied by making them princes, dukes or marquises in addition to permitting them to hold their present posts in the various provinces. It is reliably reported among Chinese official circles that if the resuscitation of the monarchy scheme becomes a fact in the not distant future, it has been caused by the sad plight of the domestic peace conference and the lack of unification of the country which is worse than in the Manchu days and that the plot is to place the Manchu ruler nominally at the head of the Chinese government while all political, financial and military powers will remain in the hands of the Chinese premier. Further, there will only be a small change in the name of the country ; that is to say, China will then be known to the world as " Chung-Hua Ti-kuo " instead of " Chung-Hua Min-kuo." The form of the government of China will then be *Chün-chu Li-hsien* or a constitutional government under a nominal king or emperor after the model of the British Empire."

The wording of this report is obviously not that of a disinterested newspaper correspondent. It is a carefully-prepared statement drawn up by someone who was in sympathy with the movement it described ; and the object of publication seems to have been to prepare the minds of the Chinese and foreign public for a new political upheaval.

That rumours of a very similar kind were still current a year or two later may be gathered from a statement published in the *North China Standard* (Peking) of March 23rd, 1921, which said that the new Manchurian empire was to be named the Pei-Chung-Hua (meaning Northern China) Empire with the seat of government at Mukden. " The rumour-mongers say that general Chang Hsün and ex-prince Tuan, Boxer ringleader, and those who failed in 1917 at the hands of marshal Tuan Ch'i-jui, are now at the back of the movement throughout North China, Mongolia and Manchuria." Another paragraph in the same paper of May 21st was as follows :

" According to reliable reports in the possession of the Chinese authorities . . . the policy of prince Su and ex-viceroy Shêng Yün aims at the restoration of the Manchu dynasty in China. If this cannot be done, adds the report, then the Manchu restorationists will raise the cry of ' Manchuria for the Manchus ' in the hope of re-establishing the decadent Manchus in Mukden at the commencement. The Chinese officials are greatly alarmed because it is feared that the joint movement of Ataman Seminov and prince Su is connected with the present serious situation in Outer Mongolia."

The common belief at the time (1921) was that the ringleaders in the monarchist conspiracy were Chang Tso-lin of Manchuria and Chang Hsün, the " kingmaker " of 1917. It is not generally known that the two families were connected by marriage, and that there was a close friendship between them. (Chang Tso-lin had supported the restoration of 1917, though he took no active part in it, and afterwards tried to persuade the world that he was a staunch republican !) Great efforts were made by Chang Tso-lin —who however kept himself carefully in the background and worked through others—to prepare the way for what was coming by bringing Chang Hsün back into official life. He was to be given an important military post on the Yangtse. It was largely due to the failure of this scheme that the monarchist *coup* was indefinitely postponed and Chang Tso-lin himself began to have other ambitions. But that he and Chang Hsün intended to restore the monarchy in 1921 was stated as a fact by ex-president Li Yüan-hung in an interview with Mr. Rodney Gilbert, correspondent of the *North China Daily News*. He declared it was bound to come, but foretold its failure.[9]

" It is said," wrote Mr. Gilbert in March, " that the plans for the monarchy movement have gone so far and are known to so many of the Manchurian dictator's military associates in various parts of China, that a public demonstration in favour of the Manchu emperor must come long before June and that it may come almost any day."[10] Mr. Gilbert added the well-justified comment : " It is also apparent that if Chang Tso-lin succeeded in restoring the Manchu emperor to the throne, he would not remain far in the background. Everyone feels that the mooted restoration is not so much in the interests of the emperor as in that of Chang Tso-lin and of his political associates, who feel that their positions are now precarious."

Some time before this, Chang Tso-lin had tried to repudiate any connection with the schemes of the monarchists, but the following statement authorised by him as early as the beginning of 1920 and published in the Chinese and foreign press on January 10th, contained a significant hint that there was to be no interference with the Articles of Favourable Treatment, of which radical politicians and their newspaper organs were already demanding the repudiation :

> "Although there may be some ex-ministers of the Ta Ch'ing court who still harbour sympathetic sentiments towards their old masters, nevertheless, *as long as the Manchu Favourable Treatment Agreement is respected and maintained by the republic of China*, it will be quite sufficient for their maintenance without aspiring for political powers as well."

I have quoted the foregoing newspaper reports because I am in a position to say that they were not mere gossip. As I knew from other sources of information which were made accessible to me, they were based on fact. Knowing this to be so, I have found it difficult to explain the statement in the Lytton Report that the Manchurian independence movement " had never been heard of in Manchuria before September, 1931,"[11] except on the assumption that the evidence for the existence of such a movement in the interests of the old monarchy had not been laid before Lord Lytton and his colleagues.

During the years from 1919 to 1924 I gradually came to know many of the persons who were interested in the various monarchist schemes, including some of those who expected to take a prominent part in carrying them out, such as the loyal old viceroy Shêng Yün, who was a Mongol. Much of the information given me was naturally of a highly confidential nature which I was under an obligation not to betray to the British or any other authorities.

No monarchist plans were discussed in the palace, and the emperor himself was not a party to any of the plots, if they can be called such. He was of course well aware that there were still

many loyalists in Manchuria and in every part of China and
Mongolia, and that they had not given up hope of seeing him
return to the throne either in Peking or in Mukden ; but as to
the nature of the various monarchist plans he knew very little
more than he gathered from the newspapers. The subject was
scrupulously avoided by his Chinese tutors and by myself, as
we were all anxious that he should not be personally involved
in anything that might be interpreted as a conspiracy against
the republic. It was only when he himself mentioned the subject
—usually in connection with a newspaper report that he had just
been reading—that some discussion of it was unavoidable. On
such occasions I did not hesitate to express my own opinion
with all the force of which I was capable. That opinion was to
the effect that anything in the shape of a conspiracy to re-estab-
lish the monarchy by a *coup d'état* similar to that attempted by
Chang Hsün in 1917 was to be condemned ; that any fraudulent
manipulation of public opinion such as that which disgraced
Yüan Shih-k'ai's Hung-Hsien movement of 1916 should also
be scrupulously avoided ; and that the emperor should refuse to
listen to any invitation to resume the throne unless it came to
him in the form of a genuine and spontaneous appeal from the
freely-elected representatives of the people. The chances of any
such invitation ever reaching him seemed to me to be very
remote, and I did not hesitate to say so ; nor was I able to
suggest any method whereby, under existing conditions in
China, the people of the country could make their will known or
—assuming it to be known—how they could make it prevail.
None of the parliaments which had yet come into being, since
the revolution, had been truly representative of the people, and
there was no prospect of any such parliament being elected.
Nevertheless it was possible—it seemed to me highly probable
—that if a genuinely representative assembly could be brought
into existence, or if the question of monarchy *versus* republic
could be made the subject of a free vote by such an assembly,
the majority in favour of monarchy would be enormous, even
if the choice of monarchy were known to involve the restoration
of the dynasty which had so lately been overthrown.

The *Peking and Tientsin Times* said in a leading article on
March 19th, 1921, that " it is probably a moderate estimate to

suggest that ninety per cent of the population would favour the return of the emperor," and I believe this was no exaggeration. But I was equally in agreement with the writer of that article when he went on to say that the anticipated monarchist movement would probably fail, because " saving or restoring the republic has become too lucrative an operation to be readily abandoned by the militarists and others seeking a short road to fortune."

As I saw no likelihood of the popular will finding a medium of expression, I could see no prospect of a restoration coming about except by means which in my opinion the emperor should refuse to employ or to allow others to employ on his behalf.

I explained to him, moreover, that if we were right in supposing that the people would welcome the revival of the monarchy, it was not so much from any deep-rooted feeling of loyalty to the imperial house, though that feeling was undoubtedly present to a far greater extent than was commonly supposed, as from the disastrous failure of the republican alternative. What the masses of the people longed for was decent government, and if they were monarchists at heart it was mainly because they thought they would be more likely to get that under the traditional system of government, which they all understood, than under the only kind of republic of which they had yet had experience.

The following paragraph is an extract from a memorandum which I wrote at Weihaiwei immediately before I left that territory at the beginning of 1919 to take up my new duties at the Manchu court.

" What most thoughtful Chinese want is a stable government, strong enough to exterminate the bands of armed robbers that now infest many parts of the country ; courageous enough to disband, or keep under control, the various ' armies ' which in several provinces are regarded as a worse evil than the brigands ; skilful enough to keep the country out of foreign entanglements and save it from the tyranny of international finance ; and conscientious enough to see that its officials do their duty faithfully and refrain from enriching themselves by corrupt means at the public expense. It seems to me that the question of ' Republic versus Monarchy ' is not the question that agitates the Chinese people to-day. They would thankfully accept any form of government that showed itself able and willing to govern."[12]

In the light of later knowledge and experience I found no reason to alter the views expressed at the beginning of 1919. They were shared to no small extent by most of the thoughtful Chinese whose acquaintance I made in Peking during the years that followed, even by those whose sympathies were not with monarchy. One of these was Dr. Hu Shih—a man who was becoming famous in several spheres of activity, including literature, education, philosophy and politics. When he was asked by someone whether it was true that Young China wanted anarchy and Old China wanted monarchy, his clever reply was that what both wanted was " euarchy." (The word actually coined and used by Dr. Hu was " eunarchy," but the obvious derivation from εὐαρχία makes the " n " superfluous and I have therefore ventured to leave it out.)

The young emperor had not the slightest inclination to take part in any monarchist conspiracy. He often assured me that in no circumstances would he consent to act again the part that had been thrust upon him by Chang Hsün. He agreed with me that the restoration of the monarchy, even if strongly desired by the people, was an improbable event, and that the republic, such as it was, had probably come to stay, at least for some years to come. Nor did this seem to cause him regret or disappointment. His familiarity with his family history, his natural pride in, and filial respect for, his imperial ancestors, could not but lead him to lament that the dynasty which had been made illustrious by such mighty rulers as K'ang-Hsi and Ch'ien-Lung should have come, in his person, to an inglorious end. But those who suspected and accused him—as many frequently did—of spending his days and nights in plotting the destruction of the republic and dreaming of grasping again the sceptre which his father the regent and the treacherous Yüan Shih-k'ai had taken out of his childish hands in 1912, were profoundly ignorant of their discarded emperor's character and personality.

CHAPTER XVII

The Dragon Restless

As EARLY AS THE LATTER PART OF 1920, before he was sixteen, the emperor had succeeded in breaking down some of the conventions and formalities that had regulated his daily life. He fixed his own hours for work and play. He walked—or ran—through the courtyards and long alley-ways that divided the palace-buildings from one another, instead of allowing himself to be carried from place to place in a huge yellow palanquin. He shocked the palace officials by the apathy or amused contempt with which he regarded many of the things that in their eyes were the be-all and end-all of his existence—court ceremonial, the etiquette of audiences and the observance of solemn anniversaries. Fully understanding the unrealities of his position, he distressed his courtiers by refusing to take them as seriously as they took themselves. Their crude flattery bored him and he detected their insincerity.

Never did Rasselas long more ardently to leave his Happy Valley in Abyssinia than did the young Manchu emperor to see something of the world that lay beyond the walls of the Forbidden City. The glimpses he had of that world from the summit of a rockery in the imperial garden or from the pavilion that crowned the Gate of Spiritual Valour merely had the effect of increasing his disquiet. Yet when he pleaded to be allowed to leave the palace grounds he met always with the same answer—the times were dangerous, emissaries of Sun Yat-sen's southern revolutionaries were lying in wait for him, he would be insulted, assaulted, perhaps done to death. Some day he might be able to come and go as he wished, but meanwhile he must be patient. The time for freedom had not yet come.

When he was at last permitted to leave the Forbidden City, the occasion was a sad one. His mother, the princess Ch'un, died on September 30th, 1921. Her death took place at the Pei Fu—prince Ch'un's residence in the northern section of

Peking, the emperor's own birthplace. At the beginning of
October he went to pay his last respects to his dead mother, and
remained at the Pei Fu for half a day. Before he left the Forbidden City the streets that led from the Gate of Spiritual Valour
due north past the Coal Hill towards the Drum Tower were lined
with police and republican troops. The road lay through the
Hou-Mên, which is the triple gateway leading from what is
known as the Huang Ch'êng or Imperial City into the outer
part of the so-called Tartar City. Normally the central gate of
the three was kept closed, only the right and left gates being
available for the public. In imperial days the central gate was
opened only for the emperor, and since the establishment of the
republic only for the president. On this occasion, and on all
similar occasions thereafter up to November, 1924, the central
gate was thrown open for the emperor's car—a sign that the
republic was still honouring its undertaking to treat the Ta
Ch'ing emperor with imperial honours.

His car was preceded and followed by the cars of his retinue.
The streets were crowded with people who had come forth
hoping to catch a glimpse of the boy who had once been their
sovereign. Needless to say, nothing occurred to suggest that
" the times were dangerous " for him. The crowd was silent,
sympathetic and respectful.

After the expiry of the period of court mourning, he expressed
a very natural desire to repeat his brief excursion into the city,
but numerous objections were immediately raised. He was
informed, for example, that no such excursions were possible
for him without costly preparations, that tiresome negotiations
had to be carried on with the republican authorities, that largesse
on a fantastic scale had to be distributed among the police and
soldiers and among the custodians of the Hou-Mên, and that a
large number of cars had to be hired for the use of his escort.
When I pleaded on his behalf that he should be allowed to visit
the city, and the country beyond it, in a purely private capacity,
without an escort, the suggestion was regarded as unworthy of
serious discussion.

Nevertheless the emperor insisted, after this experience, in
purchasing a car for himself, and it was in his own car that
on May 13th, 1922, he visited his senior Chinese tutor, Ch'ên

Pao-shên, who was seriously ill with pneumonia. The old gentleman fortunately recovered and is still (1934) hale and hearty at the age of eighty-seven.[1] On September 26th in the same year the emperor paid a similar visit to his dying Manchu tutor, I-K'o-T'an.[2] On both occasions he was accompanied, quite unnecessarily, by court officials and military officers in hired cars. Among the officers were some who wore the republican uniform, and who, as I soon discovered, were entrusted with the duty of seeing that the emperor confined his visits to the Pei Fu and his tutors' residences in the West city, and did not drive to the southern section of the " Tartar City " in which lay the foreign Legation Quarter. In this matter the palace staff and the republican authorities acted in collaboration, but on the initiative of the former. I was personally assured by president Hsü Shih-ch'ang in the course of two private interviews that so long as he was president the republic would put no restraint on the emperor's movements. On the other hand the president took no active steps, as he well might have done, to put an end to the corruption and extravagance of the court. He could have done so merely by making future payments of the stipulated subsidy (already in arrears to the extent of millions of dollars) dependent on the reform of abuses. His failure to do this was apparently due to his unwillingness to antagonise a still influential section of his political supporters, who included the household department and its large circle of friends, many princes of the imperial family, powerful " republican " leaders like Tuan Ch'i-jui, Chang Tso-lin, Chang Hsün, and Ts'ao K'un, and all the secret or avowed monarchists who through ignorance of real conditions in the Forbidden City regarded every attack on the status and privileges of the household department as an attack on the emperor or the imperial dignity, or as a violation of the Articles of Favourable Treatment.

Less than six months before the death of the emperor's mother, one of the four imperial dowagers had died in her palace in the Forbidden City. This was Chuang-Ho, a surviving *huang-kuei-fei* (imperial consort of the second degree) of the emperor T'ung Chih. She died on April 14th, 1921. Three days' full court mourning and thirty-five days' half-mourning were ordained by imperial edict, and for that period her coffin was deposited in the

Palace of Kindliness and Tranquillity which had at one time
been the residence of the empress-dowager Tz'ŭ-Hsi.[3] A few days
later it was announced in the Court Gazette that the emperor
had gone in state to pay his respects before the coffin of the late
huang-kuei-fei. On the following day the same duty was carried
out by the princes and court officials, including myself. In the
case of the princes and officials, the rites included genuflections
and prostrations before the coffin, to the accompaniment of the
wailing of a crowd of white-robed eunuchs on their knees. The
same wailing accompanied my own less elaborate salutation,
which consisted of three bows. The old lady's funeral (to the
Eastern Mausolea) took place about the middle of May.

The sincerity of the wailing may be gauged from the fact that
no sooner had Chuang-Ho ceased to breathe than her staff of
eunuchs proceeded to strip her palace of its jewellery and
treasures. The affair created a scandal in the Forbidden City, not
because of the actual thefts—it seemed to be taken for granted
that the eunuchs would steal their dead mistress's property—but
because the thieves struggled among themselves for the booty
and caused an uproar which, in a chamber of death, was regarded by the household officials as unseemly. Had the eunuchs
conducted their looting in a decorous manner, the affair would
probably have aroused very little comment. Nothing whatever
was done to punish them or even to make them disgorge their
plunder. When the emperor (who spoke of the matter to me with
deep indignation) tried to have the culprits punished he was
told not only by the court officials but also by some of the
princes (and, rather surprisingly, by the three surviving *huang-
kuei-fei*) that the affair must be overlooked in order that the
" face " of the dead lady might be saved. This is a rather
startling illustration of what " face " can be made to mean in
China. Apparently the old lady would have gone to her grave
with " lost face " if her servants had been convicted of stealing
her property after her death. It was therefore necessary that the
matter should be hushed up so that a disaster of such magnitude
might be averted.

Cases of actual theft did not often come to my knowledge, but
examples of the barefaced swindling and peculation that went
on in the Forbidden City were constantly forcing themselves

upon my attention. The outlay on the imperial kitchen-department reminded me of a possibly apocryphal story of a Chinese emperor who asked a kneeling official what he usually ate for breakfast.[4] " Two or three eggs " was the reply. " Monstrous ! " exclaimed the emperor ; " I could not afford more than one myself. How is it that you, a servant of the throne, can afford to eat two or three eggs a day ? " The official, knowing that the eyes of the court were upon him, hastened to explain that the eggs he ate were cheap and nasty : stinking eggs, in fact, quite unfit for the imperial table. Had he been acquainted with English egg-lore he might perhaps have explained that his eggs were all curate's eggs.

Such stories, whether true or not, give an accurate idea of the popular beliefs regarding the colossal " squeeze " system for which the imperial palace was notorious throughout China. A French writer tells a story of the donation of $80,000 once given by an emperor for the purpose of repairing Legation Street in Peking. By the time the money had passed through the hands of palace-officials, contractors and other middlemen and had reached the actual workmen who were to do the repairs, the amount available for distribution among them had dwindled to $80.[5]

I have a vivid recollection of a dinner-party given by one of the imperial tutors at which several of the principal officers of the household were present. The conversation turned on a recent festival at the palace, which had involved such a large expenditure that it had been found necessary to mortgage a quantity of jade and porcelain. In answer to my rather searching and probably impertinent questions regarding the reasons for so vast an expenditure on what had appeared to me to be a very simple ceremony, I was told that the greater part of the amount was payable to eunuchs for hanging up and lighting a number of lanterns. For this service, which as I pointed out could have been carried out by men hired from the streets of Peking at a total cost of certainly not more than ten dollars, it appeared that " old custom " required an expenditure of thousands. When, on this and many similar occasions, I asked why it was necessary to spend such fabulous sums in return for trivial services, I was merely reminded that in former days, before the revolution, there was no need to be stingy where money matters were concerned, and that it would be a hardship to deprive the palace staff of perquisites to which they had been accustomed. My attempts to show that as times had changed and money was no longer so easily procurable as of old, some attempt should be made to administer the affairs of the palace on more economical lines met with a frigid reception.

Having acquired his own motor-car, of which, however, he was able to make very little use, the emperor went a step further by demanding that he should be connected with the outside world by telephone. The household, of course, raised every conceivable objection to this proposal. They said, for example, that if it were publicly known that the emperor was on the telephone his enemies would make a practice of ringing him up and making insulting remarks. Finally, however, he got his way, and for the first time a telephone was installed in the emperor's private quarters. That he made abundant use of his new plaything was a fact which I soon had good reason to know.

The years 1921 and 1922 were remarkable for several convulsions in the palace for which I was directly or indirectly responsible.

One of these had reference to the emperor's eyesight. It was in 1921 that I made the discovery that he was seriously shortsighted, and surmised that headaches and other bodily ailments from which he had been suffering were due to eye-strain. The discovery was an accidental one. I happened to notice that the emperor, when seated at his table in the imperial school-room, had a habit of turning round to look at the face of a very large clock (the gift of a foreign court) of which the dial was built into the wall, to the neglect of a small clock which was conveniently placed in front of him on the table. " Why," I asked one day, " does *huang-shang* take the trouble to turn round and look at the large clock when there is a clock on the table ? " " I can't see the small one distinctly," was his reply.

I brought this obviously important matter to the notice of his father and the household officials and his Chinese tutors, and I was amazed by the indifference with which it was regarded by them. When Tuan K'ang—the most influential of the three surviving dowager-consorts—heard that the English tutor had
Sc

asked for permission to send for a foreign oculist, she replied
with emphasis that such a request could not be granted, as no
foreign doctor could be trusted with anything so precious as
the imperial eyes. When my request was repeated in a more
urgent form, her retort was to the effect that a foreign doctor
might have the presumption to prescribe spectacles, and " the
wearing of spectacles by emperors is a thing that is not done."
" I know nothing about the practice of former emperors,"
I replied ; " this one is going to wear spectacles."

Tuan K'ang's opposition was not overcome, but prince Ch'un
and the household department finally gave way with a very
bad grace, after I had intimated that if by the end of the year
(1921) I was still forbidden to send for the best ophthalmologist
in Peking, I should resign my post. By this time the household
department, who already regarded me as a nuisance, would have
been glad to see me go. Unfortunately for them, the emperor
himself put an end to the discussion by declaring that the matter
of his eyes was to be left to me, and that my resignation would
not be accepted.

It was with feelings of relief and triumph that on November
7th, 1921, I was able to write to Professor H. J. Howard, the
distinguished American head of the department of ophthalmo-
logy in the Peking Union Medical College (the Rockefeller
foundation) and invite him to pay a professional visit to the
Forbidden City. The dowager Tuan K'ang, I may add, was not
told of the decision arrived at till after Dr. Howard had come
and gone. One of the officers of the household informed me that
if she were defied in this matter she might manifest her displeasure by giving herself a fatal dose of opium. That was a
tragic possibility which I ignored.

The examination was conducted on November 8th, by Dr.
Howard and his Chinese assistant Dr. Tsing Meu Li. Their report was to the effect that his majesty had severe progressive
myopia and other ocular defects, that glasses, which they duly
prescribed, must be worn, and that the state of his eyes was
such that it would be necessary to have another examination
in a year's time to ascertain whether the trouble had been
checked. They were astonished that so grave a matter had been
neglected for many years, and Dr. Howard, at least, was almost

incredulous when I told him of the opposition which had been raised in the palace to anything being done at all.

The difference which glasses made to the emperor's comfort and general well-being was very great. Before long, indeed, he became so inordinately devoted to his spectacles that he refused to be parted from them for a moment, even for the purpose of being photographed or having his portrait painted.

I may add that no member of the palace staff or the imperial family ever expressed any satisfaction at the steps I had taken, and I think the household officials, if not the Chinese tutors, never ceased to regard my interference in this matter with resentment. Whether Tuan K'ang ever forgave me I do not know, but at any rate I have not to reproach myself with having shortened her life. What her feelings were on her first view of a spectacled Son of Heaven I can only guess.

It may be worth adding that when the Hospital authorities refused to accept a fee for the services rendered to the emperor, the imperial household was ordered by his majesty to send the hospital a donation of $1,000. It should also be mentioned that Dr. Howard subsequently added to his laurels by achieving the distinction (less common then than it became later) of being kidnapped and held to ransom by bandits in Manchuria.

The next alarming event in the palace in which I might be regarded as having been indirectly concerned was the disappearance of the imperial queue, irreverently called a pigtail. The emperor had several times expressed his desire to dispense with this ornament, but in spite of the fact that all his uncles and other members of the imperial family had got rid of theirs, he was told that he, as representative and head of the Manchu race, must show his respect for Manchu traditions by adhering to his own. He gave up arguing the matter, but one day suddenly ordered his eunuch-barber to cut it off. The barber, horror-stricken at the thought of what might befall him if he obeyed such an order, implored his majesty to call upon someone else to carry it out. The emperor said nothing, but retired to another room, took up a pair of scissors and cut off his queue with his own hands.

For a few days there was dismay at court, and many reproachful remarks were addressed to myself; but within a month there were only three queues to be seen in the Forbidden City where there had lately been at least fifteen hundred. The three surviving queues belonged to my three tutorial colleagues (soon to be reduced by death to two), who retained theirs as outward and permanent tokens of reproach and protest.[6]

Much nonsense has been uttered by both foreigners and Chinese about the queue or " pigtail " having been a " badge of servitude " imposed upon the enslaved Chinese by their Manchu masters. It was, indeed, the Manchus who required all male Chinese to show their loyalty to the new dynasty by shaving the front of the head and growing queues, but it is absurd to describe this style of coiffure as a badge of servitude, inasmuch as the Manchus themselves, from the emperor downwards, wore the same " badge." However unwilling, at first, the Chinese may have been to adopt the new fashion, they came in time to be exceedingly proud of their queues, which would hardly have been possible had they ever been regarded as badges of servitude ; and at the time of the revolution their compulsory removal often caused much bitterness and ill-feeling. In country districts in northern and western China, and also of course Manchuria, queues are by no means a rarity to this day. In some places, people who had been forcibly deprived of their queues started to grow them again. In the *North China Herald* of March 11th, 1922, ten years after the revolution, a correspondent in the province of Ssuch'uan wrote thus : " I have noticed how many people are growing queues again, and yesterday I saw a youth with a lovely one. One sees quite a number in various stages of growth." At the very time when the Chinese of that far western province were doing their best to regrow their vanished queues, the descendant of the tyrannical monarchs who were supposed to have compelled their ancestors to wear them was light-heartedly shearing off his own.

Still more remarkable is the fact that by the beginning of the twentieth century the Manchus of some districts in Manchuria had completely forgotten that it was their own ancestors who had imposed queue-wearing on the Chinese, and were under the impression that it was a Chinese custom which their ancestors had imitated. When the revolution of 1911 broke out these Manchus gave what they thought was a proof of their resentment against the Chinese " rebels " *by cutting off their own queues.*[7]

The third small earthquake in the Forbidden City for which I was held largely responsible was caused by the interest which the emperor began to take in the activities of " Young China." Without wishing to make him an iconoclast or to turn him into a disciple of the literary and social reformers of the *Hsin Ch'ing Nien* (" New Youth ") school, of which indeed I was not myself an uncritical admirer, I thought it right that a youth of the emperor's age and intelligence should at least acquaint himself with the thoughts that were fermenting in the minds of the young men of his time and should not be kept in ignorance of the existence of movements which were bound to have a profound effect, for good or evil or a mixture of both, on the cultural future of China. He learned nothing of these things from his Chinese tutors, who indeed paid little or no attention to them, and it therefore fell to me to introduce him to this new world of unorthodox thought.

I was personally acquainted with several of the leaders of the " New Youth " and the " Literary Reform " movement in Peking. many of whom were fellow-members with me of an international society—the *Wên Yu Hui* or " Society of Friends of Literature "—which met periodically to discuss the subjects in which we had a common interest.[8] For a year I held the office of president of this society, and my successor was the well-known philosopher and " literary reformer " Dr. Hu Shih. Having made a selection of his Chinese writings I presented them to the emperor, together with copies of several periodicals to which Dr. Hu and his group were regular contributors.

The result of this was that at the end of May, 1922, Dr. Hu received a summons to a private audience. Before the appointed time arrived he came to discuss with me matters of court etiquette, and was relieved to learn that the emperor would certainly not expect him to kneel. As we knew that strong opposition would be raised to the admission of a well-known radical and propagator of " dangerous thoughts " into the palace, the household department was told nothing of the summons to Dr. Hu, which had been conveyed by telephone. When, therefore, he presented himself at the Gate of Spiritual

Valour, the guard naturally refused to admit him. He was kept waiting a considerable time before peremptory orders from the emperor obliged the guard to let him pass.

The following brief account of the interview was given to me a few days later by Dr. Hu himself in a letter dated June 7th.

" The emperor was very kind and courteous to me when I called. We talked about the new poetry, its young authors, and other literary subjects. The delay at the gate having consumed a part of the time which I had calculated on for my stay in the palace, I did not stay long, and after about twenty minutes I took leave of his majesty in order to keep an important appointment outside . . . I had intended to keep this interview out of the newspapers. But unfortunately some newspapers which I do not read regularly have reported this event, which naturally seemed to them to have capital news value. . . . I must confess that I was deeply touched by this little event. Here I was, standing and sitting in front of the last of the emperors of my country, the last representative of a long line of great monarchs ! "

The remainder of Dr. Hu's letter contained a friendly reference to new influences which had come into the emperor's life, without which " the palace must have been an intellectual prison indeed."

Dr. Hu was right in saying that his interview with the emperor would be regarded as having " capital news value." It also caused him to be denounced by left-wing members of the movements with which he was associated, on the ground that he had performed the *kotow* before the emperor—which was untrue —and had addressed him as *huang-shang* (" your majesty "), which was true. Three years later Dr. Hu was still being assailed for his alleged betrayal of republican principles in these matters, in spite of the fact that in addressing the emperor as *huang-shang* he had merely shown his unwillingness to regard the Articles of Favourable Treatment as a scrap of paper.[9]

Dr. Hu had only one more short interview with the emperor in the Forbidden City. That took place nearly two years later, on March 27th, 1924.[10]

As I was held largely responsible for the various disturbing events I have described, and also for the emperor's growing dissatisfaction with existing conditions, it is not surprising that by 1922 I had come to be regarded as a menace to the stability of the palace system. In spite of the rather elaborate courtesy with which I continued to be treated by Shao-Ying—who succeeded Shih-Hsü as head of the household department—and by all the members of his staff, I became aware that I had ceased to be a *persona grata* in palace circles. Nothing but my increasing sympathy with my imperial pupil, and his personal appeals to me that I should not leave him, prevented me from resigning my post at the Manchu Court before the end of that year.

CHAPTER XVIII

The Dragon Flaps His Wings

THE FIRST HALF OF 1922 was a period of steadily increasing political tension. The Cantonese government, of course, maintained its policy of non-recognition of its northern rival, but it was not the Cantonese or the followers of Sun Yat-sen who were at this time the chief causes of anxiety and friction in the north. The trouble came from the mutual distrust and animosity of the northern political groups—the Anfu, Fêng-t'ien and Chihli parties—each of which aimed at the domination of the political life of the capital. The two chief rival personalities were Chang Tso-lin and Wu P'ei-fu. The first made it clear that he was not satisfied with the control of his vast Manchurian dominions but wished to be master also at Peking ; the second—a brave soldier if not the great general that he believed himself to be, and a true patriot if not a sound statesman—was equally determined to bring about the unification of China on a different basis than that contemplated by the warlord of the north.

I have shown in the last chapter that at least up to 1922 Chang Tso-lin was more than suspected of aiming at the restoration of the monarchy—with himself as the power behind the throne. From the middle of 1923 onwards there was a change in his attitude towards the court.

Already in the preceding year I had discovered that certain persons in the Forbidden City were his paid agents, and that through them he obtained secret and regular information regarding the affairs of the court and the political affiliations and sympathies of the household department and the Manchu princes. Up to 1922 he was regarded by them as the most powerful of their friends, and they looked to him to be their champion in the event of any danger threatening the imperial establishment. I do not mean by this that the household department or the princes were Chang Tso-lin's confederates in a monarchist plot. I cannot speak for all the princes, but I am convinced that the main concern of the Nei Wu Fu was merely the maintenance of the Articles of Favourable Treatment on which depended their own valuable privileges and emoluments. So long as Chang Tso-lin was regarded by the Nei Wu Fu as not only friendly to the imperial court but also as the strongest power in Chinese politics, they were well content to give him their undivided support and confidence.

I had evidence of this during a short and sharp civil war in the summer of 1920. For a few days it seemed possible that Peking might pass under the control of a group of politicians and military leaders who were Chang's enemies and who were believed to entertain sinister designs against the emperor. I was brought into the innermost palace councils at that time, because it was desired that I should be at the emperor's side in the event of his being threatened by personal danger, and that I should therefore be ready, at a moment's notice, to leave my own house and become a temporary resident in the Forbidden City. For several days, while battles were being fought in the neighbourhood of Peking, I kept a packed suit-case in the emperor's quarters. Suddenly, however, the situation changed. Chang Tso-lin was triumphant in his little war, and no sooner had he arrived at the gates of Peking than I was assured that all cause for anxiety on account of the emperor was gone. His majesty was now perfectly safe, and I was free to unpack my suit-case.

But the complete trust which the princes and palace authorities placed in Chang Tso-lin in 1920 had been shaken by 1923. It is unnecessary to describe here the events which gradually led to the rise of Wu P'ei-fu, who established his army headquarters at Loyang in Honan and gradually extended his power over the greater part of central and north China. It came to be a prevalent view in those regions, and especially in political circles in Peking, that Wu P'ei-fu was the coming man and that Chang Tso-lin's power south of the Great Wall, if not north of it, would soon be broken. These views were shared to some extent by several of the most influential of the Manchu princes and also by the household department ; and through those persons who, as I have said, acted in the Forbidden City as Chang Tso-lin's secret agents, the Manchu warlord learned the disconcerting news that the Manchu court was beginning to cultivate the friendship of his rival at

Loyang. Any doubts as to the truth of this story were removed
from Chang's mind when he heard that K'ang Yu-wei and other
well-known monarchists had visited and had been hospitably
entertained by Wu P'ei-fu, and that on the occasion of the
latter's birthday the Manchu Household had sent messengers to
Loyang with imperial gifts which had been placed by Wu P'ei-fu
in the central and most honourable position in his guest-hall.[1]

The fact that both Chang Tso-lin and Wu P'ei-fu were amiably
disposed towards the emperor might have provided the basis of
a common policy. But it did nothing of the kind. It merely intensified their rivalry, because the regard that each had for the
emperor was less than that which each had for himself. Chang
Tso-lin never forgave the Manchu court for what he considered
a gross affront to himself in its cultivation of the goodwill of his
rival, and although he continued to take a friendly interest in the
emperor he thenceforth assumed an attitude of cold reserve
towards the majority of the Manchu princes (there was at least
one exception) and the officials of the court. Simultaneously,
serious disagreements had arisen between himself and the president, Hsü Shih-ch'ang, whose temporising and compromising
policy, especially in connection with a quarrel between Wu
P'ei-fu and the premier (Liang Shih-yi) gravely antagonised the
Fêng-t'ien (Manchurian) party. Chang Tso-lin believed, moreover, not without some reason, that the president had been intriguing against him and had deliberately lured him into an unsuccessful war in the hope of bringing about his downfall. As soon
as it turned out that in spite of these intrigues the Manchurian
warlord's power was by no means broken, even in Peking, Hsü
Shih-ch'ang found that his presidential chair was one of increasing danger and difficulty. He had forfeited the support of Chang
Tso-lin and, by a vacillating policy which created the general
impression that he aimed at strengthening his own position by
weakening everyone else's, he also made an enemy of the Chihi
party and Wu P'ei-fu.

During the political and military turmoil of the spring of
1922 it was again believed in the palace that circumstances
might arise which would put the emperor in personal danger.
I was therefore entrusted with the duty of approaching the
British minister with a view to making arrangements for finding

a refuge for the emperor in the British Legation. Sir Beilby Alston, who had succeeded Sir John Jordan, listened sympathetically to what I had to say and finally agreed to offer hospitality to the emperor in a way which could not justifiably arouse suspicions among either Chinese or non-British foreigners that the British authorities were desirous of interfering in Chinese internal politics. What he proposed to do was to offer me for my personal use a house in the British Legation to which I, in my capacity of tutor to the emperor, could invite him as my own guest. Arrangements were made at the same time with Dom Batalha de Freitas, Portuguese minister and doyen of the corps diplomatique, and with Mr. Oudendijk, Dutch minister, for the reception, in an emergency, of other members of the imperial family.

The immediate danger, as far as the emperor was concerned, passed away, and no removal to the Legation Quarter proved necessary. The real trial of strength between Chang Tso-lin and Wu P'ei-fu was postponed for a few months. Hsü Shih-ch'ang's position as president was, however, disastrously undermined, and he was destined before long to feel the full weight of Chang's disapproval and to be isolated in a world of foes and lukewarm friends.

In view of the alliance between the " Christian General " Fêng Yü-hsiang and Chang Tso-lin which came into existence with dramatic results two and a half years later, the contribution of the former to the solution of the political problems of 1922 is worth a moment's attention. In April 1922 the " Christian General " was in Shensi. From that remote western province, to quote a Tientsin newspaper, he sent out a circular telegram announcing his intention of coming to " the defence of the republic against its foes from Mukden [Manchuria], who he alleges are attempting to destroy the being of the democracy and to set up a monarchy. . . . His telegram is a virtual declaration of war against the armies of Chang Tso-lin which have been taking up their positions during the past few days."[2]

Meanwhile, the emperor's own anxieties were not confined to matters of high politics. He was now in his seventeenth year. Not only did he find life in the Forbidden City increasingly irksome, but he became more and more clearly aware of the evils of the system of which he was the unwilling centre. He began to understand that the Nei Wu Fu was guided by one principle only—*wei ch'ih hsien chuang*—the maintenance of the *status quo*. Moreover he gradually awoke to his inglorious position as a titular monarch with none of a monarch's responsibilities. Keenly patriotic, warmly sympathetic with the undeserved sufferings of his former subjects, and zealous for the progress and prosperity of China, he began to feel the ignominy of his position as an idle pensioner of the republic. The fact that the payments of the stipulated subsidy grew steadily fewer and smaller as time went on, and that before long he was likely to be a pensioner only in theory, did not allay his discontent. The status even of a theoretical pensioner was one of which—to use his own phrase often repeated in conversation with me—he was *hsiu ch'ih*— " ashamed."

On June 2nd, 1922, Hsü Shih-ch'ang, realising that his task had become an impossible one, suddenly resigned the presidency of the republic and left Peking. His departure was hurried and unceremonious and was practically a flight. I regretted his resignation for the emperor's sake and also for my own. He was a courteous, dignified Confucian gentleman of the old school, perhaps more of a scholar than a statesman, but a man who was sincerely anxious to do his best for the long-suffering Chinese people. It was his custom to invite a few of the Manchu princes and the imperial tutors (including myself) to periodical private dinner-parties of an informal kind, and on these occasions he always showed his kindly interest in the welfare of his former sovereign. Had times been propitious and honour permitted he would gladly, I believe, have laid down his presidential functions at the foot of the throne. When in private conversation with us he referred to the fallen House he always spoke not of *ch'ien Ch'ing*—" the late Ch'ing dynasty "—but of *pên ch'ao*—" our present dynasty "—as if it were still reigning. Nevertheless he had not been cast in the mould of a Yüan Shih-k'ai, and I am confident that he would never have broken his oath to the republic. Some of my colleagues in the palace often spoke disparagingly of the president because in sending ceremonial gifts to the emperor he would not prefix *ch'ên* (" your majesty's servant ") to his name, as all loyal ministers under the monarchy were required to do when addressing their sovereign. I always expressed my unhesitating disagreement with my colleagues on this point, on the ground that for the president of the republic to describe himself as the servant of a sovereign who had ceased to reign and to whom he no longer owed allegiance would have been a meaningless compliment to the emperor and an insult to the republic.

Since his resignation Hsü Shih-ch'ang has lived in scholarly seclusion in the British Concession at Tientsin, where last year (1933) he celebrated his eightieth birthday.

By the beginning of 1922, the emperor's restiveness and dissatisfaction with existing conditions—the very conditions which the household department was determined at all costs to maintain—had become obvious to all who came in contact with him. From his own father, prince Ch'un, and from most of the other influential Manchu nobles, the emperor received no sympathy. All with the exception of Tsai-T'ao (whose relations with the ex-regent lacked warmth) were at one with the officials of the Nei Wu Fu in their determination that the emperor, for whom they professed such unbounded respect and devotion, should not be allowed to upset the *status quo* by abandoning his make-believe court and his titular dignity. They began to realise, however, that something must be done to reduce his discontent with things as they were. Their deliberations culminated in the decision that they must provide him with an empress.

On March 11th, 1922, the Court Gazette contained the following brief announcement. *Jung-Yüan chih nü Kuo Chia Shih li wei huang-hou :* " Kuo Chia, daughter of Jung Yüan, is hereby created Empress."

This did not mean that the wedding had already taken place, or even that it would necessarily take place in the immediate future. A curious feature of Chinese imperial weddings, from the Western point of view, is that the elevation of a young woman to the imperial rank is brought about not automatically by the fact of her marriage to the emperor but by the publication of the imperial rescript. She becomes empress as soon as the rescript is issued, though months may elapse (as happened in this case) between the date of the decree and that of the wedding.

When the decree was issued Kuo Chia was residing with her

parents in Tientsin, which had been their home for several years. Her father, a member of the Manchu aristocracy, is a grandson of a former Kirin general, Ch'ang-Shun. He himself, being but a young man when the revolution broke out, had not reached higher rank under the Manchu dynasty than that of expectant-taotai. His second wife, stepmother of the empress, was a daughter of prince Yü-Lang, a well-known member of the imperial clan and a direct descendant of the emperor Ch'ien-Lung.

In the same issue of the Court Gazette which notified the appointment of the empress appeared also the announcement of the selection of a secondary consort (*shu fei*) in the person of Ê-erh-tê-t'ê, daughter of one Tuan Kung, whose rank under the dynasty had been that of expectant district magistrate. The fact that both empress and *fei* were of Manchu family caused some disappointment among a good many Chinese loyalists, who had hoped that the emperor would marry a Chinese. Manchu conservatism and the dynastic house-law proved too strong for any such suggestion to be seriously considered, though at one time there was a baseless rumour to the effect that his majesty's bride would be no other than the daughter of president Hsü Shih-ch'ang.

The next official announcements relative to the approaching double wedding appeared in the Gazette of March 14th. They notified the court that Jung-Yüan had been granted audience to return thanks to his majesty for the elevation of his daughter to the imperial dignity ; and that Wên-Ch'i had returned thanks through the imperial household department for the honour conferred upon his niece Ê-erh-tê-t'ê. Simultaneously, several marks of imperial favour were bestowed upon the *hou-fu*—father of the empress. He received the button of the first rank, became an officer of the imperial bodyguard, with right of access to the imperial presence, and was granted the privilege of riding on horseback in the Forbidden City. Not long afterwards he was made a *Nei Wu Fu Ta-ch'ên*—a minister of the imperial household department.[3] Finally he was raised to the rank of duke.

That the prospect of sharing his honours with an empress did not have the effect of tranquillising the emperor's restless spirit is perhaps not altogether surprising, at least from an occidental standpoint, inasmuch as Chinese and Manchu custom, not to say court etiquette, made it impossible for him to meet his empress-elect before the wedding. He acquiesced without enthusiasm in his betrothal, but he surprised and shocked the court—especially the imperial dowagers—by vehemently protesting against being provided with more than a single fiancée. When it was pointed out to him that according to immemorial precedent there should be not only one but several *fei* or secondary consorts, he replied that civilised monarchs in the West did not practise polygamy and he saw no reason why the Manchu court should countenance the practice. After some unseemly wrangling had taken place on this point, and the dowagers had tearfully reproached him with abandoning the ways of his ancestors, the emperor compromised by consenting to the appointment of a single *shu fei*. It may be added that the most tearful of the dowagers was Ching-Yi T'ai Fei, one of the surviving consorts of the emperor T'ung-Chih.

I have been told by friendly members of the imperial family that I was counted mainly responsible for having inspired his majesty with monogamic principles. This allegation, however, is as completely untrue as is the published statement of a certain French writer that I had tried to turn the emperor into what he calls " an English dandy." The only opinion I expressed at court, or in conversation with the emperor, on any aspect of the matrimonial project was that as he was only a boy of sixteen the question of his marriage was one which might advantageously be discussed at a later date. I did not expect that opinion to make any impression on the imperial family, and it did not.

The emperor's betrothal took place in March. That it was not occupying a great deal of his personal attention during the following weeks may be surmised from an important incident which took place in June. It was fully described in the following letter which I wrote immediately after the event, to a certain English-speaking ex-official to whom reference has already been made in these pages.[4] I have omitted only a few unessential paragraphs.

Peking,
June 8th, 1922.

DEAR ——

During the recent dragon-boat festival holidays, I was absent from Peking and did not return till the morning of the 3rd. On reaching home I heard of the sudden resignation and departure of president Hsü, which had taken place the day before. In the course of the morning, his majesty, having learned by telephone of my return, sent me by confidential messenger a pencilled Chinese note asking me to go and see him in his private quarters in the palace at 3 o'clock. He also directed me to have two motor-cars waiting outside the Tung-hua Gate at the same hour, but did not state his reasons for this order. Finally, he desired me to treat his note as strictly secret, so far as the imperial household and his other tutors were concerned.

I went to the palace in my own car at the time appointed, and ordered a second car from a public garage. . . . I found his majesty awaiting me in the Yang-hsin-tien. No third person was present during the interview. It lasted over an hour, and was one of the most trying experiences of the kind I have ever gone through. The first point of importance was that his majesty wished me to take him at once to the British Legation. He had made up his mind so definitely on this subject that he was unwilling, at first, even to discuss it with me. This explained his instructions as to the motor-cars. He and I were to go together in one car, and a few of his personal attendants were to follow in the other. His majesty went on to say that as soon as he arrived at the Legation he intended to issue a telegram to the people of China, stating that he was ashamed to remain in the position of an idle pensioner of the State, and wished to surrender not only the $4,000,000 a year which the Republican Government undertook to pay him as the price of abdication, but also to renounce his imperial title and all rights pertaining thereto, including the privilege of occupying the imperial palaces. After despatching this telegram, he proposed to make immediate arrangements to visit Europe, and would trespass upon the hospitality of the British Minister only until the necessary arrangements for the foreign tour should be completed.

I should explain that this resolve on his majesty's part was only intensified, not caused, by recent political developments. As I have already informed you, he and I have often, during the past year or two, discussed the question of his position with regard to the republican government, and he has come to realise, more and more vividly, the anomalous and humiliating nature of his present circumstances. Even if there had been no upheaval in Peking politics, he would not have remained quiescent much longer. He is no longer a child. He has arrived at an age when he is perfectly well able to form opinions of his own, and having come to the definite belief that there is something fundamentally wrong about his present position, he will not rest until he has had it changed. . . .

The dramatic suddenness with which the emperor announced his intention of leaving the palace and issuing his edict of renunciation did not really take me by surprise, for I knew what had been in his mind for a long time, just as he, on his side, knew that in principle I thoroughly approved of what he proposed to do. That, of course, was why he had taken me, and no one else, into his confidence. The arguments I used to dissuade him from carrying out his purpose at this particular juncture were these. I pointed out that if he were to leave the palace and take refuge under a foreign flag on the very day after the president had been forced into resignation and flight from Peking, the two events would necessarily and naturally be regarded by press and public as a tacit admission that the fortunes of emperor and president were in some mysterious way linked together, and the denunciations of the president that were likely to follow his fall from power would more than probably be directed also, to some extent, against his majesty's person. There would be a tendency to assume that Hsü Shih-ch'ang and the emperor had been engaged in political intrigues together, and that the emperor's flight was prompted by a guilty conscience. Nor would the subsequent telegrams of renunciation of pension and title go far to remove public suspicion. It would be argued that the emperor merely wished to " save face " by making a show of giving up voluntarily what would in any case have been taken from him ere long by force.

I further pointed out that his majesty was probably wrong in assuming that the British Legation would, on this occasion, receive him as a guest. It is quite true that when civil war broke out a short time ago and there was a possibility of serious disorders in Peking, the British minister, on my representations, was good enough to promise that, if his majesty were threatened by personal danger, quarters would be found for him within the British Legation. But the present circumstances were quite different. No actual danger threatened the emperor's person, and the grounds upon which Sir Beilby Alston had agreed to grant him British protection no longer existed. It was his majesty's frankly avowed purpose to use the British Legation as a place from which, without interference from the imperial family and the palace officials, he could draft his telegram to the nation and make preparations to leave the country. Such being the case, it seemed to me practically certain that Sir Beilby Alston would find it impossible to offer his majesty the hospitality of the British Legation. Even if he were personally willing to do so, it seemed to me highly improbable
To

that the British Government would allow itself to be involved in action which might easily be construed, however unjustly, into an unwarrantable interference in China's internal concerns. I offered to settle the question at once by going to the Legation and laying the matter before the minister, and pointed out that I could easily bring back his reply within an hour. This, however, proved to be unnecessary, as his majesty very reluctantly agreed, in deference to my views, to postpone all action for the present. . . .

You will probably want to know why this matter of the proposed renunciation of the republican pension and imperial title—which has been discussed by the emperor and myself for a long time past—has suddenly become one of such urgency. I think I can assign three main reasons for this.

In the first place, let me point out that the emperor is intelligent and thoughtful, and is an omnivorous reader of newspapers of all shades of political opinion. He knows more about the present condition of China than many well-read adults, and is under no delusions whatever about his own position. He now knows far more about political and social conditions in Western countries than his Chinese tutors, whose learning is confined to the history and literature of their own country, and he is able to make comparisons which to them are impossible. He has a thorough grasp of the history of his own dynasty and of the various causes that contributed to its fall. He bears no grudge whatever against those who brought about the revolution and his own abdication, though he speaks with the utmost frankness (and with what many loyal monarchists would describe as the grossest disrespect) of such illustrious or notorious personages as the late empress-dowager T'zŭ-Hsi. During all the years of his childhood he naturally accepted things as they came, and it never occurred to him to question the wisdom of those who were responsible for the sordid bargaining which took place between the prince regent or his advisers and the revolutionary leaders at the time of the establishment of the so-called republic in 1912. During the last three years, however, as I can testify from my own knowledge, his majesty has come to feel more and more vividly the shame of taking an enormous subsidy from the State in return for no services whatever. The fact that there are at present large unpaid arrears does not affect the principle. . . .

A second reason for urgency, from the emperor's point of view, is his majesty's growing disgust with the corruption which he knows is rife throughout the palace. He has himself spoken to me with intense irritation of the malpractices of persons whom I prefer not to name even in a letter to you ; of cases of unblushing robbery, bribery and falsification of accounts, of thefts of palace treasures and the division of the spoils among high and low. He has told me with horror of how

the eunuchs attached to the palace of Chuang Ho, the imperial
consort who died last year, struggled with one another for the
treasures stolen from the very chamber in which the deceased
princess lay in state ; with even greater indignation he has told me of
how, when he wished to make an example of these ruffians, he had to
stay his hand owing to the solid wall of opposition raised against him
by princes, ministers and, of course, the whole fraternity of eunuchs.
Is it any wonder that his majesty's desire to renounce his title and
subsidy is intensified rather than diminished by his knowledge of the
fact that the renunciation would necessarily involve the collapse of
this system of organised roguery ? Naturally, the members of the
imperial household would not contemplate with equanimity the loss
of all their lucrative opportunities, and it is by no means improbable
that if they knew of the emperor's intentions they would devise some
means of forcibly preventing him from carrying them out. It is
perhaps a vague knowledge of this that suggested to his majesty the
advisability of seeking a temporary home outside the Forbidden City
as a preliminary to the issue of his proposed telegram of renunciation.
However that may be, it need cause no surprise that his majesty feels
under no obligation to cling to his subsidy for the sake of those who
now have the spending of all but the small fraction of it that suffices
for his personal requirements. That he himself should be supported
in return for no services, at the expense of his suffering and almost
bankrupt country, is humiliating enough ; but the humiliation is
many times intensified by the knowledge that by far the greater part
of the subsidy goes to support a huge staff of unnecessary and more
or less worthless parasites.

The treaty with the republic which is still in force, and which his
majesty hopes to abrogate, provides *inter alia* for the payment to the
imperial family of an annual subsidy of $4,000,000. Obviously, this
sum was vastly in excess of the amount actually needed to support
in comfort and dignity the abdicated emperor and the few remaining
princesses and ladies of the Court. For that modest purpose, indeed,
no subsidy from the republic was necessary at all, as the movable and
landed property of the imperial family was in itself far more than
sufficient for such needs. That property has, of course, been disgrace-
fully mismanaged and pillaged during the past dozen years ; but,
whatever may be its extent and value to-day, there is no doubt that
in 1912 it could, under competent and honest management, have been
made to yield a revenue which would have placed the emperor and
those properly dependent on him far above the reach of poverty.
His majesty holds the view, which is fully shared by me, that the real
object of the promoters of the treaty on the royalist side was not to
safeguard the welfare of the emperor and the imperial family, but to

provide for the indefinite maintenance in idleness and luxury of the hordes of court officials, eunuchs and hangers-on of every description, who would have been appalled at the prospect of having to go out into the world and earn their own livings, and whose one desire was to save for themselves as much as they could from the wreck of the monarchy. The impression I have gained from my three years' experience in the Forbidden City is that the real welfare of the emperor was not taken into consideration at all, and that his true interests have never been consulted from that day to this. The palace people are anxious, no doubt, to preserve his life. If they failed in that they might all be involved in a common economic catastrophe which they would find most disconcerting. So long as he is kept alive, however, they are fully satisfied, and they care little or nothing for his physical well-being. The extreme callousness shown in regard to his majesty's eyes illustrates my meaning. It was not till I had threatened to resign that the responsible officer of the household finally put the matter into my hands and allowed me to engage a foreign oculist. It is perhaps fortunate that this incident took place last year. Had it been postponed to the present time, a threat of resignation on my part would have caused the household more pleasure than dismay.

I have now given two of the main reasons why the emperor regards this proposed renunciation of title and subsidy as a matter of urgency. Firstly, he wishes to escape from a position which he has come to regard as intolerably humiliating. Secondly, he wishes to terminate the reign of corruption and roguery in the palace, and feels that a " root-and-branch " policy is the only one that will meet the case. To those who advise him to be content with introducing gradual reforms he listens with impatience. He believes that so long as the palace system is maintained and the republican subsidy (or any substantial portion of it) is available for division, corruption will maintain itself.

The third main reason for urgency is the possibility or likelihood of the revival in the near future of the so-called old parliament, or some similar assembly representative of the extreme republicans. In any such assembly there will probably be many who will favour a drastic revision of the terms of the treaty with the monarchy. If this parliament settles down to regular work it is more than likely that the question of the future treatment of the imperial house will be brought up for discussion.[5] All this is fully realised by his majesty, who is naturally anxious that the renunciation of his title and subsidy should take place as a voluntary act of his own and should be recognised as such by the whole country. It would distress him very deeply if his voluntary act of renunciation were interpreted by the people not as the outcome of his own determination to do what was right, but as the result of a mere desire to " save face " by anticipating the coercive action of parliament.

In addition to the three principal reasons I have given for the emperor's desire to have this matter settled quickly, I may mention a fourth, which is mine rather than his, and which might be regarded as comparatively unimportant by those who have never seen the inside of the Forbidden City and know nothing of the mode of life of its inmates. To my mind, however, this reason would of itself justify the emperor's immediate renunciation of his useless and cumbersome privileges. I allude to the physical and moral unhealthiness of his present surroundings. . . . Mr. Ch'ên Pao-shên, his senior Chinese tutor, tries to console him with the reflection that all the emperors of the dynasty have had to lead lives of rigid isolation, and reminds him that they were all subjected to various limitations on their freedom of action and bound by innumerable irksome conventions. The obvious answer to this is that his imperial predecessors did at least receive certain compensations. They were real monarchs and exercised real power, whereas their unhappy descendant of to-day is well aware that he has nothing but an empty title, that his only subjects are eunuchs and court officials, and that even in his own palace his most reasonable wishes are constantly thwarted by people whom he distrusts and despises. . . .

I have urged upon his majesty another reason for delay. I have pointed out that, as China is at present without a parliament (and for the moment without even a president), there is no organ or body which would be competent to accept his renunciation of the subsidy and imperial title. He might, as he desires to do, address his telegram to the people of China, but there would be no man or body of men competent to receive or acknowledge it—and surely it would deserve an acknowledgment. His majesty has admitted the force of this argument, and I think it will help me to keep him from taking any rash action. . . . Nevertheless, if there is any undue delay in the reassembly of the old parliament or in the summoning of a new one, I doubt whether his majesty will be content to allow a matter of such grave importance to himself to be indefinitely shelved while loquacious politicians are quarrelling among themselves over the prospective spoils of office.

There is one important consideration upon which I have not yet touched. When I first reported to you and Liu Chien-chih some months ago that his majesty had confided to me his wish to surrender his annual state subsidy, you advised me to remind him that it would be unwise to take this step until a thorough investigation had been made into the financial position of the imperial house. It was pointed out that, owing to the gross mismanagement, peculation

and other corrupt practices of the palace officials during the past
twelve years, it was quite impossible, at present, to say what the
assets of the imperial house really were, and to what extent, if at
all, they exceeded the liabilities. Thus it was desirable, in his majesty's
interests, to refrain from renouncing the subsidy until it had been
definitely ascertained that the real and movable estate still remaining in his majesty's possession would provide him with adequate
means of support. On my advice, he agreed to appoint a special
committee to make the necessary investigation, and as it was
obviously hopeless to expect the present ministers of the household,
if left to themselves, to conduct a scrupulously honest enquiry—
which would necessarily result in painful disclosures as to past
mismanagement and corruption—his majesty wisely decided not to
confine the membership of this committee to those who had had the
handling of the imperial finances in recent years. He therefore
willingly accepted my suggestion that you and Liu Chien-chih
should be appointed independent members of the proposed committee,
and also gladly agreed to signify his trust and confidence in yourself
by making you a Grand Guardian, which would, of course, give you
a high status within the palace and the right to audience at any
time. As you are aware, both these appointments were very strongly
opposed by interested persons, and the fact that they have at last
been made is solely due to the inflexible determination of his majesty
to have his own way. He told the ministers of the household quite
frankly, and directed them to inform the ex-regent, that he refused
to be treated any longer as a puppet, and that in this matter he
intended his will to prevail. The language which he used in addressing
the ministers on this occasion (he showed me afterwards a written
draft of what he had said) will probably never be forgotten by them
as long as they live.

Nevertheless, I think I ought to warn you that you must not expect
his majesty to allow this matter of the renunciation of the subsidy
to remain in abeyance during the long period that may elapse before
your committee has completed its investigations and drawn up its
report. Personally, I am in entire sympathy with his majesty's present
point of view, which is that the renunciation of the subsidy should not
be dependent on whether his private property is or is not sufficient
to yield him an adequate income. After all, there would be very little
courage or nobility of character shown in postponing the act of
renunciation until his majesty were fully satisfied that his private
resources were sufficient to yield him ample means of support. . . .

While I am touching on this question of enquiring into the
financial position of the imperial house, I venture to draw your
attention, as you will probably be the most influential member of

the investigating committee, to the urgent necessity of arriving at a definite understanding with the republican government as to what movable property may be regarded as belonging to the emperor and at his absolute disposal. If you read the Peking Chinese press you cannot have failed to notice the paragraphs that have appeared from time to time during the past months regarding the sale of certain palace treasures. Several protests have been raised against these transactions on the ground that the articles disposed of are State property and that the imperial family has no right to sell them. To-day's *Shun-t'ien Shih-pao* contains a paragraph to the effect that recently some articles of great value have been sent from the palace to a foreign bank, " a certain foreigner " having acted as intermediary, and it is hinted that the intention of the palace authorities is to sell them, in which case these " priceless treasures will probably be lost to China."

The emperor himself has given me to understand that the statements contained in the paragraph are accurate in the main, though, if the reference to " a certain foreigner " is meant to indicate myself, that part of the paragraph is wholly false. Anyhow, I think you will agree that this is a matter in which the honour of the emperor and the imperial family is deeply involved, and no time should be lost in separating what may rightly be regarded as Chinese national property from the personal property of the imperial family.

Mr. Liu Chien-chih, in conversation with me, has emphasised the difference between the two projects which his majesty has in view. It is not necessary and is perhaps inadvisable, he says, that the emperor should renounce both the republican subsidy and the imperial title. He may retain the latter, temporarily at least, even if he decides to surrender the former. One of your letters gives me the impression that this is also your own view. Yet I am not sure that I agree with you on this point. The abolition of the whole palace system, with all that it connotes, seems to me highly desirable in his majesty's interests. There can be little doubt that, so long as he keeps the empty title which the treaty with the republic allowed him to retain, there will be numbers of people whose personal interests will impel them to insist on the maintenance of some semblance of an imperial court and household. The result, of course, would be that the emperor would continue to live an artificial life and would have to share his private income, which then might be no more than sufficient for his own legitimate needs, with a crowd of hungry self-seekers. If you argue that the emperor must retain his title for the sake of appearances or from loyalty to the traditions of his house, I am afraid I must disagree. The more radical Chinese newspapers frequently publish more or less scurrilous and contemptuous references to his majesty, and these paragraphs will continue to appear so long as he retains his empty title and lives in the imperial palace. There is a not unjustifiable feeling among republican Chinese that one of the causes—if only a minor one—of the weakness and instability that have characterised the republic since its establishment is to be found in the fact that the emperor's abdication did not involve a complete surrender of all his imperial prerogatives. His right of conferring honours, for example, is not unnaturally objected to as wrong in principle and incompatible with a truly republican form of government. As to the views of foreigners, I would point out that the emperor's position is not generally regarded by them as essentially different from that of other sovereigns who have abdicated. To them he is simply the ex-emperor of China, and is frequently referred to as such in print and in ordinary conversation. Thus the relinquishment of the empty title would certainly not make him " lose face " among foreigners. He is an ex-emperor now, from the foreign point of view, and he would continue to be an ex-emperor if he made a public renunciation of his title.

You and others may say that if he gives up the last remnants of his imperial dignity, he will have made it for ever impossible for him to take advantage of any such changes in Chinese political conditions as might lead to a restoration of the monarchy. I do not wish to concern myself with any such remote contingency as a reversion to monarchy. I am much more concerned to see the young emperor grow up to be a healthy-minded and healthy-bodied man than to see him the centre of a monarchist movement. Nevertheless, if the people of China were to come round to the view that a constitutional monarchy would be the best solution of their country's political troubles, I cannot help thinking that his majesty's chances of restoration to the throne would be enhanced rather than diminished by the fact that from generous and patriotic motives he had voluntarily surrendered the title and subsidy which he had been allowed to retain as the price of his abdication in 1912.

Sir John Jordan once made the remark to me that perhaps some day, after the emperor had completed his education and travelled abroad, he might be elected president. That indeed is a conceivable possibility ; but only if the palace system is dissolved and the republican subsidy and the imperial title are renounced for ever. Otherwise, it is pretty certain that none but monarchists would support his candidature, and that their action would be interpreted by their political opponents as a direct challenge to republican principles. . . .

I need hardly say that my colleagues in the Yü-ch'ing Kung [the imperial tutors] have nothing whatever to do with palace scandals

and intrigues, and are morally above all reproach. As scholars of
the old school, however, they are totally out of touch with all modern
political, social and literary movements in China, and have a far
narrower general outlook than the emperor himself. They have never
been abroad, they know nothing of any foreign language, and I am
afraid they are not yet wholly convinced that outside China there
exists any civilisation worthy the name. In one respect I must
express most emphatic disapproval of the political ideas with which
one of them seems anxious to fill his young pupil's mind. His majesty
informed me, a few days ago, that when in conversation with one of
his Chinese tutors he tentatively suggested the desirability, in view
of the present financial straits of the government and the hardships
of the people, of dispensing with the stipulated subsidy, his tutor
assured him that he need not concern himself with the difficulties
of government or people, inasmuch as he should look upon the
people of China, who had dethroned him, as his enemies. His majesty's
retort to this was prompt and effective : " If they are my enemies,"
he said, " that makes it all the more urgent that I should cease to
take their money." . . . His majesty most decidedly does not look
on the people of China as his enemies. Not only does he bear them
no ill will for having dethroned him, I have never even heard him
utter a word of reproach against any individual or any political
party concerned in the revolution. On one occasion, in conversation
with him, the name of ——, the Southern general, was mentioned,
and his majesty remarked that, judging from newspaper reports,
the general appeared to be able and incorrupt, and that it might
be a good thing if he were to become a dominant power in the country.
I observed that the man was a convinced radical, and that, like most
of the Southern leaders, he probably regarded the imperial house
with no friendly eye. " What does that matter," replied his majesty,
" if he can do good to China ? " . . .

On the walls of the imperial schoolroom there is a scroll bearing
the words, " At all times think only of the people's good." I remarked
to the emperor, after hearing his account of how he had been told to
regard the people as his enemies, that if any remark of the same
character were made to him again, he should direct his tutor's
attention to that scroll and suggest that he should take it down and
hide it, as the principles on which the inscription were based were
evidently no longer valid. . . .

My relations with his majesty have always been most cordial,
otherwise, indeed, I should have resigned long ago. Externally, my
relations with the ex-regent and the other imperial princes, the
ministers of the household and my colleagues are also all that could
be desired. But I feel that they hold me (not without cause) largely

responsible for the fact that during the past year his majesty has been
growing more and more discontented and restive, less and less
willing to order his life according to the routine and conventions
of the court, and increasingly dissatisfied with his position, both in
its personal and in its public aspects. If the present conditions in
the palace are to be maintained, and the emperor is to be compelled
to acquiesce in those conditions, it will be quite impossible for me to
continue to occupy my present post, as I shall be forced to realise
that my efforts on his majesty's behalf have failed. Even if conditions
are drastically altered in the manner desired by his majesty himself,
and heartily approved of by me, I feel that I should be placed in a
thoroughly false position if I were to retain my own post after
numberless others had been deprived of theirs. As one who was
known to have had closer and more confidential relations with his
majesty than any other member of the court or household, I should
not unnaturally—and probably rightly—be held mainly responsible
for the disaster which had befallen all who had made a living out
of the palace system. The fact that I am a foreigner would add to
the bitterness of feeling with which they would regard me. This in
itself might cause me small discomfort, as I should be conscious of
having done no more than my duty ; but I could not allow it to be
assumed and believed that, while causing a multitude of others to
lose their means of livelihood, I had taken good care to safeguard
my own position as his majesty's tutor or confidential adviser. . . .

Yours sincerely,

R. F. Johnston.

This document reveals some of my reasons for dissuading the
emperor from carrying out his project, especially at that particular moment and in the manner proposed. I had other reasons
of which I thought it expedient to say little or nothing. One was
my fear that the officials of the Nei Wu Fu and their allies
among the princes, faced by the collapse of the system by which
they lived, might take desperate measures to save themselves
from that calamity. If they did nothing more drastic they might
cause the emperor to be removed from his position as head of the
Manchu imperial house and be replaced by another and more
docile member of the family. It would be difficult, no doubt, to
ensure the success of this plan, but by utilising to the full such
influence as they still possessed over men of authority in republican circles, and by the judicious expenditure of funds to be

obtained by selling some of the palace treasures, they might be able to carry it through with the tacit consent if not with the active support of the Peking government. Another very difficult task would have been to compel the officers of the Nei Wu Fu, on the eve of their disbandment, to render a full and accurate account of their dealings with the private property of the imperial house, the administration of which had been exclusively in their hands. No one else knew anything about the extent and value of that property and there would probably have been insuperable difficulties in the verification of any statement they might put forward.[6]

Another very serious consideration that weighed with me was that as soon as the emperor left the Forbidden City and became a private citizen of the republic there was a very strong likelihood that he would become the centre of monarchist plots. As I have already explained, the monarchists had not sought to implicate the emperor personally in any of their activities, because his position under the Articles of Favourable Treatment would have made it both difficult and dishonourable for him to become a party to their schemes. But the abolition of the Articles, on the initiative of the emperor himself, might make them feel free to draw him into their intrigues, as the abdication agreement would no longer be binding on him. As soon as he left the Forbidden City and was free to choose his own place of residence, he would find himself surrounded by a strong body of active monarchists who could recognise him as their leader and expect him to play his part as such. It would be unreasonable to expect that a high-spirited boy of sixteen or seventeen would remain unmoved when they called upon him not only to be the saviour of the people of China but also to imitate the emperor Kuang Wu Ti, of nineteen centuries ago, and become the second founder of the fortunes of his imperial house.

I was very doubtful, further, whether the emperor's voluntary surrender of his privileges would meet with anything like the grateful response that it would deserve. It was more than likely, in my opinion, that his motives would be misjudged and that the irreconcilable enemies of his house would accuse him of trying to rid himself of his obligations under the abdication agreement by an apparently magnanimous surrender of worthless privileges. They would suspect, and probably openly assert, that this apparent magnanimity was merely a cloak under which he would proceed to betray the republic. They would naturally consider that their suspicions had been fully justified if, after having made a public surrender of his privileges, he were subsequently to yield to the exhortations of his monarchist friends and become their active leader.

Furthermore, as stated in the letter, I felt convinced that the British minister would refuse to allow the emperor to issue public manifestos and statements of policy from behind the walls of the British Legation, and that the minister would be fully justified in his refusal.[7] Signs were already becoming apparent, among the young " intellectuals " of China, of that unreasoning hostility to Great Britain which under the direct or indirect encouragement of the Soviet embassy reached a culminating point in the violent anti-British outburst of 1925. The time was near at hand when everything that the British government might say or do in China would be made a subject of suspicion, calumny and malicious misrepresentation. There is not the slightest doubt that had I acted in accordance with the emperor's request, and had the British minister agreed to receive him at the Legation, all his subsequent activities would have been traced to British intrigue. I myself would unquestionably have become the victim of slander and denunciation from all sides. The palace authorities would probably have been even more vehement in their expressions of rage and hate than the politicians, students and journalists of Peking, though for very different reasons. The emperor's magnanimity in the renunciation of his rights would have been totally ignored or discounted. He would have been denounced as the mere puppet of the British " imperialists " who through the agency of his English tutor had induced him to lend himself to their nefarious schemes for the exploitation and spoliation of the republic and people of China.

My own plans for the emperor's immediate future were therefore not identical with his. My proposals were that he should summon the princes and the officers of the household to a palace conference ; that he should insist upon carrying out, with the least possible delay, that clause of the abdication settlement which provided for his eventual removal to the Summer Palace ;

that the proposed committee for the investigation of the financial position of the imperial house should be appointed and set
to work at once ; that this committee should be required to
draw up a scheme for the drastic reduction of palace expenditure and for the reform of the household department ; and that
as soon as possible after his removal to the Summer Palace the
emperor should on his own initiative invite the republican
government to enter into friendly negotiations with the imperial
house for the revision of the Articles of Favourable Treatment
and for the voluntary surrender of all the rights and privileges
of which the emperor not unreasonably felt " ashamed." When
these things had been carried out to the complete satisfaction
of the imperial house (as distinct from the utterly discredited
Nei Wu Fu) on the one side and the republican government on
the other, the emperor would be in a position to carry out one of
his long-cherished designs—a journey to Europe and the United
States, to be followed, perhaps, by a period of study at English
and American universities.

There is one important matter referred to in the above-quoted
letter on which I wrote without sufficient knowledge of the facts.
I was not then aware that the vast stores of valuable works of
art and other treasures which were contained in the Forbidden
City, and of which not even the emperor himself had ever seen
more than a thousandth part, had been acknowledged by the
republican government to be the private property of the imperial family. As stated in the letter, references were often made
in the Chinese press to the sale of palace treasures, and protests
had been raised against such sale on the ground that they
belonged to the State. Some time after I had written my letter,
however, I made the discovery that the republican government
did not itself regard the palace treasures as national property.
It was fully cognisant of the fact that works of art from the
palace were occasionally sold or mortgaged by the household
department in order to make good the ever-increasing deficits
in the palace accounts. The government raised no objection to
these transactions, though in my opinion it is most regrettable
that president Hsü Shih-ch'ang or his immediate successors did
not make them a reasonable excuse for pressing for the drastic
reform of the Nei Wu Fu. Instead of doing so they regretfully

and apologetically acknowledged that the financial difficulties of the imperial household, which rendered the sale of valuables necessary, were caused by the failure of the republican government to fulfil its obligations in the matter of the annual subsidy payable under the abdication agreement.

But besides the vast accumulations of treasures in that part of the Forbidden City which still remained in the occupation of the imperial family and the Nei Wu Fu—treasures of which not more than a minute fraction had been disposed of by gift, sale, or mortgage, or even by theft—there were also large collections of pictures, porcelain, bronzes, books, jewels, jade and other articles which after the revolution of 1911 had been brought to Peking from the imperial palaces at Mukden (the capital of Manchuria) and Jehol. In 1916 some of these treasures were deposited in the three throne halls taken over by the republic, but the greater portion of them were placed in the Wu-ying and Wên-hua palaces—two large buildings in the eastern and western sections of the Forbidden City.[8] These two palaces were then (towards the end of 1916) opened to the public as museums of Chinese art. Access to them was obtained not, of course, through the northern and still strictly private portion of the Forbidden City but through the gates of Tung Hua (" Eastern Glory ") and Hsi Hua (" Western Glory ").[9] During the years that followed 1916 the magnificent contents of the museum-palaces were a constant source of wonder and joy to thousands of visitors from all parts of the world.

Very few if any of those visitors had even the vaguest knowledge of the facts concerning the ownership of the treasures so displayed. It was assumed that they had been taken over by the republican government from the imperial family or had passed to the republic as a necessary result of the revolution, but there was general ignorance regarding the terms under which the transfer had taken place. I myself shared that ignorance till 1923, when in response to my own request for accurate information I was given copies of certain Chinese documents which made the matter clear.

One of these documents is here reproduced in the original Chinese, because as far as I am aware it has never been published in China, and is likely to interest if it does not

amaze any of my readers who happen to be of Chinese nation-
ality. It is dated September 11th, 1916. It explains that in
January, 1914, the republican government and the imperial
household had sent a joint deputation to Mukden and Jehol
to collect and bring to Peking the treasures contained in the
palaces there ; that these treasures were acknowledged to be
part of the private property of the imperial family; that independent experts had been called in to value the articles, which
numbered over seventy thousand ; that some of the items were
not included in the valuation on account of their exceptional
value and rarity ; that by mutual arrangement between the
imperial family and the republic, all the items except those withdrawn by the former were to be bought by the republican government at the figure named in the valuation ; that as financial
stringency made it impossible at that time for the republican
government to pay the purchase-price, the treasures were to be
regarded as on loan from the imperial family to the republic
pending a full cash settlement when the finances of the republic
permitted ; that meanwhile the Wu Ying palace, containing most
of the treasures in question, was to be opened to the public as
a national art-museum ; and that they were to be left in the
custody of an official of the household department named Chih
Ko, who would be held responsible for their safety both to the
imperial family and to the republican government.

One of the other documents relating to this matter of which
copies were handed to me gives the following interesting summary of the figures given in the valuation.

TREASURES FROM THE PALACES OF MUKDEN AND JEHOL

	Total estimated value.	Value of articles withdrawn by the imperial household and therefore not to be included in the sale to the republic.	Balance due by the republic to the imperial family.
Mukden	$1,984,315	$520,171	$1,464,144
Jehol	$2,081,732	$34,400	$2,047,332
	$4,066,047	$554,571	$3,511,476

We can see from this table that the total amount acknowledged to be due to the imperial family from the republic in respect of treasures brought to the Forbidden City from the Mukden and Jehol palaces amounted to more than three and a half million dollars (mex.), a sum which at the exchange rate of 2s., then regarded as normal, amounts to about £351,147.

I have the authority of the palace authorities for the statement that not a dollar of this sum was ever paid. In other words, after having formally acknowledged in writing that the treasures in question were the private property of the imperial family, and would remain its property until it had received the full amount of their estimated value, the republican government has ignored its own written word and has confiscated the entire collection. Its written agreement with the imperial family has been treated—like the Articles of Favourable Treatment—as " a scrap of paper."

Valuable as the treasures from Jehol and Mukden undoubtedly were (I have reason to believe that the official estimate was far too low), they were immeasurably eclipsed both in quantity and value by the huge accumulations of works of art and other treasures stored in those palaces of the Forbidden City which had remained in the occupation of the imperial family. What their total value is—or was nine years ago before they, too, were confiscated without the smallest pretence of legal right or justification—cannot be stated with any accuracy, but I have never heard a lower estimate than ten million pounds sterling. These are the treasures which, it will be remembered, were brought prominently to public notice in 1933, when a Japanese and Manchurian military threat to Peiping (Peking) caused their hurried removal to various destinations in central China. What will be their ultimate fate is a question which the future will answer ; but all lovers of China and her ancient culture will earnestly hope that they will not be dispersed or find their way to foreign countries. That some of them, at least, will never again be seen in China is a painful probability.

For all its beauty and splendour, and the inestimable value of its art-treasures, the Forbidden City was a place of tragedy. It had its hours of joyous revelry, no doubt. Of the people who dwelt there, not all lived unhappily or died in anguish. But the

wailing ghosts that haunt its palaces would make a long procession and would have piteous tales to tell us, if we had eyes
to see and ears to hear them. What agony can have been greater
than that of the last Ming emperor, when he found himself
deserted by all his ministers, all his courtiers, all his servants
but one faithful eunuch ? I have been shown the spot on which,
in the frenzy of his despair, he is said to have struck down his
empress with his own hand. I have stood upon the little hill,
overlooking the palace, on which he took his own life, following
his empress out of the thraldom of a palace into the freedom of
death—if death brings freedom. The life of the next master of
the Forbidden City should have been a happier one, for instead
of being the last monarch of a dying dynasty he was the first
of a new one that was full of energy and vitality. Yet if the
popular story of the life of the young emperor Shun-Chih (1644–
1661) has any basis of truth, the Forbidden City even for him
held little happiness. I have told that story elsewhere, and will
here repeat only its closing words, written by me in 1920.

" If ever there was a palace that deserved the name of a
prison, it is that palace in the Forbidden City of Peking, in
which the emperor Shun-Chih pined for freedom, and in which
the last but one of his successors, the emperor Kuang-Hsü,
ended his dismal days nearly twelve years ago. That ill-
omened pile of buildings was an emperor's prison two hundred
and sixty years ago, *and an emperor's prison it remains to this
day.*" [10]

Is it surprising that my young dragon was restless and had
begun, in 1922, to flap his wings ?

Uc

CHAPTER XIX

Dragon and Phoenix

WE SAW IN THE LAST CHAPTER that the emperor's betrothal—or rather the creation of an empress by imperial decree—took place on March 11th, 1922. Between that date and the wedding on December 1st of that year, various edicts were issued from time to time announcing the succeeding stages of the elaborate ritual which in China preceded and accompanied the imperial nuptials.[1]

On March 15th, the Court Gazette reported that Jung-Yüan, father of the empress, had been received in audience to return thanks for his elevation to the highest mandarin rank, for having been made a minister of the Presence, and for the privilege of riding on horseback in the Forbidden City. The same Gazette contained an edict appointing four imperial commissioners to take charge of all matters connected with the wedding (*Ta Hun Li Ta Ch'ên*). The four were prince Tsai-T'ao, Chu I-fan (an imperial tutor) and Shao-Ying and Ch'i-Ling (ministers of the household).

The next step was to have the empress conveyed to Peking. This did not mean that she was to enter the Forbidden City, far less be presented to his majesty, at this early stage, but merely that she might pass within the imperial family's sphere of influence and receive the necessary training in court etiquette. Accordingly, a number of palace officials, eunuchs and officers of the guard were sent to Tientsin, and on March 17th they brought her safely back to the capital in a special train. She was met at the station by a group of ministers of the household in their robes of dignity, some ladies-in-waiting, and by a guard of honour supplied by the republican government, which further showed its respect for the august little lady by giving orders that she should be saluted by troops and police along the streets through which she had to drive between the station and her father's Peking residence. This house, in which she spent the interval of nearly nine months between her arrival in Peking and the celebration of the wedding, was situated in a quiet street called Mao'rh Hutung (" Hat Lane ") in the north-east quarter of the so-called Tartar City of Peking, and about three-quarters of a mile from the Gate of Spiritual Valour. From the moment of the arrival of the empress this house was officially known as *Hou Ti*—" The Mansion of the Empress." Though her father continued to reside there he had to yield precedence to his imperial daughter.

Early on April 6th, the emperor, clad in ceremonial garments, paid a visit to the Shou Huang Tien, a hall at the back of Prospect Hill, containing portraits of the dynasty.[2] There, in accordance with the traditions of his house, he solemnly reported his betrothal to the august spirits of his ancestors. A day or two before the wedding, the approaching event was announced to the imperial ancestors with greater ceremony in the innermost halls (*hou tien*) of both the Chapel of the Serving of Ancestors and the Supreme Hall of Ancestors—the *T'ai Miao*. These ceremonies were conducted by the princes Li and Yi respectively.

The most important of the preliminary marriage-ceremonies were three in number : the formal " Sending of the Betrothal Presents," which took place on October 21st ; the " Marriage Contract Rites " on November 12th ; and the " Rites of the Golden Seal and Scroll " on November 30th. These dates were chosen after they had been duly declared, as a result of astrological wizardries, to be " auspicious." There was much superficial resemblance between these three ceremonies. In each case there was a state procession from the Palace of Cloudless Heaven in the Forbidden City to the residence of the bride's father, who, kneeling on a crimson cushion placed on the ground outside his front gate, received in reverent silence the emissaries of the Son of Heaven. In each case the procession was headed by an imperial commissioner—a prince of the blood—who was the bearer of a beribboned staff called the *chieh*—a symbol of imperial authority. In these and other respects the ceremonies were similar, but each had an importance and significance peculiar to itself.

The betrothal presents, sent on the morning of October 21st, were not chosen at random, but in strict accordance with dynastic precedent. Among them were two horses with saddles

and bridles, eighteen sheep, forty pieces of satin and eighty rolls
of cloth. The portable articles were carried in numbers of *lung-
t'ing*—" dragon pavilions "—draped in yellow and somewhat
resembling miniature sedan chairs.

The princes, nobles and officers of the household, whose duty
it was to convey the betrothal presents to the empress, assembled
in the great quadrangle in front of the throne-hall and fell into
their places under the guidance of grand ushers and marshals.
A herald then entered the hall, took up his position on the east
side of the throne and read aloud the following Imperial
Rescript : " WE have already issued OUR EDICT declaring
that WE have elevated Kuo-Po-Lo, daughter of Jung Yüan,
expectant-taotai and hereditary noble of the sixth rank, to the
dignity of Empress. WE now command OUR Officers of State
to take the Symbol of Imperial Authority and carry out the
ceremony of Sending the Betrothal Gifts."

The Symbol was thereupon reverently lifted from a table in
front of the throne and handed over to the principal imperial
commissioner. The latter placed himself at the head of the procession, which slowly threaded its course through the tortuous
ways of the Forbidden City, issued from the Gate of Spiritual
Valour, and passed through thronged streets to the bride's residence in Hat Lane. It was accompanied not only by a band of
court musicians and an escort of palace guards, but also by
republican soldiers on horseback and on foot. This was an
interesting indication (not lost on the Peking populace) that the
display of imperial pomp in the streets of the republican capital
was in no way resented by the president and his government.

The *Ta Chêng Li*—" Rites of the Great Proof or Marriage
Contract "—which took place a fortnight later, marked the
completion of a further stage in the ceremonial. Once more a
herald stood by the side of the throne and read an Imperial
Rescript which was identical with that read at the Betrothal
Rites except in the closing words, which enjoined the officers
concerned to " take the Symbol of Imperial Authority and carry
out the Rites of the Great Proof." This was again an occasion
for the sending of gifts to the bride and the various members of
her family. The gifts, moreover, were of much greater value
than on the former occasion. Those sent to the empress included

100 oz. of gold, 10,000 oz. of silver, one gold tea-set, two silver tea-sets, two silver bowls, 100 pieces of satin, and two horses with saddles and bridles. To her parents were sent the following: 40 oz. of gold, 4,000 oz. of silver, one gold tea-set, one silver tea-set, forty pieces of satin, one hundred rolls of cloth, two horses with saddles and bridles, two suits of court robes, two suits of winter garments, one girdle of honour. To each of the empress's two brothers, one of whom was a child of ten, were sent eight pieces of satin, sixteen rolls of cloth, and one set of writing materials. The servants of the establishment were not forgotten, for to these were sent for division the sum of $400.

The last and most imposing of the three great preliminary ceremonies took place on the morning of November 30th, the eve of the wedding. Three ceremonial tables were placed in front of the throne, the Imperial Symbol being deposited on the centre one. On the eastern table was placed the Golden Scroll or Imperial Letters Patent, while on the western table was placed the Golden Seal. Both scroll and seal were intended to pass into the possession of the empress, who would bring them back with her to the palace when she entered it as bride.

Besides the empress's Golden Scroll and Seal and the Imperial Symbol, there was one other article of great ceremonial and practical importance which was temporarily deposited, as if for purposes of sanctification, within the hall of the Palace of Cloudless Heaven. This was the great bridal sedan chair which, carried by twenty-two bearers, would shortly convey the bride from the home of her father to the palace of her imperial bridegroom. This chair, sumptuously and elaborately draped in scarlet and gold, was adorned with various emblematic devices, the most conspicuous of which were four silver birds which perched upon the corners of the roof. From these birds the imperial bridal chair derives its name *fêng yü*—the *fêng* State chair. The *fêng* is a mythical creature which is supposed to be queen of birds, and symbolises happiness and good fortune. For want of a better term the word is usually rendered by " phoenix " ; but it would be wrong to suppose that the Chinese *fêng* and the phoenix of Greek lore have much in common beyond the fact that they are both mythical birds. In China the phoenix typifies a happy and prosperous bride, and is pre-eminently the emblem of an empress; just as that other fabulous animal the *lung* or dragon, typifies a happy and prosperous bridegroom, and is pre-eminently the emblem of an emperor.

Under the eastern and western eaves of the palace roof were placed or suspended the musical instruments described in an earlier chapter. They were used exclusively for ritual purposes, and were brought out only on occasions of great solemnity. The musicians stood ready to extract from them short snatches of melody which are believed, without evidence, to date from the earliest days of China's recorded history.

When all was ready for the ceremony to commence, the emperor arrayed himself in his robes of state, entered the palace, inspected the Golden Scroll and Seal—the last and most important of his gifts to the bride—and mounted the Dragon Throne. Meanwhile the court musicians struck a few notes on their drums and hanging stones, thus giving what was supposed to be a rendering of the " Peace be with you " section of a symphony entitled " The Central Harmony." This piece of music is attributed to the emperor Shun, who—if he be not, like the phoenix, a myth—began to reign in 2255 b.c.

On the cessation of the music the princes, imperial commissioners, court officials and all concerned in the preparations for the wedding, were marshalled in order and performed the ceremony of the three-fold kneeling and the nine-fold prostration (*kotow*) on the marble terrace. Then followed the reading of a third Imperial Rescript, which was phrased like the two former ones with the necessary alterations. Immediately after this the Imperial Symbol and Golden Seal and Scroll were taken from their tables and handed over to the care of those whose duty it was to convey them to the home of the bride. While the procession was forming in the quadrangle the emperor descended from the throne, which was the signal for the musicians to strike up the " Joyous Peace " section of the symphony already named.

The ceremony which took place when the procession arrived at the bride's residence was more elaborate than on the two former occasions, and the bride was herself for the first time an active participant. She was called upon to take formal and ceremonious possession of the Scroll and Seal and personally to attend the ceremony of the reading of the Imperial Rescript. She knelt during the reading, and afterwards went through an elaborate form of salutation which consists in six times standing with arms hanging down and head slightly advanced, kneeling three times and bowing three times. This, for a woman, is regarded as equivalent to the most reverential of prostrations —the ninefold *kotow*. When the ceremony was over and the procession about to return to the palace, the bride, attended by a mistress of ceremonies, accompanied it as far as the outside of the central doorway of the inner (women's) apartments.

It was on the early morning of the same day (November 30th) that the *shu fei* or " Secondary Consort " entered the palace as bride. The fact that she preceded the empress gave rise to much ignorant and nonsensical chatter, especially among Western foreigners ; and certainly the mere existence of the *shu fei*, involving a double marriage, destroys most of the romantic glamour that might otherwise—in the eyes of foreigners, at least—be associated with the imperial nuptials. It should not be forgotten, however, that the status of secondary wife to the emperor was very far from being an ignoble one. Her position was, in fact, one of great dignity. A *fei*, in certain circumstances, might be elevated to the rank of empress, and her son might become emperor. Her betrothal and marriage rites are not described in detail in these pages merely because in all essentials they were similar to those of the empress, differing from them only in a lower degree of pomp and circumstance. The true reason why the *fei* entered the palace first is that she might be able, on the empress's arrival, to place herself at the head of all the palace women and be the first to welcome her.

The time fixed for the bride's arrival at the palace was four o'clock on the morning of December 1st. This meant that she had to be in readiness to leave the parental home shortly after 3 a.m., for Manchu weddings (unlike Chinese) are by ancient custom nocturnal ceremonies. At this hour there was bright moonlight, for the sky was serene and cloudless and the moon was nearly full.

The conveyance of the Phoenix Chair from the Palace of Cloudless Heaven to the empress's home was in itself a ceremony of great importance and solemnity. The chair was carried by

ordinary bearers belonging to the imperial equipage department as far as the front courtyard. It was then handed over to
eunuchs, who carried it into the principal hall or reception room
attached to the women's apartments. There it was set down at
such an angle that it fronted the auspicious quarter of the southeast—the region which (as had been ascertained by divination)
was at that hour presided over by the god of Happiness.

The bride, in all the splendour of her wedding robes, was ready
at the appointed hour, and when the mistress of ceremonies
formally invited her majesty to take her seat in the Phoenix
Chair, she did so without delay. The chair was immediately
raised by the eunuchs, carried out of the inner hall and through
various courtyards, and set down for a moment outside the main
gateway. There it was surrendered by the eunuchs to the regular
bearers, and the wedding procession set out on its journey to
the Forbidden City. It was not accompanied by any member of
the bride's family, but her father went as far as the outer gateway, where he knelt on his red cushion until the procession had
passed out of sight.

With the procession went an escort of republican soldiers,
cavalry and infantry, a squadron of police, soldiers of the
imperial guard, and two bands discoursing foreign and Chinese
music—fortunately not simultaneously. There was an empty
sedan chair covered with yellow satin and crowned by a silver
knob, and there were three old-fashioned " Peking carts " also
silver knobbed and draped with yellow satin and also empty.
These were intended for her majesty's personal use on future
occasions, for the Phoenix Chair could never be used again.
Among those walking in the procession were sixty bearers of
large palace lanterns, over seventy bearers of " dragon-phoenix "
flags and State umbrellas, and numerous palace servants carrying yellow pavilions containing the Golden Scroll and Seal and
the bride's trousseau. The imperial commissioner (prince Ch'ing)
carried the Imperial Symbol ; the assistant commissioner (prince
Chêng) was the bearer of the Imperial Rescript. Behind the commissioners went the bearers of portable incense burners, which
gave forth fragrant smoke, and next came the Phoenix Chair
itself with its twenty-two bearers. On either side walked eunuchs
of the Presence ; and behind the Chair went ministers of the

household, chamberlains and officers of the guard on horseback.

When the procession set out, between 3 a.m. and 4 a.m., the moon had disappeared and the night was very dark. The electric street lamps—neither very thickly clustered nor very brilliant in Peking—did little more than make darkness visible ; nevertheless, the streets were lined with crowds of well-mannered sightseers, who stood in patient silence behind the rows of republican soldiers and police, content with such glimpses as they could get of the stately court dresses then so seldom seen outside the Forbidden precincts. The centre of every street through which the imperial lady passed was strewn for the occasion (in accordance with an ancient imperial prerogative) with yellow sand and kept clear for the passage of the last—or perhaps not the last—imperial bridal procession in Peking.

It entered the Forbidden City by the central portal of one of the main gates, and did not stop until it had reached the gateway which stands some distance in front of the Palace of Cloudless Heaven. There, at the foot of a flight of marble steps, the Phoenix Chair was set down for a moment in order that the ordinary chair-bearers might be replaced by eunuchs. Slowly and with solemn deliberation the eunuchs carried their precious burden up the steps and into the great quadrangle beyond. Most of those who had formed part of the procession, including the musicians, remained outside the gateway. To them a nearer approach to the Dragon Throne was not permissible. Among those who were privileged to pass within were the incense bearers, whose portable censers, with their little chains, made a tinkling music as they swayed with the rhythmic movements of the bearers. In a few moments the Phoenix Chair had entered the Palace of Cloudless Heaven and had been set down in front of the throne. On either side stood princes of the blood, with their princesses, groups of ladies-in-waiting and eunuchs, officers of the household, and a few other high officers of what is known as the *Nei T'ing* or Inner Court, including all the imperial tutors.

The moment had now arrived when the bride was to emerge from her chair ; but court etiquette demanded that she could do this only in the presence of women and eunuchs. All the princes and officers of the court, therefore, withdrew from the throne-hall and the doors were closed.

Having been assisted by princesses and eunuchs to alight from her chair, the empress was conducted through a door at the back of the throne-hall to the Palace of Earthly Peace (K'un-Ning Kung) which stands a short distance to the north of the Palace of Cloudless Heaven.[3] There her sixteen-year-old lord and master stood waiting to welcome her, and there—after ceremoniously removing the *kai-t'ou* or head-dress which concealed her face—he gazed for the first time upon the features of his sixteen-year-old bride.

The ceremonies that followed were similar in essentials to those that take place at all old-fashioned Manchu weddings, and need not be described. The principal rites include the drinking of the Nuptial Cup and the joint partaking of the wedding feast spread at the side of the " dragon-phoenix " couch. Other essential ceremonies, such as the worship of the bridegroom's imperial ancestors, took place on the following and subsequent days. There were also court festivities of various kinds which gave a life and colour to the palaces and courtyards of the Forbidden City which they had not known since the days of the old empress-dowager. One of the most brilliant ceremonies connected with the imperial nuptials was the congratulatory ceremony on December 3rd. On this occasion the emperor sat on the dragon-throne in the Palace of Cloudless Heaven to receive the congratulations of Manchu and Mongol princes, the officers of the court and household and those ex-ministers of state who had served the throne faithfully in days gone by and still regarded the last of the emperors with affectionate loyalty. All these wore the full official raiment or court dress in vogue under the empire. In addition came a number of civil and military officials of the republic, whose garments—foreign-style uniforms and morning coats—offered a painful contrast to the old-time mandarin robes with their artistically blended colours and rich furs and silks. Some of these officials attended in their private capacity, others as representatives of the republican authorities ; for the republican government was still anxious to show that it respected, in the spirit and in the letter, the terms of the agreement between Republic and Throne. It cannot be denied that in all matters affecting the imperial wedding the government was loyal to its undertaking to treat the Manchu emperor with all the courtesy that it would show to a foreign sovereign on Chinese soil.

In one important respect this ceremony of congratulation was marked by a complete and surprising breaking-away from old custom. Only two days after the wedding, the emperor and empress, for the first time in the history of the dynasty, held a joint and informal reception of foreigners. The empress-dowager of Boxer notoriety did, indeed, receive foreigners on many occasions towards the close of her life ; but she did so as *de facto* sovereign, when she was advanced in years, and for reasons connected with state-craft. Moreover, those receptions were never wholly free from formality, and men and women were received separately, and not, as on this occasion, together. No reception held by the " Venerable Buddha " can rightly be compared with this joint reception of foreign men and women by the young emperor and empress. It took place immediately before the formal reception of Manchu notables and Chinese officials and ex-ministers, at which the empress was not present. The foreign guests, nearly two hundred in number, were first conducted to the throne-hall of the Palace of Cloudless Heaven, where they were served with refreshments and received mementoes of the occasion in the form of little silver boxes. To emphasise the informal nature of the proceedings, the emperor did not mount the throne, he did not receive his guests in the throne-hall, and neither he nor the empress was seated. The room to which the guests were admitted one by one to make their bow, and in some cases to shake hands, was a small apartment known as the *Hsi Nuan Ko*—the Western Warm Pavilion—which is entered by a door on the western side of the throne-hall. In this room their majesties stood side by side, attended by two princesses, two ministers of the household, and four persons who introduced the visitors as they came in. These four were Liang Tun-yen,[4] Lien Fang, who had served under the empire as a vice-president of the Board of Foreign Affairs, admiral Ts'ai T'ing-kan and myself. Neither Mr. Liang nor Mr. Lien has held office under the Republic. It is said that the latter was offered a high post under Yüan Shih-k'ai, but gave the answer that rather than serve the republic he would earn his living by pulling a rickshaw.

Among the foreigners who attended this reception were all, or nearly all, the foreign ministers ; but, in recognition of the fact that they were accredited not to the Manchu court but to the Chinese republic, they came as private individuals, not as the official representatives of their respective governments.

As soon as the foreigners had all been presented, they were informed that his majesty was about to join them and to speak a few words of welcome. The company maintained a respectful silence as the emperor mounted the dais of the throne. What he said was spoken slowly and clearly in English. " It is a great pleasure to us," he said, " to see here to-day so many distinguished visitors from all parts of the world. We thank you for coming, and we wish you all health and prosperity." From the hands of Liang Tun-yen he then took a glass of champagne, bowed to the company on right and left, and raised the glass to his lips.

To foreigners in Peking the emperor in the Forbidden City had hitherto been something of a mystery within a mystery. Now, for the first time, they had beheld a very human boy, conducting himself in rather trying circumstances with all the graceful dignity that seems to be inborn in the princely families of the Manchu race, and showing very clearly, by the simple frankness of his manners and his obvious pleasure at this unwonted opportunity of meeting men and women from Europe and America, that for him the old barriers between East and West had been swept away.[5]

The cost of the wedding, it need hardly be said, was enormous. On the other hand there were large quantities of very valuable presents, including over a million dollars in cash, which reached the emperor from all quarters of what had once been his empire. A "Red Book " was issued by the household department shortly after the wedding, containing lists of the presents and the names of the donors. It is an interesting compilation as it gives some indication, however slight, of the degree of loyalty to the fallen dynasty that still existed in official and unofficial circles. The names of Sun Yat-sen and his party were of course conspicuously absent, and although the " Christian General " Fêng Yü-hsiang presented " a Great Happiness *ju-i* of white jade," it is to be suspected that the good wishes symbolised by the *ju-i* were lacking in Christian sincerity. The Manchu princes and members of the imperial clan (" yellow-girdles " and " red-girdles," denoting their blood-relationship to the imperial family) and also the tutors and officers of the household, appear on the list as a matter of course. Ex-president Hsü Shih-ch'ang gave a cash present of $20,000 together with many valuable presents including twenty-eight pieces of porcelain and a magnificent dragon-phoenix Chinese carpet which covered the floor of the nuptial-chamber on the day of the wedding. Mongol princes, " Living Buddhas " and other lamas of high degree are prominent in the long list. Chang Hsün the " kingmaker " gave $10,000. Other presents of money, usually accompanied by miscellaneous gifts, came from prominent republican officials such as Wu P'ei-fu, general Wang Huai-ch'ing, admiral Ts'ai T'ing-kan, Yen Huai-ch'ing (better known in the West as Dr. W. W. Yen, not long ago China's representative at Geneva and now her ambassador at Moscow), and general Ts'ao K'un, who not long afterwards became president. Manchuria was well represented. Chang Tso-lin himself gave $10,000, the governors of the two Manchurian provinces of Kirin and Heilungkiang each gave the same amount, and many of their subordinates gave several thousand dollars apiece. Ex-officials who had served under the monarchy were naturally very numerous. They included several former viceroys, such as Ch'ên K'uei-lung, and many who had served under the throne, and also (in some cases) under the republic, as Chinese ministers abroad, such as Hu Wei-tê, who served as minister to Russia, Japan and France. (This distinguished diplomat died at Peiping in November, 1933.) President Li Yüan-hung, who had succeeded Hsü Shih-ch'ang, gave numerous presents including $20,000 in cash. It is worthy of note that by the special orders of the emperor the whole of the president's money-gift was handed over to a benevolent association for distribution among the poor of Peking.

One ex-official who wished, in spite of his poverty, to demonstrate his loyalty, gave the only treasure he possessed—a copy of the *Ch'ien Tzŭ Wên* (" The Thousand-Character Classic ") in the handwriting of the emperor Shêng Tsu (K'ang-Hsi), which had been a precious heirloom in his family for over two hundred years.

Of greater significance as evidences of loyalty than the names of the donors and the value of their presents was the manner in which the donors described themselves. Ex-viceroys and great numbers of smaller dignitaries who had served under the monarchy subscribed themselves *ch'ên*—implying that they still regarded themselves as his majesty's " servants."[6] Numerous members of parliament were neither ashamed nor afraid to use the same term. Mongols and most of the Manchus also described themselves as *ch'ên*, though some of the Manchus related to the imperial house used the rather old-fashioned terms *nu-ts'ai*— " your majesty's slave "—and *pu ju pên fên*—" one who has failed in his duty."

The republican officials were not uniform in the terms they used. Most of them omitted *ch'ên* and wrote *ch'êng chin* or *kung chin*—" respectfully presents." Dr. W. W. Yen was one of those who used the phrase *kuei chin*—" presents on his knees "— which was employed by loyalists like Chang Hsün and Chang Hai-p'êng. The last-named is now (1934) governor of Jehol, rejoicing to have had the chance, in the late evening of his life, of returning openly to his old allegiance.

Here it may be mentioned that practically all the emperor's wedding gifts, and those of the empress, were subsequently seized by the group of soldiers and politicians who, in November, 1924, made themselves masters of Peking, in spite of the fact that the republic had solemnly guaranteed that the private property of the imperial house should not be touched. The stored treasures in the Forbidden City were confiscated on the plea that they were all national property—as if the emperor and his ancestors were the only persons in the land who were debarred from collecting works of art in their private capacity. Whatever may be said for this confiscation, it can hardly be seriously argued that the wedding gifts freely given to the emperor after he had ceased to be the ruler of China were also the rightful property of the Chinese nation, and it would be interesting to learn the grounds on which he has been deprived of them. A few of the least valuable of the presents given to the emperor on his wedding and on other occasions were presented by myself. They are included in the property that has been confiscated, though it was emphatically not my intention to present them to the Chinese

people. I have no doubt that most of the donors of wedding gifts
in 1922 would say the same in respect of their own intentions.
An exception, perhaps, must be made of the " Christian General "
with his " Great Happiness *ju-i* of white jade," as he did not
take the trouble—when he had made himself master of the
Forbidden City by armed force—to pick out his own wedding gift
and return it to the person to whom he had presented it.

An imperial decree raising the three dowager-consorts to the
rank of " Grand Dowager " was issued shortly before the wedding. It ran as follows :

" Whereas the imperial consort Ching Yi [" Reverential
and Admirable "] and the imperial consort Jung-Hui [" Noble
and Gracious "] dutifully served his late Imperial Majesty
Mu Tsung Yi [T'ung-Chih, 1862–1874] and were respectful,
discreet and of blameless reputation ;

" And Whereas the imperial consort Tuan K'ang [" Upright
and Tranquil "] dutifully served his late Imperial Majesty
Tê Tsung [Kuang-Hsü, 1875–1908] and brilliantly manifested
a spirit of reverent obedience ;

" And Whereas in view of Our approaching Nuptials it is
right and fitting that We should show Our regard for the
above-named by granting them new titles of honour :

" We therefore declare that We confer upon each of the
three personages named the title of *Huang Kuei T'ai Fei*
[" imperial dowager consort of the first rank "—the first
rank below that of empress]. Let the proper department submit
a Memorial to the Throne regarding the proper steps to be
taken to give effect to this Edict.

" Such are the Imperial Commands."

" Wedding honours " were conferred upon various members
of the imperial clan and also upon the tutors and many others.
P'u-Chieh, the emperor's brother, became a *Fu-kuo Kung*—that
is to say a duke of the second order. I myself was promoted from
the second to the highest of the nine official grades (*t'ou pin ting
tai*) ; Ch'ên Pao-shên became a *t'ai-fu* or Grand Tutor ; and

Chu I-fan, my other colleague, was made a *T'ai Tzŭ Shao Pao* or Junior Guardian of the Heir-Apparent. Shao-Ying, head of the Nei Wu Fu, was made a *T'ai Pao* or Grand Guardian. Ch'i-Ling, second in rank in the household department, became a Junior Guardian. New posthumous honours were also conferred upon prince Ch'un's father—the grandfather of the emperor.

Among wedding festivities to which only members of the Nei T'ing or Inner Court were invited was a series of " command " theatrical performances in the Palace Theatre. They were held on three consecutive days corresponding to December 3rd, 4th and 5th, 1922.

An invitation to theatricals in the Forbidden City was regarded as so high an honour that it necessitated the issue of an imperial rescript in each case. As the form of invitation, being a relic of ancient palace ceremonial, is now a thing of the past, the invitation which reached me is here reproduced in facsimile. It reads :

" Communication from the imperial household department. It is respectfully intimated to you that the Office of Memorials to the Throne has passed to this department an Edict from His Imperial Majesty saying :

" The honour of attendance at the Lodge of Fresh Fragrance [the Palace Theatre] on the 14th, 15th and 16th days [of the lunar calendar] is hereby conferred upon Chuang [Johnston]. Such is His Imperial Majesty's pleasure.

" This is transmitted to you for your special information. May peace be with you."

Most of the famous Chinese actors of the day took part in the performances, and the number of plays or scenes from plays presented one after another all day long for the three days was thirty-three. There was a brilliant assemblage of Manchu and Mongol princes and nobles, all in their full ceremonial dress and peacocks' feathers. My neighbour at one of the feasts which were provided for us at frequent intervals was an elderly duke who had been one of the Venerable Buddha's favourite relatives. He told me that the Forbidden City had not known such gaiety since 1893, the year before the outbreak of the China-Japan war. Unfortunately the scene was robbed of much of its

內務府信牋

旨

敬啟者現由奏事處傳出奉

賞莊　於十四十五十六日在

漱芳齋聽戲等因欽此用特布達專此即頌

公綏

內務府啟

Wa

brilliance by the non-appearance of the empress and the princesses. They were present, and doubtless enjoyed the spectacle as much as we did, but they were concealed from our view behind screens and panels. For three winter days, the twilight of the Manchu court seemed to have broadened into something that looked like daylight—but was not.

CHAPTER XX

Plots and Stratagems

NEITHER the elaborate preparations for the imperial wedding nor the wedding itself had the result of reconciling the emperor to existing conditions in the palace or to his own life there. In face of strenuous opposition from the officers of the Nei Wu Fu and their allies among the princes, he insisted upon appointing a special committee to investigate and reform the administration of the Forbidden City and the imperial properties. The Nei Wu Fu had hitherto been a close corporation intensely jealous of its traditional " rights," and the suggestion that outsiders should be given power to pry into its secrets with the strong likelihood that they would bring to light some of its innumerable iniquities, was intolerable. Even more monstrous, from its point of view, was the proposal that the members of the investigating committee should include Chinese. The Nei Wu Fu up to that time had always been regarded as the closely-guarded preserve of Manchus, and vacancies in its personnel had always been filled up by what was practically a system of co-optation. It was quick to realise that the appointment of a plenipotentiary committee of enquiry, consisting either wholly or partially of non-Manchus, would be the first step towards the destruction of the Manchu monopoly of membership of the Nei Wu Fu itself.

With the help of prince Ch'un (to whom the Nei Wu Fu always appealed, not in vain, for support against all proposals of reform) it temporarily defeated my efforts to have a Chinese appointed to the permanent membership of its own body as a Nei Wu Fu *ta ch'ên* or minister of the household, but it failed to defeat my other recommendation, that the committee of investigation should include Chinese members. Personally, I should have preferred that the committee should consist of none but Chinese, or at least that it should not include any of the existing staff of the Nei Wu Fu. That ideal could not be realised, but I succeeded in securing the appointment of two Chinese, one being the person to whom was addressed the letter transcribed in chapter xviii, the other the person whose name is mentioned in that letter—Liu Chien-chih, a native of central China.

Most unfortunately, a long and serious illness made it impossible for the former to take up his post. He also became extremely pessimistic about the possibility of effecting any real reform in the palace system so long as the Nei Wu Fu existed and so long as it was supported by the ex-regent and other influential princes, and he anticipated the failure of any committee to achieve success. Mr. Liu Chien-chih accepted the post offered to him, but as his fellow-members were all not only Manchus but officers of the Nei Wu Fu, there was little prospect of any far-reaching results arising from his appointment. Nevertheless it was better than nothing to have broken the long-established rule whereby the affairs of the imperial household had been kept exclusively in Manchu hands.

My own share in this matter could not be kept a secret from the Nei Wu Fu, and my relations with that body became more strained than ever. A little incident which took place early in 1923 will illustrate the position as it existed at that time.

I had frequently called the emperor's attention to the fact that the methods by which money was realised from time to time by the sale or mortgage of palace treasures left much to be desired. It was not my business to complain (though I often did so) of the sale-transactions in themselves. Assuming the impossibility of abolishing the Nei Wu Fu, and the failure of the republic to fulfil its financial obligations, it was obvious that money had to be raised somehow to enable the imperial household to pay its way. The grounds of my complaints were that the treasures were disposed of in a ruinously corrupt and wasteful manner. The practice was to sell the articles to a small and exclusive ring of dealers whose close and permanent relations with the Nei Wu Fu made it easy for both parties, who thoroughly understood one another, to conduct negotiations on mutually satisfactory terms. The prices actually paid were far in excess of the amounts entered in the palace accounts, but far below the market value of the articles sold. What became of the difference between the real and the fictitious prices was a little secret which it was not to the interest of either party to disclose. Nor was it a secret about which the young emperor himself was likely to be fussily inquisitive. He had never been taught the value of money nor had he the slightest idea of the prices that ought to be realised from the sale of the articles periodically withdrawn from the palace treasure-rooms. The system worked admirably, from the point of view of the Nei Wu Fu, until a meddlesome foreigner attempted with partial success to open his majesty's eyes to the iniquitous practices of his extremely obsequious and soft-spoken staff.

On the special occasion to which I refer, the Nei Wu Fu collected a quantity of valuable articles, including a miniature pagoda of solid gold standing about four feet high, and requested the emperor's permission to dispose of them. He astonished them by accusing them of corrupt practices, and gave my name as his authority for the remark that if sold by open auction, either in Peking or elsewhere, the palace treasures would realise far larger sums than could be obtained through the customary method of private sale to a small group of specified dealers.

On the evening of that day messengers arrived at my house from the Forbidden City, bringing with them all the valuables referred to, including the gold pagoda, and an oral message from the Nei Wu Fu to the effect that it was his majesty's wish that the whole collection should be handed over to me to be disposed of in any way that I thought fit. I asked them for the emperor's written authority, which they were unable to produce. I then ordered them to take the valuables back to the palace, pointing out that any instructions which his majesty might wish to give me regarding them could be given by himself when I visited him on the following day. The messengers replied that they had definite orders to leave the articles at my house and also to obtain a receipt. To this I retorted that I refused to give them a receipt for valuables which I declined to take charge of, and that anything they might leave behind them would be deposited outside my gate on the public street. They then sorrowfully withdrew, begging me to exonerate them from all blame for not having accomplished their mission. They left nothing behind.

Next day I informed the emperor of what had occurred, and

he agreed with me that the Nei Wu Fu had acted with the deliberate intention of putting me in a false and embarrassing position. When he indignantly demanded an explanation of its action the only one offered was that his wishes had been mis-interpreted ; and there the matter dropped.

A much more thrilling episode than that of the golden pagoda has now to be told.

On Saturday, February 24th, 1923 (less than three months after the imperial wedding) the president of the republic (Li Yüan-hung) gave a reception at which I was one of the guests. There I met the wife of one of the foreign ministers in Peking who informed me that her husband, who was prevented by a bad cold from attending the reception, was anxious to see me at the earliest possible moment on urgent business. I went to his Legation forthwith. The communication he had to make to me was this. P'u-Chieh, the emperor's younger brother, had visited him during the three preceding days and had informed him that the emperor had made up his mind to leave the For-bidden City secretly, and at once, and had instructed him to beg the minister to help him to carry out his project by receiving him first at the Legation, and then facilitating his immediate departure to Tientsin.

The minister asked P'u-Chieh if he or the emperor had con-sulted me. P'u-Chieh replied no, because it was believed that I would disapprove. He added that a certain prince was a party to the scheme, and that when the emperor reached Tientsin he would live in that prince's house in the British Concession there, to which a large quantity of valuables from the palace had already been sent. The minister said he would think over the proposal and asked for P'u-Chieh's telephone number and also for that of the said prince. The numbers were given ; but later on, after P'u-Chieh had gone home he himself telephoned to the minister urgently begging him not on any account to telephone to the prince, who did not wish to be consulted.

The minister told me that he had pondered the matter care-fully and that out of pity for the young emperor who was kept in the palace against his will he had practically made up his mind to receive him at the Legation and personally accompany him to Tientsin. He would, of course, take no steps to bring his majesty out of the palace : he would merely act as his host if he presented himself at the Legation.

Having heard all that the minister had to say I proceeded to tell him confidentially of the occasion, in June of the year before, when the emperor had begged me to take him to the British Legation, and of my reasons for not doing so. I also told the minister that in my opinion it would be impossible for the emperor to leave the Forbidden City without the knowledge of the eunuchs and the palace guards, who would be sure to raise the alarm unless of course their silence had been secured by bribery.

Next day, February 25th, I wrote as follows to the minister:

" The more I think over what you told me last night, the more strongly I feel that your visitor's scheme is extremely rash and that if an attempt is made to carry it out, the results may be very unfortunate for the person whose interests we both have at heart. This being so, it is out of the question for me to be a party to the scheme, especially as I am convinced that any such action on my part would meet with the strong disapproval of my Legation and the British Government. If I am consulted on the subject by the person mainly concerned, I shall advise him not to take the action proposed, but I shall not take active steps to prevent the plan being carried out as I could not do so without betraying your confidence."

It should be explained that these events took place during the holiday-season which extended from the eve of the lunar New Year (which in 1923 fell on February 16th) to the few days after the emperor's birthday (13th of the first moon) which fell on February 28th. During such periods it was not usual for the tutors to visit the palace unless they received a summons. Had I thought it desirable to discuss this matter with the emperor, therefore, I should have had to request a special audience.

My letter to the minister failed to alter his resolution. On the afternoon of the same day (February 25th) he wrote to me as follows :

" My visitor [P'u-Chieh] informed me that the other one
was bent on the execution of his plan, that he had carefully
thought it over and that he meant to do it TO-NIGHT. . . .
I told my visitor that I had spoken with you, which did not
surprise him. But if you feel as you do, please go and see our
friend this afternoon, and if possible let me know the result
of your conversation."

To this I immediately sent the following reply :

" I am much obliged for your letter. I have decided not to
visit our friend this afternoon. I feel certain, from what I
know of his character, that I could not now change his purpose : especially as he knows perfectly well that I am in hearty
agreement with him in his general attitude and have always
been most strongly in favour of drastic changes being effected
in his way of life. It is only the particular plan which he has
finally decided to adopt that I cannot approve of. All I can
hope for now is that the plan will be successful and that my
gloomy forebodings may not be realised. He is fortunate
indeed in having enlisted the aid of so influential and sympathetic a friend as yourself."

By the time these letters had passed between the Legation
Quarter and my house, it was late afternoon. I remained at
home awaiting news. It was not till after the last train had left
for Tientsin that night that my telephone-bell rang again. The
speaker at the other end was the minister. His message was brief.
" The plan has failed," he said. " Our friend has not arrived."
Next morning I went to the Legation and heard what the
minister had to say. He knew very little. After the hour at which
the emperor was due at the Legation (according to the plan,
P'u-Chieh was to have brought him there in his own horse-
carriage), the emperor himself rang up the minister, told him
that something had gone wrong and asked him to send a car to
one of the palace gates to bring him away. This the minister
declined to do. He adhered to his decision to do nothing more
than admit the emperor to the Legation if he presented himself
there, and accompany him to Tientsin. The minister went on to

tell me that he had made all necessary preparations for the night journey to Tientsin and had secured tickets and a reserved compartment. He knew nothing as yet of the cause of the emperor's non-appearance.

Nor did I myself learn anything till the next day—February 27th. That morning—which happened to be the day before the emperor's birthday—I was sent for by him. P'u-Chieh was the only third person present. The emperor took it for granted— he had already been told—that I knew of his attempted escape. He excused himself for having failed to consult me on the ground that the prince who had been concerned in the scheme had told him that on no account must he discuss the matter with anyone connected with the court. The matter was to be a secret shared only by the emperor, the prince, and P'u-Chieh, in addition to the foreign minister whose only part in the plot was to make arrangements for his majesty's safe journey to Tientsin.

The failure of the scheme was due to a variety of causes. P'u-Chieh had made several journeys between the Forbidden City and the Legation, and on each departure from the palace he had taken with him a number of sealed attaché cases. The total number of cases brought by him from the Forbidden City to the Legation was fourteen. These journeys, and the removal of so many cases. had aroused suspicion among some of the palace staff, and there was also some reason to believe that P'u-Chieh's own servants had made a secret report to his father prince Ch'un. Meanwhile the emperor's own preparations for departure attracted the attention of some of the palace eunuchs. The consequence was that before the moment for departure came, urgent telephone-messages had summoned the ministers of the household to the palace, the guards at all the gates had been changed, and had the emperor attempted to leave the Forbidden City by any one of them he would have found his way barred. His last hope was that the foreign minister on whose aid he had been relying would devise some method of carrying him off to the Legation Quarter. Hence his personal appeal, by telephone, for the minister's car. It is extremely unlikely that had it been sent he could have used it.

Both the emperor and P'u-Chieh informed me that the prince who was mainly responsible for the scheme was determined to remain in the background and to deny that he was in any way implicated. At his instigation, or rather at his earnest entreaty, the emperor had adopted a policy of silence. When questioned by prince Ch'un and the officers of the household, he had assumed an air of blank wonderment at the suggestion that the idea of a stealthy departure from the Forbidden City had ever entered his head. In this I thought he was wrong, and did not hesitate to say so. But at that time I did not realise that had he adopted a bolder policy and insisted upon his right to leave the palace if he chose, the princes and household would have invoked the aid of the republican government to prevent his departure.

P'u-Chieh, though in the circumstances he could not deny that he had been a party to the scheme, had also refused to answer questions and told me that he would continue to do so. As the son and heir of the most influential of the princes—the ex-regent—it was unlikely that he would be harshly treated for his obstinacy. Unfortunately, as it turned out, the same immunity did not attach to those of humbler rank who had played subordinate parts in this palace conspiracy.

The emperor seemed much less despondent about its failure than I expected to find him. He treated the affair lightly, which he could hardly have done had he been intensely anxious to escape from the thraldom of the palace at that particular time. This puzzled me at first, but before our conversation was over I felt convinced that the scheme had not originated with him but with another, and that he had merely been persuaded to play a leading part in it. The real author of it, I felt sure, was the prince whom I have preferred to leave unnamed, or someone in the still dimmer background who had been using the prince as an agent.

The obstinate silence of the emperor and his brother perplexed and dismayed the officers of the household and also the princes, though in the case of one of the latter the perplexity and dismay were of course merely simulated. The suspicion that I was the principal conspirator quickly became current in palace circles. The first indication of this manifested itself on the following day—February 28th, the emperor's birthday—when in accordance with custom I went to the palace to take part in the ceremony of congratulation. On all former occasions of a similar

kind I had been shown special attention and treated with great
courtesy by the Manchu princes as well as by my official colleagues. This time I was wholly ignored by them, and I was left
severely alone in the waiting-room in which I was entertained
with the usual tea and refreshments. From the time I entered
the palace until I left it, the only persons with whom I exchanged a word were *sula* and eunuchs.

Next day my colleague Ch'ên Pao-shên paid me a visit, and
from the questions put to me by him it was obvious that he had
been deputed by the household to extract all possible information out of me and especially to find out what part I had taken
in the now notorious " plot." Naturally I was unable to inform
him of what I knew or even of what I suspected, and although I
was able to assert truthfully that I had nothing to do with the
" plot," it was obvious that his suspicions were not removed.

My next visitor on a similar errand was one of the secretaries
of the president of the republic. He gave me the rather startling
news that the affair of the emperor's attempted flight to a certain foreign Legation was known to the republican government,
to various members of parliament, and also to general Ts'ao
K'un (shortly to be president), marshal Wu P'ei-fu and ex-
president Hsü Shih-ch'ang ; and that my name had been mentioned in government circles as that of the person who was
probably the ringleader. In answer to his enquiries I said as
much as, but no more than, I had said to Ch'ên Pao-shên. We
had two subsequent interviews at which the subject was discussed, and at the second he informed me that as the government was determined to ascertain the truth, general Wang
Huai-ch'ing had been entrusted with the duty of extracting it
from those palace servants and guards who had obviously been
induced by bribery to take a humble but necessary part in the
plot. This, of course, meant that these unfortunate people might
be put to torture.

Happily it proved unnecessary to resort to these extreme
measures. The truth—or a great part of it—was brought to
light, and then the excitement died down as quickly as it had
arisen. On April 18th, I addressed a letter to a certain British
official from which the following is an extract.

" The emperor himself has not been subjected to any harsh treatment or new restrictions ; though he has himself told me that the guards at the palace gates have been warned that they will be shot if they let him pass through. Even his private telephone (which he had installed last year against the wishes of the household) has not been removed ; and everything is now going smoothly. The authorities apparently satisfied themselves that I had nothing whatever to do with the plot, and they have been rather going out of their way to be civil. I think the real reason why the matter had to be hushed up was that prince —— was deeply involved in it ; and he is too influential a man to be touched. I have discovered that it was through him that the emperor, some time ago, bought a house in Tientsin. It is situated in the British Concession and is adjacent to the prince's own Tientsin house. The prince came to see me a few days ago and told me this himself, asking me at the same time not to mention it to any member of the imperial family. It was to this house that the emperor would have gone if he had succeeded in making his escape, and it appears that I was to be sent for to join him there, pending a suitable opportunity to go abroad. . . . It seems to me quite conceivable that prince ——'s intention was ultimately to hand the emperor over to the safe-keeping of Chang Tso-lin. I happen to know that Chang and the prince are on very friendly terms."

The last sentence contains the clue to the whole conspiracy.

The emperor himself was not aware of the further ramifications of the plot in which he was to play so important a part. All he was allowed to know was that his long-cherished wish to leave the Forbidden City and to go abroad was at last about to be realised. He was first to go to the British Concession in Tientsin. He was told that when he was established there in a house of his own, free to do what he pleased, it would be time enough for him to consider his future movements.

As far as I could make out from the evidence which came to me only by degrees and in fragments, the essential part of the whole scheme was that he was to go to Manchuria. The monarchist general, Chang Hsün, was to welcome him to Tientsin and become his guardian and protector there. Soon after his arrival, it was to be explained to him that it was his duty to pay a ceremonial visit to the tombs of his ancestors near Mukden in Manchuria, in order to announce his marriage to the spirit of the great T'ai Tsung. T'ai Tsung (who ruled Manchuria from 1627 to 1643) was the first Manchurian monarch who assumed the imperial dignity, established the complete independence of his country, and adopted the dynastic style of Ta Ch'ing. Once the emperor had reached Manchuria, to which country Chang Hsün would have escorted him, he would of course have passed under the direct guardianship of its *de facto* ruler.

Thus we see that the arch-plotter was no other than the powerful Manchurian war lord, Chang Tso-lin himself. With him was closely associated his relative by marriage—Chang Hsün—who had never wavered in his loyalty to the old dynasty. The unnamed prince's part in the plot was a necessary but relatively unimportant one. He was merely to facilitate the emperor's departure from the Forbidden City, and make arrangements for his safe journey to Tientsin. The essential thing from Chang Tso-lin's point of view was that whether the plan succeeded or failed no suspicion should fall upon himself of having been in any way concerned in it. This was the reason why the carrying out of the plot, which had been under consideration for a long time, was planned for a few weeks after the emperor's wedding. What was wanted was a plausible excuse for the emperor's journey to Manchuria. That would be afforded by the ceremonial post-nuptial visit to the imperial tombs.

In spite of all the efforts made to keep the matter a close secret, there were rumours afloat in palace circles that something serious was likely to happen. On February 23rd, two days before the attempted escape, the father of the young empress visited an American friend and told him that he was greatly worried about political conditions as he had heard from a well-informed foreigner (a Frenchman who was on friendly terms with the unnamed prince) that " within five or six days something would happen that would cause considerable disturbance." It is possible, then, that on the night of the emperor's attempted flight the household and the imperial family were already on the alert, and that he was being more closely watched than he himself suspected.

It will now be clear why it was that the news of the emperor's attempt to leave the Forbidden City caused so much consternation in Chinese government circles. There was no objection in principle, on the part of those in power in north China at that time, to the emperor going where he would. He was in no sense a state-prisoner. But if there was the smallest reason to suspect that his ultimate destination was Manchuria, and that Chang Tso-lin was party to a conspiracy to bring him to Mukden, the situation was obviously one that was full of the gravest possibilities. One of these—the re-establishment of the monarchy in Manchuria—might not in itself cause much distress in political circles in north China where very few were noted for their devotion to republican principles ; but a Manchurian throne with Chang Tso-lin as the power behind it would be an ever-present menace to the stability of the political and military structure that had Peking and Loyang for its bases.

If the ultimate object aimed at by the plotters was the re-enthronement of the emperor, it may be asked why the scheme had to be kept secret from all the Manchu princes but one, and also from the palace authorities. It was because the princes and the household were known to be less interested in the fortunes of the emperor than in their own. They would have opposed his withdrawal to Manchuria because it would almost inevitably have led to the occupation of the Forbidden City by the republican authorities and the collapse of the system by which the Nei Wu Fu and many of the princes lived and throve and which the Articles of Favourable Treatment had been designed to maintain. They were therefore in complete agreement with the Peking government authorities as to the urgent necessity of preventing the emperor from taking adventurous trips to Manchuria.

Some of my readers, having read so far, may have assumed that the foreign minister to whose Legation the emperor was to have gone, and who was to have facilitated his journey to Tientsin, was the minister for Japan. The Japanese minister was not concerned in any way, directly or indirectly.

It should be added that the minister in question—whose name I cannot disclose without his consent—had no knowledge whatever of the major plot. All he assumed was that the emperor was practically a prisoner in the Forbidden City—an assumption which was not far from the truth—and that he was longing for freedom. He proposed to do nothing more than open the gates of his Legation to the emperor if he presented himself there, and accompany him, if requested to do so, to Tientsin. He was prepared, in fact, to do as much as, and no more than, would be done by multitudes of others in similar circumstances ; and what he proposed to do would have been done by him not in his diplomatic capacity but in that of a courteous gentleman.

As to the unnamed prince and his not very brilliantly-devised or chivalrous plan of action, perhaps the less said the better. I have reason to believe that Chang Tso-lin never quite forgave him for his failure and spoke of him with impatience and contempt. To Chang Hsün, the collapse of the scheme was a severe disappointment which probably hastened his end. He died in September of the same year.[1]

As far as I am aware, no whisper of the emperor's attempt to leave the Forbidden City ever reached the Press. But some time after the plot had failed, belated and in certain cases rather cryptic references were made in both Chinese and foreign newspapers to a possible visit of the emperor to his ancestral tombs in Manchuria and to political possibilities of a more serious kind. For example, the English newspapers of Peking published the following paragraph on March 23rd—a month after the plot had been discovered and thwarted.

" It is reported in Chinese circles that the ex-emperor will shortly proceed to Manchuria to Singchingfu to pay his respects at the tomb of his ancestors.

" It is pointed out that it is an ancient custom for an emperor on his marriage to take his bride to the ancestral tomb, but the rumour is causing a good deal of excitement in political circles as there are many suggestions as to what his relations with general Chang Tso-lin might be. No confirmation of the report can be obtained."

Still more significant was a communication from the Peking correspondent of the *Peking and Tientsin Times*, dated May 24th.

" Without being an alarmist, your correspondent would
suggest that the fifth revolution in the history of the 12-year-
old republic is forthcoming. . . . When this revolution will
occur and who is behind it are questions of debate. It will
emanate, principally, from Mukden and Chang Tso-lin. All
the so-called old-style politicians are behind him, financially
and otherwise. Whether the big ambition is to restore the
monarchical form of government is questionable but in this
connection it may be pointed out that it is the retired monarchists who, pooling their wealth, think they can pull the
country together. For the moment your correspondent desires
to say little except the fact that another monarchical revolution is forthcoming and that both Chang Tso-lin and Chang
Hsün are involved. The information upon which this article
is based was obtained under difficulties but from Chinese
official sources that are unquestionable."

This correspondent's sources of information were good. What
he did not know was that the plot had failed exactly three
months before he wrote this paragraph.

This episode having become a thing of the past, seldom to be
referred to even in private conversation, the emperor began to
throw himself with rather intermittent zeal into the work of the
committee which had been appointed to investigate the finances
and administration of the imperial household. Without his
personal encouragement and insistence, the committee was not
likely to make much headway against the stubborn opposition
and " non-possumus " attitude of the Nei Wu Fu. As all the
members of the committee but one were members of that body,
this was not surprising.

One of the most disconcerting announcements made by the
emperor at this time—disconcerting from the point of view of
the palace staff—was that he would not be satisfied until the
expenditure of the Nei Wu Fu was reduced from its existing figure of about six million to half a million dollars a year.
The next blow to the equanimity of the Nei Wu Fu was that he
called for inventories of the palace treasures, and frequently
caused various items, chosen at random, to be brought for his

inspection. He often sent for me in order that we might examine the treasures together, and in practically every case they were as new and strange to him as they were to me. Most of them had been stored in receptacles which, as the unbroken seals showed, had not been opened for generations. Many had not seen the light since they had first reached the palace from long-forgotten tribute-bearers and provincial viceroys. The articles in the sealed boxes had rarely or never been tampered with; but in respect of other objects it was not long before the emperor discovered that the inventories did not reveal the true state of the treasure-rooms and that many of the items which he expressed a desire to see could not be traced. The emperor's anger at these discoveries created something like a panic in the palace.

One day, in my presence, the emperor announced that he intended to make a personal inspection of some of the empty rooms and palaces in which the treasures were stored. One of the buildings designated as one destined for early inspection was the Chien Fu Kung—" the Palace of Established Happiness "—in the north-west section of the Forbidden City.

Before dawn on the morning of June 27th I was awakened by my servant with the news that my presence at the palace was required by the emperor immediately. For some time my car was impeded by a dense mass of people who, in spite of the very early hour, thronged the streets. I arrived at the Gate of Spiritual Valour to find a portion of the Forbidden City in flames. The " Palace of Established Happiness " had already ceased to exist. It had been devoured in a roaring furnace. Some neighbouring buildings had also caught fire, and had it not been for the timely arrival of a fire-engine sent by the Italian Legation it is possible that the emperor's own palace and that of the empress, both of which were not far off, might also have been reduced to ashes.

I found the emperor and empress standing on a heap of charred wood, sadly contemplating the spectacle. Several of the princes had already arrived, and the officers of the Nei Wu Fu were fussily doing their best to instruct the well-disciplined Italian firemen in the art of how not to extinguish fires.

The flames were still raging when I arrived. Just after I had reached the emperor I was astonished to see three Europeans
Xc

—one of them a lady—all in evening dress that at an earlier hour had been immaculate, smilingly emerging from clouds of smoke. The first impression I received from their appearance was that their dress clothes would never again be fit to wear. The second was that all three were personally known to me. They were Mr. Gascoigne and Mr. Carson of the British Legation staff, and Mrs. Carson. After I had presented them to the emperor and empress, who at once thanked them for the zeal and courage they had shown in helping to fight the fire, they told me they had seen the fire from the roof-garden of the Grand Hotel de Pékin and had at once driven to the Forbidden City. Baffled at first in their attempts to pass the guards they had succeeded in making their way through the gates by mingling with the Italian firemen.

Apart from the historical and architectural value of the buildings destroyed, the losses were enormous. According to the statements afterwards submitted to the emperor, the articles of value totally destroyed by fire numbered 6,643. Those saved were 387. The lost or irremediably damaged treasures included 2,685 gold Buddhas ; 1,157 pictures, mainly Buddhistic ; 1,675 Buddhist altar-ornaments of gold ; 435 articles of porcelain, jade and bronze, including pieces of the Chou, T'ang, Sung and Yüan periods ; thousands of books ; and 31 boxes containing sables and imperial robes.

The great fire in the Forbidden City naturally caused excitement in Peking, and the general belief which found full expression in the Chinese press was that it had been caused by eunuchs who dreaded the imminent discovery of their malpractices. The following is an example of the statements which appeared in the local newspapers and were allowed by the Nei Wu Fu to go uncontradicted.

" Peking, June 29 :—It now appears that an inventory of the property in the buildings of the Forbidden City destroyed by fire on Wednesday had actually been started. A close tabulation of the treasures had been ordered by the young emperor and two rooms had been gone over when the fire occurred. This strengthens the view taken that culprits who had been gradually denuding the palaces of the property saw that they would soon be caught and adopted this desperate measure of covering their tracks.

" The Chinese cite a similar instance of this sort of dastardly crime that happened several years ago. The Temple of the Ten Thousand Buddhas in the Pei Hai, which was sacred to the Mongols, was being robbed, and to prevent discovery it was suddenly burned down. It is now an empty court just back of the well-known Dragon Screen in the north part of the Pei Hai."

The enquiry into the origin of the fire was conducted by the Nei Wu Fu and therefore had no decisive result. The real causes of the disaster were never discovered, or if discovered were never disclosed. Attempts were made to persuade the emperor that it arose from the fusing of an electric wire, but this he refused to believe. A few of the eunuchs attached for duty to the destroyed buildings, and also the men in charge of the electric-lighting of the Forbidden City, were placed under arrest. Several were dismissed, but it was not long before some of them, at least, were reinstated. No satisfactory explanation was ever vouchsafed as to why no fire-alarm had been raised till it was too late to save the flaming buildings and their precious contents. The attitude of the Nei Wu Fu seemed to be that as the damage had been done and could not be remedied, the less said about it, and the sooner it was forgotten, the better for all concerned.

But the emperor refused either to forget it or to cease asking inconvenient questions about it. For a few weeks the Forbidden City presented an outward appearance of calm, but it proved to be the calm that came before a storm.

The storm broke eighteen days after the fire. On July 15th something happened which produced an even greater thrill among the Chinese and Manchu population of Peking than the incident of the fire. A system which had existed at the Chinese court for thousands of years—for it was known under the Chou dynasty—was on that day abruptly abolished by the expulsion from the Forbidden City of the entire staff of eunuchs.

In order to attain his object the emperor acted with an energy and determination that did him credit. I was aware of his intention, and on general grounds (quite apart from the suspected but unproved causes of the great fire) I was heartily in favour of what he proposed to do. I had often discussed the eunuch-system with him, and he was aware that it was regarded by the Western world as a relic of barbarism. Up to the middle of 1923, however, he had despaired of being able to abolish it in face of the obstinate and united opposition of the imperial family, his father the ex-regent, the Nei Wu Fu and even his Chinese tutors. By July 1923, however, he had decided on a plan of action which he kept secret from them all up to the very day decided upon for its execution.

He informed his father that he wished to pay him a visit. Having arrived at the Pei Fu he immediately interviewed the prince in private and told him that he had made up his mind to get rid of the eunuchs and to do so at once. His father begged him to reconsider the matter. Failing in this, he suggested that if the eunuchs were to go they should be given reasonable notice and dismissed by degrees. This the emperor flatly refused to agree to, pointing out that unless his father were prepared to see the entire Forbidden City share the fate of the palace of Established Happiness, it was essential that the dismissal of the eunuchs should take effect without a day's or even an hour's notice, and that all should be expelled simultaneously. They might subsequently be readmitted one by one, under careful observation, for the purpose of collecting their personal be-longings and for that purpose only. To act upon the prince's suggestion and merely inform them that they must be prepared to leave the Forbidden City within a prescribed limit of time would be a fatal mistake, as it would enable them to conspire with one another to loot the palace, and possibly set fire to it, before they left.

A somewhat painful interview, subsequently described to me in detail, ended in a statement by the emperor that not only was he inflexibly determined that the eunuchs should go but that he would refuse to return to the Forbidden City until they had gone.

Prince Ch'un, in a state bordering on hysteria, gave way. After a brief interval, another interview between father and son took place at which the emperor outlined the method by which he thought his purpose might best be carried out. General Wang Huai-ch'ing—a republican officer but a good friend of the imperial family, who commanded the troops stationed between Peking and the Summer Palace—was to be sent for at once and requested to send a small body of well-disciplined and trustworthy troops into the Forbidden City. Simultaneously, Shao-Ying, the comptroller of the household, was to be instructed to marshal the whole corps of eunuchs (there were over a thousand of them) in one of the palace courtyards and inform them briefly that by the emperor's orders they were to leave the palace at once. If they showed any restiveness or any indication that they might break into disorder, they were to be surrounded by general Wang's troops and shepherded out of the Forbidden City.

The emperor's plan was carried out and was successful. Under the eyes of general Wang's soldiers the eunuchs assembled to learn their fate. They received the news of their dismissal in silence. In less than an hour they had all passed through the Gate of Spiritual Valour and the Forbidden City knew them as permanent residents no more.

For three or four days the Peking populace enjoyed the unwonted spectacle of palace-eunuchs sitting in disconsolate groups on the parade-ground between the northern wall of the Forbidden City and Prospect Hill, awaiting their turn to return to the palace in twos and threes to collect their personal property and to receive the grants of money which each one received according to his age and seniority.

In respect of one difficulty which the emperor had to encounter in this matter, he felt obliged to agree to a compromise. He was now old enough and more than strong enough to contend successfully with a timid and incompetent father; he found it a less simple matter to cope with three women in tears. The three were the *t'ai fei*, who when they learned that their indispensable and more or less faithful eunuchs would no longer be there to anticipate every want and obey their lightest whispers, were filled with woe and dismay. Whether it was their tears or their quasi-maternal authority that gave them a measure of victory in a struggle in which the regent was utterly defeated, I am unable to say; but it is true that the order of dismissal was withdrawn by the emperor in favour of about fifty eunuchs whose duties were restricted to the service of the three old ladies.

The Chinese press was uniformly eulogistic over the action of the emperor in the abolition of the eunuch-system, and numerous complimentary references were made to the development of his character and intelligence and his accessibility to modern ideas. One Chinese news agency referred to the matter thus:

" This action on the part of the ex-emperor Hsüan-T'ung is welcomed by the vernacular press and the people in general. Hsüan-T'ung is now hailed as one of the very few progressive Manchu princes of the present day, and probably there would have been no Chinese republic had he been born thirty or forty years earlier."[2]

Some of the press-comments contained references to myself and my supposed influence over the emperor, but the tone of such comments was not unfriendly.[3] The same cannot be said of some of the remarks contained in numerous anonymous letters which I received during the months that followed the expulsion of the eunuchs. Every form of flattery and threat was employed to induce me to persuade the emperor to reverse his decision. Some of my correspondents were considerate enough to warn me that if I failed to bring about the reinstatement of the eunuchs they would see to it that I paid the forfeit of my own life.

CHAPTER XXI

The Imperial Garden

THE TOTAL DESTRUCTION of the palace of Established Happiness was a calamity for which nothing could compensate, but it had a minor result which was wholly beneficial. It provided the emperor with a large area which, after the ruined buildings had been cleared away, was turned into an admirable recreation ground. Hitherto no adequate space existed for this purpose, for the delightful *Yü Hua Yüan* or " Imperial Garden " was of small size and full of rockeries, pavilions and ancient trees. In the new recreation ground there was ample space for various outdoor amusements, and on October 22nd, 1923, the game of lawn-tennis was for the first time played within the walls of the Forbidden City. The first players were the emperor and his brother P'u-Chieh on one side and the empress's brother (Jun-Ch'i) and myself on the other. It is unnecessary to mention the result of the game, which would probably be reversed if the same partners were to meet again in 1934.

The emperor had other things to attend to besides out-door recreation. Having got rid of the eunuchs he was anxious to carry out many other drastic reforms in the palace, but was hampered at every turn by the obstructiveness of the Nei Wu Fu. He became convinced that no headway would be made until he could find an able, incorrupt and experienced man to replace Shao Ying as comptroller of the household ; and he also realised, with natural regret, that he was unlikely to find anyone possessing the necessary qualifications among the Manchus.

Having come to the conclusion that the post must be given to a Chinese, the emperor found his task simplified by the fact that there were already several very distinguished Chinese scholars and ex-statesmen who during the past year or two had been attached in an honorary capacity to what was known as the Nan Shu-Fang, formerly the office of the Hanlin secretaries attached to the imperial court.[1] They had been chosen

not merely because the prestige of their names added lustre to
the court in its time of twilight, but also because they had
remained devotedly loyal to the dynasty and had in several
cases sacrificed brilliant careers owing to their refusal to serve
the republican government. Two of these were men whose fame
as historians and archæologists had spread to Europe—Lo
Chên-yü and Wang Kuo-wei. A third Chinese loyalist of great
distinction, but not at that time so well known outside China as
he is now, was Chêng Hsiao-hsü.

This remarkable man was received in audience for the first
time in the second half of 1923. He was introduced by his fellow-
provincial, my colleague Ch'ên Pao-shên. In the course of two
interviews the emperor was deeply impressed by his personality,
and expressed a desire that I should make his acquaintance.
We met several times, and both with him and with one of his
sons I discussed the affairs of the emperor and the corruptions
of the Forbidden City. A short time afterwards the emperor
asked me what I thought of Chêng Hsiao-hsü. I told him that in
twenty-five years of experience in China I had never met a
Chinese for whom I had conceived a greater respect and
admiration.

Chêng Hsiao-hsü—or Su-k'an as he is known to his friends
and in literary circles—was not a politician. He had held both
civil and military office under the empire and was regarded in
official circles as one who was certain of a brilliant future. Like
many other loyalists he resigned office when the republic was
established and devoted himself to literature and calligraphy.
He is undoubtedly one of the most learned and accomplished
men of his generation in China, perhaps the most distinguished
of living Chinese poets and calligraphists, and a true Confucian
gentleman. When I made his acquaintance he was in the sixties,
but had the strength and vigour of a much younger man. He
had been opposed to the revolution from the beginning, not
only because of his loyalty to his sovereign—with men like
Su-k'an loyalty is part of their religion—but also because as a
Chinese patriot he sincerely believed that the revolution was a
terrible blunder and a calamity for China. A poem written by
him in 1912, after receiving the news of the emperor's abdication, contains a melancholy prophecy which events have shown

to be only too true—*ta luan ts'ung t'zŭ shih*—" from this event will anarchy take its rise."

In another poem addressed to his eldest son Chêng Ch'ui, he warned him that " riches and honours are worth no more than a wild swan's feather," and Su-k'an had shown by the facts of his own career how little he cared for the trappings or the spoils of office. He refused again and again to take office under a government the authority of which he did not recognise. He would not serve the republic unless he could do so single-heartedly, and he could not do that without ceasing to be the loyal and faithful servant of his emperor and without being false to his own conception of the true needs and interests of China. In 1923, when I first met him, he might have been one of the richest men in China had riches been his goal. As it was, he preferred to live in obscurity and comparative poverty, deriving most of his income from the sale of specimens of his calligraphy.[2]

But though he steadfastly refused to take office under the republic he dutifully obeyed his imperial master's commands to assist him in the work of reorganising the household department. He became first Chinese head of the Nei Wu Fu. Nominally he held the post jointly with Shao-Ying, whose " face " it was considered necessary to save ; but it was quickly realised throughout the Forbidden City that the real control of affairs was to be in the hands of Chêng Hsiao-hsü.

The hostility and opposition that he immediately encountered from the corrupt fraternity whose vested interests were menaced would have daunted a less courageous man than Su-k'an. A few days after his appointment he was the principal guest at a luncheon party given by a Mongol prince, a relative of the imperial family. He showed me two letters which he had just received. In both of them he was threatened with assassination unless he resigned his new post forthwith. He tore them up in my presence.

Threats of this kind he treated with contempt ; but he was soon faced with a real difficulty which he had not foreseen—an alliance between the officers of the Nei Wu Fu by whom he was regarded with fear and hate, an influential group of Manchu princes, and a powerful clique within the republican cabinet.

One of the underhand methods by which the Nei Wu Fu tried to force the resignation of their new chief was to spread the report in republican government circles that his object in accepting the appointment was to get control of the palace treasures. Fortunately Chêng Hsiao-hsü's reputation stood too high for the accusation to be taken seriously. Meanwhile he carried on his work unperturbed, and within three months he had already effected reforms which reduced the palace expenditure by many thousands of dollars a month. There was every indication that if not interfered with he would be able, within a reasonably short period, to present the emperor with a balanced budget.

Before the end of 1923 my relations with the emperor had become completely informal, and my position was that of companion rather than tutor. His regular studies in the Yü-Ch'ing palace had been given up after his wedding, and although I still paid him daily visits, and spent a considerable part of each day in his company, I had no fixed hours of attendance. We met as a rule in his own quarters, or on the new recreation ground, or in a portion of the Forbidden City that had formerly been regarded as reserved for the exclusive use of the emperor and the ladies of the court—the *Yü Hua Yüan* or "Imperial Garden."

This delightful haunt of ancient peace—destined before long to lose its right to be so-called—is situated in the centre of the northernmost portion of the Forbidden City, behind the palaces of Cloudless Heaven and Tranquil Earth. Its rockeries, grottoes, venerable trees and winding pathways made it a place of rare charm and beauty, in which my happiest memories of the Forbidden City will always be centred.

It was early in 1924 that the emperor bestowed upon me a mark of favour which according to the palace officials was unique in the history of the dynasty. He assigned to me a building in the Imperial Garden for my private use both as a residence (when it might happen to be convenient to me to spend a night there), and as a place where I could read and write during the day and in which the emperor himself could see me alone and without formality. It was a large two-storied pavilion in the south-west corner of the garden, and only a few minutes'

walk from the Yang Hsin Tien—the emperor's own palace. Its
name was *Yang Hsing Chai*, which means " Lodge of the
Nourishment of the Nature." My generous host caused it to be
furnished for me in European style—though had I been consulted I should have preferred Chinese furniture—and I added
to its attractions by bringing in a quantity of books from my
own library. It contained several sitting-rooms and a bedroom.
Next door, rooms were provided for my own servants or for
those of the palace servants who were told off to wait upon me.
There I spent the greater part of each day, sometimes alone
with my books, sometimes in the emperor's company. Occasionally he would invite himself to lunch in my pavilion, on which
occasions the materials for the feast were always brought by
servants from his own kitchen. Several times he brought one
or two of the young Manchu princes to share our meal. Not in-
frequently we were joined, either in the pavilion or in the
garden, by the empress or the dowager-consort, Tuan K'ang,
and on such occasions the former was often accompanied by
Miss Isabel Ingram, the empress's American friend who had
been her teacher of English both before and after the empress
entered the Forbidden City as a bride. From time to time I was
summoned from the Lodge of the Nourishment of the Nature to
join the emperor and empress at a meal in the empress's residence
—" the Palace of Treasured Beauty." All these meetings were
completely informal.

Among the visitors whom the emperor brought to see me in
my Lodge was the stout old loyalist Ku Hung-ming, of whom
something has been said in an earlier chapter.[3] The emperor had
summoned him to a private audience in the Yang Hsin Tien,
and afterwards brought him to lunch in the garden. The old
man had never seen the emperor before and he was almost over-
powered by the honour conferred upon him. When he came to
luncheon he was still in a state of awe-stricken speechlessness
(I had met him before and had never known him speechless on
an ordinary occasion), and even the youthful spirits and informal
gaiety of the emperor failed to strike a responsive chord that
was audible to me—though doubtless there were unheard
melodies, of which he alone was conscious, deep down in the
old man's soul. Ku Hung-ming regarded this as the proudest

day of his life, and I have heard that the memory of it consoled him when he lay dying, a few months afterwards.

Although Ku Hung-ming, who received his foreign education in Scotland, had many foreign friends, he was no lover of Western foreigners in general, and his dislike of them increased after the revolution, which he attributed to Western influences. He resented the introduction into China of democratic ideals of a type that was alien to the Chinese spirit. " This religion of the worship of the mob," he wrote, " imported from Great Britain and America into China, which has brought on this revolution and the present nightmare of a republic in China " was now " threatening to destroy the most valuable asset of civilisation of the world to-day "—the real Chinese spirit. And he added that this mob-worship, if not soon put down, would " destroy not only the civilisation of Europe but all civilisation in the world." There are Europeans who have thought so too.

Ku Hung-ming was never a first-rate Chinese scholar, for like many Chinese who have been educated abroad he neglected his Chinese studies for English and other foreign languages and subjects, and after his return to China he never succeeded in making up leeway. Yet he was a passionate believer in Confucianism as the best basis for the development of Chinese civilisation, and made a highly characteristic, though diffuse and not always accurate, translation of the Confucian *Analects*. His faults were mostly of the kind that are readily forgiven. He was vain of his knowledge of Western languages, which included a smattering of Latin ; he held exaggerated notions about the merits of his English literary style, which was poor compared with that of many of his younger contemporaries ; he was dogmatic and pugnacious when discussing matters in which he was emotionally interested ; he obstinately refused to admit the possibility of any good emerging from the chaos of the China of his day ; he was never weary of insisting that his own country-men were the most courteous people in the world and therefore the most civilised, yet failed only too frequently to exemplify that admirable characteristic in his own conduct. He could, indeed, be both arrogant and rude, though most of his friends came to understand that he was never intentionally discourteous. In many respects he was an admirable and likeable figure,

a picturesque relic of the Old China that is passing or has passed
away. It should be added that he never made money out of any
work he ever did, and that though he had held various small
official appointments, some of which offered manifold opportunities for " squeeze," he lived and died a very poor man.

The Chinese courtesy of which Ku Hung-ming was so rightly
proud as one of the characteristics of his race was woefully
lacking in the reception accorded by a certain section of Peking
students to a very distinguished stranger who was also, in 1924,
one of the emperor's visitors. Rabindranath Tagore came to
Peking in April that year at the invitation of a literary group
which included men of the high standing of Dr. Hu Shih and
that brilliant young poet and leader of the " Crescent Moon "
coterie, Hsü Chih-mo (Tsemou Hsu), who was unhappily cut
off by a tragic death a few years later. Tagore came to China at
a time when alien influences were at work in academic and other
circles which caused his message to fall on stony ground ; and
his appeal to Young China to cherish what was noble and beautiful in the cultural heritage of the race met with a cold and even
hostile reception by some of his student-audiences. I was anxious
that Tagore should not leave Peking without catching a glimpse
of the courteous and dignified China that has never failed to
rouse the homage of foreign visitors, and I therefore spoke of
him to the emperor and requested permission to bring him to
the Forbidden City. I also showed the emperor some English
and Chinese translations of Tagore's poetry. The permission
asked for was most readily granted, and the meeting, when it
took place in my pavilion in the imperial garden, gave pleasure
certainly to the emperor and I think also to the poet.

Chêng Hsiao-hsü was one of those who were in attendance
on his majesty on that occasion, and I felt glad to have brought
together, under imperial auspices, the foremost poets of two
great countries once closely linked together by bonds of spiritual
kinship.

During the same year the gradual dissolution of court conventions and formalities made it possible for the emperor to make
the acquaintance of many more foreigners than he had opportunities of meeting in earlier days. Among the visitors introduced by myself in an informal way were the British naval

commander-in-chief on the China station, Admiral Sir Arthur Leveson, and his family, the general officer commanding in Hong Kong (Sir John Fowler), and many members of the foreign Legations in Peking. The place of meeting on the occasions of such visits was nearly always the imperial garden.

During 1923 and 1924 the majority of the foreign visitors received by the emperor were Europeans, but they also included a few Japanese. One of these was introduced by myself—namely, my friend Mr. Yoshida, then Counsellor at the Japanese Legation, who many years afterwards accompanied the League of Nations commission of enquiry into the Manchurian affair, and recently died at his post of Japanese ambassador to Turkey. The only other Japanese, as far as I am aware, who visited the emperor were the members of a deputation sent to convey to him the thanks of the Japanese Government and people for his magnificent donations to the earthquake relief fund. I was the first to inform him, on September 3rd, 1923, of the great earthquake in Japan. He was deeply affected by the news of the devastation and suffering caused by that great calamity, and wished to give a much larger cash-donation to the relief fund than the comptroller of the household thought he could afford. He insisted, therefore, on augmenting his subscription by sending to the Japanese minister a quantity of art-treasures with the request that they should be sold and the proceeds added to his cash-donation. Mr. K. Yoshizawa, the Japanese minister, recognised the exceptional interest attaching to the collection, and when transmitting the articles to Japan he made the suggestion that as it would be a pity to disperse them it might be found possible to pay out of the imperial Privy Purse a sum of money corresponding to their assessed value so that the articles might be preserved intact in the imperial collection at Tokyo. This suggestion, I was afterwards told, was carried out, and according to a Japanese statement the value was assessed at no less than $200,000. It was at the beginning of November, 1923, that the Japanese deputation was sent to thank the emperor for his liberality and sympathy. It was received by him in one of the pavilions of the imperial garden. I was not present at the interview, but I was informed by one of the members of the deputation that the unconventional little ceremony which took place on that occasion was the most impressive and moving he had ever attended.[4]

I can confidently assert that there was no political motive underlying the emperor's action in this matter, as I was a personal witness of his emotion when he heard the details of the great tragedy. Generosity and kindliness and sympathy with suffering are indeed among the most striking features of his character. He took a real pleasure in acts of charity, and the great majority of his gifts were bestowed anonymously. He was always a most liberal subscriber to funds for the relief of the poor of Peking and sufferers from flood or famine in other parts of China, but he never allowed his own name to appear on any subscription-list, and even the promoters of the innumerable funds to which he subscribed were in most cases ignorant of his identity.[5]

As for Chinese visitors, I usually declined to request audiences on their behalf, though I was frequently asked to do so, as I considered that the proper channel of communication for them was the Nei Wu Fu ; but I was the means of making the emperor personally acquainted with a native of China whose distinguished ancestry, if nothing else, seemed to me to make him worthy of an emperor's notice.

It was in September, 1924, that I first made the acquaintance of this obscure nobleman. On several occasions I had noticed in the Court Gazette announcements such as these :

" The marquis Chu (*Chu Hou*) on this day set out on his journey to the Ming Tombs to offer sacrifice " ; " The marquis of Extended Grace having duly fulfilled his mission to the Ming Tombs, returned thanks for the imperial bounty."

The marquis's name was Chu Yü-hsün. His surname, Chu, was that of the Ming emperors who ruled China from 1368 to 1643. His personal name, Yü-hsün, may be translated " Shining Merit." The hereditary dignity of marquis was bestowed upon one of his ancestors by the Manchu emperor Shih Tsung (Yung-Chêng, 1723–1735), with the title *Yen-Ên*—" Extended Grace." The title referred, of course, to the " grace extended " by Manchu imperial magnanimity to the descendants of the dynasty which the Manchu house had supplanted on the throne. In return for

the imperial favour, each Ming marquis had one duty to perform—namely to pay ceremonial visits twice a year to the *Shih-
San Ling* or " Thirteen Imperial Tombs " of the Ming emperors,
which are situated a few miles to the north-west of Peking. He
was required to report the dates of his departure and return,
and the due fulfilment of the sacrificial rites, and he received in
return a grant of money which was understood to cover his
travelling and other expenses. His reports were submitted
through the household department, and before 1924 the emperor
had never seen him. Nor had any of my colleagues made his
acquaintance. He was outside their social circle, and indeed
very few Chinese, and still fewer foreigners, were aware of his
existence.

In August, 1924, I little knew how soon the lingering twilight
of the Manchu court was going to deepen into night, but when
I happened during that month to notice the marquis's name in
my copy of the Gazette I was seized by a strong desire that the
last of the Manchu emperors should stand face to face with the
representative of the last of the Mings. I spoke of the matter to
the emperor, with the result that his interest in the marquis of
Extended Grace was for the first time aroused.

Early in September the household department was surprised
to receive from his majesty an intimation that he wished to
receive the marquis in private audience. The interview took place
in the emperor's palace on the 7th of that month. On the afternoon of the same day I happened to be at home in my own house
north of Prospect Hill when a visitor's card was brought in. The
characters on the card (here reproduced) intimate that it is the
card of " Chu Yü-hsün, descendant of the imperial Ming house,
marquis of Extended Grace, bearing the additional personal
name of Ping-nan, dwelling in Yang-kuan Road, Little Street,
north of the Tung-chih Gate."

He came in, attired in official coat and hat, and explained very
apologetically that he had come to see me in obedience to his
majesty's direct commands. He had come straight from the
Forbidden City, where his majesty had received him most
graciously and had informed him that it was to me that he
owed the privilege of the audience. For this he wished to give
me thanks.

I found him a very quiet and unassuming man, obviously without much book-learning but by no means unintelligent. He told me he was forty-three years of age and had two sons, aged nine and four. He assured me, deprecatingly, that they were both contemptible little brats, brainless and ill-mannered—a subject on which I should have preferred to form my own opinion. As he allowed me to photograph him, my readers may judge of his outward appearance for themselves.

When I told him I would shortly return his call he besought me most earnestly not to do so as he lived in a hovel and had no guest-room. "You mustn't think," he went on, "that the official coat and hat I am wearing are my own. I borrowed them for the audience." So saying he stood up and opened his coat, to show me the poor and well-worn garments underneath. He was evidently sincere in his desire that I should not return his call, for after leaving me he spoke privately to my servants, begging them to dissuade me from visiting him and pointing out that the borrowed garments had to be handed back to their owner that day.

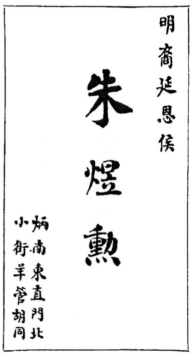

A short time afterwards I sent him a small present together with copies of the photographs I had taken ; and my messenger reported to me that his house was indeed a ramshackle hut and that he had found the marquis sitting in rags on a broken bench. Out of consideration for him—he would have " lost face " if he had had to receive me in such lowly surroundings—I refrained from returning his visit ; but he called on me a second time to thank me for my little gifts. The general impression of him that I formed was that the marquis was a gentleman, and

Yc

deserved the " extended grace " that he had inherited from his ancestors.

The founder of the Ming dynasty, Chu Yüan-chang, who reigned (under the Hung-Wu title) from 1368 to 1399, was buried, not near Peking, which had not yet become the capital, but at Nanking. It may be remembered that when the republic was inaugurated in 1912, Sun Yat-sen (inappropriately attired in a frock-coat and top hat) paid a ceremonial visit to the tomb of the first Ming emperor and formally conveyed to that august spirit the gratifying intelligence that the throne had been wrested from the alien Manchu usurpers and that China once more belonged to the Chinese people. If ever a dynasty in China had forfeited the " mandate of heaven " by its own incompetence and the corruption of its court, it was the Ming, and the founders of the republic knew better than to pretend that even the greatest of the Ming emperors were comparable with such rulers as K'ang-Hsi and Ch'ien-Lung. This may perhaps partially explain why nothing was done to associate the living descendants of the Mings with the ceremonies conducted at the tomb of Hung-Wu. The tomb itself they repaired ; but neither at that time nor later was any interest taken by the republican authorities in the fortunes of the living members of the Ming house. Nor has anything been done to show respect and courtesy to the marquis of Extended Grace or even to extricate him from his dire poverty. His title of dignity, moreover, is no longer recognised by the republic.

If any excuse is wanted for slighting him it may perhaps be found in the fact that after the revolution of 1911 he remained " loyal " to the Manchus and continued as before to carry out his ceremonial visits to the tombs of his imperial ancestors under the auspices of the Manchu emperor.

Later events showed that his loyalty was sincere. The audience took place on September 7th, 1924. Two months afterwards, as we shall see, the emperor was the state-prisoner of the republic— or rather of half a dozen self-elected persons calling themselves the government of China and the representatives of the people— and was shortly to become an exile in a foreign Concession. Before long, the marquis of Extended Grace scraped together a few dollars for his travelling expenses to Tientsin.

Never, I think, did the name of Shining Merit become him better than when he knelt before his exiled sovereign—soon, it might be, to sink into obscurity and poverty like his own—returning loyal thanks for " grace extended."

Chapter XXII

The Summer Palace

It will be remembered that in the Articles of Favourable Treatment there was a clause to the effect that while the court might continue temporarily to occupy the Forbidden City, the permanent residence of the Manchu emperor was to be the Yi-Ho Park, the country residence of the court known to foreigners as the Summer Palace.[1]

From the first year of my tutorship I had repeatedly drawn the attention of the Manchu princes, the household department, and latterly the emperor himself, to the existence of this clause and had urged them to give effect to it on their own initiative. My main arguments in favour of a voluntary retirement to the Summer Palace were the following.

In the first place, although the manner in which the republic had hitherto discharged its obligations under the Articles left a good deal to be desired, that was not a sound reason for any failure on the part of the imperial House to observe its part of the compact. It was true that (apart from Yüan Shih-k'ai's move in that direction) the republic had not yet formally called upon the emperor to fulfil clause 3 by vacating the Forbidden City and removing to the Summer Palace, and that he could not justly be convicted of a breach of the clause until he had replied to such a formal demand with a blunt refusal. Nevertheless his " temporary " occupation of the Forbidden City had already extended (by the end of 1923) to twelve years, and the imperial household had not yet given the slightest indication of its intention to move. This might easily be made a serious ground of complaint and become the basis of a charge against the emperor that in the spirit if not in the letter he had broken the abdication agreement. Those who wished to bring about the cancellation of the agreement—and among them were a large group of very active and venomously anti-Manchu politicians and a growing army of turbulent students already falling under the influence of communist propaganda—would naturally be glad to shift the responsibility for such cancellation from their own shoulders to those of the emperor, and if they could find no better evidence of his faithlessness than his failure to move his court to the Summer Palace, they would undoubtedly seize upon that fact to justify their action in declaring the agreement null and void.

In the second place, I argued that by moving to the Summer Palace, where the Manchu court had always lived in a much simpler way than in the Forbidden City, it would be possible to effect an enormous reduction in expenditure and even enable the emperor to accumulate reserve funds which in a few years would suffice to make him independent of his present precarious sources of income. Drastic reductions in staff could be carried out, and excellent opportunities would arise for the abolition of sinecures.

The very soundness of this argument made it most repulsive to the officers of the court and their horde of satellites. I remember a long conversation I had on this subject in 1923 with one of the ministers of the household—Ch'i-Ling. His main objection to the proposal that the emperor should move to the Summer Palace was that the residential quarters would be too small for the requirements of the officers and staff of the Nei Wu Fu ; and when I pointed out that there was certainly far more than enough room to accommodate the imperial family and all the court-officials and servants for whom any semblance of work could be provided, I met with nothing but a blank refusal to admit that this had anything to do with the matter or that the reduction of the existing staff was either feasible or desirable. Nor was he in any way moved by my suggestion that a drastic reduction in court expenditure would make possible the accumulation of a financial reserve for the emperor's own use in the days of adversity that obviously (to me) awaited him in the near or distant future.

The attitude of Ch'i-Ling's colleagues with whom I often discussed these questions was identical with his own. Their imperial master—for whom their lip-and-knee loyalty was beyond criticism except in respect of its sincerity—might go down to hopeless ruin and tragedy, but on no account should they be expected to save him from catastrophe by the sacrifice of their own rice-bowls. Reductions in staff, salaries, or perquisites, the abolition of sinecures and the withdrawal of funds which had hitherto gone to the maintenance of a huge and utterly useless establishment, would all constitute an intolerable outrage which must at all costs be resisted.

Their callous indifference to the fate of their master except in so far as his interests were bound up with their own, made it hopeless to expect them to pay any attention to my third main argument in favour of removal to the Summer Palace, which was that the change of surroundings would be immensely advantageous to his physical, mental and moral welfare. I could hardly conceive of there being any honest difference of opinion on this point. No reasonable person, acquainted with the unhealthy conditions under which the emperor had been brought up since infancy in the Forbidden City, and conscious of the wholesome atmosphere in which he might work and play in the Yi-Ho Park, could possibly hesitate as to which of the two palaces was the better fitted to be his home. In my opinion, Chang Hsün acted from a mistaken sense of loyalty when (no doubt at the urgent entreaty of a multitude of interested persons) he dissuaded Yüan Shih-k'ai from carrying out his intention of requiring the imperial family to move to the Summer Palace ; and the imperial family was equally at fault in accepting and profiting by Chang Hsün's intervention.[2]

So intensely hostile was the Nei Wu Fu to the idea of the emperor's removal to the Summer Palace that they used all their influence—with success—to prevent his going there even on a visit. They led him to suppose that the place was in a ruinous condition and quite unfit even for his majesty's inspection far less for his residence. They also asserted that the neighbourhood of the palace was infested with bandits and that if he were to go so far from the city his life would be in danger—if not from bandits then from political conspirators or from those " patriots " who believed that the emperor, so long as he was allowed to live, would be a danger to the State.

There was only one argument in favour of holding on as long as possible to the Forbidden City that seemed to me in any way plausible: namely, that to move the vast stores of treasures and

inestimably valuable works of art to the Summer Palace would
be impracticable, and that to leave them behind would mean
that they would promptly be seized by the republican authorities. I agreed that if the treasures were left behind in the Forbidden City they would probably never be seen again by the
emperor, and that his rights of ownership would be disputed or
(more probably) ignored. Nevertheless it seemed to me that the
problem of ownership should be straightened out once and for
all. There was an obvious and ever-growing possibility that by
clinging too tightly and too long to the Forbidden City and its
enormously valuable contents, the imperial family would
finally be forcibly deprived of both ; whereas by showing a
willingness to compromise, and by taking the initiative in
suggesting the appointment of a joint commission of enquiry
with a view to allocating to the State such articles as might
reasonably be regarded as *kuo pao* or " national treasures," the
imperial family might be left in undisputed possession of all
that remained.

The appointment of Chêng Hsiao-hsü to the control of the
household department gave me a welcome opportunity to
bring up these matters for a fuller discussion than they had yet
received. I was delighted to find that though he differed from
me in minor points of detail, on general principles we were
unanimous. He agreed with me that preparations should be
made for compliance with clause 3 of the Articles of Favourable
Treatment and for the emperor's voluntary removal to the
Summer Palace. He was strongly of opinion, however, that
those preparations would take some time to carry out, and that
it would be necessary in the first place to reform and reorganise
the administration of the Summer Palace and its extensive
adjacent properties, which included farm-lands and also the
Jade Fountain estate, to bring its unwieldy staff of useless
functionaries down to manageable dimensions, to carry out
certain minor repairs and alterations, and to put the palace-
finances—which invariably showed a very large deficit in spite
of several valuable sources of revenue—into something like
order.

Hitherto the Summer Palace had been under the control of
the Nei Wu Fu. What Chêng Hsiao-hsü now recommended to the

emperor was that I should be appointed imperial commissioner (*pan shih ta ch'ên* or " amban ") in charge of that palace with the fullest powers over its administration and with direct responsibility to the emperor alone.

Thus it was that early in 1924 the Nei Wu Fu received a shock comparable only with that of the abolition of the eunuch-system and the appointment of a Chinese as their own comptroller. It was bad enough, from their point of view, that they should for the first time in the history of the dynasty be placed under the authority of a Chinese ; it was almost worse that a considerable portion of the imperial domain should be wholly withdrawn from their control and placed under that of a Western barbarian. Perhaps the bitterest pill of all was that the imperial edict conferring the appointment upon me had to be officially communicated to me through them. This unprecedented document will be found on the opposite page in its Chinese original. The following is a translation :—

Communication from the Nei Wu Fu

" You are respectfully informed that on this day the Comptroller of the Imperial Household Department has personally received the following Edict from His Majesty the Emperor.

" ' Chuang Shih-tun [Johnston] is hereby commissioned to assume control of the Yi-Ho Yüan [' Park of the Cultivation of Harmonious Old Age,' known to Europeans as the Summer Palace], the Ching-Ming Yüan and the Yü-Ch'üan Shan ' [Jade spring Hill and adjoining park, both known to foreigners as the Jade Fountain].

" Such is His Majesty's Edict, which is hereby formally communicated to you for your information and guidance.

" This special communication is sent to you with compliments."

The Nei Wu Fu were learning by painful experience that shocks never come singly. On the very day after the issue of this edict, another thunderbolt fell among them. After a brief consultation with me the emperor announced that he and the

内　務　府　信　箋

敬啟者本日總管內務府大臣面奉

諭旨著派莊士敦管理

頤和園靜明園玉泉山事務欽此用特肅函奉

聞即希遵照可也專此籍頌

時綏

內務府啟

empress proposed on that day to pay their first visit to the Summer Palace, and he ordered that his car and that of the empress should be prepared for his departure in two hours. Up to that date the emperor's longest journey had been to his own father's residence, the Pei Fu, in the north of the city. He had never been outside the walls of Peking. Every possible argument and prognostication of evil were used to induce him to change his mind. When these methods failed, Shao-Ying, who still held the nominal post of comptroller, appealed to me to dissuade his majesty from embarking on this foolhardy adventure ; and when, to his profound annoyance, I replied that the adventure was one of which I thoroughly approved, he tried to intimidate me by declaring that if any harm happened to his majesty I should be held personally responsible. My only answer to that was that the responsibility was one which I gladly accepted.

The next move of the Nei Wu Fu was to communicate with the republican government, in the hope that the trip to the Summer Palace would be vetoed. In this manœuvre also they were unsuccessful, except in so far as the authorities sent an " escort " of troops in six motor-cars to accompany the emperor on his daring journey, doubtless to ensure that he would not suddenly change his destination and visit the Legation Quarter instead of the Summer Palace. The Nei Wu Fu also engaged another six cars for the use of some of their own number, including Shao-Ying himself ; so that when at the appointed time we set out from the Gate of Spiritual Valour we formed a procession of fourteen cars. In the first car went the emperor and myself, while in the second followed the empress and the *shu fei*.

The expedition was in every way successful, except from the point of view of the Nei Wu Fu, and the emperor was delighted with his first visit to the country and to the Summer Palace that he had never seen. The palace itself, which was by no means in ruins, far surpassed his expectations, and he rambled through its park and over its numerous scattered buildings with evident pleasure. After exploring the buildings and climbing to the summit of the Hill of Imperial Longevity we embarked on one of the barges—the empress and *shu fei* and their ladies following in another—and visited the little island of the Dragon King which is one of the gems of the palace.

On the same day I formally entered upon my new duties and held a preliminary interview with the numerous palace officials, many of them of mandarin-rank, who were now my direct subordinates. From that time onward I divided my time between the Forbidden City and the Summer Palace, with an occasional too-brief visit to that one of my four residences which was the most delightful of all—my mountain-retreat in Cherry Glen. The emperor thereafter paid frequent visits to the Summer Palace—always followed by a fleet of cars occupied by functionaries and soldiers whose company on his excursions was entirely superfluous and very costly. Sometimes he lunched at the Summer Palace as my guest, and on these occasions he made the acquaintance of many of my foreign friends and a few discreetly-selected Chinese.

In August, 1924, I accompanied him on his first mountain ramble, when he visited the group of temples (one of them a favourite resort of his great ancestor Ch'ien-Lung) at Pa Ta Ch'u on the slopes of the Western Hills.

The only boats on the K'un-ming lake in the Summer Palace grounds were cumbersome barges which had doubtless been suited to the needs of the Venerable Buddha and her eunuchs but were of very little use to a young monarch who proposed to learn to row, or to his foreign tutor whose function it was to teach him that art. For his benefit—and also, incidentally, for my own—I caused three boats to be built at Tientsin, Chefoo and Shanghai respectively. One was an outrigger with sliding seat which I named " Ariel " ; another was a small rowing-boat with fixed seats to which was given the name of " The Witch of Atlas." The third—a canoe which had been completed but had not arrived at the palace when the events of November, 1924, brought my wardenship there to a sudden end —was named " Alastor." Both " Ariel " and the " Witch," but more especially the former, caused great wonderment among the palace-staff who had never seen anything like them before ; and their wonder was at first tinged with horror when they observed the Son of Heaven toiling at an oar when he might very well have left that arduous and menial occupation to his bargemen.

Being free to choose my own living quarters in the Summer

Palace I first selected the island of the Dragon King. Finding that delectable situation inconvenient for the transaction of business I moved to a secluded garden surrounded by a wall of its own, with pavilions and a running stream. The name of this delightful retreat was *Chi Ch'ing Hsien* or " Pavilion of Clearing Skies." It was a kind of annexe to a larger enclosure of the same general character— the *Hsieh Ch'ü Yüan* or "Garden of Harmonious Delight."

But charming though my surroundings were, there was very little " harmonious delight " in the difficult work that I had undertaken or in my relations with the throng of people whose interests were threatened by the activities of a " new broom." Some of my European friends in Peking congratulated me on having taken up what they thought would be a delightful hobby. They had little conception of the wearisome nature of the work I had to do, the jealousy and hostility of which I was the object, or the sullen opposition which met every attempt to reform abuses inherent in the Chinese system of palace-administration. The palace officials, though always courteous and respectful, gave me very little active assistance, especially in my extremely delicate task of cutting down expenditure by reducing the staff and revising the scale of salaries. During the summer, one of the principal palace-officials died, and I was immediately confronted with a series of recommendations regarding the promotions which, it was assumed, would result from his death. Great was the disgust openly manifested when I announced that the post was superfluous and would be abolished.

Equally emphatic was the disapproval of my methods when it came to deciding how certain repairs to various buildings should be carried out. I was given the names of two contractors in the neighbouring village of Hai-Tien who, I was assured, had for many years past been entrusted with all such work. Having called for provisional estimates from these two men I found them ridiculously high and then proceeded to advertise for sealed tenders from contractors in the city of Peking. This was a procedure which caused so much surprise that it was commented upon in the Chinese press ; but the result of it was that the work was efficiently carried out at a figure which was less than one-seventh of the amount considered necessary by the two privileged contractors—an amount which my staff had tried to convince me was reasonable.

By degrees I succeeded in convincing a few of the more intelligent of my subordinates that there was something to be said for a policy of reform and retrenchment, and that it was our joint duty to do the best we could for the imperial master whom we all served. Some of them began to take an interest in the work I was doing and to co-operate with me. Success did not come as rapidly as I should have liked, but before the end of the summer I had satisfied myself that instead of being a heavy drain on the emperor's resources, which it had always been in the past, the Summer Palace could be made to maintain itself out of its own sources of revenue, which included the rents of farm-lands, tickets of admission to the palace and to the Jade Fountain on visitors' days, the sale of fish from the palace lake, and shares in the profits of certain local enterprises such as an hotel and a soda-water factory at the Jade Fountain, tea-houses and a photographer's shop.

Various more or less childish attempts were made to bring about my resignation. Among many threatening letters received by me during 1924 was one which purported to be from someone who regarded me with the highest respect and who therefore thought it his duty to warn me that an attempt was to be made on my life. I was to be shot by hired bandits during one of my journeys between the Forbidden City and the Summer Palace— journeys which I usually accomplished on horseback. The bandits must have been a clumsy or pusillanimous crew wholly unworthy of their hire, for my rides to the Summer Palace and back were frequent, yet they never availed themselves of many excellent opportunities of earning it.

The opposition and hostility I had to face came not only from the jealous Nei Wu Fu in the Forbidden City and from the throng of useless hangers-on in the Summer Palace itself but also from that section of the Press which was patronised by the student-class. The politically-minded students of that period were largely influenced by ultra-radical politicians who were in close touch with the Soviet embassy. The newspapers which represented their views welcomed any opportunity of attacking either " imperialism " (especially the British variety) or the emperor,

to whom of course they always referred contemptuously as
" P'u-Yi." During 1924 they found many welcome opportunities
of killing (or wounding) two birds with one stone. One example
of how they did this is perhaps worth quoting.

About the beginning of September, 1924, a Peking evening
paper called the *Ta Wan Pao* came out with a most scurrilously-
worded paragraph in which it was declared that the English
tutor of " P'u-Yi," actuated by foul motives, had brought his
daughter into the Forbidden City and had introduced her to
" P'u-Yi " ; that " P'u-Yi " had gazed upon her and found her
fair ; and that the English tutor—for a consideration—had left
her in " P'u-Yi's " hands.

As so stated in English, the wording of the paragraph was
sufficiently offensive ; the Chinese phraseology was worse. Had I
thought it worth while to reply to the base accusation brought
against both the emperor and myself I might have resorted to
various lines of defence, but perhaps one would have been
sufficient. The daughter in question did not exist.

Dr. Hu Shih, in a letter to me, was good enough to express his
regret that the Peking press should be capable of descending to
these and similar scurrilities. On October 10th, 1924, he wrote
as follows :

" Your work in the imperial palace, however strongly those
little men may try to blacken it, has been and will always be
appreciated and honoured by those whose opinion will, I
believe, in the long run count more than the lies and attacks
that are now being circulated. There is still a sufficient amount
of Chinese chivalry left to recognise and honour a chivalrous
act."

In this letter Dr. Hu Shih was not referring only to the contemptible rubbish of Peking's gutter press. He also had in mind
various attacks that were being made upon me in political circles.
Several times I was denounced by a group of politicians in the
most corrupt of the whole series of China's disreputable parliaments. The leader or spokesman of this group was one Li
Hsieh-yang, who professed to believe, *inter alia* that the Summer
Palace revenues were being accumulated by me for the purpose

of financing a restoration of the emperor. These attacks, unlike those published in an obscure evening newspaper, seemed to me to call for a public reply. I replied at some length in letters which were published in English and Chinese ; and my reply elicited the following comment from the *North China Daily News.*

"THE EMPEROR AND AN M.P.

" We publish to-day Mr. R. F. Johnston's most interesting and trenchant reply to the unfounded and slanderous attack made by Mr. Li Hsieh-yang M.P., on the Manchu Emperor and, in passing, on Mr. Johnston himself. No one who has read the article will grudge the time spent in doing so, and assuredly it must be felt that such a reply was entirely necessary. Under existing conditions in China it was impossible to leave Mr. Li's venomous attack unnoticed. Circumstances might arise at any moment when, popular feeling running high, it would only be remembered that such accusation had been made, and the emperor's life might easily be endangered. One cannot help thinking that the political conditions of the day are at the bottom of Mr. Li's onslaught. As the failure of the republican *régime*, or what pretends to that name in China, becomes more glaringly conspicuous, men's minds are turning more and more to the idea of a monarchy as the only refuge from the intolerable anarchy which everywhere prevails. Everything that is heard of his majesty Hsüan-T'ung disposes the public to think sympathetically of the last of the Ch'ing emperors ; and just as Milton was compelled, after the beheading of Charles I, to remonstrate with the people on their unaccountable sorrow at the tragedy, so perhaps Mr. Li conceives himself similarly appointed to do the best he can to blacken the emperor's character, and disgust the Chinese people with him. Let it be said at once that we are not trying to thrust his majesty or any other emperor down China's throat. We are merely trying to get at what may have been the motive in Mr. Li's mind. Whatever that motive may have been, he has been guilty of an inexcusable slander, of suggesting falsehoods the truth of which could easily have been ascertained, and incidentally, of libelling Mr. Johnston himself, whom he presents to the Chinese as using his position in order to intrigue for a monarchical restoration. No more telling exposure could well be imagined than that we have published from Mr. Johnston. It only remains for Mr. Li to do what his position as a member of Parliament requires, and that is to apologise for his unfounded charges as publicly as he delivered them."[3]

It is superfluous to say that no apology was ever forthcoming ; though two months later a Chinese friend at my own suggestion brought me face to face with Mr. Li Hsieh-yang at a private dinner-party on which occasion (under pressure from others) he personally admitted to me that he had been misled.

That I should be regarded with coolness and hostility by the Nei Wu Fu (apart from Chêng Hsiao-hsü) and by the majority of the Summer Palace staff was only to be expected ; but the persistence and viciousness of the attacks made upon me in the Chinese press and in political circles were not so easily understood. It was not till the beginning of October, 1924, that light was thrown on the matter by a certain Chinese friend who revealed to me the existence of a plot to have me removed, by fair means or foul, from the service of the emperor. I referred to the matter in a letter written by me on October 4th to another Chinese (Cantonese) friend named Hsü Shan-po, who was an enthusiastic disciple of K'ang Yu-wei and therefore loyal to the emperor. The letter is perhaps worth quoting in view of the last sentence which I have italicised, and the events which took place exactly a month later.

" . . . came to see me yesterday and told me that a number of members of parliament and senators are hatching a plot to have me removed from the palace. They have begun a campaign of lies and slander against me in the newspapers and are going to accuse me of having become a millionaire in his majesty's service. *Their ultimate object, of course, is to ruin the emperor himself and have him expelled from the palaces and deprived of his property.*"

I was not the only one against whom a campaign of lies and vituperation was being carried on during the summer and autumn of 1924. My good friend and colleague Chêng Hsiao-hsü was the victim of similar attacks, though his most irreconcilable antagonists were within the Forbidden City and not outside it. He struggled nobly and unselfishly for several months and carried through various extensive reforms in the teeth of the persistent opposition of the Nei Wu Fu and several of the most influential of the Manchu princes. There was a time when he felt utterly discouraged, and in the middle of 1924 he applied for indefinite leave of absence. But he had no intention of abandoning his task or leaving his young sovereign to face alone the difficulties and dangers that loomed ahead.

Chêng Hsiao-hsü, it is unnecessary to say, and also his son Chêng Ch'ui, were always welcome guests at the Summer Palace. So were our friends Wang Kuo-wei and Lo Chên-yü, two brilliant scholars who, as was mentioned in an earlier chapter, held honorary posts in the imperial secretariat.[4] These two men, whose names are well known in Europe and America to all serious students of Chinese history and archæology, had been instrumental in saving from destruction a mass of extremely valuable unpublished historical material, relating to the earliest days of the Manchu monarchy, which the republican authorities had been on the point of destroying or selling as waste paper. They were anxious to find a safe and commodious place in which this vast mass of papers could be stored, studied and edited, and were glad to hear from me that there were unused buildings under my control that I thought would be admirably adapted to their purpose. They spent a day with me at the Summer Palace, and I conducted them to a great roofed building on the west side of the hill of the Jade Fountain—a building which dated from Ch'ien-Lung's time and had successfully resisted at least two great fires. They agreed with me that no more suitable building than this could be found anywhere in or near Peking, and on our return to the Summer Palace we sat for some time by the side of the lake happily discussing a project to make that romantic spot on the Jade Fountain Hill a great centre for historical and archæological study, a meeting place and a haven of refuge for scholars and students from all nations. It was only a dream that never came true.

One of the three who sat by the lakeside that day is now serving his emperor, to whom he has always been loyal, in the privy
Zc

council of the new state of Manchuria. Another is trying to teach Chinese in the murky caverns of Finsbury Circus. The third—a gentleman and a scholar if ever there was one— revisited the Summer Palace alone on June 2nd, 1927, and made his way, unattended, to the margin of the lake where we three had discussed our plans and dreams exactly three years before. He saw nothing but darkness ahead for China and for his emperor, and therefore the light in his own life had quite gone out.

It was late in the afternoon of that day before they found his body and took it out of the water.[5]

When the Summer Palace came under my control I became the custodian of a large number of documents relating to the origin and history of the various country residences and pleasure-parks established by Chinese emperors on the same or neighbouring sites from the twelfth century onwards. As one of these documents purports to explain the origin of the Yi-Ho Park, and has a bearing on what I have already said regarding the character of the Venerable Buddha and her relationship with her nephew the emperor Tê Tsung (Kuang-Hsü), I have made a translation of it for these pages. It is an imperial edict issued by the emperor in 1888, shortly after his marriage and coming of age, when the empress-dowager had relinquished the regency and was about to take up her residence in the new palace. It professes to show that the idea of building (or rather rebuilding) the Summer Palace originated with the emperor himself, who is thus made responsible for this unnecessary extravagance ; and evidently it was also intended to stifle any awkward questions that might arise as to the financial arrangements made for so costly an undertaking. It quotes an edict issued by the empress-dowager herself, who is represented as having accepted the gift of the palace with modest reluctance and as an indulgent response to the urgent entreaties of her grateful and loving nephew.

"IMPERIAL EDICT OF THE 1ST DAY OF THE SECOND MOON OF KUANG-HSÜ 14 (1888)

" Ever since We, in Our childhood, succeeded to the Great Inheritance, the direction of state affairs has been in the hands of Her Imperial Majesty the Empress-Dowager Tz'ŭ-Hsi-Tuan-Yu-K'ang-I-Chao-Yü-Chuang-Ch'êng [" Loving and Blessed, Upright and Helpful, Vigorous and Careful, Brilliant and Pleasing, Decorous and Sincere "].[6] who in Her anxious toil has denied Herself adequate food and sleep for over twenty years. Through Her efforts, peace has been maintained in internal and external affairs and the Chinese people have enjoyed prosperity.

" Last year We received Her Imperial Majesty's commands to assume full imperial responsibilities.[7] Having compassion on Our youthful inexperience She graciously assented to Our entreaties that She would continue to instruct Us in the art of government. Ever since the beginning of the T'ung-Chih reign [the reign of the emperor Mu Tsung, 1862–1874], a period of over twenty years, Our Holy Mother has laboured on behalf of the Empire, looking upon nothing as too insignificant for Her personal attention, never allowing Herself the slightest relaxation from the endless cares of state even for the sake of Her own health.

" Awakening to a sense of these things and turning them over in Our mind We could neither sleep nor eat in tranquillity. We then remembered that in the neighbourhood of the Western Park there was a palace which had been occupied by His Majesty the Emperor Shêng Tsu [K'ang-Hsi, 1662–1722] and that many of the buildings were still in fair condition and only required some restoration to make them fit for use as a place of solace and delight. On the Hill of a Myriad Years [Wan-Shou Shan, the name given by the emperor Ch'ien-Lung to the hill overlooking the Summer Palace Lake] there was the building called the Great Monastery of Gratitude and Longevity, in which His Majesty the Emperor Kao Tsung [Ch'ien-Lung, 1736–1795] thrice invoked blessings on the Empress-Dowager Hsiao-Shêng-Hsien [" Dutiful, Holy and a Pattern to All "].

" Reverently following such exalted precedents and being desirous of perpetuating the auspicious influences of that favoured spot, We conceived the idea of restoring the Ch'ing-I Yüan [" Park of Clear Rippling Waters "] and conferring upon it the new name of Yi-Ho Yüan [" Park of the Cultivation of Harmonious Old Age "]. Our desire was to make it a fitting place for the reception of Our Gracious Sovereign Lady and for the celebration of the approaching Joyful Anniversary.[8]

" We looked forward to proceeding to the new Park on that solemn occasion at the head of Our Ministers of State and humbly laying before Her Imperial Majesty Our respectful congratulations. By so doing We should be testifying, however inadequately, to Our loyal and reverent devotion.

" In all sincerity We submitted Our proposal for Her August Majesty's gracious approval, but not until We had done so on several occasions were Her commands conveyed to Us in the following Edict :

" EDICT BY THE EMPRESS-DOWAGER

" From the time when I first lowered the curtain and attended to State affairs, I have been filled day and night with fear and awe, as though I were travelling along the edge of a chasm. Although the Empire is now fairly peaceful, this is no time for leisurely relaxation or for any diminution of strenuous endeavour. I am conscious of the fact that the former sainted Emperors of our dynasty laid upon Their Successors the necessity of devoting Themselves to the duties of government and to relieving the sufferings of the people. All parks and gardens created by our sainted Predecessors were intended to provide facilities for martial exercises, and not for purposes of sumptuous display and the pleasures of the chase, as was the case with the parks established by the sovereigns of earlier dynasties.

" I am, however, aware that the Emperor's desire to restore the palace in the West springs from his laudable concern for my welfare, and for that reason I cannot bear to meet his well-meaning petition with a blunt refusal.

" Moreover, the costs of construction have all been provided for out of the surplus funds accumulated as a result of rigid economies in the past. The funds under the control of the Board of Revenue will not be touched, and no harm will be done to the national finances.

" Nevertheless there are current rumours which show that all the facts of the case are not fully understood, and the

audacious suggestion has even been made that the proposed
works, include the gradual rebuilding of the Yüan-ming Yüan
[the old Summer Palace destroyed in 1860 by the Anglo-
French allies]. This is a gross error, which has filled me with
consternation.

" Having regard to the present circumstances of the State,
there can be no thought of entering upon building operations
for Court or Government on anything like the scale adopted
in the Yung-Chêng period [reign of the emperor Shih Tsung,
1723-1735]. The proper objects of present endeavour are the
happiness and welfare of the people, and peace for all within
the four seas.

" I do not know how many there are who are capable of
reverently following the counsels of our Imperial Predecessors
and transmitting Their glorious traditions. It is particularly
necessary to adapt our actions to the times in which we live
and to confine our attention to essentials. That the desires of
my heart are not directed towards idle relaxation will assuredly be recognised throughout the land.

" The Emperor has now reached manhood. He will henceforth devote himself with all diligence to his administrative
duties and learn how to combine self-control with love of the
people. He must not let his filial devotion lead him for my sake
into lavish expenditure on idle luxuries.

" Furthermore I enjoin all servants of the State, great and
small, in the capital and in the provinces, to be loyal, diligent
and strenuous, and to beware of wasting their substance on
frivolity and extravagance. Let them act in accordance with
the highest principles and not disappoint the deepest longings
and aspirations of my heart.

" Having reverently received Her August Majesty's commands,
it only remains for Us to obey them with trembling, not daring
to embark upon any extravagant expenditure. All our officers
of State must also act in accordance with Her August Majesty's
benign wishes, and strive to carry out their duties with the
utmost diligence, each thereby helping to inaugurate an age of
peace and prosperity.

" The work at the Western Park is now gradually approaching
completion, and We have respectfully selected by divination the

tenth day of the fourth moon of this year [1888] as the date
upon which We will reverently escort Her August Majesty's
equipage to Her new residence. Let all necessary measures be
taken forthwith for the appointment of a guard-of-honour and
for the allocation of duties in accordance with the programme
to be submitted to the Throne by the princes and ministers of
the proper departments.

" Let this Decree be communicated to those concerned."

It would be difficult to imagine a more revealing testimony to
the make-believe and insincerity of the Manchu court than this
document. We may well wonder whom it was intended to
deceive : certainly neither of the imperial personages in whose
names the two edicts were issued. The Venerable Buddha was
not so simple-minded as to suppose that her imperial nephew's
devotion and affectionate solicitude for herself were as profound
as his words implied ; nor was the emperor so witless as to dream
that there was any real reluctance about his imperial aunt's
acceptance of his jubilee gift of a nice new Summer Palace, or
any sincerity in her demand for economy in the building of it.

No doubt, however, she looked forward to spending a mellow
old age in a delightful retreat from which she could make
periodical excursions into the political and domestic world of
the court when she wearied of posing as goddess of Mercy among
the lotuses ; and no doubt he, for his part, looked forward with
eagerness to the day when she would betake herself to any
paradise, earthly or heavenly, that would keep her out of the
Forbidden City.

As neither the nominal authors of the two edicts, nor the
departmental officials who had to read them, were in the least
likely to take them at their face value, presumably they were
intended to go on record as constituting the authorised explanation of how it was that in a time of national distress and financial
stringency the court had found it possible to provide itself with
a new and most costly palace. There is nothing in the edicts to
hint at the truth—that the palace was paid for out of funds
diverted from the Chinese navy. On the contrary, as we have
seen, it was carefully explained that the whole expenditure had

been met out of surpluses arising from rigid economies in the past. Did the court of Peking ever try to economise or succeed in doing so ? Not, surely, since the days of the great K'ang-Hsi, who, for his pains, was accused of parsimony.

Perhaps it would be unfair to say that the Venerable Buddha did nothing for the Chinese navy in return for the diversion of its funds to her " stately pleasure dome." Her contribution to her country's naval forces exists to this day in the form of a Marble Boat in the Summer Palace lake, of which the best that can be said is that while the rest of the Chinese fleet perished ingloriously at Weihaiwei, it was destined to survive both the China-Japan war and the Manchu dynasty. Unfortunately it does as little credit to the Venerable Buddha's æsthetic sensibility as to her patriotism.[9]

The empress-dowager has left in the Summer Palace a more infamous monument to her character than the marble boat.

On the edge of the lake, and almost immediately behind the Venerable Buddha's throne-hall—the *Jên Shou T'ang*—in which it was her custom to hold formal audiences when such were necessary, stands the building which was the Summer Palace dwelling-place—more fittingly described as a prison—of the unhappy emperor Kuang-Hsü. Its name was Yü-Lan T'ang— " the Hall of the Waters of Rippling Jade." In an earlier chapter I said that the jade-like waters of the lake rippled against the walls of Kuang-Hsü's prison, but not for his ears to hear nor for his eyes to see.[10] What I meant by that remark must now be explained.

When I took charge of the Summer Palace the Hall of the Waters of Rippling Jade was one of the few buildings in that palace which were never opened to visitors. Its outer and inner doors were all sealed, and the dates on the transverse paper strips which constituted the seals showed they had not been touched for several years. The building had not been used since it was last occupied by the emperor. A few days after my appointment I caused the seals to be removed. Passing through the gateway I found myself in a large paved courtyard, with the main building (*chêng tien*) in front and two lesser buildings (*p'ei tien*) on either side. The main building contained four apartments, the centre one being that which should have been the emperor's reception-room or throne-hall but which was practically his only living-room. It contained a small throne, however, which in accordance with custom faced south. On each side of the throne there was a doorway. That on the west side opened immediately into the emperor's bedroom. It was a small and ill-ventilated apartment, twelve feet three inches from west to east, sixteen feet eight inches from north to south. On one of the walls were a painted landscape by Hsü Liang-pien and the drawing of a deer and crane (emblems of long life) by Huang Chi-ming.

The door on the east side of the throne opened into another bedroom containing specimens of the calligraphy of Hsü Hui-fêng and a delicate flower-painting by Shên Shih-chieh. There was another room to the west of the throne-hall and imperial bedroom, containing an inscription by Wu Shih-chien. Here, hanging on the wall, was a fine specimen of carved blackwood representing a landscape.

There remain to be described the two p'ei-tien or side-buildings which, had it been possible for the imperial prisoner to use them, would have given him several additional rooms. On unsealing and opening the doors of these buildings I made a startling discovery. Throughout the whole length of the inside of each of the two side-buildings there was a solid unbroken brick wall. Between the wall and the door and windows that faced the courtyard there were only a few inches of space, scarcely leaving enough room for the door to be opened inwards. The walls in the two buildings could not be seen from the courtyard unless the doors were opened. It was the building on the west side of the courtyard that should have given the emperor a view of the rippling waters of the lake, but the two interior walls shut him off from every view on both east and west, while his own living quarters and the locked gate in front of his courtyard shut him off equally effectually from north and south.

I turned to the palace staff for an explanation of the existence of these walls. They were the Venerable Buddha's playful and ingenious device for making her victim realise that he was a criminal and a prisoner. Apart from the fact that the walls made the rooms within which they were built wholly useless for residential or any other practical purposes, they served as a

perpetual reminder to the emperor that he was a captive ; and
it was with the deliberate object of adding to his misery and
humiliation, as well as for the purpose of depriving him of room-
space and of the possibility of beholding the waters of the
beautiful adjoining lake, that his cruel and vindictive jailoress
had conceived the brutal idea of constructing the interior walls.

Had her intention been merely that he must be prevented
from communicating with the outside world, she might have
contented herself with walling up the windows that looked out
on the lake on the one side and on the eastern section of the
palace grounds on the other. He would at least have been able
to make use of the two buildings as additional sitting-rooms.
But that would not have given her the same malicious gratifica-
tion that she derived from the knowledge that on opening the
door of each building her captive would be faced with nothing
but a blank wall.

This discovery was to me a new revelation of the spiteful
hatred actuating the old dowager in her treatment of the
wretched Kuang-Hsü during the last ten years of his life. It
was also new to Kuang-Hsü's imperial nephew when I told him
of it ; and on his next visit to the Summer Palace he accompanied me to the Hall of the Waters of Rippling Jade and gazed
upon those blind walls for the first time.

I am unable to say whether they are still in existence or
whether the local authorities who have had control of the
Summer Palace since its confiscation by the republican government have caused them to be demolished. If they are still in
existence it is greatly to be hoped that they will be maintained
intact as a permanent memorial of the hate and spite of a
bigoted and vindictive woman who not only blighted an
emperor's life and brought his dynasty to ruin, but was largely
responsible for the disorder and misery that have afflicted the
long-suffering Chinese people for the past twenty years.

If ever a roll of honour is prepared to commemorate the
names of martyrs to the cause of political and social reform in
China, one of the highest places on that roll should certainly be
assigned to the unhappy Kuáng-Hsü, for whom the young
Chinese patriots of to-day, whose fathers left him to his fate,
are rarely heard to utter a word either of respect or of pity.

CHAPTER XXIII

The Fifth of November

IT IS UNNECESSARY for our purposes to discuss the political events which led to one of China's recurrent civil wars in 1924. At first the quarrel was one between the rival military leaders of the provinces of Chehkiang and Kiangsu, namely Lu Yung-hsiang and Ch'i Hsieh-yüan. It was obvious to all onlookers that the strife could not be confined to central China, for the Man-churian war-lord Chang Tso-lin was an ally of Lu, while Wu P'ei-fu and Ts'ao K'un (the latter having bribed himself into the office of president in October, 1923) were allies of Ch'i. The war between the Yangtse war-lords soon developed into an armed struggle between the two great rivals—Wu P'ei-fu and Chang Tso-lin.

Wu P'ei-fu came to the north with his " punitive " army and spent several weeks in and near Peking, making his final prepara-tions for his advance to Shanhaikuan, the gateway of Manchuria, where the Great Wall comes down to the sea. He seemed to be confident of victory and boasted that he would be in Mukden in a month.

During September and the greater part of October, 1924, the war caused no great anxiety in palace circles. Fêng Yü-hsiang, " the Christian General," who had one of the most important commands under Wu P'ei-fu in the north, was always regarded as a potential menace, but so long as he was loyal to Wu P'ei-fu, or was overawed by the armies under Wu's direct control, he could do no harm.

Wu P'ei-fu had good qualities that had won him many friends and admirers. He was honest and courageous, he cared nothing for money, he was an indulgent and considerate chief and a sincere patriot, and he was honoured for his consistent refusal to demean himself in time of trouble, as so many of his contem-poraries did, by taking refuge in foreign Concessions. But he had faults and weaknesses, among them being inordinate vanity and an exaggerated notion of his own military genius. He had been known to compare himself with Napoleon—not to his own disadvantage—and he had a dangerous tendency to despise his opponents. A minor peccadillo was his love for the brimming wine-cup. It is said that the Christian General, whose principles were shocked by this genial peculiarity in the warlord of Lo-yang, once sent him, as a birthday-present, a bottle of water. The Christian General's principles, had they been more stable than they were, would probably have received an even greater shock if he had heard Wu's language when he uncorked it.

Wu's most serious defect was that he was a bad judge of human character. He placed too much faith in unworthy associates, and he was constantly being deceived and led astray by some of the men whose positions enabled them to interpose themselves between him and the outside world. Again and again he was " let down " by his subordinates. This, as we shall see, was the cause of his undoing.

On the whole, Wu was for some time a more popular hero in north China than any other prominent figure since the so-called republic came into being. If he did not embody all the ideals of " Young China " he had at one time the gift of inspiring many able young men with feelings almost of devotion—feelings certainly of a much warmer and less artificial kind than were ever inspired by the living Sun Yat-sen. Some of these young men were nicknamed *Wu mi*—" infatuated with Wu "—and I have known them accept the nickname with equanimity.

By the early days of October, Wu P'ei-fu at the head of his large army was battering at the gates of Manchuria. Accounts from the front were optimistic, and a triumphal entry into Mukden, the Manchurian capital, seemed a possibility of the near future. Fêng Yü-hsiang had been ordered by Wu to lead his forces to Ku-pei-k'ou, an important pass in the mountain range that forms the northern boundary of China proper and the southern boundary of Jehol. The duty assigned to him was to hold the northern passes against any flanking operation by Chang Tso-lin.

Wu's generalship was not amiss, but he made the most costly blunder of his life in selecting the Christian General for the task of defending the northern passes. It may be that he did not want

Fêng's company on what he hoped would be his victorious march to Mukden, and that at the same time he was afraid to leave him in control of the Peking area. Apparently it never entered his head that he was playing into the hands of a man who was nursing an old grievance against him and whose reputation for loyalty and soldierly obedience was already dubious.

On October 17th I found the emperor in a pensive mood not because of the political outlook, which seemed to give no pressing cause for anxiety, but because Tuan-K'ang, the surviving consort of the emperor Tê Tsung, was ill and reported to be dying.

I set out on that day on a short visit to my retreat in the mountains—Cherry Glen. On the evening of the 21st, after a walk and ride over the hills, I reached the Summer Palace, where I spent the night. There I heard the news that Tuan-K'ang was dead.

It was a beautiful autumn night, and I sat long by the margin of the lake. Whatever might be in store for us in the near future, nothing could have seemed more remote from a world afflicted by warlike excursions and alarums than the Summer Palace lake. It was as tranquil as that Scottish loch which Wordsworth saw with his mind's eye—real wild duck taking the place of the poet's dream-swan.

I returned to Peking by car next day. Strange rumours of various kinds were flying through the city, but outwardly all was calm. I did not visit the Forbidden City that day.

Early on the morning of the 23rd, one of my servants, greatly excited, came to tell me there had been a case of *ping pien* (mutiny of troops) in the northern section of the Tartar city, that the Hou-Mên (the great street gate a few dozen yards to the north of my house) was closed and guarded by troops, and that telephones were not working. People in the streets were terrified, and rich families were already flocking to the Legation Quarter (as they always do in Peking when danger threatens) and were taking rooms in the Wagons-Lits Hotel.

That the trouble was due to a local mutiny was of course only a guess and it turned out to be untrue. What had happened was that Fêng Yü-hsiang had carried out an amazingly successful *coup d'état*. It subsequently became known that he had never gone as far as Ku-pei-k'ou at the Great Wall but had halted halfway from Peking. Two generals named Sun Yüeh and Hu Ching-yi, who had under their command considerable bodies of troops left behind by Wu P'ei-fu in the Peking area, were his fellow-conspirators, and it was they who opened the gates of Peking to Fêng's returning troops in the dark hours of the morning of the 23rd. The railway station and telegraph offices had been occupied and telephonic communication cut off. Troops had been placed round the presidential palace with such promptitude that by the time the unfortunate president had been awakened from his slumbers his way of escape to the Legation Quarter had already been cut off.

Not knowing what had taken place, and still assuming that a mutiny of troops (a not unusual occurrence in republican China) was the most probable explanation of the excitement, I drove to the Forbidden City. The first ominous sign that I noticed, other than the deserted appearance of the streets, was the presence of armed men at the gate of the Chi An So—a ceremonial building belonging to the imperial family. On reaching the open space between the Forbidden City and Prospect Hill I found further cause for anxiety. The hill, which owing to its height and central position dominates the city of Peking, was not, as usual, silent and unpeopled but had become a scene of martial activity. Groups of men in uniform stood on the slopes and crowded the pavilions. At the gateway, which directly faces the Forbidden City, stood armed soldiers whose uniform was not that of the imperial body-guard.

At the Gate of Spiritual Valour everything seemed normal. My own chair was waiting to carry me into the Forbidden City, and the guard presented arms as usual.

On arriving at the emperor's quarters I was told that he was awaiting me at my own pavilion in the imperial garden and wished to see me at once. I found him in my study, attended by a few servants whom he immediately sent away.

He knew even less than I did about the events of the morning. At first I made no allusion to the subject, but referred to the death of Tuan K'ang and expressed my sympathy. He asked if I knew that troops had occupied Prospect Hill. I replied that I had seen them. " They went there without permission," he went on, " and I don't know what they mean to do. Shao Ying has sent them tea and food, as he thinks we must treat them as our guests." I asked if they had expressed gratitude. " No," said the emperor, " but they asked for more." They would.

After a few minutes' conversation, during which we paced the pathways of the garden, he said, " Let us go and see them." We went up the rockery that is crowned by a pavilion overlooking the walls of the Forbidden City and inspected Prospect Hill through field-glasses. It was crowded with soldiers.

We went to the Yang-Hsin Tien where I lunched with the emperor. Shao-Ying and other members of the Nei Wu Fu came in to discuss matters. They told us that criminals were being released from the gaols and that bands of excited students were going about the streets distributing communist leaflets. The arrival of prince Ch'un and others was announced and I left the emperor in consultation with them, promising to obtain what information I could from the Legation Quarter.

At the Peking Club the *coup d'état* was of course the one topic of conversation. No one seemed to know exactly what had happened, or why, but theories were numerous. The ignorance of the club reflected that of the foreign Legations. I walked home slowly through two miles of streets hoping to learn more there than I could glean from the caves of the diplomats. Two pieces of information which I picked up on my walk turned out to be true—Ts'ao K'un, the president, had tried and failed to escape to the Legation Quarter and was a prisoner in his own palace. His treasurer and friend—many would call him his accomplice in evil doing—had been arrested and was in close military custody.

The events of the next few days must be briefly summarised. The presidential treasurer, having failed to disgorge all the money that he was suspected of possessing, underwent a ten minutes' trial and was publicly executed. Parliament was dissolved on the ground of the gross corruption of its members in having sold their votes to elect Ts'ao K'un to the presidency ; and to add irony to the proceedings the wretched Ts'ao K'un was compelled, under a veiled threat of a punishment similar to that which had befallen his treasurer, to sign the mandate of dissolution. This part of the *coup d'état* gave dissatisfaction to very few except the members of parliament themselves. There has been no parliament

in China since that date. As for my antagonist Li Hsieh-yang, I
never heard of him again.

Besides being required to dissolve the parliament by which he
had been elected, the luckless Ts'ao K'un was also compelled to
issue presidential mandates dismissing marshal Wu P'ei-fu from
all his posts, ordering an immediate cessation of the civil
war, and appointing a new cabinet. Of another mandate,
similarly extorted, something remains to be said in the next
chapter.

Having done everything that the authors of the *coup d'état*
considered necessary to give a colour of legality to their proceedings, Ts'ao K'un was then called upon to resign the presidency.
When he had done this he was allowed to leave Peking. He made
his way to the foreign Concession-area in Tientsin without a
moment's unnecessary delay, but apparently with the secret
intention of revoking all the mandates issued by him under
duress as soon as he found himself safe under foreign protection.
With this purpose in view he carried off the presidential seals.
Unfortunately for Ts'ao K'un, the disappearance of the seals was
discovered before his train reached Tientsin. The train was
stopped and Ts'ao K'un was given firmly to understand that his
liberty if not his life depended upon the handing-over of the
seals. They were surrendered at once, and the train carried him
safely to Tientsin.

Most of the prominent officials who had served in Ts'ao K'un's
cabinet and were known to have been his or Wu P'ei-fu's
nominees were quick to realise the importance of seeking
immediate change of air. One of these was the foreign minister,
Dr. Wellington Koo, who was sheltered for some weeks in the
Legation Quarter and subsequently—with the help of a Canadian
friend—made his escape by motor-car to Tientsin. Even there
he did not consider himself quite safe from pursuit and arrest,
and shortly afterwards went by steamer to Weihaiwei. The fact
that he should have selected what was then British-administered
territory as his place of refuge is not without its piquancy, for in
his capacity of Chinese foreign minister he had recently been
negotiating with the British authorities for Weihaiwei's rendition
to China. The negotiations had ended in temporary failure, and
he now had reason to congratulate himself that such had been

382 TWILIGHT IN THE FORBIDDEN CITY

the case. As we shall see, he had further reason for self-con-
gratulation in connection with the same matter four years later.
The new cabinet—practically self-elected—was so small that
each member had to take charge of two or more portfolios. The
premier was general Huang Fu and the foreign minister Dr. C. T.
Wang.

According to the Christian General's own statements, the
object of the *coup d'état* was to save the tortured Chinese people
from the pains and horrors of further civil war. As far as this
laudable object was concerned it proved to be an utter failure.
Civil wars became more frequent, more brutal, more disastrous
to China and the Chinese people than they had been before, and
they have continued almost without intermission up to the
present day. But Fêng's real purpose was to ruin marshal Wu
P'ei-fu, and in this he was successful. I do not propose to discuss
the stories told concerning the vast sums of money alleged to
have been paid or promised to him in return for his services in
overthrowing Wu P'ei-fu, because the subject is one which does
not concern us in these pages.

On receipt of the startling news from Peking, Wu P'ei-fu
was compelled to withdraw from contact with Chang Tso-lin's
forces at the Great Wall and to turn his attention to the generals
who had betrayed him. Into the details of the brief campaign
that followed it is needless to enter. Wu and Fêng met in battle
between Tientsin and Peking, with results disastrous to Wu.
His forces were scattered, and Wu himself had to embark with
a remnant of his followers on his little fleet of supply-transports.
He retired by sea to the Yangtse Valley and for a short period
ceased to count in Chinese warfare or politics. Fêng and his
military and civilian colleagues were left for the moment in a
position of unassailable supremacy in north China south of the
Great Wall. The Manchurian warlord was still, to be sure, a
mighty force to be reckoned with ; but inasmuch as he had been
saved from what might have been a colossal defeat solely by
the great betrayal carried out by the Christian General, there
was no obvious reason to suppose that he would be otherwise
than grateful. A close alliance between Chang Tso-lin and Fêng
Yü-hsiang seemed to be almost a certainty of the immediate
future.

Thus it was that at the end of October and the beginning of November, 1924, Fêng's daring *coup* seemed to have been crowned with complete success. It is not surprising that the *Peking Leader*, in an article of October 26th, described it as " unquestionably one of the most extraordinary *coups d'état* in Chinese history."

Had the writer of that article known what was to follow in a few days, and also what might have followed if certain very dangerous counsels had prevailed, his language would have been even stronger.

Meanwhile in the Forbidden City there was growing consternation. Preparations were being made for the funeral of the late dowager-consort Tuan K'ang, but the ceremonies that in normal times would have accompanied the lying-in-state were much curtailed. The troops of Sun Yüeh—one of the Christian General's allies—who occupied Prospect Hill, became more insolent every day towards those officers and men of the imperial guard who showed themselves outside the walls of the Forbidden City, and incidents were related to me which indicated that Sun Yüeh's men were seeking an excuse for an open quarrel.

On Sunday, November 2nd, shortly after dawn, I was summoned to a conference at the emperor's palace. On arrival there I found only the emperor, his father-in-law, duke Jung, and Chêng Hsiao-hsü. The two latter gave various reasons for their belief that Fêng was contemplating another *coup* aimed at the emperor. We discussed the advisability of taking his majesty at once to the Legation Quarter, but it had been ascertained that every gate into the Forbidden City was now closely watched from the outside. I had myself observed that the sentries of the imperial guard usually stationed at the Gate of Spiritual Valour had withdrawn to the inside and that a force of Sun Yüeh's troops was drawn up outside.

The emperor collected a bundle of important documents and a parcel containing articles of great value. These he handed to me to put in a place of safety. I subsequently deposited them in the Hong Hong and Shanghai Bank.

I returned to the palace later, partly for the purpose of paying my ceremonial visit to the room in which Tuan K'ang was
AAC

lying in state. This duty performed, I went to the emperor's
quarters again and told him that the valuables with which he
had entrusted me were safe. He opened a cabinet and took out
a small basket which was nearly full of jewelled rings. " They
were all Tuan K'ang's," he said ; adding, with a sad smile,
" they would have been stolen if they had been left in her palace.
Choose the one you like best and keep it in memory of her." I
made my selection—it was a ring containing a piece of exquisite
green jade.

On November 3rd I was again in the Forbidden City, which
presented a ghostly and forlorn appearance. Many of the staff
were in hiding or had disappeared. Others were engaged in
carrying out the ceremonies connected with Tuan K'ang's
funeral, and flitted about in the white garb of mourners.

On Tuesday, November 4th, I had lunch alone with the
emperor, and we then visited the empress. From her palace of
" Treasured Beauty " we went to my pavilion in the garden
and discussed schemes for his escape. Chêng Hsiao-hsü had by
this time evolved a plan which seemed feasible, and it was
decided that an attempt should be made on the following day
to get the emperor out of the Forbidden City in disguise.

The long twilight in the Forbidden City was deepening into
darkness.

At breakfast-time on Wednesday, November 5th, I was
called to the telephone, which by that time was again in working
order. The agitated voice that spoke to me I recognised as that
of prince Tsai-T'ao. His news, though it can hardly be said to
have surprised me, was nevertheless disturbing in the extreme.
A body of Fêng Yü-hsiang's troops had entered the Forbidden
City and had seized and closed the Gate of Spiritual Valour. No
one was allowed in or out. His majesty's telephone had been
cut. There was no means of knowing what was happening to the
emperor. Would I accompany him to the gate and make an
attempt to get through ?

In ten minutes he was at my house in his car, which he drove
into my front courtyard and left there. He preferred to drive to
the Forbidden City in my car rather than in his own. I was awaiting him and we wasted no time. In a few minutes we had arrived

at the Gate of Spiritual Valour, all three doors of which we found
closed and closely guarded. My car was stopped in front of
Prospect Hill and a soldier came up to investigate. I produced
my Chinese card, telling him that I had the right to enter the
palace. He took the card and went to consult an officer. During
the two minutes of his absence the prince, who was deeply
moved, said, " If they let you in, tell them I am your servant."

That remark made an impression on me that time will not
erase. The prince was torn between two emotions—dread of the
fate that might be awaiting him if he ventured inside the Forbidden City at this crisis, and the loyalty that bade him risk his
own life, if need be, in an effort to save the emperor. The spirit
of *noblesse oblige* won the day ; yet although he had braced himself to the ordeal of going into the Forbidden City if permission
to enter it were granted to me, he hugged the hope—doubtless
a vain one—that he himself might escape the notice of the
soldiers if he were to follow me into the palace as my humble
personal attendant.

Dismal indeed was the plight to which the proud and imperial
Manchu race had been reduced before such words could have
passed the lips of a prince of the blood. What would the mighty
K'ang-Hsi or Ch'ien-Lung have said had they lived to see the
day when a member of their House—the brother of one emperor
and uncle of another—would seek to crawl into the palace of his
conquering forefathers in the guise of a foreigner's servant?
What would the " Venerable Buddha " have said had she foreseen this pitiful result of her wild efforts to expel the hated and
despised " foreign devil " not only from the sacred ground of
her capital but from every yard of the soil of China ?

Our suspense was brief. The soldier who had taken my card
returned with the message that on no account whatever could
I be admitted to the Forbidden City. Orders had been issued on
the subject by the high command and they were peremptory.

We turned the car and drove away. Tsai-T'ao was in tears.
" What are we to do ? " he asked. " There is only one thing to
be done," I replied ; " we must go at once to the Legation
Quarter and ask the foreign ministers to do whatever they
can do to protect the emperor."

The Dutch minister, Mr. W. J. Oudendijk, was the doyen of

the diplomatic body, and we drove straight to the Netherlands Legation. Just as we arrived there we met the British minister, Sir Ronald Macleay, coming down the steps of the minister's house. I stopped him at once, told him that we had very important news to communicate, and asked him to return with us to interview the Dutch minister. He did so, and in a few minutes the four of us were seated at a round table in the minister's study.

Neither the British nor the Dutch minister had heard about the invasion of the Forbidden City that morning. It did not take long to give them our own scanty information, but there was some discussion before any concrete proposal was adopted. It was finally agreed that the two ministers should call on Dr. C. T. Wang (the new foreign minister) that afternoon and make whatever representations might be necessary to save the emperor from personal violence. It was also agreed that the Japanese minister, Mr. K. Yoshizawa, should be informed of the circumstances and invited to join them. This he willingly agreed to do.

Meanwhile a state of panic had arisen among the Manchu aristocracy of Peking. There were wild rumours that a massacre had taken place in the Forbidden City, that the emperor and empress and the two surviving t'ai fei (consorts of the emperor T'ung-Chih) were dead, and that all members of the Manchu imperial family were to be sought out and put to the sword. Panic is a thing that feeds upon itself and expands in the process. During this eventful day dozens of the upper-class Manchus —princes and nobles and their wives and children—crowded into the Legation Quarter and found a temporary lodging-place in the empty buildings of the German Legation Guard. Here I visited them and gave them what consolation I could, while I awaited the result of the visit of the three ministers to the Chinese Foreign Office.

It was when I was still in the Legation Quarter that the happy news reached me that the worst of the rumours were untrue and that the emperor was alive. During the afternoon he had been expelled from the Forbidden City and conveyed under guard in his own car to his father's residence—the Pei Fu—in the northern section of Peking. The Forbidden City, however, was still under the exclusive control of Fêng Yü-hsiang and his colleagues, the imperial body-guard had been disarmed and the Nei Wu Fu had ceased to exercise its functions. A detachment of troops had been sent to the Pei Fu, and the emperor was now a state-prisoner in the house of his own father.

The news that the emperor was alive and unharmed spread rapidly among the Manchus who had fled to the Legation Quarter, and the panic among them slowly subsided. Most of them began to wend their way back to the city, though many were afraid to return to their own homes and accepted the hospitality of Chinese friends.

Though naturally anxious to see the emperor as soon as possible, I wished to be able to give him news about the action taken by the Dutch, Japanese and British ministers and its results. I therefore waited in the Legation Quarter till I could ascertain what had taken place at the Chinese ministry of Foreign Affairs.

It was to the Dutch minister, Mr. W. J. Oudendijk, that I applied and from whom I received the first news. The three ministers had seen Dr. C. T. Wang together and had pressed for information regarding the reported invasion of the Forbidden City. They also asked for assurances as to the safety of the emperor and the imperial family. Dr. C. T. Wang was at first inclined to be arrogant and reticent, and more than hinted that the foreign Legations had no *locus standi* inasmuch as what had taken place related solely to Chinese internal politics and had nothing to do with international relations. The ministers, however, did not allow the matter to rest there and replied that in the interests of humanity, if on no other account, they had the right to satisfy themselves that the emperor was not being treated with cruelty or subjected to indignity. They added, with emphasis, that any ill-treatment of the emperor would be regarded by their respective governments with grave displeasure.

A somewhat acrimonious discussion ended as satisfactorily as in the circumstances could be expected. Dr. Wang, perceiving that the ministers were taking the matter seriously, changed his tone and assured them that the emperor was in no danger, that he was not being ill-treated, and that his personal liberty would not be interfered with. For the first time in his life, in fact, he had become a free agent. He then explained in greater detail that " Chinese public opinion " had for some time demanded that the abdication agreement should be modified, that the imperial title should cease to be used, that the court and the household department should be abolished, and that " P'u-Yi " should take his place as an ordinary citizen of the republic. The cabinet, obedient to what it had satisfied itself was the will of the people, had therefore prepared a new " agreement " with the ex-imperial house embodying a statement of the altered status of the emperor, and it was this agreement which had that day been placed before " P'u-Yi " for his acceptance.

Such in rough outline, as far as I could gather, was the explanation given by Dr. Wang of that morning's proceedings in the Forbidden City. Nothing was said of the circumstances in which the emperor left the palace or of the fact that he was treated as a prisoner even after his departure, because at the time when the interview between the three ministers and Dr. Wang took place the emperor was still within the Forbidden City or had only just left it. It is quite possible that Dr. Wang himself knew very little of the brutal and cowardly manner in which Fêng Yü-hsiang (or his henchman Lu Chung-lin, who personally directed the affair) was carrying out the policy of the "cabinet."

Dr. Wang's statement obviously left a good deal unexplained, but on the whole it sounded plausible, in spite of the nonsense about " the will of the people." At any rate the ministers had to content themselves with the assurance, for what it was worth, that the emperor's life was not in imminent danger.

The statement of the Dutch minister only slightly relieved the anxiety that was in my own mind as I drove through the three or more miles of streets separating the Legation Quarter from the mansion of prince Ch'un. It still remained to be seen whether I should be admitted. By this time it was late in the evening and the streets were dark. I found the outer gates closed and a strong body of Fêng Yü-hsiang's soldiers drawn up outside. I handed my card to a soldier who came forward as my car stopped, and told him I had an engagement with the prince. After a short delay the gate was opened and my car was allowed to drive into the courtyard. I was recognised at once by some of the servants of the house who told me I was expected and that the emperor was awaiting me.

He received me in a large reception room which was nearly

full of Manchu notables and of officers of the imperial household. The least agitated of the whole crowd was the emperor
himself—indeed he was quite calm and gave me a friendly smile
of greeting as I entered. The most agitated was his father, the
prince, whose manner and appearance would have suggested to
anyone ignorant of the facts that it was he, not the emperor,
who had been through a nerve-racking ordeal. My first duty was
to announce the result of the visit of the three ministers to the
Foreign Office. They had already heard from Tsai-T'ao of the
consultation in the Netherlands Legation that morning and were
naturally eager to know what had happened at the interview
with Dr. Wang. They listened attentively to what I had to say,
all but prince Ch'un, who while I was speaking moved nervously
round the room for no apparent purpose. Several times he suddenly quickened his pace and ran up to me uttering a few half
incoherent words. The slight impediment in his speech seemed
to be more marked than when he was in a normal state. The
purport of his words was the same each time he spoke : " Ask
huang-shang (his majesty) not to be frightened "—a totally unnecessary remark from one who was himself obviously in a state
of much greater alarm than the emperor. When he had run up
to me four or five times with this inane observation I became
slightly irritated and said, " His majesty is here, standing beside
me. Why not address him direct ? " But he was too much upset
to notice the rudeness of my remark and resumed his aimless
circumambulations.

The emperor took me to his private rooms and there we had
a quiet talk. He showed dignity and self-possession, and referred
with amused contempt to the alarm and bewilderment shown
by others in the room we had left.

His brief story of the events of the morning was told me afterwards in greater detail by the officers of the household. It was
about nine in the morning when a force of Fêng Yü-hsiang's
soldiers under the command of one of his staff officers, Lu
Chung-lin, presented themselves at the Gate of Spiritual Valour
and gave peremptory orders for the immediate disbandment
and disarming of the palace guard. Leaving a detachment of
troops at the gate to collect the arms and prevent unauthorised
persons from going in or out, Lu Chung-lin and his men and a

civilian, well known in academic and other circles, named Li Shih-tsêng, then entered the palace and compelled some of the disarmed guard to lead them through the labyrinthine ways that led to the offices of the Nei Wu Fu. There they demanded an interview with " P'u-Yi *hsien-shêng* "—" Mr. P'u-Yi." One of the chamberlains replied that *huang-shang*—" his majesty the emperor "—was in the palace of the empress. Speaking in loud and aggressive tones they announced they had come to order " Mr. P'u-Yi " and his wife and the two surviving dowager-consorts to leave the Forbidden City within three hours. " If they stay a moment longer, we cannot be answerable for the consequences."

They then produced a document which they presented to the comptroller, Shao-Ying, and demanded that it be shown to " Mr. P'u-Yi," whose immediate acceptance of the formula which it contained was imperative. No alteration of any kind could be considered, and the document must be accepted as it stood. It purported to be a " revision " of the Articles of Favourable Treatment, and the opening clause was so worded as to make it appear that the revision was carried out on the initiative of the emperor himself. The document, according to the copy afterwards shown me, may be translated as follows :

Whereas the emperor of the Great Ch'ing dynasty is desirous of entering into full sympathy with the spirit of the republic and its five constituent races and is unwilling to persist in maintaining a system which is incompatible with republican institutions, the Articles of Favourable Treatment of the Manchu imperial house are hereby revised in the following manner :

1. From this date the imperial title of the emperor Hsüan T'ung is for ever abolished ; and henceforth he will enjoy all the privileges which are accorded by law to the citizens of the Chinese republic.

2. From this date the republican government will grant to the Ch'ing household an annual subsidy of $500,000, and will also pay $2,000,000 for the purpose of creating an industrial establishment to provide employment for the poor of Peking, with the understanding that Manchu bannermen will have the first claim to admission.

3. In fulfilment of the third clause of the original " Articles of Favourable Treatment " the Ch'ing family will leave the Forbidden City forthwith. They will be at liberty to select their own

place of abode, but the responsibility of protecting them will continue to rest with the government of the republic.

4. The sacrificial ceremonies hitherto observed in the ancestral temple of the Ch'ing family and at the imperial tombs will be maintained for ever, and the republic will devise means of providing military guards in order that the temple and the tombs may be adequately protected.

5. The whole of the private property of the Ch'ing family will remain in their possession, and the government of the republic will have the duty of seeing that they are left undisturbed in the enjoyment of it. All public property, however, will belong to the republic.

The document was dated the fifth day of the eleventh month of the thirteenth year of the Republic (November 5th, 1924) and the signatures appended to it were those of Lu Chung-lin, Wang Chih-hsiang, governor and mayor of Peking, and Chang Pi, head of the police. All these men belonged, of course, to the little clique who, together with the self-appointed "cabinet" of Huang Fu and his colleagues had usurped the control of the capital and called themselves the government of the republic of China.

The document was brought to the emperor by the comptroller, who was speechless with indignation. As may be readily imagined, the terms of the " revised " agreement were much more disturbing to him than to his imperial master. Nevertheless neither he nor the other officers of the household had the folly or the hardihood to advise the emperor to defy a group of men who obviously had both the will and the power to use force.

The only serious opposition to the demand that the imperial family should leave the Forbidden City forthwith came from the dowager-consorts. These two old ladies promptly replied that they would die rather than go. " I don't know what has happened to them," remarked the emperor ruefully when he came to this part of the story ; " they both threatened to kill themselves if they were turned out by force."

The emperor and the empress put a few of their personal belongings together—they were not allowed to take more than what a servant or two could carry—and walked into the imperial garden, at the northern end of which their cars awaited them. They were given no option as to their destination, in spite of

the fact that the emperor had just been officially notified that
he was now a free citizen of the republic and could choose his
own residence.

They entered their cars, each accompanied by only a single
attendant. A soldier took his place beside each driver, and two
other soldiers, with arms obtrusively displayed, stood on the
running boards of each car. No sooner had they passed—perhaps
for the last time—through the gate of Spiritual Valour, than
several other cars, full of soldiers bristling with arms, joined
the procession. The cars were driven rapidly northward past
Prospect Hill, past the walls of my house, and through one of
the side portals of the Hou Mên or Northern Gate that leads
out of the so-called *huang chêng* or " imperial city." For the
first time in the emperor's experience the central portal, always
closed to the public, was not opened to let his car pass through.
Evidently " Mr. P'u-Yi " was to be taught, without delay, that
there was nothing to differentiate him from his fellow-citizens
—except perhaps certain regrettable limitations on his personal
freedom.

The Pei Fu, his father's mansion, was not the place that the
emperor or his friends would have chosen for his abode at this
critical stage in his career. It was in the extreme northern
section of the city, more than three miles from that one part of
Peking in which he knew he would have found a welcome and
a sanctuary. Mainly, no doubt, for that very reason the foreign
Legation Quarter was the very place to which his custodians
were determined that he should not go.

That he was a state-prisoner was a fact which was impressed
upon him in a disagreeable fashion only an hour after his arrival.
For the express purpose of putting the matter to the test he
gave orders that his car should be prepared as he intended to
take a drive in the city. By this time prince Ch'un's own police-
guard had been turned out of their quarters and in their place
an armed party of Fêng's troops had stationed themselves not
only at the main entrance to the house (which is a very large and
rambling one with many courtyards and a large garden) but
also at all other possible exits ; and no sooner had the officer
in command of the troops learned that the emperor proposed
to go out of doors than he intimated that according to the orders

he had received " Mr. P'u-Yi " was required to stay at home.

By the time the emperor had given me his account of all that had occurred, it was about eight o'clock at night. I asked whether he would like me to spend the night at the Pei Fu, and at first he replied with an eager affirmative. But after a little reflection he said it was important that I should keep in touch with the foreign ministers and that he therefore wished me to return to the Legation Quarter. " I shall expect you to-morrow morning," he said as we parted, " and tell the foreigners all that has happened."

Without waiting to say good-night to prince Ch'un I went out to the courtyard and got into my car. The outer gate was closed and barred. It was opened at my request, but before I was allowed to drive out the officer of the guard came up to my car and searched it thoroughly. It was apparently supposed that the emperor might be concealed under my rug.

After spending about two hours in the Legation Quarter giving and receiving news I returned home anxious and despondent. On the one hand, the overthrow and final collapse of that useless, costly and irremediably corrupt body, the Nei Wu Fu, was a consummation which no one had desired more earnestly than myself. Nor was the final extrication of the emperor from the entanglements of the demoralising palace system a thing to be deplored. Unfortunately, the relief and exhilaration which I should have felt if those happy events had come about by the emperor's own volition and in the way I had been planning and working for, were submerged in feelings of deep regret and foreboding. The manner in which the affair had been carried out was discreditable to China and the Chinese government, or rather to the little group of irresponsible soldiers and politicians who had usurped the functions of government, and would I knew be deeply resented by the large if usually inarticulate body of Chinese who were still loyal to the old order and who still regarded what had been the imperial throne with respect or even reverence. I knew it would be resented no less keenly by that perhaps still larger body of decent-minded republicans who were jealous of the honour and good name of their country.

What I had often anticipated had unfortunately come to pass. The abolition of the palace-system and the imperial title with their attendant privileges had, after all, been brought about not by the voluntary action of the generous and high-spirited young monarch but by the exercise of brute force put in motion by persons who did not know, and probably could never be made to believe, that he had himself earnestly desired to surrender those privileges. " It is more than likely," I had written in my letter of June 14th, 1922, " that the question of the future treatment of the imperial House will be brought up for discussion. All this is fully realised by his majesty, who is naturally anxious that the renunciation of his title and subsidy should take place as a voluntary act of his own and should be recognised as such by the whole country. It would distress him very deeply if his voluntary act of renunciation were inter-preted by the people not as the outcome of his own determina-tion to do what was right, but as the result of a mere desire to ' save face ' by anticipating the coercive action of parliament."[1]

The long foreseen coercive action had been applied at last—not, indeed, by parliament, for there was no parliament left, but by a self-elected " cabinet " composed of men who were devoid of the least trace of kindly feeling for the boy who had been their reigning sovereign and who yielded to none of them in his love for China and the Chinese people. Never would the emperor get the smallest fragment of credit or gratitude for his unselfish and patriotic intentions. Few Chinese, and probably few foreigners, would believe that such intentions had ever been his.

I had a further cause for the deepest anxiety. It was far too soon to be sure that Fêng and his colleagues harboured no designs of taking such further action as would ensure that never again would the ex-emperor willingly or unwillingly threaten the stability of the state. There was a party of hotheads, in Peking and in the provinces, who believed or pretended to believe that political conditions in China would never be tranquil so long as the ex-emperor was allowed to remain alive. That Fêng Yü-hsiang shared this view was more than a possibility. Already it was clear to me—it was to become clearer on the following day—that Dr. C. T. Wang had not told the truth when he informed the three foreign ministers that " Mr. P'u-Yi " was now a free citizen of the republic.

As for the revised terms of treatment of the former imperial house, there was little or nothing in them that to me seemed intrinsically unsatisfactory, however inadequate they might and certainly would seem to the jaundiced eyes of the officers of the imperial household and the other hangers-on of an extravagant court. So far from objecting to the terms as such, I considered them immeasurably more satisfactory than the original terms of 1912. There was only one flaw in them, but unfortunately it was a fatal flaw. They contained no guarantee of any kind that the new terms would be faithfully observed by the republic. For my own part I had no faith in the honour of the men who had drawn them up ; and even if I misjudged them, there was no guarantee that the unilateral agreement, which had been drawn up and imposed by force by an ephemeral " cabinet," would be observed by the cabinets of days to come. A study of the document embodying the new terms convinced me that it had been drawn up for the sole purpose of throwing dust in the eyes of Chinese and foreigners and deluding them into the belief that the emperor was being treated with fairness and generosity. Subsequent events proved that in holding these views I did no injustice to the men in whose honesty of purpose and good faith I had no confidence.

In the loneliness of my own library my thoughts turned to the Summer Palace and to the well-ordered and tranquil little world I had hoped to create there. That little world, in which the emperor was to have begun a free and happy and useful life, such as he had never known before, dissolved, as I thought of it, like the baseless fabric of a vision. The Palace remained, but it was no longer the Palace of my dreams. The old empress-dowager's spirit seemed about to resume its sway over that beautiful domain in which, after all, I had been only the intruder of a day. Never again would her ghostly picnics and merry-makings be marred by the presence of a meddling foreign devil. Without fear of unseemly interruption the bodhisattva Kuan-yin might arise once more out of a lotus-sea before the adoring gaze of a shadowy throng of winking and worshipping eunuchs. And if the spirit of the Venerable Buddha found it possible to reconcile such conduct with the character of the goddess of Love and Mercy, she might also resume her gloatings over those blind walls built by her to remind the imperial victim of her hate that his share in her fairy-palace was a prison-cell.

I wondered whether that other emperor to whom a few hours earlier I had said good-night was destined also to experience thenceforth the same death-in-life that had been the lot of his martyred predecessor ; and thinking of that dreadful possibility I found myself almost hoping that Fêng Yü-hsiang's final blow, if it was to come at all, would come quickly.

Such was China's Fifth of November—the date on which the twilight that had lingered in the Forbidden City for thirteen years at last deepened into night. English schoolboys used to be exhorted to remember that date—perhaps for inadequate reasons ; it may be that Chinese schoolboys of the future will be expected to remember it too—as a day of repentance and humiliation.

CHAPTER XXIV

The Dragon Caged

WHEN I reached home late at night on November 5th I found my domestic staff in a state of nervous tension. Wild rumours had reached them of tragic happenings in the Forbidden City, and my own prolonged absence had increased their alarm. They told me that my house had been kept under close observation by police and detectives all day long and that Chinese visitors had been turned away. Not till later did I learn that one of these visitors was a friend and well-wisher named Fu Ching-po who for some time had been seriously concerned for my personal safety and had wished to repeat his warnings of what he thought was my own imminent peril.

If any such danger had ever been more than imaginary, it was probably during the weeks that preceded the *coup d'état.* Now that the emperor's expulsion from the Forbidden City was an accomplished fact, the principal motive for the elimination of his foreign tutor (regarded as a possible obstacle to the success of the *coup*) no longer existed. But I soon had evidence that the action taken by me in invoking diplomatic intervention on behalf of the emperor had made me an object of deep resentment. On the morning of the 6th my car was stopped at prince Ch'un's gates and I was told that my entrance was strictly forbidden. I did not see the emperor again for three weeks.

At first, others besides myself were included in the prohibition. During the 6th and 7th no one was allowed in or out of the Pei Fu except a few members of the prince's family. After these two days my Chinese colleagues were admitted, and also Chêng Hsiao-hsü and Shao Ying, but the exclusion order against myself continued to be rigorously enforced. The only result of my protests (and those of the emperor himself) was that the prohibition was extended to all foreigners.

The ringleaders of the *coup d'état* regarded it as an unpardonable offence that I had extinguished their hopes of persuading the world that the action taken by them in the Forbidden City had not involved the use of force or intimidation. What they had wished the world to believe was that no compulsion, physical or moral, had been applied to the emperor, that he had left the Forbidden City of his own accord, rejoicing in his new-found freedom, and that the revised " agreement " was the result of friendly negotiation. This was the impression they tried to convey through the medium of a subsidised press (foreign as well as Chinese) and by other means ; and they had hoped not only to induce the Chinese and foreign public to accept this explanation of the affair, but also to intimidate the imperial family and their adherents into giving it at least the endorsement of silence.

This ingenious plan was thwarted at the outset by the publicity given to the protest and warning addressed to the " foreign minister," C. T. Wang, by the three European envoys. It was impossible to persuade Peking or China that the action taken by Fêng Yü-hsiang had been prompted by a benevolent interest in " the prisoner of the Forbidden City," or that the " prisoner " himself had welcomed Fêng's soldiers as liberators. The only people who believed in this version of the affair were some of Fêng's missionary friends who were jealous of their hero's reputation and extremely reluctant to modify their belief in the sincerity of his Christian principles.

One of these foreign admirers was an evangelist and revivalist of " fundamentalist " views, the Rev. Mr. Goforth. There is a story to the effect that when someone in Mr. Goforth's hearing declared that the Christian General had " gone Red," his prompt reply was " Yes, he is red—red with the blood of Jesus."[1] But shortly afterwards the Christian General, having been disastrously worsted in warfare, went on a pilgrimage to Moscow, where according to Dr. Hu Shih he spent much of his time drawing portraits of Lenin with a Chinese brush. Since that time the enthusiasm for the Christian General in missionary circles has to some extent evaporated.

The new authorities were careful to provide themselves with an alternative justification for the action taken against the emperor. It was that Fêng Yü-hsiang and his colleagues had acted just in time to save the State from a royalist restoration. As it was no longer possible, in the circumstances, to accuse

Chang Tso-lin of being the leader in this conspiracy, that rôle was assigned to his beaten rival, Wu P'ei-fu.

There is good reason to believe that Fêng Yü-hsiang and his colleagues hoped, if they did not expect, to find among the emperor's papers incriminating evidence against him, and that it was a great disappointment to them when they found nothing that could with any plausibility be described as proofs of his complicity in a plot for his restoration. Nevertheless although C. T. Wang was subsequently obliged to admit that no such evidence had been discovered, his " cabinet " at first not only allowed the story to go uncontradicted but gave it the widest publicity in their own press. One English newspaper in Peking —the bilingual *Far Eastern Times*, owned and edited by B. Lenox Simpson (better known outside China by his pen name of Putnam Weale)—was base enough to lend itself to the propagation of this lie, and there is no doubt that the endorsement by a prominent foreign journal of the false charge against the emperor not only furnished Fêng Yü-hsiang's party with an excellent excuse for their harsh treatment of his majesty and for the cancellation of the original abdication agreement but also made the emperor's position as a state-prisoner one of very grave peril. Many of the emperor's friends believed that Fêng Yü-hsiang was deterred only by fear of foreign complications from putting the young emperor on trial for his life—or rather from having him executed without trial—and nothing seemed more likely to embolden him to proceed without further hesitation to this extreme than his knowledge that responsible foreigners, who presumably had no axe to grind, were prepared to endorse Chinese allegations concerning the emperor's guilt.

The following is an example of the infamous lies deliberately disseminated by a British subject during these critical days. It appeared in the *Far Eastern Times* on November 6th, the day after the outrage had taken place.

" A monarchist plot, as great as any formulated two hundred years ago in Europe on behalf of ' Bonnie Prince Charlie ' was frustrated yesterday afternoon in Peking. Attempting to take advantage of the unsettled state of the country, several groups of Manchus and their adherents were

BBC

plotting for the return of the youthful Hsüan T'ung, as emperor—*in fact* instead of *in name only*. Final details awaited settlement, details regarding the proper costumes to be worn at the enthronement ceremonies, precedence, titles to be bestowed and other trivialities. . . . Now comes the amazing part of the stroke and possibly the inner reason. There is little doubt that Wu Pei-fu was set on a restoration had he been successful in his warfare, with himself as guardian of the Throne. Certain very curious details, which are still veiled in secrecy, go to prove that he was making dispositions in that sense."

Four days later the same newspaper added the following information.

" It is no longer disputed in Manchu circles that a high emissary was sent to Loyang before the present civil war to sound Wu Pei-fu on the subject of a Restoration. The reply given by Wu Pei-fu was considered sufficiently encouraging to report to the ex-emperor Hsüan T'ung that Wu Pei-fu was certainly favourable to the idea and that all would depend on the march of events. . . . The very careful steps taken to surround and sandbag the Palace entrances since November 1st, prior to the clearing of the Palace and the handing-over of all the imperial seals, were dictated by these considerations, the ever-present possibility of a *coup* in what is after all a Manchu city, being one which cautious men could not ignore."

The only fragment of truth in all these allegations was the fact which no well-informed person in China was ignorant of, that there were great numbers of people in all classes of society who would have welcomed the collapse of the crazy political structure that called itself a republic and the re-establishment of the only system of government that the Chinese people really understood. That neither Wu P'ei-fu nor Chang Tso-lin was a republican at heart was also true, though it will be observed that in the allegations of the *Far Eastern Times* a discreet silence was observed concerning Chang Tso-lin, whose monarchic sympathies had formerly been a subject of public comment to a much greater extent than those of his rival. But it was utterly false to say that the emperor had taken a personal part in any monarchic conspiracy. The monarchists had themselves been scrupulously careful to avoid involving him in their own schemes. As for the Nei Wu Fu, I have already explained why that body was careful to keep aloof from all political activities that might jeopardise their own interests.

The *North China Standard* voiced the common view among both foreigners and Chinese when it declared in its issue of November 11th that the report of a monarchist plot for which the *Far Eastern Times* had made itself responsible was, " as everybody knows, a swindle pure and simple." Similarly, the *Peking and Tientsin Times* of November 17th wrote as follows :

" There has been no monarchical plot in which the emperor has been in any way implicated. The alleged restoration conspiracy was a fake invented with the object of justifying a wanton outrage. Try as he may Mr. C. T. Wang can find no plausible pretext for tearing up the Abdication Treaty. And it is now obvious that the virtual imprisonment of the emperor is designed to prevent his public repudiation of the agreement forced upon him by the unscrupulous men temporarily in power of the capital."

The mention in this paragraph of the Abdication *Treaty* was not due to a careless misapprehension of the nature of the Articles of Favourable Treatment. The following remarks on this subject are taken from the same article :

" Mr. Wang scoffs at the idea that the abdication agreement can be regarded as a Treaty. Yet Marshal Tuan Ch'i-jui, whose memorial to the Throne was the decisive factor in securing abdication, is our authority for the statement that ' the People's Army ' had undertaken ' if the Throne accepts its terms, to register the latter with the Hague Tribunal.' Is it customary, we should like to ask, to register agreements which are not in the nature of treaties, at the Hague Tribunal ? Is it possible to construe this undertaking in any other way than as revealing an intention on the part of the republicans to give the abdication agreement a treaty status ? The terms of abdication themselves reveal that the intention of both parties was to enter into a binding pact, which could be altered or modified only by mutual agreement—not, as in the present case, by a handful of Bolshevik upstarts temporarily in power in Peking."

In spite of the facts which I have tried to establish, that the Articles of Favourable Treatment were drawn up by persons who were working for other purposes than the good of the emperor, and that in his endorsement of those Articles Yüan Shih-k'ai tricked both the republic and the throne, it can hardly be doubted that whether we regard the Articles as equivalent to a treaty or not, neither the republic nor the throne had the right to cancel or amend them without the willing consent of the other. I have already made it clear that the emperor, if properly approached, would gladly have consented to their amendment. *Their unilateral cancellation by an act of brute force, and by virtue of a presidential mandate extorted by an illegal cabinet from a president who was not a free agent,* cannot be defended.

The actual mandate which constituted the only authority for the act of November 5th has never, as far as I am aware been published either in English or in Chinese, and as it is worthy of preservation as a historical curiosity a copy of it which was handed to me by the comptroller of the household is here reproduced in the original Chinese.

It purports to be a mandate issued by president Ts'ao K'un, who was at the time a prisoner in his own residence and was being compelled under threats to issue all the mandates that his captors saw fit to extract from him. It states that Lu Chunglin and Chang Pi are " appointed to negotiate the amendment of the Articles of Favourable Treatment of the Ch'ing house " without any specification as to lines on which the amendment was to be carried out. There were no " negotiations " of any kind. The document embodying the " amended " Articles was prepared by the " cabinet " and taken into the Forbidden City, and the household department was merely informed that they superseded the Articles of 1912.

The mandate purports to be endorsed by the following members of the " cabinet " :
Premier : Huang Fu.

Minister for War : Li Shu-ch'êng.

Minister of Justice : Chang Yao-tsêng.

Minister of Finance
Minister for Foreign Affairs } Wang Chêng-t'ing [C. T. Wang].

Minister for Home Affairs : (blank).

Minister for the Navy : (blank).

Minister of Education
Minister of Communications } Huang Fu.

Minister for Agriculture and Commerce : (blank).

大總統指令

派鹿鍾麟張璧交涉清室優待條件修正事宜此令

中華民國十三年．十一月

國務院代行國務院總理黃郛

陸軍總長李書城

司法總長張耀曾

外交總長王正廷

財政總長王正廷

內務總長

海軍總長

教育總長黃郛

農商總長

交通總長黃郛

An interesting feature of this document is that although two ministers held five portfolios between them, no one had been found for three of the remaining portfolios.

Is it surprising that the Manchu imperial house and its friends deny the legality of this instrument and hold that the Articles of Favourable Treatment have never to this day been legally and constitutionally abolished? It is for this reason that the emperor has never abandoned his title, in spite of his former willingness to do so.

The belief of the emperor's friends that Fêng Yü-hsiang entertained sinister designs against his majesty's person was greatly strengthened by his deliberate attempts to create in Peking an attitude of hostility to the emperor. We have seen that such an attitude existed already among certain small sections of the population, especially among those members of the student-class who had fallen under extreme radical or communistic influences, but there was not, and never had been, any ill-will towards the imperial family among the Peking populace, and Fêng's attempts to stir up such ill-will were miserably ineffective. He soon discovered that so far from obtaining recognition as a national hero he had made himself the least trusted and most hated man in China. Vigorous denunciations of his betrayal of Wu P'ei-fu found their way into print and were reproduced in pamphlets and leaflets; and his cowardly treatment of the defenceless emperor checked the applause which men were undoubtedly ready to give him for his summary obliteration of the contemptible body of *chu tsai* or "Piglets" (to use the derisive Chinese epithet for their legislators) that called itself a parliament.

A western writer who certainly cannot be accused of monarchist sympathies described the popular attitude in these words :

" The arbitrary cancellation of the abdication act by the government caused widespread consternation. The impression of it was even greater than that of the stabbing in the back of marshal Wu P'ei-fu. . . . Only a few approved the action of the government—the Chinese politicians who were in lively communication with the Soviet embassy, and Dr. Sun Yat-sen."[2]

The leading foreign newspaper in north China declared that Fêng Yü-hsiang's second *coup* in Peking, like his first, was " rooted in dishonour." It constituted " one of the most un-savoury chapters in the whole chequered history of the so-called Chinese republic."[3]

The leading Shanghai newspaper was equally emphatic. After condemning the *coup* it referred to the " flimsy tale " of a restoration plot ; and it adds that although there was no plot it could not be denied that sympathy with the monarchic idea was " becoming more vocal with China's sorry display of pseudo-republicanism." That sympathy, it said, would not be silenced by the action taken against the Manchu house ; " for it has developed, not at the instance of monarchical plotters and schemers, but as a reaction against a political experiment which instead of a republican authority has produced so far only com-petition among a congeries of military cliques. Many Chinese are coming to believe in monarchy for no better reason than they believe in bridles for undisciplined horses."[4]

Among the views expressed by responsible leaders of Chinese political opinion, none were more significant and important than those of T'ang Shao-yi, who as we know had taken a prominent part in the negotiations that led to the abdication of the emperor and the drawing-up of the Articles of Favourable Treatment. He declared in an interview that " if China wants to change the relations between the republic and the Ch'ing emperor, we must do it in a fair and gentlemanly way." " We agreed," he said, " to the Articles because, by abdicating, the Manchus made it unnecessary to prolong the period of the revolution, saved human life and gave us an opportunity to settle down to reconstruction. Wang Ching-wei, an ardent revolutionist, was the most earnest pleader for concessions to the house of Ch'ing[5]. . . . No matter what our personal opinions may have been, we, the representa-tives of the Chinese people, entered into a solemn agreement with the Ch'ing emperor by which we have to abide until a new arrangement is made. . . . But perhaps general Fêng is no longer conscious of the ethical foundations of the Chinese race. . . . This is not a political question ; it is a moral question. This is not a matter of the form of government for China ; it is a ques-tion whether there is any sense of decency left in the land. . . .

You can tell all the foreigners, through your newspaper, that the events which are happening in these days are not examples of China's attitude towards political and ethical problems. We are faced by an ugly situation, but the ethical character of the Chinese people will reassert itself as it has always done in the face of even uglier situations."[6]

The views of Dr. Hu Shih, one of the intellectual leaders of Young China, were of a similar character. In an open letter to Dr. C. T. Wang he insisted that the abdication agreement could only be revised or abrogated by mutual agreement and through peaceful channels, and that the methods adopted by Huang Fu's " cabinet " and Fêng Yü-hsiang would go down to history as " the most unsavoury act of the Chinese republic."

It is not unnatural that some of the most powerful protests came from representatives of the Mongol and Manchu princes, inasmuch as they, like the Manchu imperial house, held rights and privileges under agreements or guarantees similar to the Articles of Favourable Treatment.[7] They were quick to perceive that if the latter could be unilaterally abrogated by the republic, their own rights also might at any time be taken from them by a republican mandate. The Mongols and Tibetans had not taken part in the revolution and had had no desire to overthrow the Manchu dynasty ; apart therefore from all questions of their own interests they regarded the abrogation of the Articles of Favourable Treatment of the Manchu house with the strongest disapproval.

It was mentioned in the last chapter that one of the members of Ts'ao K'un's cabinet who fled for sanctuary to the Legation Quarter was Dr. Wellington Koo. The mere fact that C. T. Wang was a prominent member of the new " government " was sufficient to account for Dr. Koo's sudden disappearance from the political world of Peking, for the two had long been known to be keen rivals if not enemies, and the rise of one of them to cabinet rank almost inevitably involved the eclipse of the other. They were two stars which could not shine in the same firmament. My own acquaintance with Dr. Koo was slight, but in the middle of November we were both denounced in Wang-Fêng circles as colleagues in evil doing.

On the 15th of that month a Chinese newspaper called the

Shih Chieh Wan Pao (" The World's Evening News ") came out
with an announcement that the source of the numerous false
rumours which were creating unrest in the capital had been
traced to two villains—Dr. Wellington Koo and myself—to
" a certain English newspaper," and to " a certain English news
agency." Recent events, it was said, had destroyed Dr. Koo's
" rice-bowl "—the ministry of Foreign Affairs—and had given
great dissatisfaction to Chuang Shih-tun [Johnston], the English
tutor of " P'u-Yi " ; these two had therefore put their heads
together with a view to upsetting the newly-established régime
and were daily holding secret meetings in " a certain room " in
the Wagons-Lits Hotel (in the Legation Quarter) and concocting
plots in collaboration with representatives of the *Peking and
Tientsin Times* and of the unnamed English news agency. The
two latter, it was stated, had been heavily bribed by provincial
governor Ch'i Hsieh-yüan, the ally of Wu P'ei-fu. I need hardly
say that the " secret meetings " in question were as mythical
as the daughter whom I was accused of having taken into the
Forbidden City.

I have reason to believe that the first authentic account of
Fêng's seizure of the palace and expulsion of the emperor reached
Chang Tso-lin in Manchuria through British channels. It produced an effect which caused an English eye-witness to remark
that although he had often seen Chang Tso-lin in a bad temper
he had never seen such an explosion of wrath as that which
convulsed the warlord on that memorable occasion. He did not,
of course, object to Fêng's seizure of Peking or to the betrayal
of Wu P'ei-fu. To that betrayal Chang owed his own triumph,
and he was undoubtedly an accomplice. But in seizing the Forbidden City and tearing up the abdication agreement Fêng and
his colleagues had acted on their own initiative and without
consulting him. This would have been an unpardonable offence,
even if he had approved of their action in principle, which he
did not. Whatever gratitude he may have felt for Fêng's oppor-
tune betrayal of Wu P'ei-fu was swallowed up in his indignation
against the violator of the sanctities of the Forbidden City.
Certain Chinese cynics subsequently declared in my hearing that
his wrath may have been partly due to his belief that the violator
of the imperial sanctities was also likely to be the plunderer of

the imperial treasure-vaults. Chang Tso-lin probably felt, indeed, that if the treasures of the Forbidden City had to pass out of imperial custody, he himself would make quite as suitable a custodian of them as anyone else ; yet later events showed that he still retained some regard for the safety and welfare of the emperor, and that his indignation against Fêng Yü-hsiang for his brutal treatment of their fallen sovereign was at least to some extent genuine.

It will perhaps never be known to what extent Fêng Yü-hsiang and his confederates were prompted to act as they did by the knowledge that they had powerful friends in Communist circles. A grim story was told in the Legation Quarter to the effect that when a certain prominent Communist was asked what he thought of the expulsion of the emperor from the Forbidden City, he replied with a sinister smile, " Why is the line drawn there ? We in Russia know how to deal with emperors." It is to be hoped that this anecdote is apocryphal.

It was not till nearly six years later that I was given an astonishing piece of information which as far as I am aware never reached the ears of the foreign diplomats. My informant was a Chinese official who had himself been a minor member of the little group of politicians and militarists who made themselves masters of Peking towards the close of 1924.

If the information given me by this official was correct, the authors of the *coup d'état* were not satisfied with unseating the president of the republic, abolishing parliamentary government (such as it was), expelling the emperor from the Forbidden City and annulling the abdication agreement, but seriously considered and discussed a further proposal to crown their achievements by a forcible occupation of the Legation Quarter. This portion of the " Tartar " city of Peking had been under the exclusive military and administrative control of the foreign Powers represented in China ever since the siege of the Legations by the Boxers in 1900. As the right of such control had been conceded by treaty, it is inconceivable that the interested Powers could have tamely acquiesced in the unilateral abrogation of such right. Moreover, any attempt by Fêng-Yü-hsiang to carry out a military occupation of the Quarter would certainly have been resisted by the various Legation Guards, and an

armed clash between foreign and Chinese troops would necessarily have had consequences of a very far-reaching and disastrous kind for China. Presumably this probability was not overlooked by the more level-headed members of the Huang Fu
" cabinet." At any rate, fortunately for China, the project was
abandoned or postponed.

One of the ugliest features of the molestation of the imperial
family in the Forbidden City, especially from the point of view
of the traditional social code of China, was that it took place at
a time of mourning, while the funeral ceremonies of the dowager-
consort Tuan K'ang were actually in progress. Her death had
indeed come at an embarrassing moment for the conspirators, if
only because the two surviving consorts flatly refused to leave
the Forbidden City with the emperor and empress, and gave it
as one of their principal reasons for refusal that they had ceremonial duties to carry out in connection with the obsequies of
the deceased *t'ai fei*. These two ladies refused to be intimidated
by the threats of personal violence that reached them through
their terrified eunuchs, and when warned that if they did not
go of their own accord they would be expelled by force, they
declared they would prefer to die by their own hands.'

The suicide of the old ladies would undoubtedly have intensified the detestation which Fêng's treatment of the imperial
household aroused in Peking and elsewhere, and would almost
certainly have had unpleasant consequences for himself and the
members of the Huang Fu " cabinet." That they were quick to
realise this was shown in a very significant way. Lu Chung-lin—
Fêng's second in command—was deputed to visit the emperor
and persuade him to use his personal influence with the dowagers
to make them leave the palace voluntarily and without unnecessary fuss. The emperor not unnaturally felt himself under no
special obligation to help the " Christian general " out of an
awkward predicament ; but he knew that if he took no action
in the matter, and the two old ladies carried out their threat of
suicide, his enemies would undoubtedly try to throw on him
the responsibility for their death. So after stipulating that they
should be allowed to remain where they were till after Tuan
K'ang's funeral, he finally consented to persuade them to leave
the Forbidden City.

The funeral ceremonies in the palace ended on November 19th, and on the afternoon of that day a modest little procession, shorn of all imperial splendour, escorted the coffin of Tuan K'ang out of the Gate of Spiritual Valour to a temple near the Drum Tower in which it found a temporary resting-place pending its final removal to the imperial mausolea.

Two days later the two surviving dowagers passed through the same gateway of the Forbidden City for the last time. A little band of more or less faithful eunuchs accompanied them to their new home in the eastern part of the Tartar city. Perhaps only those eunuchs could give an adequate account of the mental sufferings which the two old ladies had endured since the tranquillity and seclusion of their palaces in the Forbidden City had been shattered. They themselves never spoke of their experiences except to members of the imperial family and household, and their lips are now closed for ever.

Though the betrayal of Wu P'ei-fu and the dispersal of his forces made it an easy matter for Chang Tso-lin to walk into Peking, he was in no hurry to meet the man who had turned possible defeat into overwhelming victory. He came as far as Tientsin and there he remained for over a fortnight. During that time Fêng, very reluctantly, paid him a visit. The two warlords took a dislike to one another which neither attempted to conceal. According to the stories which reached Peking, they had a violent quarrel at their first interview, the main cause of the quarrel being the episode of the Forbidden City. However this may be, there is no doubt that the " Christian general " was given a thoroughly uncomfortable reception at Tientsin. It was not only with Chang Tso-lin that his relations were strained. He was also received very coldly by Tuan Ch'i-jui, who was Chang Tso-lin's nominee for the presidential vacancy. Tuan had already publicly expressed his strong disapproval of the arbitrary cancellation of the Articles of Favourable Treatment. His opinion of Fêng's *coup* against the emperor carried great weight in influential republican circles, if only because it was he who had been the " saviour of the republic " in 1917, when Chang Hsün carried out the short-lived imperial restoration, and he had earned a right to be consulted before any revision of the abdication settlement was effected. At that time Tuan

Ch'i-jui had it in his power to abrogate that settlement and to deprive the emperor of his privileges, and for reasons which were generally regarded, outside Kuomintang circles, as entirely valid and just, he had refrained from doing so. It is not surprising that Tuan was indignant with Fêng for having had the effrontery to take drastic action in a matter in which he had earned no right to interfere.

Fêng Yü-hsiang returned to Peking in a thoroughly bad temper and announced that he was about to resign his military command and go into retirement. Chinese military (and civil) leaders are fond of talking about resignations which they have no serious intention of carrying into effect. The question people asked was not why Fêng was resigning but at whom or at what would he aim his next blow.

Meanwhile it came to be known in Peking that Chang Tso-lin and Tuan Ch'i-jui were about to arrive in the capital and that Tuan would be the head—real or nominal—of the new government. There was much speculation as to whether this would mean the disappearance of the Huang Fu " cabinet," which, as we know, had put itself into office by virtue of a bogus mandate extracted from a captive president. Speculation was soon set at rest. No sooner had the two marshals arrived in Peking from Tientsin than the Huang Fu " cabinet " passed out of existence.

With the constitution of the new ministry we are not concerned, but a very significant fact was that Tuan Ch'i-jui, who had long been a warm friend and admirer of Chêng Hsiao-hsü, made a strong effort to persuade that loyal servant of the emperor to enter the new government. As a member of the cabinet Chêng Hsiao-hsü would have been in a position to protect the interests of the emperor, and for this reason it was naturally hoped that he would accept the appointment. But without a moment's hesitation he refused it. Tuan then tried to force his hand by causing him to be gazetted to a cabinet post as minister of the Interior, but even this move was unsuccessful. Chêng Hsiao-hsü had never taken office under the republic and never would. He could not serve two masters.

CHAPTER XXV

The Flight of the Dragon

TUAN CH'I-JUI entered Peking on November 22nd, 1924, and Chang Tso-lin followed on the 23rd. The former brought no troops, the latter only a bodyguard. On the 24th, Tuan Ch'i-jui assumed office under the title of *Chih Chêng*—" Chief Executive." The assumption of this title, instead of that of *Ta Tsung T'ung* (" President ") was due to the fact that as Parliament had ceased to exist there was no constitutional means of holding a presidential election. *Chih Chêng* implies a temporary and provisional régime, and it was as provisional head of the government that Tuan Ch'i-jui took office.

On the next day the Chinese and foreign newspapers contained the following announcement:

" Yesterday Marshal Tuan Ch'i-jui assumed the post of provisional chief executive. One of his first acts was to remove the restrictions over the Manchu emperor which have caused such an outcry and to inform Mr. R. F. Johnston, his tutor, that he could visit him."

This was followed by a further statement to the effect that " by order of marshal Tuan Ch'i-jui, Fêng Yü-hsiang's men were withdrawn from prince Ch'un's palace yesterday and replaced by guards provided by the headquarters of the metropolitan police."

Another more curious item of information given to the public at the same time was that Chang Tso-lin on arrival at Peking had refused to see any of the members of the Manchu imperial house but that " he was interested in the work of the emperor's foreign tutor " and would probably see him.

All these published statements were true. I received an official intimation from the chief executive's office that I was free to visit the emperor, and almost simultaneously a messenger from the emperor brought me the happy intelligence that Fêng Yü-hsiang's soldiers had indeed disappeared from the Pei Fu and that my presence was desired immediately.

I drove to the Pei Fu and was admitted at once. The emperor was awaiting me in the courtyard of his quarters. He grasped my hand and for some moments did not speak. Then he led me into a private room where we had a long talk which need not be recorded. While we were conversing, a private message was brought to me direct from marshal Chang Tso-lin, requesting me to visit him that evening as soon as possible after dark. I sent back an oral message saying that I would do so. I spent the rest of the daylight in the emperor's company, and before I left him he gave me a signed photograph of himself to present to Chang Tso-lin together with a topaz ring set with diamonds.

By six o'clock it was dark, and I drove to the marshal's head-quarters in the west of the city. My only companion was prince Ch'un's steward, a man named Chang Wên-chih, an old friend of the marshal's and a namesake, but not a relative. On arrival we passed through a series of courtyards occupied by the marshal's armed bodyguard. He received us in a friendly and informal way (he was in Chinese civilian dress) and after a few minutes' conventional conversation in the presence of members of his staff he asked us to accompany him to a small private study. During the hour's talk that followed, the door remained closed. Not even the usual tea-attendants entered the room.

I handed the emperor's presents to the marshal. He took the photograph, looked at it long and thoughtfully, and after a glance at the ring, handed it back to me. He accepted the photo-graph but not the ring.

He then explained in some detail that he regarded the action taken against the emperor by Fêng Yü-hsiang and his colleagues as infamous. He wished to help the emperor and to undo the evil that had been done, but said it was essential that he should take no action that might give rise to the suspicion, in republican circles, that he was aiming at the restoration of the monarchy. He then proceeded to unfold a plan whereby the emperor might be reinstated in his privileges without any colour being given to the notion that his reinstatement was due to Manchurian support. Of this plan I cannot here give details ;

it must suffice to say that he wished the initial steps to be taken by Mongols, Manchus, and by those Chinese who desired, either from loyalty or from their regard for the national honour, that there should be no unilateral cancellation or amendment of the Articles of Favourable Treatment. In order that his plan might be effective, it was desirable that certain information should be conveyed to the diplomatic body ; and it turned out that his main object in discussing the matter with me was that he wished me to be the bearer of this information to the ministers of friendly Powers.

I agreed to do as he wished, whereupon he asked me to pay him another visit in a few days' time and inform him of the result of my action in the Legation Quarter.

When the interview was over, Chang Wên-chih returned to make his report to the emperor and to prince Ch'un, and I went home to prepare a memorandum of the interview for the information of the foreign diplomats. I made three copies and handed them personally that night to the three who had acted so promptly on the emperor's behalf on November 5th—the ministers for Great Britain, Japan and the Netherlands. The Dutch minister was the doyen of the diplomatic body and was in a position, if he thought fit, to communicate the contents of my memorandum to the rest of his diplomatic colleagues. Whether he did so or not I am unable to say, and what followed the presentation of my memorandum is not a matter which I feel at liberty to discuss.

For a brief period all went well. I paid daily visits to the emperor, who had borne the dangers and anxieties of the preceding three weeks with courage and dignity. He was naturally disgusted at the manner in which he had been treated and the insults to which he had been subjected, but he was happy in the belief that Fêng Yü-hsiang and C. T. Wang and their confederates had not spoken truly when they declared themselves to be the representatives and spokesmen of the people of China. It also consoled and gratified him to learn from me how outspoken and practically unanimous (apart from Lenox-Simpson's subsidised paper) had been the condemnation of their action by the foreign press.

But in two or three days the skies began to cloud again. Strange rumours began to be current about the possibility of another *coup d'état* in the immediate future. Fêng Yü-hsiang had been sulking ever since his return from Tientsin. He had talked about resigning and had retired to a Buddhist temple in the Western Hills where he would see none but his most intimate associates. But no one believed that he was sincere when he talked of resignation. That he had " lost face " was obvious to the world. The forced withdrawal of his armed guard over his imperial prisoner was one of several proofs that this was so. It was common knowledge that Chang Tso-lin, in spite of the fact that he owed his victory in the civil war entirely to the Christian general's betrayal of Wu P'ei-fu, hated and despised him. The " alliance " between them, such as it was, could not be a lasting one. Sooner or later, the two " allies " would be at war.

No one realised this more clearly than Fêng Yü-hsiang himself. But Fêng had already declared himself to be a man of peace. War, therefore, must at all costs be avoided. How was it to be done ? There was only one practicable method and it seemed almost ridiculously easy. Fêng was still in military control of the Peking area. Chang Tso-lin had only a bodyguard. What could be simpler than to surround and disarm the bodyguard and invite the marshal to a tea-party in his own headquarters, to be followed by a walk in one of the interior courtyards—a walk which would terminate in a little accident which would eliminate the marshal for ever from the battlefield of Chinese politics ?

That the Christian general was meditating some such masterstroke as this may or may not be true : certainly it was believed to be true by some of the emperor's friends who, as I knew from experience, were in touch with much more trustworthy sources of information than were accessible to the chancelleries of the foreign Legations. When I mentioned in the Legation Quarter some of the rumours I had heard I was regarded as a scaremonger. When I told my British friends that marshal Chang might at any moment disappear from view, either through some mysterious " accident " or by a hurried journey by train or car to Tientsin, I was assured that the political waters of Peking
Ccc

were unruffled and that the marshal had accepted an invitation to dine at the British Legation in ten days' time—which was, of course, proof positive that he had no intention of leaving Peking.

Chang Tso-lin had many remarkable qualities, good as well as bad. One of his characteristics, which perhaps contains the secret of his remarkable rise from the status of a bandit to that of supreme rulership over a region as large as France and Germany combined, was that he had boundless confidence in himself. A much more dangerous peculiarity was that he was apt to hold his rivals in contempt. The haughty disdain which he felt and often expressed for Wu P'ei-fu nearly brought his dazzling career to a disastrous close. His refusal, for several days, to pay serious attention to repeated warnings concerning the sinister designs of Fêng Yü-hsiang, seemed likely to prove fatal. It was not that he believed in Fêng's honesty and good faith : on the contrary, as I had learned from his own lips, he regarded him as capable of any treachery. But he could not, until confronted by convincing evidence, bring himself to believe that the contemptible Fêng would dare to raise his hand against him, the triumphant warlord of Manchuria.

The emperor's friends did not share the marshal's optimism, and I found them increasingly anxious about immediate prospects. Several times we discussed the question as to whether, now that the emperor was no longer a prisoner, he should not take the opportunity—an opportunity which might be lost for ever at any moment—to leave his father's residence and take refuge in the Legation Quarter. Each discussion, however, ended in the unanimous agreement among the princes, tutors and officers of the Nei Wu Fu that in view of what had already been done for the emperor by Tuan Ch'i-jui and Chang Tso-lin his departure to the Legation Quarter would be strongly resented by them, as it would imply that he had no belief in the stability of their régime or no faith in their good intentions.

On November 28th Chêng Hsiao-hsü and Ch'ên Pao-shên came to my house for a consultation. They were becoming seriously alarmed at the news they were getting from sources that they believed to be trustworthy, and told me they had communicated their fears to the emperor who had instructed them to consider the question of finding him a new place of residence, as near as possible to the Legation Quarter. By this time the rumours that a new *coup d'état* was expected in Peking had reached the foreign newspapers, though the Chinese press —not through ignorance of the rumours—said nothing about them. I pointed out that the foreign Legations still seemed to be blissfully ignorant of any impending trouble, but this did not reassure them. We finally agreed that the risk of offending the chief executive and the marshal must be faced, and that when we met on the following morning we would do what might be necessary to remove the emperor to a safer place than his father's residence. The place we had in view was a large empty dwelling-house in a street called Soochow Hutung near the Hatamen city gate which is close to the eastern entrance to the Legation Quarter. The Nei Wu Fu had already begun negotiating for the lease of this house to be used as offices for their own department.

When I arrived at the Pei Fu on the following morning, November 29th, Chêng Hsiao-hsü had not arrived but Ch'ên Pao-shên was anxiously awaiting me and told me that according to his latest information Fêng Yü-hsiang was reinforcing his troops in the city and had suddenly summoned some of his senior officers to a conference at his temple in the Western Hills. At any moment he might send an armed guard of his own men back to the Pei Fu, from which Tuan Ch'i-jui and Chang Tso-lin had compelled him to withdraw them, and in that case the emperor's last hope of escape would have vanished. Even now it might be too late, as Fêng Yü-hsiang had troops in every part of the city. I agreed with him that there must be no further delay and that the attempt must be made at once. He proposed that we should first tell " wang yeh " (prince Ch'un) what we intended to do. I strongly disapproved of this suggestion on the ground that the prince, from fear of the possible consequences to himself of the emperor's escape, might refuse to let him go. Ch'ên Pao-shên admitted the justice of my remark and gave way.

We then went to the emperor's room and told him that the times were dangerous and that we had decided that he should go forthwith to the Legation Quarter and place himself under the protection of one of the foreign ministers. His immediate reply was that he was in our hands and would do what we thought best. I stressed the extreme importance of not saying a word about

our plans to any one else in the Pei Fu : not even to the empress
or to his father. The empress could follow later. If she accompanied us, her presence in the car would certainly attract attention and we might be stopped. He followed our advice.
In order to avoid arousing any suspicion as to our intentions,
the emperor made no preparations for his departure and packed
nothing, but he handed me a bundle of pearls and other jewels
which I thrust into the recesses of my fur coat. We did not order
his car—which fortunately had no distinguishing mark—until we
were already in the front courtyard, ready to start. Just as the
emperor was stepping into the car prince Ch'un's steward,
Chang Wên-chih, suddenly appeared from the house and asked
where we were going. Ch'ên Pao-shên replied that we were going
for a short drive. Chang Wên-chih seemed surprised and suspicious and asked if he might accompany us. No objection was
raised to this proposal. As the emperor took his seat he invited
me to sit beside him and give whatever directions might be
necessary to the chauffeur—who, as it fortunately happened, was
one of the emperor's very loyal servants. Another servant—a
young Manchu boy—was ordered to mount the car and sit in
front beside the chauffeur. Ch'ên Pao-shên sent home his own
horse carriage, telling the coachman that we were going to
Soochow Hutung. He then took his seat in my car, in which he
was joined by Chang Wên-chih.
The main gate was opened and the two cars passed through it
to the public road. A guard of police was stationed at the gate
and it remained to be seen whether they would interfere with us.
Evidently they had no instructions to do so, but two armed
constables jumped on the running-boards of the emperor's car
and accompanied us on our journey.
My object now was to avoid all the main streets in which it
was likely that we might meet Fêng Yü-hsiang's soldiers. More
especially was it advisable to avoid the great central thorough-
fare that leads through the Hou-Mên past Prospect Hill and the
Forbidden City. Before leaving the prince's courtyard I had
already told the chauffeur to drive through the eastern section
of the city as we intended to inspect the house in Soochow
Hutung which the Nei Wu Fu proposed to lease. Ch'ên Pao-
shên had already sent a secret message to Chêng Hsiao-hsü, who

had not yet arrived, telling him that we were about to make an attempt to take his majesty to the Legation Quarter and hoped to lodge him temporarily in the German hospital there.

Our route was a tortuous one—I made the chauffeur change his direction twice in order to avoid meeting two detachments of Fêng Yü-hsiang's troops—and what ought to have been a drive of not much more than three miles was one of nearly five. But we were fortunate and the drive was uneventful. The elements were favourable to us, for there was a strong wind and the air was hazy with dust. When we had reached Hatamen Street, with Soochow Hutung on the east side and the Legation Quarter on the west, I suddenly told the chauffeur not to go at once to Soochow Hutung but to turn to the right (the west) and go on till we arrived at a certain photographer's shop (kept by a German named Hartung) where his majesty wished to inspect a few photographs of which I had spoken to him.

" I know the shop," said the chauffeur ; " it is in the Legation Quarter." " It may be," I replied ; " go straight on till you come to it, then stop." The two armed constables, to my great relief, said nothing.

Another two minutes, and we had passed through the eastern entrance of the Legation Quarter and had stopped in front of the photographer's shop. We dismounted from the car and walked in. We looked at and purchased a few photographs, and while we were doing this I committed a slight blunder which fortunately was now of no great consequence. From force of habit I addressed the emperor by his imperial title—*huang shang*. The Chinese in the shop looked up startled, and one of them ran into the street. By the time we left the shop we found a crowd of Chinese awaiting us : but they were merely inquisitive, silent and harmless. They were gazing upon their former emperor for the first time.

My own car had followed us all the way, and I was amused to observe the quiet and contented look on the face of my venerable colleague, Ch'ên Pao-shên, and the bewildered expression on that of his companion. " Why have we come here ? " he demanded excitedly. " Why did we not go to Soochow Hutung ? "

I paid no attention to Chang Wên-chih but turned to the emperor. " Dr. Dipper," I said, " is quite close by. Let us go and

see him." Dr. Dipper, it should be explained, was a well-known
German doctor who during the preceding year or two had frequently been summoned to the Forbidden City. His consulting-
room was in the German hospital, well within the Legation
Quarter and only a minute's drive from where we were standing.

We resumed our places in the car and drove to the hospital.
We alighted and went in, and I sent my card to Dr. Dipper, requesting an interview as soon as possible. He came out of his
room and recognised the emperor. I asked him to take us at
once to a private room as I had something important to say. He
took us upstairs to an empty ward.

I told him briefly what had happened and what we proposed
to do. "Meanwhile," I said, "I am going to interview the
foreign ministers. I leave the emperor in your charge. Please
see that he is well protected."

I took out the bundle of pearls and jewels which the emperor
had entrusted to me and handed it to him. Then I left him in the
company of Ch'ên Pao-shên. Chang Wên-chih had not accompanied us upstairs. Speechless with amazement or indignation or
both he had hurried away by himself, to report the startling
events of the morning to an equally horrified and amazed
prince Ch'un.

I went first to the Japanese Legation. I did so because I felt
that of all the foreign ministers the Japanese minister was the one
who was most likely to be both able and (I hoped) willing not
only to receive the emperor but also to give him effectual protection.

By this time it was about one o'clock. The Japanese minister
was not at home. He was lunching out. I then went to the
Netherlands Legation. The Dutch minister, also, was out.
Finally I visited the British Legation. Sir Ronald Macleay was
at home. I told him briefly what had happened. Knowing as I did
that the British Legation attitude was strongly hostile to any
action on the part of a British subject which might be construed as interference in Chinese internal politics I referred as
lightly as possible to my own share in the emperor's escape, and
merely remarked that acting on the emperor's instructions I had
driven with him into the Legation Quarter.

I went on to say that I had already called at the Japanese

Legation, as it was my opinion that if Mr. Yoshizawa would consent to give him protection he could not be in better hands. The minister agreed, and was considerate enough to add that if matters were arranged in the manner proposed he would expect me to become his guest at the British Legation in order that I might be as near as possible to the emperor. The two Legations are almost face to face.

I went back to the Japanese Legation but the minister had not yet returned, and it was nearly three o'clock by the time my interview with him took place. He listened to what I had to say, and when I begged him to extend to the emperor the hospitality of his Legation he did not answer immediately. He walked up and down the room considering the matter and then gave me his decision. He would receive the emperor, but wished to arrange suitable accommodation for him and therefore asked me to return to the German hospital and await a message. I discovered later on that the " suitable accommodation " which Mr. Yoshizawa and his wife prepared for the emperor was their own private apartments—the best rooms that the Legation contained.

I returned joyfully to the German hospital and found that a member of the Nei Wu Fu—T'ung Chi-hsü—had just arrived. He was one of the few members of that body who were sincerely loyal to the emperor and he was the first to follow him to the Legation Quarter. He asked me where his majesty was and I took him upstairs. On the way we met a German male nurse, who asked where we were going. " To see the emperor," I said. " What emperor ? " he said, " there is no emperor here." " Nonsense," I said, " I brought him here myself ! "

He looked at me and seemed slightly reassured. " The emperor was here," he said, " but he has gone."

T'ung Chi-hsü and I looked blankly at the man. " Where has he gone ? " I demanded.

" I haven't the faintest idea," was the prompt reply.

" But I have just made arrangements for him to go to the Japanese Legation," I exclaimed in bewilderment.

" That is precisely where he has gone ! " answered the honest fellow.

This was reassuring, but I was still puzzled. Where was Dr.

Dipper? " He has gone home," said the nurse, " and he told me that if any strangers came and asked for the emperor I was to say we had no emperor here."

I congratulated the man on the way he had answered me and hurried back to the Japanese Legation with T'ung Chi-hsü. There we found the emperor not in the minister's house but in the quarters of Colonel Takemoto, the commandant of the Japanese Legation Guard. Chêng Hsiao-hsü and Ch'ên Pao-shên were both with him. There was no sign of the minister.

The mystery was soon solved. It appeared that Chang Hsiao-hsü on going to the Pei Fu that morning had met Ch'ên Pao-shên's carriage coming away. The coachman told him that his master had gone with the emperor and myself in two motor-cars to Soochow Hutung. Chêng Hsiao-hsü had driven there at once in his own carriage and had found no trace of us. He then went on to the German hospital where to his profound relief he found the emperor in safety.

He was most anxious, however, that the emperor should be sheltered in one of the Legations as soon as possible, and as he was personally acquainted with Colonel Takemoto, who had already expressed his sympathy with the emperor in his misfortunes and his strong desire to help him, Chêng Hsiao-hsü suggested that as a temporary measure the emperor should accept Colonel Takemoto's hospitality. The emperor agreed, and Chêng Hsiao-hsü paid a preliminary visit to the commandant's quarters just at the time when I was in the minister's own library. The commandant agreed to receive the emperor, and gave Chêng Hsiao-hsü the impression that he would report the matter at once to his minister, which, however, he did not do.

Chêng Hsiao-hsü then returned to the hospital and brought the emperor to the Japanese Legation in his own carriage. Inadvertently or through ignorance of the precise limits of the Legation Quarter the coachman drove the carriage along the Ch'ang-an street, that is to say for a few dozen yards outside the Legation Quarter. Fortunately the dust-laden wind which had been favourable to us had by this time developed into a dust-storm, and this helped to conceal the carriage and its occupants from the public view. In a few minutes the carriage turned south again into the Legation Quarter and along the side of the creek

that separates the British from the Italian and Japanese Legations. The Japanese commandant was awaiting them at the gate
of the Japanese Legation, and they had not been long in his
quarters when I joined them. It was only after their arrival
that the commandant had communicated with his minister ; and
it was after my own arrival that Mr. Yoshizawa opened the door,
walked in, and greeted the illustrious visitor who was destined
to be his guest for months to come.

Within an hour the emperor was resting in the comfortable
rooms assigned to him in the minister's house ; and before night-
fall he was sitting in an equally comfortable reception room
listening to alternate reproaches and congratulations from a
nervous and excited father, distracted Manchu nobles and a
chattering crowd of Nei Wu Fu officials. Prince Ch'un's contribution to the discussion was a pressing invitation to his son to
return to the Pei Fu—an invitation which was politely declined.

The escape of the emperor produced a sensation in Peking
only less than that caused by his expulsion from the Forbidden
City. Various accounts of it appeared in the press, but being
based on inadequate information and mostly on rumours they
were all inaccurate. The Japanese minister was of course loaded
with abuse, though in an interview which was reported in the
Peking newspapers of December 2nd he gave a straightforward
and entirely truthful account of how he had come to be the
emperor's host. The most abusive of the newspapers, which
included myself among the main objects of their attack, were the
Ching Pao, generally understood in Peking to have influential
Communist support, and the Ch'ên Pao, which was regarded as
the organ of the students.

The two police who had entered the Legation Quarter on the
running boards of the emperor's car did not dare to return to
their duty, as they expected to be held responsible for not having
stopped the car while it was still within Chinese jurisdiction.
They begged to be allowed to remain in the Legation Quarter
(which, it will be remembered, was wholly under foreign control),
and their petition was granted. Nominally and temporarily they
became members of the emperor's suite. The police guard had
had no orders to prevent the emperor from leaving the Pei Fu
and could not reasonably be held responsible for what had

happened ; but they felt a very reasonable dread of the punishment that might befall them if Fêng Yü-hsiang resumed full
control of Peking. Thus when the empress attempted next day
to join the emperor, her car was stopped at the outer gate and
she was politely informed that she must remain where she was.

The emperor received from her a piteous little note which he
showed me, imploring him to devise means of rescuing her.
The matter was mentioned to Mr. Yoshizawa, who took prompt
action. He sent one of his diplomatic secretaries (Mr. Ch'ih Pu)
to the Pei Fu with orders to bring the empress back to the
Legation and *not to return without her*. In a short time the secretary telephoned from the Pei Fu saying that the empress was
ready and anxious to accompany him but was not allowed to
leave.

Without a moment's loss of time Mr. Yoshizawa ordered his
car, visited the chief executive Tuan Ch'i-jui, and requested
politely but firmly that immediate instructions be issued to the
guard at the Pei Fu that no restrictions of any kind were to be
placed on the empress's movements. Within an hour Mr. Ch'ih
Pu returned to the Legation in triumph, bringing the empress
with him.

On the night of the 30th November I decided to pay my
second visit to Chang Tso-lin, partly to fulfil my promise to
return and report the result of the action I had taken at his
request in the Legation Quarter and partly to convey a message
from the emperor explaining as tactfully as possible why he had
taken refuge in a foreign Legation.

The Chang Tso-lin whom I encountered on this occasion was
a very different person from the Chang Tso-lin of a few days
earlier. I found myself confronted not by a suave, sympathetic
and courteous Chinese gentleman but by a Manchurian bandit,
arrogant, ill-mannered and tempestuous. To what extent his
attitude was simulated it is difficult to say ; but it was noteworthy that on this occasion he received me not in a private room
but in a hall with three open doors at each of which stood interested listeners. It seemed obvious that this time he wished to
make no secret of what he had to say.

Without any of the usual conventional preliminaries he
plunged at once into a vehement denunciation of myself for

having brought the emperor into the Legation Quarter. From what he said I gathered that the Pei Fu had been careful to put the whole responsibility for the incident upon my shoulders. I attempted a few words of explanation, but it was obviously difficult to justify my action without touching upon the very delicate subject of the insecurity of Chang Tso-lin's own position. This I could hardly do in the presence of others. The warlord interrupted me by asking what harm could possibly have befallen the emperor at the Pei Fu so long as he, Chang Tso-lin, was in Peking ; and it was hardly possible for me to reply, except in a very guarded way, that it was precisely because I believed that he would not be in Peking long that I had considered it urgently necessary to withdraw the emperor from danger before he left.

On the subject of our earlier conversation Chang Tso-lin refused to say a word or to hear a word from me. He brought the interview to a sudden conclusion and left the room abruptly without any of the customary words of farewell.

Whether Chang Tso-lin had already realised, at the time of this interview, that his own position was becoming dangerous and that he might have to follow the emperor's example, it is difficult to say. If he had not realised it then he did so in a very few days. Very early on a cold December morning my servant entered my room at the British Legation (where I was then a guest) and gave me the latest news. Chang Tso-lin had left Peking by his own special train in the grey dawn that morning. The capital was once more under the undisputed military control of Fêng Yü-hsiang.

In the circumstances it is not surprising that the details of the plot that the Christian general had been hatching against Chang Tso-lin have never been fully disclosed. Possibly not more than half a dozen men were entrusted with those details, and in view of the Manchurian marshal's escape, to be followed before long by a war between Fêng and Chang which resulted in the former's defeat, it is not likely that the sharers in Fêng's secret would be eager to confess their own participation in a plot that had miscarried. Yet scraps of information have appeared from time to time in the Chinese press and also in at least one little book—not as well known as it should be—which

has been written in English by a Chinese writer. I refer to
Chi-Hung Lynn's *Political Parties in China*.[1] In that book
Fêng Yü-hsiang is curiously described as " the Master Mind of
China." According to the account given in this book—an
account which corroborates the information gathered from
Chinese sources by myself—a *coup d'état* aimed at Chang Tso-lin
and also at the emperor and others was decided upon at " a
secret meeting in the Western Hills." It may be noted that
Fêng Yü-hsiang was at that time living in pretended retreat
at a Western Hills temple called the T'ien-T'ai Ssŭ.[2]

" The first item on the programme was the death sentence
to be meted out to Chang Tso-lin, Tuan Ch'i-jui, Ts'ao K'un
and the ex-emperor Hsüan T'ung now known as Mr. Henry
P'u-Yi. General Li Ching-lin who hated the Mukden leader in
his fight with Lu Yung-hsiang over the tupanship in Chihli,
was a party to the scheme.
" One bright afternoon in early December of 1924 Li Ching-lin
suddenly left Peking for Tientsin. . . . After a very careful
investigation had been made it was learned that Li's mission
to Tientsin was to cut off the retreat of the Mukden soldiers
once their old marshal was executed in Peking. Alarmed by the
disclosure of the Western Hills plot, Chang Tso-lin and Chang
Hsüeh-liang headed for Tientsin at midnight leaving Tuan
Ch'i-jui and others bewildered by the new turn of events.
" Seeing that Chang Tso-lin and his son had been allowed to
flee, the Master Mind of China thought it unwise merely to carry
out the rest of the programme. Consequently Tuan Ch'i-jui,
Ts'ao K'un and Henry P'u-Yi, who were then either puppets
or prisoners in Peking, were saved from the fate of facing a
firing squad."

It may be added that the personage erroneously described as
" Henry P'u-Yi " would in any case have been " saved from
the fate of facing a firing squad " by the fact that by the time
the plot was to have been carried out he was already safe in
the Japanese Legation.
" The Flight of the Dragon " has been commemorated in
both literary and pictorial art by that brave and devoted loyalist

who is also, as my readers know, one of the most distinguished of living Chinese men of letters—Chêng Hsiao-hsü.

The poem consists of an eight-lined stanza in the so-called *ch'i ku* style (seven characters or syllables to a line) which was brought to perfection by the author's eighth-century T'ang dynasty models. My English version of it is far from conveying an adequate idea of the force and beauty of the original.

The title may be rendered " Accompanying His Imperial Majesty on his drive to the Japanese Legation on the third day of the eleventh moon."[3] Under the title is the following note. " Ch'ên Pao-shên and Chuang Shih-tun [Johnston] accompanied His Majesty to the German Hospital. I, Hsiao-Hsü, followed them, and we subsequently went on to the Japanese Legation." Then follows the poem.

Aided by the eddying wind, with cloud-banners streaming overhead,
Driven rapidly onward by ghostly rather than by human hands,
The Son of an Imperial race was rescued from the tiger's den.
What have all the annals of the past to show more wonderful than this ?

On this of all days, what created the Mongolian hurricane,
When Kung-Kung revealed himself in crashing heaven and riven earth ?
No valiant knight-at-arms came forward as champion,
But still there was among the living one bald-headed old man.

The two last lines mean that although there was no armed champion to protect the emperor in this great adventure, he had at least a bald-headed old man to guard him—namely Chêng Hsiao-hsü himself. Like most Chinese poetry of the classical type this one contains allusions which are apt to escape the notice of the uninitiated. The reference to a great storm and " a valiant knight-at-arms " shows that the poet had in mind a famous little poem known as the *Kao Fêng Ko* or " Song of the Storm " attributed to the Emperor Kao Tsung of the Han dynasty, who reigned 206–195 B.C.[4] The personage referred to as Kung-Kung was a mythical superman who tried to destroy the world with storms and floods. The phrase " bald-headed old

man " (*t'u wêng*) may have been borrowed from a passage in
the Annals of Ssŭ-ma Ch'ien (second century B.C.).

Su-k'an's poem is followed in the printed text by an extract
from his diary of which the following is a translation.

" On the first day of the eleventh moon,[5] the Communists
scattered leaflets among the people and also songs about the
dictatorship of the proletariat. Among the leaflets, of which
there were tens of thousands, were some which denounced
' Imperialism.' On the following day it was reported in the
foreign newspapers that Fêng Yü-hsiang was about to carry
out a third *coup d'état* in Peking. I was sent for by his majesty
and ordered to find a new place of residence for him as quickly
as possible.[6]

" On the third day [November 29th] I received a secret
message from T'ao-An [one of the names of Ch'ên Pao-shên]
saying that a most critical moment had arrived and that the
plan decided upon was to take his majesty to the German
Hospital. It was then past noon. I drove to the Pei Fu [prince
Ch'un's residence], but when I got as far as the Drum Tower I
met T'ao-An's empty carriage coming away, and was told that
he had already gone to Soochow Hutung. I went there as quickly
as possible, but found no trace of him.

" Then I went on to the German Hospital, and went upstairs,
where I found his majesty walking up and down below a window.
No one was with him but T'ao-An, who told me that Johnston
had already gone to the Dutch and British Legations, that
Chang Wên-chih had hastened off to report matters to prince
Ch'un, and that they would return. I begged his majesty to
proceed forthwith to the Japanese Legation. His majesty ordered
me to go there first and interview the Japanese authorities.
I immediately went off to call on Chu Pên [Colonel Takemoto,
commandant of the Japanese Legation Guard] and told him of
the emperor's arrival in the Legation Quarter. Chu Pên reported
the matter to his minister Fang Tsê and told me to inform his
majesty that he was at liberty to decide for himself whether
he should come to the Legation or not.

" By this time a violent storm had arisen and the sky was
obscured by clouds of yellow sand. It was impossible to see
anything more than a few paces in front.

" On my return to the hospital I feared that the chauffeur might disobey orders, so I thought it best that his majesty should go to the Japanese Legation in my horse-carriage. I was also afraid of the people who had collected in great numbers in front of the hospital, so I took the carriage round to the door at the back of the hospital.

" A female nurse and a German who had the keys conducted his majesty downstairs. The backdoor was then opened and his majesty and I got into the carriage. A young servant-boy accompanied us.

" From the German hospital to the Japanese Legation there were two routes, each nearly a third of a mile long, one going from east to west and turning north, entirely within the Legation Quarter, the other leading into Ch'ang-an street and turning south.[7]

" I ordered my coachman to drive back to the Japanese Legation, but he, knowing that the northern route was slightly shorter than the other, proceeded to drive us along Ch'ang-an street. His majesty exclaimed in alarm, ' Look at all those Chinese police in the street. Why did we come this way ? ' However, the carriage was being driven along swiftly, and I replied, ' It is no distance, and how can any one know that the emperor is in the carriage ? There is no cause for alarm.' Then. we turned south along the side of the stream [the channel in the Legation Quarter between the British and Japanese Legations] and I said, ' We are in the Legation Quarter now.'

" We entered the Japanese Legation grounds, where Chu Pên was awaiting us, and we were brought into the quarters of the Legation Guard. T'ao-An joined us there.

" During the time that we were driving along Ch'ang-an street there was a violent sandstorm, and we could hardly see where we were going through the murky air.

" While we were resting in a room his majesty said, ' The people in the Pei Fu know now that I went to the hospital. Johnston and Chang Wên-chih are sure to go back there to look for me. They must be told where I am.' So I returned to the hospital where I found prince Ch'un and T'ao beileh [prince Tsai-T'ao]. I accompanied them, and several officers of the household who had arrived, back to the Legation.

" His majesty then ordered me to inform Tuan Ch'i-jui of
what had happened, and instructed Chang Wên-chih to report
to Chang Tso-lin. I went home and wrote several letters and
despatched them by the hand of my son Yü. By that time it
was night. The storm had passed and the whole sky was brilliant
with stars. My two sons Ch'ui and Yü both came to the Japanese
Legation with refreshments for his majesty. The Japanese
Minister Fang Tsê gave up his own three upstairs rooms for his
majesty's use as sleeping quarters.

" The servant-boy who accompanied us in the carriage was
Li T'i-yü, aged fourteen.[8] The coachman was Wang Yung-
chiang and the groom was Wang Hsiao-lung."

It will be seen that the explanatory note contains a correct
description of the facts except that Chêng Hsiao-hsü erroneously
assumed that Colonel Takemoto had consulted the Japanese
minister before he agreed to receive the emperor in his own
quarters. The relations between the civil and military branches
of the Japanese Legation were not as close and friendly as
those between the corresponding branches of the British and
other Legations, indeed it is doubtful whether Colonel Takemoto
regarded himself as subject to the minister's authority. He did
not, therefore, feel himself under any obligation to report to
Mr. Yoshizawa his conversation with Mr. Chêng Hsiao-hsü, and
he did not do so. He was in fact prepared and anxious to be
himself the emperor's host, and had no desire to be deprived
by the minister of his illustrious guest. It was therefore not till
after the emperor had arrived at the commandant's house that
Mr. Yoshizawa was informed that the emperor was already
within the precincts of his Legation.

I have said that Chêng Hsiao-hsü commemorated the incident of the emperor's escape in pictorial as well as in literary
art. In his picture, which is here reproduced in miniature,
will be seen a small portion of the walls and pavilions
of the Forbidden City only dimly discernible through the
mirk of the dust-storm. The storm is also characteristically
shown by the straining branches of trees. The ancient pine in
the left foreground is specially noteworthy. Chêng Hsiao-hsü
has a high reputation among contemporary Chinese painters
for his drawings of pine-trees, and this is a good specimen of

his artistry. Nothing can be seen of the Peking streets—they are totally shrouded in the whirling dust, amid which, in the upper right-hand corner, is the suggestion—nothing more—of an object faintly indicating the dragon in his flight. The dragon, it will be remembered, is in China one of the symbols of majesty.

When the picture had been mounted, in the usual Chinese way, on a long roll of silk, Ch'ên Pao-shên and I (as participators in the drama of "the flight of the dragon") were invited to make our written comments concerning the picture on that portion of the silk roll which, in accordance with the usual Chinese practice, had been left blank to allow space for the autographs, seals and "appreciations" of critics and brother-artists. My own notes were written in English, and as they consisted merely of a brief narrative of the events already described, they need not be reproduced. Ch'ên Pao-shên's contribution, which is reproduced, along with the picture, in his own delicate and graceful calligraphy, consists of two large Chinese characters meaning "A Storm and a Marvel," followed by a brief note and a poem of which my translation is as follows :

"Su-k'an [Chêng Hsiao-hsü] drew this picture to commemorate the events of the third day of the eleventh month of the year *chia-tzŭ* (November 29th, 1924), and I, Pao-shên, wrote on it the following stanza :

There was the roar of a sandstorm as the sun sank in the west.
Where was a refuge to be found in this hour of crisis ?
The poetic spirit of Ch'ang-Li animates this picture
Portraying the flight of the dragon through murky skies and over
   a darkened earth."

Ch'ang-Li, it should be explained, is one of the literary names of the famous T'ang dynasty poet Han Yü (768–824) who is known to be one of Chêng Hsiao-hsü's most admired models. It has been said by his literary friends that his poetry shows the influence both of Han Yü and of his great friend and contemporary the poet Liu Tsung-yüan (773–819), and it was a compliment to Chêng Hsiao-hsü to suggest that Han Yü's influence was traceable not only in his verse but also in this picture.

Ddc

Such is the true story of the emperor's escape to the Legation
Quarter. To the many inaccurate versions of the episode, it
is unnecessary to refer ; but a protest must be made against the
remarkable account recently given to the world by an American
writer.

> " In October, 1924, while P'u-yi and his wife were at break-
> fast, her serving matron ran in crying that hordes of rough
> Chinese soldiers were at the gates shouting ' Kill the deposed
> Son of Heaven and his Consort.' The Emperor and Empress
> escaped by back passages. They fled to the British Legation,
> but the sentry refused them entrance. Fleeing on through the
> Legation Quarter, they debated concerning the American
> Legation, and decided that they would be refused. They
> hesitated regarding the Japanese Legation, but the Japanese
> sentry ran to their aid and closed the Legation gates against
> their pursuers. The Legation people were gentle and kind.
> The Minister's wife insisted that the refugee Emperor and
> his Empress, who had soiled and torn their clothes, change
> to garments from her husband's and her own wardrobes."[9]

Although these statements are erroneous, it would perhaps
be unnecessary to draw attention to them were it not for the
very grave indictment of British honour and hospitality which
is implied in the assertion that the sentry of the British Legation
denied sanctuary to the fleeing emperor and empress. It is
pleasant to be able to contradict, with equal emphasis, the
statement that " they debated concerning the American
Legation and decided that they would be refused." I am convinced that the American Legation authorities, who in former
years had more than once given shelter and generous hospitality
to hunted Chinese with whom they can have had little political
sympathy, would not have shut their gates against two imperial
fugitives whose death-sentences had been pronounced by
" hordes of rough Chinese soldiers."
Discerning readers, English or American, are not likely to
have been misled by statements of this kind. More serious,
in view of later political events involving China, Manchuria
and Japan, is the charge which has persistently been brought

against Japan in the Chinese press, and elsewhere, that the emperor's reception by the Japanese Legation was the result of crafty manœuvres on the part of the Japanese " imperialists " who foresaw that he might become a useful pawn in the game of high politics. It will be seen from the foregoing pages that the Japanese minister knew nothing whatever of the emperor's arrival in the Legation Quarter until I myself informed him of it ; that it was at my own earnest entreaty that he agreed to grant him protection within the hospitable walls of the Japanese Legation ; and that Japanese " imperialism " had nothing whatever to do with " the flight of the dragon."

The Dragon goes Home

TWILIGHT IN THE FORBIDDEN CITY had deepened into night. The darkness that followed does not come within the limits of my tale, nor the new dawn that in the opinion of many is now discernible elsewhere. A brief summary of the events of the long night is all that can be attempted in these pages.

The emperor remained an honoured guest at the Japanese Legation for several months—from November 29th, 1924, to February 23rd, 1925. He was still there when Sun Yat-sen arrived in Peking, a dying man.

During those months the emperor never left the Legation Quarter, but he returned the visits of some of the foreign diplomats, he came frequently to my quarters in the British Legation, and occasionally we walked together on that short section of the city wall which, being the southern boundary of the Quarter, is excluded from Chinese control. From that wall he had his first view of the wooded park that surrounds the Altar of Heaven. The great white marble altar itself, at which in happier days he would have officiated as Son of Heaven and Father of his people, was invisible. From the same wall he saw the gleaming yellow roofs of the Forbidden City, which though it may have been in some respects a prison had also been his home since infancy. On one of our evening walks on the wall I caught sight of a solitary dark figure coming towards us. I told the emperor in a whisper to observe him closely as he passed by. He was Karakhan, the Soviet ambassador.

Then followed a long and dreary sojourn of nearly seven years in the unattractive Japanese Concession in the treaty-port of Tientsin. It lasted from February, 1925, till November, 1931. Lying allegations were made in the Chinese press, and by a society which called itself *Fan Ch'ing T'ung Mêng* or the " Anti-Manchu League," that the Japanese were trying to induce him to go to Japan, where they might use him as a political instrument in their imperialistic designs on China, and had promised to give him a palace to live in. Had the Japanese government, at any time between 1925 and 1931, conveyed to him the merest hint that he would be hospitably welcomed in Japan, he would have rejoiced at the opportunity of exchanging his drab and colourless life at Tientsin for the free and spacious life he might have led in a country residence in the beautiful neighbourhood of Kyoto or within sight of the peerless Fujiyama. He was given no such hint. On the contrary, it was intimated to him, through me, that his presence either in Japan or in the Japanese leased-territory of Kuantung in Manchuria would " seriously embarrass " the Japanese government.

By the autumn of 1925 Fêng Yü-hsiang and Chang Tso-lin had ceased to be even nominal allies. A new alliance against Fêng was formed by the two who had recently been at war with each other—Wu P'ei-fu and Chang Tso-lin—and the civil chairmanship of the movement was offered to the veteran statesman T'ang Shao-yi. Though he had taken little part in recent politics he was highly respected in nearly all political circles and was generally regarded as honest and capable. He returned a non-committal reply to the invitation, saying that he could not promise his support to the new alliance unless Wu P'ei-fu (who had been nursing his wounds and gathering new strength in the Yangtse Valley) would give assurances that it was not his intention to restore Ts'ao K'un to the presidency or to recall the discredited parliament which had been bribed to elect him.

T'ang Shao-yi took the opportunity to refer in a courageous and remarkably outspoken manner to the prevalent rumours that the new alliance intended to declare null and void the illegal action taken against the emperor and restore the privileges guaranteed by the Articles of Favourable Treatment. Not content with a mere approval of this proposal (which for various reasons was never carried out) he went on to make a statement which attracted comparatively little notice at the time but which is of the deepest interest and importance when we read it in the light of the events of a few years later. His words are here quoted as they were published towards the end of October, 1925.

" As regards the restoration of Manchu privileges, T'ang Shao-yi said that the Manchu conquerors brought Manchuria as a dowry in the China-Manchuria union. The Chinese people had thrown out the Manchu House, but Manchuria seemed still the rightful heritage of the Manchus, and the ex-emperor Hsüan-T'ung ought to be allowed to resume his sovereignty over that territory."[1]

During a visit to Shanghai a few months after T'ang Shao-yi had made this very remarkable statement, I had a long conversation with him and satisfied myself from his utterances on that occasion that the report as published had not misrepresented his views.

T'ang Shao-yi did not re-enter politics either at that time or later, though he was frequently pressed to do so. The new alliance, however, succeeded in some of its objects, one of the most important of which was the overthrow of Fêng Yü-hsiang, who then seems to have arrived at the conclusion that his spiritual home was Moscow. It was there, in 1926, that he spent a portion of the period of his enforced retirement from active political life in China.

This " master-mind of China " has since made many re-appearances on the political stage of his native country but his sinister figure seems destined to inspire distrust wherever he goes, and he has few friends in China to-day. To those friends, however few, Fêng was and is a disinterested hero and patriot. By a far greater number he has been denounced as an un-scrupulous traitor, false and treacherous to both friends and foes. He has been crowned with laurels and roses, bespattered with mud and filth. Some have seen in him a true democrat, a devoted worker on behalf of the toiling masses, the staunch friend of the poor and oppressed. In the eyes of others he is a hypocritical rogue, wearing the mask of piety, humility, simplicity and frugality, merely in order that he may the more easily accomplish his own dark designs and fulfil his selfish ambitions by posing as the people's friend and champion. Foreigners have differed among themselves almost as widely as the Chinese in their estimates of the man's character. Protestant missionaries, who with natural pride spoke of their most distinguished convert as a sincere and pure-hearted " soldier of Christ," now mention his name with diminished enthusiasm. Lay Christians like Sir John Jordan, whose natural bias was entirely friendly to him on account of his conversion to Christianity, but who were frankly shocked by some of his words and deeds, remarked apologetically to their mystified country-men that Fêng was " an Old-Testament Christian." This was supposed to explain if it did not justify some of his frequent lapses from the ethical standards of the Sermon on the Mount. " I salute the Christian general, the Cromwell of China," said the Rev. Jonathan Blunt, a zealous missionary, " and agree with Sir John Jordan that he is a highly creditable specimen of the Old Testament Christian, and I fervently pray that . . . he may yet prove to be, under God, the saviour of his country."[2]

Yet in 1929 we find him described by an " anti-Fêng " society as a rebel, the embodiment of northern militarist wickedness, and " a crafty secret wolf." He was accused of " ten great crimes," among which were the surrender of Outer Mongolia to the Russians, rebellion against the national government, breaking up the lines of communication so as to " hinder the funeral obsequies of our late leader " (Sun Yat-sen), destroying the lives of several hundred thousand young men, using relief-money and grain for financing his own wars, joining the com-munists, forcing the farmers of the north-west to grow opium, and robbing the people. " These ten charges," declares the society's manifesto, " show what a wicked man he is. For the crimes he has committed, death would be an inadequate penalty."[3]

As long ago as 1920 Fêng's Christian friends informed the world that at a time " when all crop prospects seemed to be blasted by drought," he had called upon the Buddhists and Taoists of his neighbourhood to pray for rain. " They were in consternation and hopeless confusion as they begged off." Then Fêng prayed, " and soon there was a great rain."[4] Nevertheless exactly ten years later he was described by the people of the province of Shensi as " the demon of drought " because his very presence seemed to prevent the rains from falling.[5] " Curiously enough," said the Shensi correspondent of an English newspaper in China—one who happened himself to be a missionary—" the break-up of the drought coincides with the end of Fêng Yü-hsiang's régime in Shensi. . . . His coming to Shensi in 1927 heralded three long years of famine. The very day he telegraphed his resignation one of the heaviest downpours we have had for years took place. And it only needed the final departure of the remainder of his troops to ensure the complete break up of the drought, for it has been raining ever since ! "⁶

Fêng Yü-hsiang's friends may possibly find some consolation in the fact that his pilgrimage to Moscow took place *after* he had been honourably known as a rain-maker and *before* he came to be regarded as a demon of drought.

I do not myself propose to attempt a final estimate of this strange man's character. The time for that has not yet come. As I write, he is sulking in his tents—or rather in a Buddhist temple in which I myself have spent many delightful days without sulking—on the slopes of T'ai Shan, the most celebrated of the Holy Mountains of China. I have strong faith in the cleansing and regenerating power of mountains, and T'ai Shan possesses that power in high degree. It has been for thousands of years a sacred hill, and during those years it has been a source of inspiration to poets, saints, sages, emperors, soldiers, monks, hermits, artists and mystics. Fêng is a soldier and possibly something of a mystic. He may be an artist, too, if his portraits of Lenin were such as to entitle him to that description. Great things may happen when he grows tired of sulking and turns to serious meditation.

> *Thou hast a voice, great Mountain, to repeal*
> *Large codes of fraud and woe : not understood*
> *By all, but which the wise, and great, and good*
> *Interpret, and make felt, or deeply feel.*

I doubt whether the Christian general's past activities in politics or war or practical morals have earned him the right to be described as wise, great or good ; but he may descend a new man from the heights of T'ai Shan. Dr. W. R. Inge has told us that " the ' land which is very far off ' is always visible to those who have climbed the holy mountain." We may hope that Fêng Yü-hsiang has at least caught a glimpse of it. If he comes down to the plains no wiser, greater or better than he was before he went up, he will have shown himself unworthy of the privilege granted him of communing with the spirit of the holy mountain. In that case he will have no share in the repealing of those " large codes of fraud and woe " with which his unhappy country is so sorely afflicted to-day.

During nearly three months' residence in the Legation Quarter and also during the earlier years of his sojourn in Tientsin, the emperor was the target of the most scurrilous, unscrupulous and unchivalrous abuse. Not only was he denounced for imaginary political crimes and intrigues and for his alleged intention to overthrow the republic if he could, but he was held up to public ridicule and contempt and his personal character shamefully assailed. He was also declared to be a vicious degenerate. The propaganda against him was intended to influence foreigners as well as Chinese, and it met with very considerable success, both at home and abroad. It was during the early days in Tientsin that the practice grew up among certain foreign journalists of referring to him, not without a strong tincture of contempt, as " Mr. Henry P'u (or rather Pu) Yi," in flagrant disregard not merely of the fact that neither he nor his friends ever used these names in combination but also of the conventional courtesy which prescribes that ex-monarchs should be described not as " Mr ——" but as " ex-king ——" and very frequently as " king " without the " ex." It was also in ignorance or defiance of the fact that by the Articles of Favourable Treatment the Ta Ch'ing emperor was entitled to retain the full imperial style (without the prefix of " ex ") and that those Articles had never been abrogated by any legal or constitutional process.[7]

The Anti-Manchu League existed for the purpose of keeping up a continual agitation against the imperial house. It advocated the total abolition of the last vestiges of " favourable treatment," including the arbitrarily-imposed " agreement " of November, 1924, and the drastic punishment and even the execution of all " monarchists " including the emperor himself.

In the latter part of 1925 the enemies of the Manchu house published certain correspondence which had been found in a box in the emperor's bedchamber in the Forbidden City. They declared that this correspondence revealed the existence of a plot to restore the monarchy and implicated several persons prominent in the Chinese political world. None of the letters published did in fact prove the existence of any plot, though they showed—greatly no doubt to the disgust of republican readers—that the emperor still had warm friends and sympathisers in all parts of China. One of the documents in question, which was described as being of primary importance because it was supposed to involve me in monarchist conspiracies, was a long letter addressed to me by the famous reformer (now regarded in " advanced " circles as a reactionary) K'ang Yu-wei. It contained loyal messages to his majesty, an account of his recent journeys in central China, and references to the friendly and sympathetic attitude towards the emperor which he had observed in influential quarters. I had handed the letter to the emperor for his perusal and he had put it away among his papers. Certainly it contained no evidence whatever that the emperor or the Manchu court or I myself had been concerned in political intrigues. The League for the total suppression of all monarchists was delighted, however, to seize upon this letter (which, along with others, was reproduced in facsimile and circulated throughout China) as a positive proof that the English tutor of " P'u-Yi " had been engaged in plots for the restoration of the emperor.

The emperor's enemies went further than this, for they publicly declared that I was still engaged in these nefarious enterprises and was exercising a malign influence in the world of diplomacy. A typical example of the accusations directed against myself is the following, which was translated from a Chinese newspaper called the *Min Pao* and appeared in the English press on August 11th, 1925.

" Ever since the arrival of the former emperor in Tientsin, Mr. Johnston has been making overtures to all the ministers and consuls of the European imperialist countries in China in the name of his pupil. He did his best to win their support in a restoration movement by offering various concessions. As a result of his intrigue, the British chargé d'affaires has come under his influence. Since the Shanghai outrage of

May 30, Mr. Johnston has been taking a more prominent part in this monarchical plot together with the British chargé."[8]

These contemptible lies were followed up a few weeks later by the publication of an open letter from the Anti-Manchu League to the British minister in Peking demanding my expulsion from China. The League professed to represent 400,000,000 Chinese in making this request. It declared that all Chinese monarchists were to be executed ; and that as my crimes were unpardonable my punishment should also be of a drastic nature.

The accusations against myself were puerile and might have been disregarded, but I received a private intimation from Tuan Ch'i-jui's government that they would be glad if I would make a public reply as it would facilitate their efforts to keep the activities of the anti-Manchu agitators within bounds. I therefore wrote a reply which was published on August 12th in the *Peking and Tientsin Times* and other foreign newspapers, and also (in Chinese) in various prominent Chinese periodicals. It would be superfluous to give the full text of my reply in these pages, but as the last paragraph refers to the base attacks which were still being made upon the emperor, it may be found of interest.

" Even in his retirement in Tientsin, the nineteen-year-old emperor is not free from the bitter and unchivalrous attacks of his enemies. Not content with having deprived him by force of the rights and privileges accorded to him in the original abdication pact, they are now attempting by every possible means to deprive him of such privileges as remain to him under the revised pact imposed upon him at the time of the *coup d'état* last November. Charges are incessantly being made against him of intriguing for a monarchist restoration. In this morning's Chinese press, for example, it is stated that he is surrounded at Tientsin by active members of the monarchist party ; that he has established close relations with the various foreign consuls in Tientsin ; that he has recently applied to a certain foreign Power for protection, and has promised *when restored to the Throne* to grant that

Power various valuable privileges in China; and that he is allying himself with a certain military party, also with a view to a monarchist restoration. It is hardly necessary to say that not the smallest fragment of evidence is produced to support these wild assertions."

The Anti-Manchu League made determined efforts to compel Tuan Ch'i-jui's government to have all suspected monarchists arrested and tried on the capital charge of treason and was much disgusted when the government declined to take any action. One of its most prominent spokesmen, one Tu Hsiao-shih, summarised its views in a memorandum which was published in English and Chinese during the latter part of August, 1925.

Nothing roused the Anti-Manchu League to fiercer indignation than the current rumour that Tuan's government proposed to restore to the imperial house some of its confiscated properties. "What the government means by taking such action" said Tu Hsiao-shih in his memorandum "is hard to understand. The action, if it gives rise to no other surmises, will give an ample ground for the belief that the government itself is implicated in the monarchical restoration movement."[9]

In 1926 it was necessary for me to pay a short visit to England (my second in twenty-eight years of residence in China) in connection with the administration of the British share of the "Boxer" indemnity. Early in 1927 I returned to China to take up the post of British commissioner at Weihaiwei. In this "leased territory," in which I had formerly served for many years as district officer and magistrate, I remained until the British government carried out its long-standing promise to restore the territory to China nearly four years later, though during that time I kept in touch with the emperor and paid him several visits.

I spent some days in his company at Tientsin before proceeding to Weihaiwei, and it was on the occasion of his birthday, which that year fell on February 14th, that I met for the last time the staunch old royalist-reformer with whom my name had been associated in charges of monarchist intrigues. K'ang Yu-wei, who was accompanied by his devoted disciple Chui Leong (Hsü Liang) called on me on the morning of the birthday, and after a long conversation concerning the emperor and his past and future we went together to Chang Yüan, the emperor's house in the Japanese Concession. The emperor greeted us warmly, and when the old man knelt before him the emperor rose from his seat, touched him on the shoulder and bade him sit down. I never saw K'ang Yu-wei again. He returned to Shanghai, and on the 8th of the following month celebrated his own birthday—his seventieth. Large numbers of his friends and disciples made this the occasion for a great demonstration of respect and affection. But the greatest joy that came to him that day was a gracious message from his sovereign, who had sent Chui Leong from Tientsin to convey his congratulations and some presents. A few days afterwards he went north again to occupy a new house which he had taken at Tsingtao, and we had arranged that during the summer he was to come to Wei-haiwei and pay me a long visit. But the only news of him that reached me from Tsingtao was the news of his death. He had died on the very morning of the day on which I arrived at Weihaiwei to take up my new duties—March 31st, 1927.

One of the most moving of the addresses spoken at his funeral was that of the most famous of all his disciples—Liang Ch'i-ch'ao, himself destined to follow his master very shortly into the shadows. In his oration he gave K'ang Yu-wei the fullest credit for having been the great pioneer of reform in China, and as the one who saw earlier and more clearly than others that the choice for China lay between progress on modern lines or hopeless decay and ruin. " Those who will write the history of the New China," said Liang Ch'i-ch'ao, "cannot do otherwise than take the events of 1898 as the first chapter in that history." In this book I have acted upon that hint.

It was while I was at Weihaiwei that the emperor and the Manchu imperial family were plunged into mourning by a catastrophe the magnitude of which can hardly be estimated except by those who know something of the Chinese cult of ancestors and the deep reverence with which the Chinese and Manchus regard the graves of their forefathers.

The devastation and violation of the imperial tombs (the Tung Ling, to the east of Peking) took place between the 3rd and the 11th July, 1928.

It matters little whether we describe the perpetrators as
soldiers or bandits—too often there is not much to choose
between them in these days of internal disorganisation and
disruption in China. The principal motive for the outrage, if
not the only one, was plunder, for it has been the custom in
China to bury enormous quantities of jewels and other valuables
in the graves of imperial personages. The mausolea were immensely strong and it required dynamite to burst them open.
Coffins were broken open and the bodies flung out on the floor.
The remains of one of the greatest sovereigns who ever occupied
the Chinese throne—Kao Tsung (Ch'ien-Lung)—and also the
body of the empress-dowager Tz'ŭ-Hsi, "the Venerable Buddha,"
were hacked to pieces and their bones scattered.[10] The scene,
when it was afterwards visited by the emperor's messengers,
was indescribably hideous. A full description of it was prepared
for the emperor's information and for preservation in the records
of the imperial family, and copies of this document were sent
to me together with the letter which the emperor wrote in reply
to my letter of sympathy.

A special court was set up to try a few of the minor offenders,
but they were only lightly punished, if at all. No serious attempt
was made to arrest the ringleaders, who included military
officers of rank. They escaped all punishment, and were even
allowed to retain possession of their loot, much of which has
since been dispersed throughout the world. The emperor waited
for a word of sympathy or regret from the national government
of China, which had twice given solemn undertakings to afford
adequate protection to the imperial tombs. He waited in vain.
Not a sign of sorrow or compunction came either from the all-
powerful Kuomintang or from the government at Nanking.

Everything else could be forgiven—insults, ridicule, threats
of death, confiscation of property, the tearing up of agreements—
but not this appalling act of savagery and sacrilege. From this
time on there was a change in the emperor's attitude to China—
or rather towards those who were responsible for its misgovernment. By nature he is generous and forgiving, and I had never
heard him utter a word of angry complaint against the most
violent of his enemies. But this was something he could
never overlook. Up to that time he had taken no part in the

independence movement that he knew was gathering momentum in Manchuria, and the possibility of his being invited to return to the Manchurian home of his ancestors was a subject to which he had hardly given a serious thought. He had never ceased to hope that China would recover her sanity and that all would be well. But now that hope was dead. When I next visited him the change was very marked. So marked was it that it seemed to me as though he had been in communion with the spirits of his outraged ancestors and that they had urged him to turn away from the China that had disgraced herself and them and to fix his gaze on the land in which they had laid the strong foundations of their empire three hundred years ago.

Other grave events were happening in north China during this time besides the violation of the imperial tombs. The Nationalist advance toward Peking was making rapid progress. Chang Tso-lin was in Peking, and he appeared to have all north China completely in his grasp ; but his position was strong only in outward semblance. Dissensions and radical differences of opinion among the different sections of his own party made it impossible for him to present a strong front to his enemies, and though he had the best-equipped army in China he feared —and had good reason to fear—that if he sent it southwards to meet the invaders he would receive a stab in the back which might be fatal. With extreme reluctance, and bitterly distressed at the collapse of all his schemes for the consolidation of his power in China proper, he made up his mind to withdraw with his army to his own realm of Manchuria. What took place on his return journey to Mukden is well known to all the world, though how it happened is still—more or less—a mystery. Only a few miles from his capital, the special train in which he was travelling was bombed and Chang Tso-lin was killed. So ended the career of a man who had had one of the most varied and brilliant careers of which the annals of modern China hold record.

It seems to have been anticipated in certain quarters that his death would be the signal for a breakdown of such law and order as existed in Manchuria ; but the news of his death was carefully concealed until all the necessary precautions had been taken to ensure the peaceful succession of his son Chang Hsüeh-liang.

Manchuria, be it remembered, was at that time a monarchy in all but name, owing only a shadowy allegiance to the central government of the Chinese republic. Chang Tso-lin had wielded a power that was greater than that of most monarchs, and it was taken for granted that he would be succeeded by his son. Peking fell into the hands of the nationalists without a battle. Many of the officials fled, and among them was the foreign minister, Dr. Wellington Koo, whose name was included in a list of about a dozen persons—mostly members of the now discredited An-Fu party—for whose arrest warrants were issued by the Nanking government. Dr. Koo left Tientsin in a British steamer on July 20th and arrived at Weihaiwei on the 21st. This was not the first time he had taken refuge in the British leased-territory of Weihaiwei to escape the persecution of his political opponents, but on this occasion he made a longer stay. He remained there under the protection of the British flag for a period of five months. In December he left for Europe. When he returned to the Far East, by way of Canada, some months later, his name was still on the Nanking government's " black list." He returned however, not to China proper but to Manchuria, where for a considerable time he remained as the honoured guest and friend of the Manchurian ruler, Chang Hsüeh-liang. When Chang Hsüeh-liang decided to change his father's policy and recognise the authority of the Kuomintang and the Nanking government, it was essential that that government should do something in return. In spite of the fact that his old antagonist C. T. Wang was at that time the Nanking government's foreign minister, Dr. Koo's name was taken off the black list, his confiscated property (including his house in Peking) was restored to him, and before long he had re-entered the service of the Chinese government. In 1932, having been nominated Chinese assessor to the League of Nations commission of enquiry, he accompanied the commissioners on their visit to Manchuria.

Two weeks before the rendition of Weihaiwei I paid a farewell visit to the emperor at Tientsin, for I was about to leave China and it was uncertain whether we should ever meet again. We discussed the possibilities of the future and he gave me reasons for the belief that his long exile in Tientsin would soon come to an end. . . .

He came to my hotel very early on the morning of my departure—September 15th, 1930—and remained with me till it was necessary for me to go on board my steamer. We drove together in his car to the wharf, and he sat in my cabin till the last possible moment. It took nearly half an hour for the steamer to turn round before going down stream. During that time he sat in his car on the wharf and remained there as long as the ship was in sight.

His last present to me was a fan on which he had copied an ancient Chinese poem of farewell, of which the following is a rough translation."[11]

The road leads ever onward,
And you, my friend, go this way, I go that.
Thousands of miles will part us—
You at one end of the wide world, I at the other.
Long and difficult is the journey—
Who knows when we shall meet again ?
The Tartar horses breathe the northern winds,
The birds of Yüeh build their nests in southern trees.
Our farewells are said, we are far apart ;
Already I grow weak with pining.[12]
The sun is hidden by drifting clouds,
The traveller journeys on, turning his head no more.
Thinking of you, I seem to have grown old.
The months have swiftly passed, a whole year has gone.
It is all over. There is no more to be said,
I must make myself strong for the strenuous days to
*   come. . . .*

Out of the city's eastern gate I go on foot,
To gaze longingly at the road that leads to far Kiangnan.
On that day of storm and snow,
Here it was that we parted, and my friend went away.
I want to follow him across the river,
But the river is deep and has no bridge.
Oh that we were a pair of herons,
That we could fly home together.

On October 1st, 1930, on behalf of the British Government I conducted the rendition of Weihaiwei. Since 1898 that Territory, with a population of nearly 200,000 and an area about double the size of the Isle of Wight, had been governed by a British commissioner directly responsible to the Secretary of State for the Colonies. It was now handed back to China, and the people of the Territory passed under the jurisdiction of the Chinese republic for the first time, for China was still a monarchy when it was " leased " to Great Britain.

Immediately after the rendition I returned to England, not knowing when, if ever, I should return to the country in which I had spent over thirty years. Rather unexpectedly, I returned almost exactly one year later, partly on business connected with the " Boxer " indemnity, partly as a member of the British group participating in the biennial Pacific Conference, which that year was held in China.

The famous Mukden incident of September 18th, 1931, took place a few days before my ship reached Japan on my outward journey. I went on to China, and almost immediately after my arrival at Shanghai I travelled by train to Tientsin, which I reached on October 7th. The emperor expected me, and I was met at the station by one of his suite. There was a very prevalent rumour in Tientsin that he had already left for Manchuria. That, of course, I knew to be incorrect. I spent the next two days in his company, and was given information which enabled me to foresee what was to happen in the near future. The information which he himself gave me was corroborated by Chêng Hsiao-hsü. That night we were both the emperor's guests at dinner, the only others present being Chêng Ch'ui, Ch'ên Pao-shên and Chui Leong. As may be readily understood, there was only one topic of conversation.

On the 8th I left for Peking. There I met marshal Chang Hsüeh-liang, the dispossessed warlord of Manchuria. He allowed me to know that he had heard of my visit to the emperor at Tientsin, and he showed obvious anxiety to extract information from me about the emperor's probable movements. From me he learned nothing. During my stay in Peking I received visits from various loyalists who could not be persuaded that my sudden return to China was not connected with the startling events in Manchuria. They were in a state of subdued excitement and expectation.

On October 15th I returned to Tientsin for further conversations with the emperor. On the 21st I reached Shanghai, and during the days that followed I attended the meetings of the Conference. The Chinese press at that time was full of rumours that the emperor was about to ascend a Manchurian throne. My own supposed influence over him was mentioned in several of the papers, and I was approached by some Chinese who wished me to use that influence in, dissuading him from leaving Tientsin. I may add that similar appeals reached me after he had already gone to Manchuria. I answered one of them in a long letter which was subsequently published in the *National Review*.[13]

On November 10th I was in Nanking and received an urgent request to visit Mr. T. V. Soong, Chinese minister of finance and also at that time acting minister for foreign affairs. At the interview he showed me a telegram from the north in which he had been asked to inform me that P'u-Yi was " in danger and in need of Johnston's help." It was apparently hoped by the Chinese authorities that I would return to Tientsin and make an effort to dissuade him from embarking on the Manchurian adventure. I told Mr. Soong that the emperor knew of my movements and could communicate with me direct at any time. If he were in danger and needed my help, he had only to say the word and I would go to him. But the word must come from himself.

On November 13th I returned to Shanghai and learned from a private telegram that the emperor had left Tientsin for Manchuria.

The Chinese endeavoured to make out that the emperor had been kidnapped by the Japanese and carried off against his will. This statement was widely circulated among Europeans, many of whom believed it; but it was wholly untrue. The extraordinary statements recently published to the effect that the emperor and empress had telegraphed to Chiang Kai-shek at Nanking and to Chang Hsüeh-liang at Peking " asserting their loyalty and asking for sanctuary " are equally false. So is the allegation that the emperor had " sworn a pact with his wife to commit suicide before he would consent to be king of Manchuria."[14] I need hardly say that the last persons in the world to whom the emperor would have appealed for sanctuary were Chiang Kai-shek and Chang Hsüeh-liang ; and that had he wished to escape from the danger of being kidnapped and carried off to Manchuria, all he had to do was to walk on board a British steamer bound for Shanghai. His loyal and devoted servant Chêng Hsiao-hsü was most emphatically not his jailor. He left Tientsin and went to Manchuria of his own free will, and his faithful companions were Chêng Hsiao-hsü (now his prime minister) and his son Chêng Ch'ui.

I do not propose to describe the events that followed. After some weeks spent in the Kuantung peninsula and at the hot-springs of T'ang Kang-tzŭ, the emperor received a formal in-vitation to become provisional head of the new government. The term *chih-chêng* (the same as that which was assumed by Tuan Ch'i-jui in 1924) is a vague term meaning " chief executive" and, as students of the Chinese language will readily understand, it was a temporary and provisional one and never meant to be anything else. The ultimate intention of the leaders of the move-ment, from the beginning, was to establish a monarchy.

As he went north, the special train in which he travelled stopped at various points to allow local and other officials to pay their respects to their sovereign. They went on their knees before him and addressed him by his imperial title. One touch-ing incident occurred when the train was passing the tombs of the early Manchu rulers near Mukden. A brief halt was made, so that the emperor, without leaving the train, might do obeisance to the spirits of his forefathers.

The Dragon had come back to his old home.

One of the tombs is that of the emperor T'ai Tsung, who died in 1643, just before his armies entered Peking after the fall of the Ming dynasty. He was the monarch who, in the third decade of the seventeenth century, completed the work begun by his immediate ancestors—that of establishing the complete in-dependence of Manchuria. As a demonstration to the world that he had repudiated all allegiance to the Chinese court and had rejected all Chinese claims to suzerainty, he assumed the im-perial style and status and became emperor of *Ta Manchoukuo—*

the empire of Manchuria. A little more than three hundred years after T'ai Tsung ascended his Manchurian throne, his direct lineal descendant has returned to the land of his fathers—a land which his family had never ceased to regard as " home "—and has reassumed the imperial style and status of Manchurian emperor. He has done what that veteran Chinese statesman T'ang Shao-yi declared in 1925 that he was entitled to do—having been rejected and thrown out by the Chinese people he has resumed possession of the " rightful heritage " which had been the dowry brought by his Manchurian forefathers to the China-Manchurian union.

Long ago a Chinese sage taught his countrymen this saying : *Ta nan pu ssŭ pi yu hou fu* : " He who emerges with his life from great perils will have a happy and prosperous future."

That the emperor has come successfully through great perils, no one will deny. There were perils of the revolution in China, the crafty ambition of Yüan Shih-k'ai, the rash loyalty of Chang Hsün, the clashing of rival military cliques at the gates of the palace, the callous brutality of Fêng Yü-hsiang, the murderous designs of anti-Manchu fanatics, the impetuous zeal of his own loyal supporters, the manifold plots and conspiracies aimed at his life both before and after that dark night of November, 1931, when he fled from the dearly-loved land of his birth, where he had been spurned, insulted, robbed and denounced as an alien, and returned to the old Manchurian home of his ancestors. Not less serious were those dangers to his moral and intellectual life that lurked in the dark corners of his own palace—the noisome miasma of the Forbidden City, the subtle poisons of a corrupt court. From all the external dangers that threatened him he has emerged in safety ; and even from the deadlier internal dangers he has suffered no permanent hurt. If the Chinese sage's words are true, his future should indeed be prosperous and happy. But those who have a knowledge of his character are sure that he will never be satisfied unless the prosperity and happiness that may be in store for himself are shared in ample and ever-increasing measure by the people over whom he has now been called to rule.

NOTES

INTRODUCTION

1. Almost eighteen years after my first meeting with prince Ch'un I entered the service of his son the emperor in the Forbidden City. After the lapse of another fourteen years, the prince's first grandchild was born (on February 15th, 1933) in my house on the banks of the Thames.

2. *The Break-up of China*, by Lord Charles Beresford (Harper & Brothers, 1889), pp. 196—200.

CHAPTER I

1. Lord Charles Beresford, *op. cit.*, pp. 44 and 60.

2. " The steps taken by Russia . . . amounted to the informal annexation of Manchuria. . . . Manchuria is not only to all intents and purposes a Russian province, but is already invested by Russian troops, pending the time when it shall be opened up and developed by Russian capital." (Alexis Krausse, *China in Decay*, London : 1900, p. 184.) In view of present or recent conditions in Manchuria, the following additional remarks by Krausse are of interest. He says that the population of the country, " amounting to some fourteen millions, may be roughly divided into two broad classes, the agriculturists and the brigands. The latter have always preyed upon the former. . . ." (*Ibid.*, p. 189.) Krausse wrote at the end of the nineteenth century. The same remarks might be applied with equal truth to the conditions of a generation later, the only necessary alteration being that the population since then has rather more than doubled.

In a review of Professor C. Walter Young's book, *The International Relations of Manchuria* (Cambridge Univ. Press, 1929), *The Times* made the following remark : " It is certain that Manchuria and Mongolia would have been absorbed into the Russian Empire long ago had Japan not fought a war to prevent it." The article from which these words are taken was published in *The Times Literary Supplement* of February 6th, 1930, more than nineteen months before the Japanese action in Manchuria of September 18th, 1931.

3. In the *Fortnightly Review* of November, 1928, p. 581, Mr. Lewis Einstein (United States Minister to Czechoslovakia) informs us that when Mr. Herbert C. Hoover (recently president of the United States of America) went to China in 1899 he owed his appointment as Government Engineer to the fact that " the young Kuang-Hsü, *advised by Sun Yat-sen*, was then attempting to introduce Western reforms into China and wanted an American engineer to head the newly-founded Bureau of Mines." It is scarcely necessary to say that Sun Yat-sen never " advised " the emperor Kuang-Hsü in this or in any other matter. It would be difficult to imagine anything that could distress the spirit of K'ang Yu-wei more than to be confused with Sun Yat-sen. Now that they have both passed " to where beyond these voices there is peace," perhaps each will recognise in the other one who tried, in his own way, to do his best for China.

4. Not to be confused with Ch'ên Pao-shên, subsequently tutor to the emperor Hsüan-T'ung. See Index of Names.

CHAPTER II

1. She had acted as regent for her son T'ung-Chih from the beginning of his reign in 1862 till his marriage ten years later ; and for Kuang-Hsü from 1875 to 1888.

2. Miss Eliza R. Scidmore (in *China the Long-Lived Empire*, London : 1900, p. 120) says : " She rose from the harem's ranks, uneducated, ignorant of public

affairs ; but by sheer ability, by her own wits, will, and shrewdness, she attained the supreme power. Hers is the greatest of personal triumphs, her strength of mind and force of character and dominant personality, having won every step : centuries of precedent and all the shackles of Oriental etiquette overborne by her masterful strategy and remorseless will." This shows an extraordinary misconception of the forces and conditions that put the supreme power into the hands of the dowager-empress, but it is a view that many Western writers have adopted.

3. See below, p. 59.

4. See p. 271.

5. One of many indications of the superior rank of an empress-dowager is afforded by the phraseology of written communications addressed to her by the reigning emperor. Students of Chinese know that in memorials addressed to the emperor by all Chinese officials, however exalted, each memorialist was obliged to refer to himself as *ch'ên*—" Your Majesty's servant." But it may surprise many to learn that an emperor was obliged to use the same term when he addressed the empress-dowager. He was also obliged by immemorial usage to use such expressions as *shang yen*, which convey the meaning that he is on a lower level than the august personage whom he is addressing and " submits his words " to her from below the throne. This practice was not confined to such cases as that of the emperor Kuang-Hsü in his relationship with the empress-dowager T'zŭ-Hsi. It was the regular procedure, whether the empress-dowager happened to be acting as regent or not. For example, the emperor Hsüan-T'ung, under whom I served, was obliged, in addressing the empress-dowager Lung-Yü (the widow of the emperor Kuang-Hsü) to refer to himself as *ch'ên*. It should be noted that the emperor, though a Manchu, did not apply to himself the more abject term *nu-ts'ai*—" slave." That term was only used by Manchus addressing the emperor. Manchu princes, when addressing the imperial head of their House, were allowed to use either *ch'ên* or *nu-ts'ai*.

6. A very conspicuous illustration of this may be found in the writings of Ku Hung-ming, who was educated in Edinburgh and wrote fluently in English. He referred to the emperor in terms of respect, to the empress-dowager in terms of almost fanatical loyalty.

7. *Wu-hsü* is the name of the year 1898 in the Chinese sixty-year cycle. The year of the Boxer movement (1900) was *Kêng-tzŭ*. Cf. Preface, Notes 1, 4, and 5.

8. On this subject, see " Wen Ching," *The Chinese Crisis from Within* (London : 1901), p. 57. " Many friends of the reformer have charged K'ang Yu-wei with rashness in precipitating the conflict between Kuang-Hsü and the Manchus. There was indeed no rashness on the part of K'ang Yu-wei, because at an audience the emperor pointed out to him the powerful opposition to reform among the elder mandarins, and requested his advice. . . . But the conflict was inevitable. . . . In fact, reforms could only succeed if the reformers had sufficient power to compel obedience." See also Gowen and Hall, *An Outline History of China* (New York : 1929), p. 312.

9. There were and are many, however, who believe this to be true. See, e.g., Stanley P. Smith's *China from Within* (London : 1901), pp. 11–16.

CHAPTER III

1. *Ta Nei*—one of the terms used to describe the Forbidden City.

2. As to why the foreign Powers did not intervene to save Kuang-Hsü and the cause of reform, see Alexis Krausse, *China in Decay* (London : 1900), pp. 359 ff.

3. See Introduction, p. 17.

4. *Shang Pin :* a conventional phrase for the death of an emperor.

5. This will be explained in a later chapter. See pp. 373 f.

6. An illustration of Hsü T'ung's hatred not only for foreigners but for all their works is given by A. H. Smith in *China in Convulsion*, vol. i., p. 186. We are there told that " he would not use the Legation Street entrance to his residence because the road had been metalled and provided with gutters."

7. Sir Robert Hart's views were discussed by me in the *Chinese Social and Political Science Review* (Peking: October, 1926, vol. x., No. 4, p. 958), and in the *Quarterly Review* (January, 1927, pp. 160 ff.). See also George Lynch, *The War of the Civilisations* (London : 1901), pp. 225 f., where he says : " I have the utmost and most complete admiration for the leading motives which actuated the Boxers."

8. F. L. Hawks Pott, *A Sketch of Chinese History*, p. 185. Alexis Krausse says : " I have not the least hesitation in asserting that the rising . . . is the direct outcome of the activity of the supporters of the dowager-empress " (*China in Decay*, London : 1900, p. 366).

9. Headland, *Court Life in China* (New York : 1909), p. 55.

10. See A. H. Smith, *China in Convulsion*, vol. i., p. 168.

11. " Malgré tous les efforts d'un siècle philosophique, les empires les plus civilisés seront toujours aussi près de la barbarie que le fer le plus poli l'est de la rouille." Antoine de Rivarol, *Essai sur les causes de la révolution française* (1827).

12. This official explanation of the tragedy is accepted by I. T. Headland in his *Court Life in China* (New York : 1909), p. 204. It would appear that he had heard of no other explanation. But he wrote in the lifetime of the empress-dowager.

CHAPTER IV

1. This was so, but Mencius laid down certain conditions, which the empress dowager can hardly be said to have fulfilled.

2. My account of the Boxer indemnities and their partial return to China may be found in the *Report of the Advisory Committee* (Blue-book China No 2, 1926) presented to both Houses of Parliament and published in 1926 by H.M.'s Stationery Office.

3. See R. K. Douglas, *Society in China* (London : 1901), p. 446.

4. See above, chap. i., pp. 19 f., and A. H. Smith, *China in Convulsion*, vol. i., pp. 101 ff.

5. The following significant remarks are from an article published in 1925 (therefore long before the present Manchurian controversy between Japan and China broke out) by the well-known authority on Manchuria and its railway-system, Dr. C. C. Wang. " Taking as a pretext the suppression of the Boxers, Russia sent a large army to occupy the Three Eastern Provinces [Manchuria]. At the outset, the whole Chinese population of Blagovieschensk, a Chinese settlement on the right bank of the Amur, of about 5,000 men, women and children, were driven into the Amur at the point of the bayonet. In consequence, the Three Eastern Provinces were soon over-run by Russian troops. Proclamations were posted by Russian commanders which amounted to declarations of conquest." (*The Annals of the American Academy of Political and Social Science*, November, 1925, p. 61.) Even after the overthrow of Russia by Japan in the war of 1904–5, Russia did not give up the struggle for predominance in Manchuria. In the same article (p. 61) Dr. C. C. Wang goes on to say : " Since the Portsmouth treaty, Russia has exerted every effort to consolidate her position in North Manchuria by colonisation and other methods. It was said that Russia intended to make Manchuria a second Bokhara."

These facts should not be overlooked by students of recent political developments in Manchuria. Of the atrocious massacre of Chinese by the Russians at Blagovieschensk, Mrs. Archibald Little wrote a gruesome account in *The Times* of July 15th, 1900, which is quoted in the Appendix to George Lynch's *The War of the Civilisations* (London : 1901), pp. 307 f.

6. Some observations on this subject may be found in an article in the *China Social and Political Science Review*, 1926, p. 958, written by me under the pen-name of " Reginald Irving." See also *China Under the Empress Dowager*, by Bland and Backhouse (Heinemann, 1911), pp. 266, 284–5, 291, 400, etc. Ching Shan's Diary, included in this book, in itself constitutes a vindication of Jung-Lu's attitude towards the Boxers. Professor Duyvendak's faithful re-translation of the Diary is fuller and more accurate than the earlier version.

7. The influential Liang Chi-ch'ao was one of those who disbelieved in the empress-dowager's sincerity, and it was this disbelief that gradually led him to despair of the dynasty and to join the republicans.

8. See above, pp. 19 and 53.

9. A good recent account of the reforms of this period may be found in *The Reform Movement in China, 1898–1912*, by Meribeth E. Cameron, Ph.D. (Stanford University Press, 1931). I do not, however, concur in all the views of the author, especially with regard to the abilities and " educability " of the empress-dowager.

10. See above, p. 29.

11. See above, pp. 28 f.

12. P'u-Lun was, however, the son of a secondary wife, not of a *fu-chin* or princess.

CHAPTER V

1. *The Chinese Crisis from Within*, by Wen Ching (London : Grant Richards, 1901), pp. 281–3.

2. The " China Reform Party " (to which of course K'ang Yu-wei belonged) published in 1900 (immediately after the relief of the Legations) a manifesto which is well worth reading as showing that the reformers were prepared to support the dynasty provided (1) that Kuang-Hsü were restored to the throne and freed from the domination of the empress-dowager, and (2) that the autocracy were converted into a constitutional monarchy. The document was published in the *North China Herald* of October 10, 1900, and is reproduced in full in Stanley Smith's *China from Within* (London : 1901), pp. 234 ff. The Second Resolution contained in the manifesto was as follows : " Resolved, that it is our firm conviction that the simplest solution of the present complicated problem is for the Allied Powers to depose and banish the Usurper and her crew of servile bigots and reactionaries, and to reinstate the emperor Kuang-Hsü, who stood as the exponent and representative of Reform. This resumption will at once restore public confidence, allay popular discontent, and remove a possible cause of international complications."

3. Dr. Meribeth E. Cameron, *op. cit.*, p. 182.

4. *The China of To-day* (London : 1927), p. 15.

5. *Op. cit.*, p. 182.

6. *History of China*, p. 65.

7. *Op. cit.*, p. 97.

8. *China, the Long-Lived Empire*, by Eliza R. Scidmore (London : 1900), p. 120.

9. Headland, *op. cit.*, p. 109.

10. Mrs. Conger (wife of an American Minister at Peking), *Letters from China* (Foreword).

11. Colonel Denby, formerly United States Minister at Peking. It is only fair to add that it is not only Americans who have eulogised the " Venerable Buddha " in extravagant terms. George Lynch in his book *The War of the Civilizations* (London : 1901) describes her as " the greatest ruler China has ever seen " (p. 229) and as " one of the greatest women the world has ever seen " (p. 232). What would all these Western admirers of T'zŭ-Hsi have said had they studied the history of that truly astonishing woman Wu Tsê T'ien of the T'ang dynasty, in the seventh century of our era ? Some of T'zŭ-Hsi's Western admirers have allowed their enthusiasm to mislead them into endowing her not only with greatness of intellect and character but also with superlative physical beauty, which as a matter of fact she never possessed. George Lynch, in the work cited above, informs us that " as a girl all accounts agree that amongst this race of beautiful women she was easily the first " (p. 227).

12. *Buddhist China* (John Murray : 1913), p. 355.

13. The view of " A. E. Grantham " in *Pencil Speakings from Peking* (London : 1918, p. 287) is worth quoting. " She has been called great, but she really only

was strong, for, having the opportunity to guide the dynasty into the way of progress and safety, she actually hastened the threatening *débâcle* through a fatal clinging to narrow family prejudices and considerations when only the widest outlook could save the situation : a failing which seems the bane of all dynasties from whom the mandate of Heaven is passing away."

14. Reprinted in the *North China Standard*, September 18th, 1921.

15. *Two Years in the Forbidden City* (New York : 1924), p. 356.

16. See *China in Convulsion*, by A. H. Smith, vol. i., p. 28. For a different view of the empress-dowager and her tea-parties, see Ku Hung-ming's *Papers from a Viceroy's Yamen*, pp. 8–9.

17. If Mr. H. Belloc's estimate of Queen Elizabeth and her circle is true, as stated in his recent " Charles the First, King of England " (Cassell : 1933), it suggests a parallel with the situation in China under the empress-dowager. He denies that Elizabeth was in any sense a great woman or ruler ; she was merely " a figurehead and symbol," used for their own purposes by others. It was the "others " who governed (or misgoverned) China, not the empress-dowager, just as (if Mr. Belloc's view be correct) it was " William Cecil who governed England, not the Queen." But see Prof. J. E. Neale's *Queen Elizabeth* (Cape : 1934).

18. See the photograph facing p. 454 in *China Under the Empress Dowager*, by Bland and Backhouse. Cf. *Buddhist China* (John Murray : 1913), p. 355. See also Headland, *op. cit.*, frontispiece and to face p. 90 ; and P. W. Sergeant, *The Great Empress Dowager of China* (London : 1910), to face pp. 284 and 316.

19. *Memoirs of Father Ripa*, English trans. (John Murray : 1855), p 87.

20. My interview with the Dalai Lama is described in an article in the *New China Review* (Shanghai), vol. i., No. 2, May, 1919, written under the pseudonym of " Christopher Irving." In later years the Dalai Lama quarrelled with the Chinese Government, and for a time was a refugee in British India. His distrust of China was intensified by the revolution of 1911, with which he had no sympathy. He made Tibet practically independent of the Chinese republic till his death in December, 1933. His death coincided almost to a day with a celestial phenomenon, namely the simultaneous lunar occultation of both Venus and Saturn, which " is computed to occur only once in several thousand years." It was immediately reported from Peiping (Peking) that the lamas in that city " regard the double eclipse as a heavenly omen marking the death of the Dalai Lama " ; and it was added that " the successor to the Dalai Lama will be the first to be chosen without the consent of the Chinese government." (See the *Daily Telegraph*, London, December 21st, 1933.)

21. Those of my readers who have heard some of the scandalous stories once current in Chinese and foreign circles about the empress-dowager's private life, may be surprised that I have omitted to touch upon her alleged intimacy with Li Lien-ying (assumed for the purposes of the scandalmongers to have been no eunuch) and others. The omission has been intentional, because in spite of the emphatic statements of such writers as " Wen Ching," whose hatred of T'zŭ-Hsi reduces the value of their evidence, I do not believe the stories to be true. Perhaps the " Venerable Buddha " might have been a better woman than she was, and also a wiser ruler, if they had been based on fact. It seems possible that the warping of her character, so far from having had anything to do with over-indulgence in sensual pleasures, was due in part to an inner conflict arising from sex-repression. (The statements of " Wen Ching," the accuracy of which I question, may be found in his book *The Chinese Crisis from Within*, pp. 133–58.)

22. See above, p. 43.

23. Yet a third story, which I prefer to relegate to a note, is that Yüan Shih-k'ai bribed a Chinese doctor with $33,000 to have the emperor put out of the way. This story is told by Headland (*op. cit.*, p. 323), who adds : " We are told that the empress-dowager in reality died first and then the emperor, though the emperor's death was first announced, and the next day that of the dowager." See also P. W. Sergeant, *The Great Empress Dowager of China* (London : 1910), pp. 302 f.

24. It is said to have cost over £1,000,000. See P. W. Sergeant, *op. cit.*, p. 306.

The cost of the funeral and the value of the pearls, jade, and precious stones deposited in the tomb were of course very much greater.

25. καὶ μὴν ἔμοιγε ζῶντι μέν, καθ' ἡμέραν
κεἰ σμίκρ' ἔχοιμι, πάντ' ἂν ἀρκούντως ἔχοι·
τύμβον δὲ βουλοίμην ἂν ἀξιούμενον
τὸν ἐμὸν ὁρᾶσθαι· διὰ μακροῦ γὰρ ἡ χάρις.

Euripides, *Hecuba*, 317–20.

CHAPTER VI

1 See Bland and Backhouse, *China under the Empress Dowager*, p. 465, and *Annals and Memoirs of the Court of Peking*, pp. 494–5.

2. See above, p. 29.

3. For my contemporary comments on the naval scheme, see *Lion and Dragon in Northern China* (London : 1910), pp. 436–7.

4. G. G. Coulton in his *Five Centuries of Religion* says : " Revolt generally comes not when things are at their worst, but when they have already begun to improve ; when men have already tasted enough of progress to fight for a radical change " (p. 274). Coulton refers to religious reforms, but his words apply equally well to political conditions. Conditions in China were certainly mending under the Manchus when the revolution came.

5. Dr. Meribeth E. Cameron, *op. cit.*, p. 192.

6. " The battle near Hankow led to the recapture of Hankow and Hanyang by the imperial force, and it is almost certain that it could have captured Wu-ch'ang and destroyed the nerve-centre of the revolutionaries. But by this time, December 1911, both sides sought peace and arranged an armistice." *Modern China*, by Sih-gung Cheng (Clarendon Press, 1919), p. 15. This Chinese writer says later (p. 34) : " The rank and file of the northern army showed little sympathy with revolutionary doctrines. They would have fought their opponents to the bitter end, had the imperial government not consented to accept peace."

7. Père Léon Wieger, S.J., an exceptionally well-informed student of modern Chinese politics, writes thus of Yüan's exploits at Hankow. " On se bat un peu, oh ! combien peu, à Han-k'eou, juste assez pour montrer qu'on pourrait si on voulait." He also says : " Feignant de travailler pour les Ts'ing [Manchu Court] il travaille en réalité pour soi-même " (Chine Moderne, Tome iv.: *L'Outre d'École*, 1923, p. 11).

8. See the *Nineteenth Century and After*, July, 1912, p. 51.

9. " It will be seen that the imperial government did not suffer, or even acknowledge, a military defeat. The emperor retired in a dignified manner under a noble impulse. . . . The provisional president was virtually appointed by an imperial edict, though the appointment was confirmed by the votes of the National Assembly " (Sih-gung Cheng, *Modern China*, p. 18).

10. The *Nineteenth Century and After*, July, 1912, pp. 52–3.

11. *Ibid.*, p. 52.

12. The *North China Standard* (Peking), November 29th, 1922.

13. The *Nineteenth Century and After*, July, 1912, p. 50.

14. H. A. Giles, *The Civilisation of China* (Williams & Norgate : 1911), p. 248.

15. *The Times*, in a leading article of May 28th, 1933, on the subject of Herr Hitler's influence in Germany, observes that Germany is " a nation peculiarly sensitive to mass-suggestion." Is it more so than any other nation ? That the Chinese are extremely " sensitive to mass suggestion " has been proved repeatedly in recent years, in spite of the old and now discredited theory that they are a singularly imperturbable and unemotional people. Père L. Wieger, discussing " crises de frénésie populaire " in China, gives the following advice : " Relire certaines pages de l'histoire des *Grands Ancêtres* par H. Taine. Il en sera toujours ainsi." (*L'Outre d'École*, p. 365). Yes, but not only in China.
If we want a modern parallel to Defoe's cynical remark about Popery, let us

NOTES 461

turn to the little American story told by Sir Norman Angell in his book *The Public Mind* (London : 1926, p. 108).

" Says Jones, ' What is this I hear, Smith, about your not believing in the Monroe Doctrine ? ' Smith retorts, ' It's a wicked lie. I never said I did not believe in it. I do believe in it. I would lay down my life for it. What I did say was that I do not know what it means.' "

16. *A Short History of Chinese Civilization*, English trans., London, 1929, p. 256.

17. *Manchuria, Cradle of Conflict* (New York : 1932), p. 72.

18. *The Middle Kingdom*, rev. ed. 1883, vol. i., p. 565. With reference to the policy of " direct action " often resorted to by Chinese villagers and townsfolk when exasperated by the malpractices of local officials, see my *From Peking to Mandalay* (London : 1908), pp. 372-5. Cf. A. R. Colquhoun, *China in Transformation* (1912 ed.), pp. 91 f., and H. A. Giles, *China and the Chinese* (New York : 1902), pp. 90 f.

19. *These from the Land of Sinim*, pp. 96-7.

20. See above, pp. 65, 66.

21. *Op. cit.*, p. 97.

22. *China and the Chinese* (New York : 1902), p. 93.

23. *The Three Principles of the People (San-min-chu-i)*, English trans. published by the *North China Daily News*, 1927, pp. 59-64. The closing words are an interesting admission that the revolution had not been an unqualified success.

24. *Ibid.*, p. 63.

25. J. O. P. Bland in *The Times Literary Supplement*, August 3rd, 1933.

26. " Sun Yat-sen, as many thinking Chinese now agree, is not the real hero or China's example " (Lady Hosie, in the *Observer*, August 27th, 1933). The fact is, Dr. Sun Yat-sen did not understand his own countrymen or their civilisation, of which he was neither part nor product. The statement by Père Wieger (*op. cit.*, p. 11), that he was " né en 1866 à Honolulu, a étudié la médecine à Hong-Kong, a intrigué et comploté à New York et à Londres," is inaccurate only as regards his birthplace. The Kuomintang would deny his foreign birth even if it were true. I have heard American residents in Honolulu, however, claiming him, without enthusiasm, as a native of their island, and A. R. Colquhoun in his *China in Transformation* (London : 1912), p. 279, also states that he was born there. That he attended a Honolulu school is a matter of certainty, but it must be assumed, for lack of evidence to the contrary, that the Cantonese are correct in claiming him as a native of the district of Hsiang-shan, in the Canton province.

CHAPTER VII

1. See, for example, the *two lines* dealing with the subject in Dr. Meribeth E. Cameron's *The Reform Movement in China*, 1898-1912, p. 197.

2. As I have repeatedly come across evidence that the Articles here translated into English have never been seen by many educated Chinese of the present day, a copy of the original Chinese document is printed on the next page. This Chinese document, and the similar agreements relating to the treatment of the Manchu imperial clan, the nobles and people of Mongolia, the Tibetans and the Chinese Mohammedans, were readily available for the perusal of all Chinese up to and including 1924. Since then, they have been excluded from such Chinese official publications as I am acquainted with. They may all be read in the edition of the *Fa Ling Ta Ch'üan* (" Complete Laws and Ordinances of the Republic of China ") which was published by the Commercial Press, Ltd., of Shanghai, under Chinese Government authority, in June, 1924, the thirteenth year of the Republic. The " Articles of Favourable Treatment " are given a very prominent place in this official publication, for they are printed immediately after the Provisional Constitution of the Republic. It will be noted that the date of their last official publication (June, 1924) was only five months before the " Christian general " and his associates turned them into " a scrap of paper," as narrated in the twenty-second chapter of this book.

關於大清皇帝辭位後優待之條件

中華民國元年二月十二日公布

今因大清皇帝宣布贊成共和國體，中華民國於大清皇帝辭退之後優待條件如左

第一款　大清皇帝辭位之後尊號仍存不廢，中華民國以待各外國君主之禮相待

第二款　大清皇帝辭位之後歲用四百萬兩俟改鑄新幣後改為四百萬元，此款由中華民國撥用

第三款　大清皇帝辭位之後暫居宮禁，日後移居頤和園，侍衛人等照常留用

第四款　大清皇帝辭位之後其宗廟陵寢永遠奉祀

第五款　德宗崇陵未完工程如制妥修，其奉安典禮仍如舊制，所有實用經費均由中華民國支出

第六款　以前宮內所用各項執事人員可照常留用，惟以後不得再招閹人

第七款　大清皇帝辭位之後其原有之私產由中華民國特別保護

第八款　原有之禁衛軍歸中華民國陸軍部編制，額數俸餉仍如其舊

3. The latter part of this clause was not taken seriously by any one concerned, least of all by the Nei Wu Fu itself. Nothing was done to reform abuses, curtail expenses or dismiss superfluous members of the staff.

4. See above, p. 85.

5. " It was believed that after the recapture of Hanyang, Yüan Shih-k'ai did not pursue his policy of suppression to the end, because he was not loyal to the imperial government, but wished to make himself emperor." Sih-Gung Cheng, *op. cit.*, pp. 16–17. And cf. chapter vi., note 7.

6. *The Chinese-Japanese Puzzle*, by Neville Whymant (Gollancz, 1932), p. 101.

7. See note 2, p. 461.

8. The following is an extract from an article by J. H. Dodge, which appeared in the *China Illustrated Review*, Tientsin, more than ten years ago : " In 1911, China became a Republic, and, at the same time, Mongolia declared its independence and stated that whenever China restored the monarchy under a Manchu emperor Mongolia would voluntarily rejoin China." Many of the Mongol princes have more or less openly remained loyal to the emperor from the time of the revolution to the present day. I have myself met them in the Forbidden City, bringing tribute to the emperor whom they treated with all the marks of respect which they would have paid him had he still been their reigning sovereign. I may even claim to have shared some of the tribute ; for a Mongolian pony given to me by the emperor in 1922 was one of many presented to him by Mongolian princes.

9. The Greek city-states, as Mr. John Buchan has said, " failed because they had no ultimate mystical point of unity." China, since the collapse of the monarchy, seems to be failing for much the same reason.

10. See above, pp. 62–3.

11. See p. 82.

12. One of the latest recruits to Buddhist monasticism is the once ambitious and powerful Sun Ch'uan-fang, concerning whom a Reuter's telegram published in the English press on October 16th, 1933, contained the following announcement. " Sun Ch'uan-fang, at one time in control of five of the richest provinces of China, has decided to become a Buddhist monk." The fortunes of this satrap were discussed by me, shortly before his fall, in the *Quarterly Review*, January, 1927, pp. 153–8.

13. It will hardly be believed that in the fourth year of the Republic the Peking authorities applied *whitewash* to the old marble steps and terraces of the Altar of Heaven. A letter of protest by Mr. E. T. C. Werner (formerly of the British Consular Service in China) appeared in the *Peking Gazette* of November 20th, 1915, and was followed up on the 23rd by a letter from Mr. Bernard Leach on the general subject of the vandalism then rampant in China, the pulling down and defacing of ancient monuments and the perpetration of a hundred architectural abominations in the once-beautiful city of Peking. It is to be feared that these and other protests by Western lovers of Chinese art have hitherto met with only a languid response from republican China.

CHAPTER VIII

1. See above, chapter iv., p. 57.

2. In the English versions of treaties between foreign countries and China the custom was to use the phrase " the emperor of China," but in the Chinese originals the term used is *Ta Ch'ing Kuo Ta Huang Ti*—" Great Emperor of the Realm of the Great Ch'ing dynasty." Doubtless it was because this use of a dynastic instead of a territorial title was unfamiliar to and would be misunderstood by foreigners that it was thought necessary when preparing English versions of treaties to convert the dynastic title into " emperor of China." Presumably, however, it was the foreign translator who was responsible for the change. In the treaty of 1871 between Japan and China " no title for either of the sovereigns of the two contracting Powers is employed in the Treaty." Japan is *Ta Jih-pên Kuo*—" the Realm of

F Fc

Great Japan " ; China is *Ta Ch'ing Kuo*—" the Realm of the Great Ch'ing (dynasty)." See Mayers, *The Chinese Government* (London : 1897), pp. 142, 144. Although the Japanese, imitating the Chinese custom, use *nien-hao* (reign-titles) for chronological purposes, they do not follow the Chinese example in the use of a dynastic title as a substitute for the name of the country, for the simple reason that there has been no more than one dynasty in Japan. The name of the country (*Ta Jih-pên*—" Japan ") is therefore used as it is in Europe, where in China the term used would be dynastic—not *Chung Kuo* (" China ") but *Ta Ch'ing Kuo*—the Realm of the Great Ch'ing dynasty.

3. The following paragraph is taken from a leading article in the *Peking and Tientsin Times* of December 4th, 1925 :

" Dr. Sun came to Peking in 1912 in an atmosphere of glamour created by the sedulously fostered belief that he had shown great self-abnegation in resigning from the Presidency of the Republic in favour of Yüan Shih-k'ai. As there was little likelihood that the Republic would ever have come into existence had he insisted on retaining the Presidency his merits in this connection were probably greatly exaggerated. Ex-President Li Yüan-hung is our authority for the statement that Sun Yat-sen ' had nothing to do with the actual work of overthrowing the Monarchy.The Revolution was finished when he reached China' —finished, that is to say, so far as actual hostilities were concerned. The Northern generals, who looked to Yüan Shih-k'ai for leadership, would never have submitted to Sun Yat-sen. His claims, therefore, to be the actual founder of the republic are based only upon his willingness to forgo an office which he could never have obtained."

4. See above, p. 60.

5. See chapter ii., note 5.

6. P'u-Lun not only took steps to ingratiate himself with Yüan Shih-k'ai but also attempted, immediately after the revolution, to win the favour of Sun Yat-sen. He actually presided at a feast given by various members of the imperial family in honour of Sun Yat-sen when the latter paid an official visit to Peking shortly after the emperor's abdication.

7. Messrs. Gowen and Hall, in their *Outline History of China* (p. 386), describe Liang Shih-yi as " an unscrupulous plunger in frenzied politics and high finance." The *Peking and Tientsin Times* of February 3rd, 1921, described Liang as " the chief organiser of Yüan Shih-k'ai's monarchical project, who did not scruple to cripple the Government banks in the interests of his patron." He died in Shanghai on April 9th, 1933, and was buried at his native place of Sam-shui, on the West River near Canton.

8. See my *Confucianism and Modern China* (Gollancz : 1934).

9. I discussed this and other cases of canonisation or quasi-deification in China in an article entitled " The Chinese Cult of Military Heroes " in the *New China Review*, vol. iii., Nos. 1 and 2 (1921). I may add that among Yüan Shih-k'ai's flatterers were some who not content with giving him a quasi-divine ancestor of the Ming dynasty but tried to prove that he was a descendant of the " Yellow Emperor " whose mythical reign is assigned to the twenty-seventh century B.C.

10. The article was originally delivered as a lecture.

11. The career of Ch'ên Tu-hsiu has been a tempestuous one. During my residence at the Manchu Court, from 1919 onwards, he was arrested and imprisoned in Peking for distributing inflammatory pamphlets. One of his friends, believing that his life was in danger, asked me to beg the emperor to intercede on his behalf with president Hsü Shih-ch'ang. He was saved, however, from the deep humiliation of owing his liberty or his life to the intervention of the head of the hated Manchu house, and it was not through any action taken by myself that he was set free. While in custody, he seems to have experienced a temporary " change of heart " and mind, and shortly afterwards wrote an article which seemed to indicate that he was about to become a Christian. The article was eagerly welcomed by the missionary press. That phase soon passed, however, and Ch'ên Tu-hsiu then became one of the most active members of the Chinese communist

party and finally its acknowledged leader. He was in hiding for a long time and was arrested again by the Nanking Government a year or two ago. After a long trial he received a sentence of indefinite duration, which apparently he is still serving. For some notes on his activities, reference may be made to my article on " The National Movement in China " in the *Quarterly Review*, January, 1927, p. 158.

12. A. M. Tracey Woodward, in an article on " The Influence of Yüan Shih-k'ai on Chinese Coins " in the *New China Review*, vol. iv., No. 2, p. 103.

13. See p. 78.

14. The Chinese characters for the reign-title chosen by Yüan Shih-k'ai were those which are transliterated *Hung-Hsien*. The Chinese reverence for the written characters of their language often leads them to find in certain characters hidden or mystical meanings. For example, it has been suggested that the character *hung* has a fateful significance for the Manchu dynasty. It is pointed out that *Hung*-Wu was the reign-title of the first emperor of the dynasty which preceded that of the Manchus. Again, a certain high Chinese official who at first fought against the Manchus but afterwards went over to them and became one of their leading advisers in the organisation of their new Chinese empire, was a native of Fuhkien province named *Hung* Ch'êng-ch'ou. Further, the character representing *hung* also appears in the name of the leader of the T'ai-p'ing rebellion, *Hung* Hsiu-ch'üan, who brought the Manchu dynasty into imminent peril in the nineteenth century. The same character reappears in one of the names given to the dangerous Triad Society—*Hung* Chia—a secret fraternity which had as one of its aims the restoration of the Ming dynasty. We find it again in the name of the (nominal) leader of the revolutionary forces at Wu-ch'ang in 1911—Li Yüan-*hung*. Finally, it occurs, as stated, in Yüan Shih-k'ai's reign-title.

A Chinese writer on this subject, whose article was published in a Tsingtao Chinese newspaper of the 24th July, 1928, points out that the Manchu dynasty supplanted that founded by a *Hung*, organised its own empire through a *Hung*, nearly lost it through a *Hung*, and finally did actually lose it through two *Hungs*.

15. *Saving China*, by V. K. Ting (Tientsin Press, Ltd. : 1922 ?).

16. In the *North China Standard* (Peking) of March 22nd, 1922, appeared an article in English from the pen of the well-known foreign-educated Chinese Ku Hung-ming, on the subject of " The Religion of the Gentleman in China." A few sentences from this article, including his comments on the character of Yüan Shih-k'ai, are worth quoting.

" I predicted that the republic in China would be a failure. Why ? Because, I said, the man who succeeds in becoming the supreme head of the government must possess transcendent moral qualities to touch the imagination and command the respect of the whole nation. *But Yuan Shih-k'ai, in the way he acted, has not shown an average sense of honour and duty, such as one would expect from thieves and gamblers.* Remember, Yüan Shih-k'ai was called upon to defend and uphold the *Ta Ch'ing* dynasty. He responded to the call. But instead of doing his duty as a man of honour, he first meekly surrendered to the revolutionists, then, by intrigue and machination, debauched and destroyed the loyalty of the troops entrusted to his command and, with their help, forced the emperor to abdicate, and finally became the president of the republic. How can a plain man with ordinary common sense reconcile such conduct with the simplest rule of honour and duty ?

" Foreigners admire Yüan Shih-k'ai as a great statesman who saved the situation in China without bloodshed, not knowing that he only postponed the necessary little blood-shedding for the present for the terrible anarchy and the greater blood-shedding of the future. Indeed, if what I have tried to show in the above is true, then Yüan Shih-k'ai has done something infinitely worse than shedding human blood—he has destroyed not only the sense of honour and duty in the Chinese nation, but also the *religion,* the civilisation of the Chinese race.

" Many of my foreign friends are amused at what they call my foolish and fanatic loyalty to the Ta Ch'ing dynasty. But my loyalty is not merely a loyalty to the imperial house under whose beneficent rule my father and my forefathers have lived, my loyalty in this case is *a loyalty also to the religion of China*, to the cause of the civilisation of the Chinese race.

" I say that my loyalty to the Ta Ch'ing Dynasty is a loyalty to the religion of China. Now what is the religion of China ? The religion of China, I say, is the religion of the *Law of the Gentleman*, and the great code of this religion of the Law of the Gentleman is called the Great Code of Honour and Duty—in Chinese *Ming fên ta yi* . . . in short, the religion of China, the moral basis of the social order in China, rests upon these two simple Chinese words, *Chung Hsiao*, Filial Piety and Loyalty. In fine, this Great Code is the Constitution, the moral Constitution of the State, in what I have called the religion of good citizenship in China. It is for that reason that I say that my loyalty to the Ta Ch'ing dynasty is a loyalty to the religion of China.

" It is also for that reason that I have again and again said that the great unpardonable crime of Yüan Shih-k'ai is that he broke this Great Code, the religion of Loyalty in China."

CHAPTER IX

1. Père Wieger, *L'Outre d'École*, p. 13.

2. *Op. cit.*, p. 17.

3. *Human Nature in Politics* (Constable : 1908), pp. 232 f.

4. A letter in which this subject was well discussed and emphasised was published by Mr. J. O. P. Bland in *The Times* of July 29th, 1938.

5. See my *Confucianism and Modern China* (London : 1934).

6. Poultney Bigelow in *Prussian Memories* (New York : 1915), p. viii.

7. See above, chapter viii., p. 119.

8. J. O. P. Bland, *China, Japan and Korea* (1921), pp. 313–14.

9. *Op. cit.*, p. 60.

10. *Op. cit.*, p. 63.

11. " On July 2nd, 1917, Chang Hsün knocked at the door of the imperial palace and suddenly put the Manchu emperor on the throne without the previous knowledge or consent of the imperial family." S. G. Cheng, *Modern China*, p. 26.

12. His colleague Liang Tun-yen, whom I first met when he was head of the Chinese Foreign Office (then called the *Wai Wu Pu*) under the monarchy, and with whom I became intimately acquainted in 1921, died in Peking in May 1924. Like many of the loyalists, he was a Cantonese.

13. Mr. George E. Sokolsky, who ought to have known better, described Chang Hsün as " a glorified bandit "—a description which has been applied, accurately in many cases, to a large number of China's military leaders of the republican era. (See *North-China Daily News*, October 10th, 1925.) Mr. Frank Goodnow in his *China, An Analysis* (Baltimore : 1926) describes him as a Manchu. This also is an error. He was a pure Chinese, a native of the province of Kiangsi.

CHAPTER X

1. See Mayers' *Chinese Government*, No. 465. Bat'uru is a Manchu word meaning " Brave." Mayers observes that the distinction may be regarded as similar to that of the *légion d'honneur*.

2. Tz'ŭ-chou is a town in the extreme south-west of Chihli, south of Shun-tê. The imperial cavalcade, returning to Peking with the empress-dowager and emperor from their exile in Hsi-an, passed through this town after crossing the provincial boundary into Chihli, the metropolitan province. It was therefore at Tz'ŭ-chou, in 1901, that Chang Hsün, already a high military officer, first met the " Venerable Buddha."

3. This honour, which was one of those bestowed upon General Gordon, is described by Mayers (*op. cit.*, No. 458) as " the most coveted form of reward for military services."

4. The ill-feeling referred to seems to have been caused by jealousy between the new empress-dowager and the four surviving imperial consorts in connection with trifling points of precedence and etiquette. The Forbidden City was seldom wholly free from unpleasant incidents arising from such causes.

5. This refers to the Revolution of 1911.

6. See above, pp. 117-20.

7. See my *Confucianism and Modern China* (Gollancz: 1934).

8. This refers to the strengthening of the position of Yüan Shih-k'ai after the collapse of the so-called "Second Revolution." See above, p. 116.

9. This was the Society which came into existence for the purpose of preparing the way for Yüan Shih-k'ai's ascent of the throne. See chapter viii., p. 120.

10. The reference is to the rebellion against Yüan Shih-k'ai started in Yunnan by Ts'ai Ao. See chapter viii., p. 124.

11. See above, p. 135.

12. This refers to the fact that on Hsü Shih-ch'ang's election to the presidency of the republic towards the close of 1918 he received a free pardon for his share in the affair of the Restoration.

13. Shao-hsien was one of Chang Hsün's personal names.

CHAPTER XI

1. See above, p. 56.

2. The same reference to the astrologers had taken place when the emperor first began his Chinese studies, in 1911. See P. H. Kent, *The Passing of the Manchus* (London : 1912), p. 87.

3. The strictness with which the inviolability of the *Tzŭ-chin-ch'êng* or " Purple Forbidden City " was observed in the days of the monarchy may be gathered from the following paragraph taken from R. K. Douglas's *Society in China* (London : 1901), p. 67. " Anyone passing without proper authorisation through any of the gates of the Forbidden City incurs a hundred blows of the bamboo. This law is invariably enforced, and quite lately the *Peking Gazette* announced the infliction of the penalty on a trespasser and the degradation of the officer of the guard at the gate through which he had entered. Death by strangulation is the punishment due to any stranger found in any of the emperor's apartments ; and with that curious introspection which Chinese laws profess, any one passing the palace gate with the intention of going in, although he does not do so, is to have a definite number of blows with the bamboo."

4. A short description of the T'ai Miao has recently appeared in the *Journal of the North China Branch of the Royal Asiatic Society* (Shanghai), vol. lxiv. (1933), p. 72. The article is by Dr. Emil S. Fischer.

5. The use of " moon " instead of " month," here and elsewhere, indicates that the date in question is in accordance with the lunar calendar.

6. See *Confucianism and Modern China* (London : 1934).

7. See above, p. 121.

8. Mencius, book vii., part ii. 35. A Chinese scholar writing in English in the *International Journal of Ethics* (April, 1922, p. 252) observes on this passage : " To develop reason on the one hand is to diminish the lower desires on the other." He adds : " Teachers and rulers are not to be separated. Most of the Chinese political ideals are the same as Plato's. King must be philosopher ; philosopher must be king."

9. See above, pp. 26, 27.

10. She " began by taking the little golden key and unlocking the door . . . and *then*—she found herself at last in the beautiful garden, among the bright flower-beds and the cool fountains." (*Alice in Wonderland*, chapter vii.) Is it surprising, in the circumstances, that *Alice* found a sympathetic reader in the person of the emperor Ch'ien-Lung's imperial descendant of the twentieth century ?

11. See above, p. 48.

12. See below, pp. 409, 410.

13. See above, chapter vii., p. 106.

14. Those who are interested in the fascinating subject of the symbolism of the Forbidden City should consult Mrs. Florence Ayscough's article in the *Journal of the North China Branch of the Royal Asiatic Society*, vol. lii. (1921), pp. 51, f.

15. *Society in China* (London : 1901), p. 12.

16. See *Sacred Books of the East*, vol. xxvii., p. 91.

17. See above, p. 78.

18. *The New China* (English trans. from the Dutch) (London : 1912), pp. 55–8.

CHAPTER XII

1. *The Lore of Cathay* (Fleming H. Revell Co., 1901), p. 287.

2. See my Bristol Lectures on *Confucianism and Modern China* (Gollancz : 1934).

3. For Legge's translation of the passages of which I have given my own version, see *Sacred Books of the East*, vol. xxvii., pp. 70, 121 ; vol. xxviii., pp. 82, 88. An excellent essay in Chinese on the theory of the place of Education in the social and political system of China and on the relationship between teacher and pupil was published by Liu I-chêng in the *Hsüeh Hêng* (the *Critical Review*), No. 28, April, 1924. He quotes illustrative passages from the *Ta Tai* edition of the *Li Chi (Records of Rites and Ceremonies)* and other ancient authorities. " The Son of Heaven," he observes, " occupied the most exalted position in the State, yet the ancient books declare that there was one to whom even the Son of Heaven had to yield precedence—namely, his Teacher. Therefore according to the old Chinese system no title was more exalted than that of Teacher, for he owed no obedience to any one in the land, however rich or noble or influential."

4. See above, p. 89.

5. Yung-chêng, 1723–1735.

6. K'ang-hsi, 1662–1722.

7. *Op. cit.* (1811 ed., vol. xxi., pp. 273 f.).

8. A short account of his career is given in the *Chinese Biographical Dictionary* by Dr. H. A. Giles.

9. See p. 195.

10. *Op. cit.*, p. 109.

11. The account of this and other incidents given by Mr. J. O. P. Bland in his *China, Japan and Korea*, pp. 300–8, is in the main correct, though there are a few minor inaccuracies, such as his description of Shih-Hsü as an imperial tutor and as a fanatical leader of the Boxer movement.

12. Sister of the murdered *Chên Fei* or " Pearl Concubine." See above, p. 26.

13. See p. 32.

14. As already stated, Ch'ên Pao-shên is not the Ch'ên Pao-chên who was governor of Hunan in 1898. The two are confused by Mr. J. O. P. Bland in his *China, Japan and Korea*, p. 302.

15. See pp. 22 ff.

16. For a picture (from a Chinese woodcut) of an imperial prince kneeling at the bedside of his sick teacher, together with some interesting notes regarding the duty of an emperor or imperial prince to pay this tribute of respect to his teacher, see P. Léon Wieger's *Chine Moderne*, tome i, " Moralisme " : pp. 19–21. He translates the following from authoritative texts. " Qui vous a enseigné ? Qui vous a appris tout ce que vous savez ? N'est-ce pas votre maître ? Le vénérez-vous comme vous devez ? . . . Dans son école, le maître est le réprésentant de votre père, et vous devez le vénérer comme tel. . . . Voyez ce prince prosterné. Le vieillard est son maître. Ts'ao-p'ei, un fils de roi, le vénère en conséquence. Il juge son rang de prince héritier, inférieur à la dignité de son maître. . . . La reconnaissance de l'élève, traduite en actes à l'occasion, doit durer autant que sa vie."

17. Mr. P. H. Kent, in his book *The Passing of the Manchus* (London: 1912), p. 197, records the bestowal of posthumous honours on the Canton " Tartar-general " Fêng Shan, who was murdered on October 25th, 1911. " This outrage," he says, " was noticed by imperial decree, which derives an interest from the fact that it was destined to be the last occasion for the Manchu exercise of the picturesque prerogative which grants those posthumous honours which have been so highly prized." (He was made a Junior Guardian of the heir-apparent besides being given a title.) Mr. Kent was mistaken in supposing that this imperial prerogative ceased to be exercised after the establishment of the republic. The emperor continued to bestow honours on both living and dead up to November, 1924, when, as we shall see, the Articles of Favourable Treatment were abrogated by the arbitrary action of the " Christian General " and a self-appointed Cabinet which held office for a few days.

CHAPTER XIII

1. See chapter xi., p. 170 f.

2. See chapter xi., p. 170.

3. Hsün Tzŭ, *Wang Chih P'ien.*

4. All these ladies are now dead. The empress, it may be noted, is not exempted from kneeling to the emperor on ceremonial occasions.

5. J. O. P. Bland, *China, Japan and Korea*, p. 312.

6. Many years ago I expressed some views which I still hold on the famous " kotow " question in my *Chinese Appeal to Christendom Concerning Christian Missions* (London : 1911), pp. 219 f.

7. The Manchu rulers, who belonged to a warlike race, did on ceremonial occasions carry swords, at least before they became emperors of China. In 1923 the emperor showed me the ancient state sword which was said to have been brought from Manchuria when the Manchus entered China. It was not an impressive article and had very little ornamentation. Its sheath was covered with black lacquer. On the blade, some characters which appeared to be intended for Roman lettering had been written by some sharp-pointed instrument, but I was unable to make out their meaning. Presumably the weapon is now among the imperial possessions which were confiscated at the time of the *coup d'état* in November, 1924, though surely it cannot rightly be regarded as a *Chinese* heirloom ?

8. *Daily Telegraph*, February 6th, 1924.

CHAPTER XIV

1. See above, chapter vii.

2. For a good illustration of how a Manchu prince's property could be mismanaged by his unfaithful steward, see Richard Wilhelm's *The Soul of China* (New York), p. 189. See also Owen Lattimore, *Manchuria, Cradle of Conflict* (New York : 1932), p. 261. Cf. also p. 180, where Lattimore says : " It is a matter of common knowledge that at the present time a great deal of land in Manchuria is held by the descendants of slaves and stewards who usurped in time the estates of their proprietors."

3. See pp. 81–2.

4. *Things Chinese*, by Dyer Ball and Werner (Shanghai : 1925), p. 1.

5. *A Glossary of Reference* (Shanghai : 1900), p. 1.

6. It may be that the disdain for what were regarded as the sordid details of finance was partly the result of a bad interpretation of a passage near the end of the Confucian " Higher Learning," part of which is translated by Legge as follows : " When he who presides over a State or a family makes his revenues his chief business, he must be under the influence of some small, mean man," etc. (See Legge's *Chinese Classics*, vol. i., p. 380). Cf. also the first chapter of Mencius, with its disapprobation of mere " profit."

7. Montaigne's *Essays* (Oxford ed. : 1927), vol. ii., p. 461.

8. See chapter vii., p. 103.

9. In this respect, Shao Ying flagrantly disobeyed one of the teachings of Confucius, which was to the effect that " the gentleman is slow to speak, quick to act." See my Bristol Lectures on *Confucianism and Modern China* (Gollancz : 1934).

10. Eliza R. Scidmore in *China, the Long-Lived Empire* (London : 1900), p. 112.

11. *Op. cit.*, p. 337.

12. From " The Higher Learning " (*Ta Hsüeh*), chapter ix.

13. See H. St. J. B. Philby, *Harun Al Rashid* (Peter Davies : 1933).

CHAPTER XV

1. See above, chapter xii., p. 181.

2. See above, chapter xiv., p. 220.

3. See above, chapter iv., p. 220.

4. Among the emperor's possessions were suits of ancient Japanese armour which had been presented by former emperors of Japan. On one occasion the emperor commanded Yü-Ch'ung to don one of these suits and had him photographed in it. The photograph is reproduced in this book.

5. See above, chapter vii., pp. 106–7.

6. A glance at the Pedigree of the Imperial Family will make this matter clearer.

7. See above, pp. 60, 120.

8. The imperial taboo on the emperor's Chinese personal name " P'u-Yi " may be regarded as having ceased to exist when he became head of the new Manchurian state, where his position up to the early part of 1934 was nonimperial. After March 1932, therefore, it became no longer either disrespectful or technically incorrect to refer to him as " P'u-Yi," and he himself used that name in official and other documents. On no occasion does he call himself " Henry P'u-Yi." Those who remained loyal to the Manchu dynasty have always continued, of course, to address him as *huang-shang*—" his majesty the emperor." It may be argued that they are technically correct in doing so, as the Articles of Favourable Treatment by which he retained the right to the imperial title have never yet been abrogated by any legal or constitutional process.

9. See my Bristol Lectures on *Confucianism and Modern China* (Gollancz : 1934).

10. This line is meant to indicate the first signs of autumn. The *wu-t'ung* tree, frequently met with in Chinese poetry, is the *sterculia platanifolia*.

CHAPTER XVI

1. I have discussed the beginnings of the student-movement in the *Quarterly Review*, January, 1927, pp. 148–52. For a Chinese account of it from the Nationalist point of view, see M. T. Z. Tyau's *China Awakened* (Macmillan : 1922), chapter ix.

2. *Shu Kuang*, vol. ii., No. 8, pp. 16–17. Cf. above, pp. 79 f. Similar admissions were made by the red-hot revolutionary Ch'ên Tu-hsiu (now undergoing penal servitude for his communist activities), in a Chinese article published in the *Hsin Ch'ing Nien*, vol. iii., No. 3, pp. 1–2. The article was published about two months before Chang Hsün's restoration movement of July, 1917.

3. The term " Man-Mêng " (which became a very familiar one in the Chinese press during the years that followed the revolution) is made up of the first syllables of *Man-chou* (Manchuria) and *Mêng-Ku* (Mongolia).

4. The allegiance of Tibet to the Chinese republic, like that of the Mongolians, has never been more than nominal. The Tibetans, as Owen Lattimore says, " during the twenty years of the Chinese Republic, have actually been encroaching on lands once conquered from them by the Chinese, and have been driving out the Chinese and establishing themselves again ; and this movement appears to

be spreading over an ever wider territory and to be gaining speed." (*Manchuria : Cradle of Conflict*, New York, 1932, p. 281.)

5. Her title appears in full in Chinese characters above the portrait of the empress-dowager given as frontispiece to *China Under the Empress-Dowager*, by J. O. P. Bland and E. Backhouse (London : 1910).

6. The *Fortnightly Review*, October, 1933.

7. Lytton Report, p. 27.

8. The *Peking Leader*, March 28th, 1919.

9. See *North China Daily News*, March 14th, 1921.

10. *Ibid.* In the circumstances it was not surprising that telegrams reached the American press to the effect that the restoration of the emperor had actually taken place. See *Asia*, December, 1920, p. 1047.

11. Lytton Report, p. 97.

12. That I was by no means alone in views of this kind may be gathered from much that has already been said and quoted, and also from the following extract from an article by the well-known writer Mr. Rodney Gilbert in the *North China Herald* of March 18th, 1922.

" We frequently hear it said that the people do not favour democracy and would heartily welcome the restoration of the monarchy. Seemingly this statement can be verified by diligent inquiry among the people in any province in China. It could nowhere be better demonstrated at this moment to the satisfaction of the superficial observer than in Kuangsi, which was last year invaded by foreign trained, frock-coated, ultra-constitutional democracy. The truth, of course, is that the rank and file prefer peace to riot and chaos. Under the monarchy they may not have had perfect government but they did enjoy some peace ; under the republic, except in very isolated cases, they have consistently enjoyed neither good government nor peace. Naturally in minds in which the rival theories of autocracy and democracy find no place or arouse no interest, monarchy connotes order, and republicanism, hell. This is all there is to the notion that the Chinese people favour the restoration of the Empire, and it explains fully the much advertised popular yearning after the strong man, selfish or benevolent, who can and will restore order."

CHAPTER XVII

1. In 1933 he joined his imperial master in Hsin-king (Ch'ang-ch'un), the new Manchurian capital.

2. See chapter xii., p. 195.

3. See chapter ii., p. 27.

4. There are various versions of the story, of which one is given by Bland and Backhouse in their *Annals and Memoirs of the Court of Peking* (London : 1914), p. 337.

5. Reclus, *La Chine*, quoted by Émile Hovelaque, *China* (trans. by Mrs. Laurence Binyon), p. 57.

6. Rumours of the disappearance of the emperor's queue reached England, and Sir John Jordan, who had recently completed his long term of office as British Minister at Peking, was questioned on the subject by English journalists. "The emperor," said Sir John, according to the newspaper reports, "is a most enlightened young man who has imbibed Western ideas from his English tutor. . . . The abandonment of the queue may be taken as visible evidence on his part that he is in favour of progress and reform, which will certainly strengthen his popularity." (Reproduced in the *North China Herald* of October 28th, 1922.)

A few days after the emperor appeared queueless before his tutors, the following lines were laid before him :

> *Those ugly foreign devils wear no queue,*
> *And if they did, they'd still be far from pretty.*
> *In China, queues are also getting few,*
> *And that, we all agree, is such a pity.*

7. There is a reference to this in S. M. Shirokogoroff's *Social Organisation of the Manchus* (Shanghai : 1924), p. 148.

8. The Society flourished from 1920 to 1924. Its members came from China, the United States, Great Britain and the British dominions, France, Holland and Russia.

9. The matter was discussed in the foreign press in China as well as in Chinese newspapers, and in a letter dated August 11th, 1925, which was published in the *Peking and Tientsin Times*, I gave an account of what had actually happened at the interview.

10. Mr. George E. Sokolsky's account of the relations between Dr. Hu Shih and the emperor, in his able and illuminating work *The Tinder Box of Asia* (New York : 1932), pp. 272–3, contains several inaccuracies. There was no "schooling over the telephone," and Dr. Hu never became the emperor's teacher. There is no foundation for the statements that it was only in the emperor's bedroom that "the ceremonials of the court" could be dispensed with and that the interviews therefore took place in that apartment.

CHAPTER XVIII

1. The reference is to Wu P'ei-fu's birthday in 1923. The following remark, based on private information, was made in a letter written by myself to a British official on May 18th, 1923. "Among the numerous birthday presents which reached him from all parts of the country was an autograph scroll from the emperor. He received a similar scroll from president Li, but he caused the emperor's to be hung in the centre of his main hall, whereas the president's was given a subordinate place at the side. He also gave the emperor's deputy precedence over the president's."

2. *China Illustrated Review* [Tientsin], April 29th, 1922.

3. See chapter xiv., p. 221.

4. It was to this ex-official that I addressed the letter of July 17th, 1919, quoted in chapter xv., p. 243. Some unessential passages have been omitted.

5. This turned out to be a true prophecy.

6. See above, chapter xiv.

7. I subsequently ascertained that I was correct in this view. The action I had taken received the full approval of the British authorities, to whom a copy of the letter I have transcribed was transmitted. I personally handed another copy to the emperor himself, and in all probability it is still among the documents seized by those who evicted him from his palace in November, 1924, unless they have thought it expedient to destroy it. Subsequently, as narrated in pp. 489–40, they published some of the papers found in the emperor's quarters in the vain belief that they would discredit him in the eyes of the Chinese public and in the equally vain hope that they would show that I myself, among others, had been involved in monarchist plots. It is not difficult to guess why the letter I have quoted, assuming that they found it among the papers stolen by them from the emperor's quarters, was not among the documents which they decided to publish. It was not part of their scheme to permit the people of China to learn that their dethroned emperor had shown himself to be magnanimous and patriotic.

8. For references to these throne-halls and palaces see chapter xi., p. 169.

9. See above, p. 226.

10. "The Romance of an Emperor," in the *New China Review* (Shanghai), vol. ii., Nos. 1 and 2, February and April, 1920, p. 194.

CHAPTER XIX

1. The description of the wedding ceremonial is mainly based on three articles contributed by me to *Country Life* of February 3rd and April 14th, and *The Times* of January 22nd, 1923. They were the only full accounts of the wedding which

appeared in print either in China or abroad, as no Chinese journalists were admitted to the Forbidden City and no foreigner besides myself was present at the principal ceremonies.

2. See chapter xi., p. 178.

3. See chapter xi., p. 171.

4. See above, p. 136.

5. A writer in the *Peking Leader* of December 5th, 1922, describing the reception, said : " Sunday was a memorable day because it gave those really interested, in a friendly way, the chance to note that the ' Boy-Emperor ' and his bride are exactly what folks hoped they were—a young bride and groom with human, natural feelings that charm and win friends."

6. See above, chapter xviii., pp. 282–3.

CHAPTER XX

1. See chapter x., p. 158.

2. This was reported in the foreign press of Peking on July 18th, 1923.

3. A reference of this kind appeared in the Chinese *Shun-t'ien Shih Pao* of July 17th.

CHAPTER XXI

1. See chapter xi., p. 171.

2. For a fuller account of the life and character of Chêng Hsiao-hsü, reference may be made to my article, " Manchuria and its Prime Minister," in the *English Review*, May, 1932. I have here borrowed some passages from that article.

3. See chapter vi., pp. 88–9, and chapter viii., note 16.

4. I gave a brief account of this matter in the *National Review*, May, 1933.

5. I may add that poverty and exile made no difference to his unselfish generosity and kindliness of heart. During the dreary years of his narrow life at Tientsin, from 1925 to 1931, he was never so poor that he had not something to spare for others even less fortunate than himself.

CHAPTER XXII

1. See chapter vii., p. 96.

2. See above, chapter x., p. 153.

3. See the *North China Herald*, August 9th, 1924.

4. See chapter xxi., p. 342.

5. On the subject of Wang Kuo-wei, a few words should be added. He loyally refused to leave the emperor after the latter's escape to the Japanese Legation, though the post he had held in the Forbidden City was purely honorary, and he was a very poor man. He was offered a good position as professor of history at Ch'ing Hua University, which is situated near the Summer Palace. The post was one for which he was eminently suited, and he would have liked to accept it ; but he refused it because he could not bring himself to leave the emperor at a time when the latter was in danger. The president of the University, with whom I was well acquainted, wrote to me on the subject, saying that there was only one person who could induce Wang Kuo-wei to change his mind—namely, the emperor himself. Would I ask his majesty to speak to him ? I thereupon explained the circumstances to the emperor, with the result that Wang Kuo-wei accepted the professorship in obedience to his sovereign's direct commands.

Wang Kuo-wei was, of course, of pure Chinese—not Manchu—race. He retained his queue to the end of his life, and I have been told that he won the respect and affection of the students to such an extent that he was never harassed by them on account of his well-known loyalty to the Manchu house. He taught at Ch'ing Hua from early in 1925 to June, 1927. By that time the advance of the Nationalist armies towards Peking and the apparent hopelessness of the political outlook for his sovereign drove him to despair. One day at the beginning of June he went in a hired rickshaw to the Summer Palace, bought a ticket of admission, and walked alone to the margin of the lake. . . . His body was brought back to Ch'ing Hua University that evening.

6. These were the titles she had received, or caused to be bestowed upon herself, up to that date. Several others were conferred upon her during the later years of her life, and yet others after her death.

7. See chapter ii., p. 26.

8. The reference is to the empress-dowager's sixtieth birthday, for the sumptuous celebration of which great preparations were made for several years. This edict was issued in 1888, and the " joyful anniversary " did not arrive till 1894. When it did arrive, the occasion was shorn of most of its splendour by the fact that the country was then in the middle of the disastrous war with Japan, and the empress-dowager was reluctantly compelled to give orders for the cancellation of most of the ceremonies and festivities, which were to have been held on a scale of unparalleled splendour.

9. Contrary to the common belief, however, it was really only the tawdry superstructure of the marble boat that owes it existence to the empress-dowager. The hull dates from the time of Ch'ien-Lung. It may be added that Lady Susan Townley in *My Chinese Note-Book* (London : 1904), p. 285, unaccountably describes the marble boat as " built in perfect imitation of a Chinese junk."

10. See above, chapter iii., p. 43.

CHAPTER XXIII

1. See above, chapter xviii., pp. 290-1.

CHAPTER XXIV

1. For some references to Mr. Goforth's activities, see my *Chinese Appeal to Christendom Concerning Christian Missions* (London : 1911), pp. 40 f.

2. Kotenov, *New Lamps for Old* (1931), p. 197.

3. *Peking and Tientsin Times*, November 8th, 1924.

4. *North-China Herald*, November 29th, 1924.

5. Wang Ching-wei was the man who tried to assassinate the prince-regent. See chapter vi., p. 82.

6. *North-China Herald*, November 8th, 1924.

7. See chapter vii., pp. 97-8.

8. See my article, " A Letter to a Chinese Official," in the *National Review*, November, 1932, pp. 588-9.

CHAPTER XXV

1. Published in 1930 by Henri Vetch, Peking.

2. The temple in question, well known to me, is that which I have described in the *New China Review* (Shanghai), vol. ii., No. 2, pp. 180 f.

3. This was the date in the lunar calendar which corresponded to November 29th, 1924.

4. A description and translation of Han Kao Tsu's poem in French may be found in Chavannes' *Mémoires Historiques*, vol. i., p. clxi. See also the *New China Review*, vol. i. (1919), p. 680.

5. Corresponding to November 27th.

6. This question of finding a place of refuge for his majesty and of devising some means of enabling him to reach it was discussed that night by Chêng Hsiao-hsü, Ch'ên Pao-shên and myself at a meeting at my house. See above, p. 416.

7. Ch'ang-an Street is the broad high road that bounds the Legation Quarter on the north side, but is outside that Quarter and is therefore under Chinese jurisdiction. Hence the risk for the emperor involved in taking that route.

8. This boy is still (1934) in the emperor's service in Manchuria.

9. See article by Nora Waln in the *Atlantic Monthly*, May, 1933, p. 583. Is it possible that she was misled by the story about Kuang-Hsü which is told above at the beginning of chapter iii. ? There are many other inaccurate statements concerning the emperor in the article referred to. The long letter said to have been written to the author by a Manchu princess living in the emperor's abode in Manchuria was not written by any member of the imperial family, and there is no such princess. Two princesses—the emperor's sisters—were his guests in Manchuria at the time the alleged letter is supposed to have been written. Both were unmarried, though the letter-writer describes herself as the mother of "nine healthy sons." One has since married and is with her husband (a brother of the empress) in Japan ; the other is also married, and since December 1932 she and her husband (a grandson of Chêng Hsiao-hsü, now prime minister of Manchuria) have been visitors in England. Other inaccurate statements concerning the emperor and empress appear in the same writer's book *The House of Exile* (London : 1933), e.g. on p. 317.

EPILOGUE

1. The words were recorded by Reuter's Agency and published in the *North China Herald* (Shanghai) of October 26th, 1925, and in many other papers in both English and Chinese.

2. The *North China Herald*, November 22nd, 1924.

3. The framers of these charges were not monarchists or friends of the emperor. They were anti-Manchu Kuomintang nationalists, and it is for this reason that the action taken by Fêng Yü-hsiang against the emperor in 1924 is not numbered among the Christian general's ten crimes.

4. *China's Millions*, February, 1920, p. 16. The story is told by the Rev. J. Goforth, to whom reference has already been made.

5. What is meant by "demon of drought" in China is explained in my *Lion and Dragon in Northern China* (London : 1910), pp. 295 f.

6. *Peking and Tientsin Times*. The date of the communication is October 29th, 1930.

7. It follows from this that the full imperial title has never ceased to be his majesty's by right, and that even his proclamation as emperor of Manchuria in 1934 effected no alteration in his imperial status but merely marked a dynastic transition. The title of Ta Ch'ing emperor was discarded and was replaced by a new imperial title intended to indicate the beginning of a new dynastic era. As Chief Executive (*chih chêng*) of Manchuria he was not officially described as emperor, because the new Manchurian state had not yet been declared to be a monarchy, and the official use of the imperial title which was his by virtue of his succession to the Ta Ch'ing throne and of the Articles of Favourable Treatment would have caused confusion and misunderstanding. But throughout his tenure of the provisional and temporary office of *chih chêng* or chief executive he was invariably addressed as emperor, at least in private, by all those who had remained loyal to his dynasty or who had not recognised the legal validity of the action taken by the unconstitutional "cabinet" of November, 1924.

8. The British Chargé d'Affaires at this time (during the absence on leave of Sir Ronald Macleay) was Mr. C. M. Palairet.

9. Tu's memorandum was published in the *Far Eastern Times*, August 20th, 1925.

10. See the closing words of chapter v.

11. Owing to the fan not having been fully spread out by the photographer, the first seven characters of the poem are missing in the photograph.

12. Literally, "already I walk with looser belt."

13. See the *National Review*, November, 1932, pp. 581 f.

14. These statements appear in *The House of Exile*, by Nora Waln (London : The Cresset Press), pp. 317 and 318.

INDEX OF NAMES

GENERAL INDEX

Printed in the United States
208018BV00001B/500/A